GREEK MYSTERIES

Mystery cults represent the spiritual attempts of the ancient Greeks to deal with their mortality. As these cults had to do with the individual's inner self, privacy was paramount and was secured by an initiation ceremony, a personal ritual that established a close bond between the individual and the gods. Once initiated, the individual was liberated from the fear of death by sharing the eternal truth, known only to the immortals.

Because of the oath of silence taken by the initiates, a thick veil of secrecy covers those cults and archaeology has become our main tool in deciphering their meaning. In a field where archaeological research constantly brings new data to light, this volume provides a close analysis of the most recent discoveries, as well as a critical re-evaluation of the older evidence. The book focuses not only on the major cults of Eleusis and Samothrace, but also on the lesser-known Mysteries in various parts of Greece, over a period of almost two thousand years, from the Late Bronze Age to the Roman Imperial period.

In our mechanized and technology-oriented world, a book on Greek spirituality is both timely and appropriate. The authors' inter-disciplinary approach extends beyond the archaeological evidence to cover the textual and iconographic sources and provides a better understanding of the history and rituals of those cults. Written by an international team of acknowledged experts, *Greek Mysteries* is an important contribution to our understanding of Greek religion and society.

Michael B. Cosmopoulos is the Hellenic Government–Karakas Foundation Professor of Greek Studies and Professor of Greek Archaeology at the University of Missouri-St Louis. He has excavated at several ancient Greek sites and is the director of three archaeological projects, at Eleusis, Oropos, and Iklaina. He has published ten books and over seventy papers in archaeological journals and conference proceedings. His recent publications include *The Mycenaean Pottery from Grotta, Naxos* (2002), *The Rural History of Ancient Greek City States* (2001), and *The Bronze Age Pottery from Eleusis* (in press).

Contributors: Pierre Bonnechere, Kevin Clinton, Susan G. Cole, Michael B. Cosmopoulos, Fritz Graf, Madeleine Jost, Mark Lawall, Noel Robertson, Albert Schachter, Christiane Sourvinou-Inwood.

GREEK MYSTERIES

The Archaeology and Ritual of Ancient Greek Secret Cults

Michael B. Cosmopoulos

LONDON AND NEW YORK

First published 2003
by Routledge
11 New Fetter Lane, London EC4P 4EE

Simultaneously published in the USA and Canada
by Routledge
29 West 35th Street, New York, NY 10001

Routledge is an imprint of the Taylor & Francis Group

© 2003 selection and editorial matter, Michael B. Cosmopoulos; individual chapters, the contributors

Typeset in Garamond by Wearset Ltd, Boldon, Tyne and Wear
Printed and bound in Great Britain by St Edmundsbury Press,
Bury St Edmunds, Suffolk.

All rights reserved. No part of this book may be reprinted or reproduced or utilised in any form or by any electronic, mechanical, or other means, now known or hereafter invented, including photocopying and recording, or in any information storage or retrieval system, without permission in writing from the publishers.

British Library Cataloguing in Publication Data
A catalogue record for this book is available from the British Library

Library of Congress Cataloging in Publication Data
Greek mysteries : the archaeology of ancient Greek secret cults / edited by Michael B. Cosmopoulos.
p. cm.
Includes bibliographical references and index.
1. Mysteries, Religious–Greece. 2. Greece–Religion. 3. Mysteries, Religious–Turkey. 4. Turkey–Religion. I. Cosmopoulos, Michael B., 1963–
BL795.M9 G74 2002
292.9–dc21

2002031736

ISBN 0-415-24872-8 (hbk)
ISBN 0-415-24873-6 (pbk)

TO THE MEMORY OF MARY E. CRITZAS

CONTENTS

List of illustrations   ix
List of contributors   xi
Preface   xii
Note on abbreviations and transliteration   xv

1 Mycenaean religion at Eleusis: the architecture and stratigraphy of Megaron B   1
MICHAEL B. COSMOPOULOS

2 Festival and Mysteries: aspects of the Eleusinian Cult   25
CHRISTIANE SOURVINOU-INWOOD

3 Stages of initiation in the Eleusinian and Samothracian Mysteries   50
KEVIN CLINTON

4 "In the Sanctuary of the Samothracian Gods": myth, politics, and mystery cult at Ilion   79
MARK L. LAWALL

5 Evolutions of a mystery cult: the Theban Kabiroi   112
ALBERT SCHACHTER

6 Mystery cults in Arcadia   143
MADELEINE JOST

7 Trophonius of Lebadea: mystery aspects of an oracular cult in Boeotia   169
PIERRE BONNECHERE

CONTENTS

8 Landscapes of Dionysos and Elysian Fields   193
   SUSAN G. COLE

9 Orphic Mysteries and Dionysiac ritual   218
   NOEL ROBERTSON

10 Lesser Mysteries – not less mysterious   241
   FRITZ GRAF

11 Concluding remarks   263
   MICHAEL B. COSMOPOULOS

   Index   265

ILLUSTRATIONS

Figures

1.1	Plan of the area of the Peisistrateian Telesterion, Eleusis, with the Mycenaean walls	3
1.2	Plan of the Middle Helladic walls under the Peisistrateian Telesterion, Eleusis	4
1.3	Schematic section (SW–NE) at the Telesterion, Eleusis	5
1.4	Plan of wall 7, Megaron B, Eleusis	6
1.5	View of the steps, the anta of wall 6 and the platform from the SE	7
1.6	Plan of the platform and the east end of Megaron B, Eleusis	8
1.7	Plan of the "tower" of wall 7 and the paved courtyard, Megaron B, Eleusis	9
1.8	Section (a) and top view (b) of the drain, Megaron B, Eleusis	11
1.9	Section of the anta of the east part of B1a, Eleusis	12
3.1	Plan of the sanctuary at Eleusis	60
3.2	Plan of the sanctuary at Samothrace	61
4.1	Southern area of the West Sanctuary, Ilion: Upper and Lower sanctuaries	79
4.2	View of the northern area of the West Sanctuary, Ilion: Temple A	80
4.3	State plan of excavations in the West Sanctuary, Ilion, 1992–2000	82
4.4	Archaic West Sanctuary, Ilion	83
4.5	Early Hellenistic West Sanctuary, Ilion	85
4.6	Mosaic Building, Ilion	86
4.7	Late Hellenistic West Sanctuary, Ilion	88
4.8	Roman West Sanctuary, Ilion	90
4.9	Terracotta figurine of Cybele from the West Sanctuary, Ilion	96
4.10	Terracotta rider plaque from the West Sanctuary, Ilion	98
5.1	Rock formation	115
5.2	Theban Kabirion: to the end of the fourth century BC	116

ILLUSTRATIONS

5.3	Theban Kabirion: late fourth/early third century BC	117
5.4	Theban Kabirion: second quarter, third century BC	119
5.5	Theban Kabirion: late Hellenistic	120
5.6	Theban Kabirion: Roman	121
5.7	Theban Kabirion: large tub found in Lower Tholos (12)	123
5.8	Name incised on the tub from the Lower Tholos	123
5.9	Kabirion-ware vase, 410–400 BC	124
5.10	Vase attributed to the Mystes Painter, c. 400–375 BC	125
5.11	Bronze statuette from the Kabirion	127
5.12	Terracotta statuette from the Kabirion	129
5.13	Procession scene on vase attributed to the Mystes Painter	131
6.1	Demeter of Lykosoura	145
6.2	Lykosoura: the temple and the steps	147
6.3	Lykosoura, reconstruction of the *Megaron*	148
6.4	Figurine with criomorphic head	158
6.5	Criomorphic head	159
6.6	The veil of Lykosoura (1)	160
6.7	The veil of Lykosoura (2)	161
6.8	The veil of Lykosoura (3)	162

Tables

6.1	Mystery cults in Arcadia	143
8.1	Gold tablets: dispersal, date, and content	202–205

CONTRIBUTORS

Pierre Bonnechere, Université de Montréal

Kevin Clinton, Cornell University

Susan G. Cole, State University of New York, Buffalo

Michael B. Cosmopoulos, University of Missouri-St. Louis

Fritz Graf, Princeton University

Madeleine Jost, Université de Paris X-Nanterre

Mark L. Lawall, University of Manitoba

Noel Robertson, Brock University

Albert Schachter, McGill University

Christiane Sourvinou-Inwood, Oxford, UK

PREFACE

Since the beginning of our existence, humans have pondered the mysteries of life and death and have strived to find meaning in a constantly changing world. Above and beyond the world of the senses and the triviality of our existence there has always been a belief in another kind of reality, one of eternal powers, powers that affect and impact human lives. To comprehend that supreme reality and to be in harmony with it, humanity has relied on religion.

Religion in ancient Greece had a strong public character and was, in many respects, a way of integrating the individual into the community. Within this public religion, which often was sponsored and even imposed by the polis, there were special cults that addressed people on an individual basis and were voluntarily selected by each person. The ancient Greeks called them Mysteries ("Mysteria") and they represented a special opportunity for dealing with the gods of the polis on an individual basis. As these cults had to do with the individual's inner self, privacy was necessary and was secured by an initiation ceremony, a personal ritual that brought the individual to a new spiritual level, a higher degree of awareness in relation to the gods. Once initiated, the individual was entitled to share the eternal truth, to catch a glimpse of the eternal reality.

Mystery cults are the spiritual attempts of the ancient Greeks to deal with their mortality. The phenomenon is by no means restricted to Greece, but it is in Greece that it found its philosophical explanation and justification. Exactly because Mysteria deal with the spiritual aspects of our existence, they have fascinated both scholars and the public. Looking back in order to understand those cults is especially timely today. We live in an age of rapid technological progress, an age of virtual realities and an abundance of material goods that are redefining our society. And yet our age experiences a surge of private cults and religious sects, of drugs and abuse, of violence and materialism, forcefully proving how desperately we need to regain our spirituality. It is one of the greatest paradoxes of our time, that those of us who are fortunate to live in the developed countries seem to have all the material objects we could possibly desire, but our lives appear to be emptier than ever. Unless we redefine our priorities to focus on our humanity, rather than our technology, we may never regain a deep connection with ourselves and with each other.

Within this framework, a book on ancient Greek mystery cults is both timely and appropriate. This volume will not solve the great mysteries of life and death or settle the unanswered questions about our spirituality. Its purpose is to take you, the reader, on a fascinating intellectual journey, a journey through the minds, lives, and souls of hundred of thousands of people who lived before us, people who loved, suffered, rejoiced, and aspired to happiness, much like we do. There are many lessons to be learned from their experience. As you turn each page of this book, please remember that the picture so painstakingly reconstructed by each author is part of a greater canvas – the painting of ancient Greek religious and spiritual life. Although the contributions found in this volume are the fruits of the rational and meticulous work of scholars, they offer valuable new pieces to the great puzzle of ancient Greek mystery cults.

The chronological range of this book spans a period of almost two millennia, from the Late Bronze Age to the Roman epoch. In an area of study where archaeological fieldwork constantly brings new data to light, this volume provides a close analysis of the new information and a critical re-evaluation of the older evidence. Although archaeology is the backbone of the book, the authors' interdisciplinary approach extends beyond the archaeological evidence to cover also textual and iconographic sources. The ten chapters cover a wide variety of topics relating to Greek mystery cults. The first three study Eleusis: the beginning and early development of the sanctuary (Cosmopoulos), as well as issues of the Eleusinian ritual and how it relates to festivals (Sourvinou-Inwood) and to the cult of the Kabeiroi in Samothrace (Clinton). The archaeological evidence for Mysteria at Troy, Boiotia, and Arcadia is examined by Lawall, Schachter, and Jost. The next three chapters are devoted to the mysteric elements of the cults of Trophonius (Bonnechere), Dionysus (Cole) and Orpheus (Robertson). The final chapter (Graf) deals with the lesser-known but equally important cults of mainland Greece and Asia Minor.

This project would have been impossible without the collegial and interactive relationship of the authors. For the editor, a Bronze Age archaeologist, who for the last thirteen years has been studying pottery sherds in the basement of the museum at Eleusis, working with the contributors of this book has been a wonderful opportunity to place the Eleusinian cult within the greater context of Greek religion; more importantly, the warm atmosphere and scholarly interaction among the scholars involved with this project has been a great source of personal and intellectual pleasure. To each and every one of the contributors I am grateful for accepting to participate in this venture and for their professionalism and cooperation. Many thanks also go to the staff of Routledge, especially Richard Stoneman, Senior Editor for

PREFACE

Classics and the staff of Wearset, especially Claire Dunstan, for their support and assistance with the production of this volume.

The book is affectionately dedicated to the memory of a remarkable person and a great enthusiast of Eleusis. Mary Critzas and her husband, Evangelos, were born in Smyrna and came to St. Louis in the early 1930s. Here, they became the life-long friends of George and Lella Mylonas, a friendship that lasted until their deaths. Although Evangelos Critzas passed away before I came to St. Louis, I was privileged to have known Mary Critzas during my graduate years at Washington University, when she became my family away from home. Her passing a few years ago at the age of 92 was a great loss to the Greek-American community in St. Louis and to Hellenic studies in our area. Throughout her long life not only did she keep her passion for Greece alive by teaching Greek and by promoting Hellenic studies, but for over half a century she remained an ardent supporter of archaeological work at Eleusis. The dedication of a book on Greek mystery cults to her memory is a small recognition of her silent but substantial contribution to Eleusinian studies, and to the nobility and humanity of her character.

Michael B. Cosmopoulos
University of Missouri
St. Louis, March 2002

NOTE ON ABBREVIATIONS AND TRANSLITERATION

Abbreviations of periodicals and series are those listed in the *American Journal of Archaeology* (2000) (http://www.ajaonline.org/shared/s_info_contrib_7.html). The transliteration and English spelling of Greek names follows the preference of individual authors, although in the index I avoid the latinized versions of Greek names (e.g. Amphiaraos instead of Amphiaraus, Trophonios instead of Trophonius).

1

MYCENAEAN RELIGION AT ELEUSIS

The architecture and stratigraphy of Megaron B*

Michael B. Cosmopoulos

The function of Megaron B at Eleusis is one of the most controversial issues in the history of the site. The excavators of Eleusis, Kourouniotes and Mylonas, had suggested that the Mycenaean building known as Megaron B and its adjacent units B1, B2, B3 (Figure 1.1) were in fact a Mycenaean temple to Demeter and possibly an early Telesterion (Kourouniotes 1935; Mylonas 1961, 38–49).[1] Thus, they proposed that the cult of Demeter originated in the Late Bronze Age. In view of the lack of objects that could be characterized as ritual, Mylonas supported this theory with three arguments: (a) chronology (he dated the introduction of the cult of Demeter to the Mycenaean period on the basis of his interpretation of the events narrated in the Parian marble and the *Homeric Hymn to Demeter*); (b) continuity of location (the later Telesteria were built right above Megaron B); and (c) architectural elements (use of a *peribolos* wall to isolate Megaron B from the rest of the settlement, and a raised platform which could have been used as an altar). A religious function for Megaron B was also proposed by Travlos (1970, 60; 1983, 329; cf. Mazarakis-Ainian 1997, 347–348) who, on the basis of an earlier suggestion by Nilsson (1950, 468–470), suggested that Megaron B served not only as an early temple of Demeter but also as the residence of a prominent family of Eleusis, perhaps the Eumolpids.

A religious function for Megaron B was generally accepted by scholars[2] until the early 1980s, when it was seriously challenged by P. Darcque.[3] Darcque's arguments are: (a) the lack of continuity in material remains between the Mycenaean period and the second half of the eighth century, when for the first time evidence for cult activity appears; (b) the fact that the events mentioned in the Parian Marble and the *Homeric Hymn to Demeter* are not likely to refer to events in the Mycenaean period; (c) the observation that Megaron B had primarily a residential function, as indicated by the utilitarian character of its finds; and (d) doubts about the use of the platform as an altar and also about the existence of a peribolos wall, which in turn cast serious doubt on the architectural isolation of Megaron B and, therefore, its sacred character.

The uncertainty about the function of Megaron B stems largely from the summary way in which the finds were published. Mylonas' book on *Prehistoric Eleusis* (1932a) was written before Megaron B was excavated, so the only published descriptions of the building are interim reports in the *ArchDelt* and the *AJA* (Kourouniotes 1930–1931, 18–23; 1931–1932, 2–3; Mylonas and Kourouniotes 1933), as well as the description of the building in Mylonas' classic *Eleusis and the Eleusinian Mysteries* (Mylonas 1961, 31ff.). As a proper interpretation of the function of Megaron B can only be based on a detailed analysis of its architectural elements and finds, in this chapter I use the unpublished excavation records and the evidence provided by the recent study of the finds, in order to reconstruct the architectural development and stratigraphic sequence of the building and to shed new light on the issue of its function. This chapter does not discuss the more general issue of continuity of cult from the Late Bronze Age to the Dark Age, but only the function of Megaron B in the Mycenaean period.

The bulk of the Mycenaean remains under the Roman Telesterion (Figures 1.1, 3.1: 7) were brought to light during two long excavation seasons in 1931 and 1932. Further exploration in the same area took place in 1933 and 1934, but produced little evidence that could be of use to the reconstruction of the stratigraphy of Megaron B. The director of the excavation was Konstantinos Kourouniotes, assisted by George Mylonas (except in 1933), Ioannis Threpsiades, and Ioannis Travlos, who was also the architect of the project. The excavation was difficult, as most Bronze Age strata were covered by later remains; the excavators were confined to digging in deep and narrow trenches and tunnels under the bases of the columns of the later Telesteria, and even had to remove temporarily two column bases of the Peisistrateian Telesterion (Kourouniotes 1930–1931, 18). An added difficulty was that in the 1880s Philios had already excavated parts of the Telesterion down to the bedrock (Philios 1884, 64–65) and then refilled his trenches, in many cases without marking the already excavated areas. Kourouniotes and Mylonas excavated in artificial layers 0.20 to 0.30 m thick, but also recorded in their notebooks changes in natural stratigraphy.

The architectural elements of Megaron B and its adjacent structures

The building known as Megaron B[4] is a rectangular structure located under the Peisistrateian Telesterion. The earliest remains at that location were parts of walls dating to the late MH period (Figure 1.2; Kourouniotes 1930–1931, 18; Mylonas and Kourouniotes 1933, 279).[5] Although their

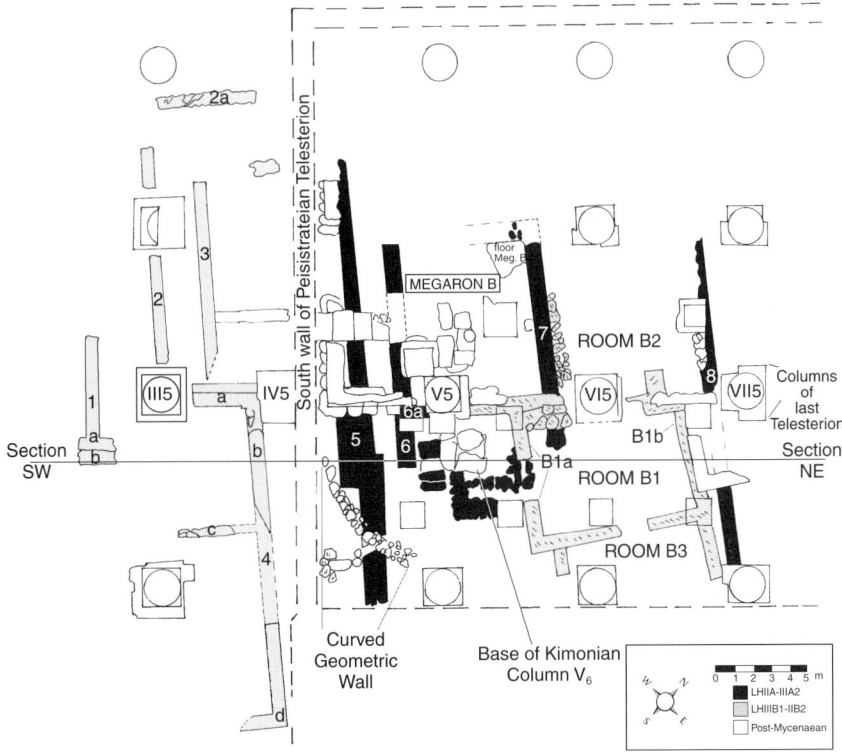

Figure 1.1 Plan of the area of the Peisistrateian Telesterion with the Mycenaean walls (based on an unpublished plan by I. Travlos)

state of preservation was very fragmentary, parts of at least one rectangular building was discerned, oriented roughly from east to west: a cross wall running from north to south divided the building into a smaller back room and a larger room that stretched towards the top of the hill. Notable was the fragment of a wall running north–south, underneath the LH wall 6a (Figures 1.1, 1.2; Notebook 1932, 21). Several MH burials were also found associated with these walls. The pottery associated with these walls consists of Grey Minyan, Yellow Minyan, polychrome, and matt-painted sherds, dating to the late MH period.[6]

Megaron B (Figures 1.1, 1.3) overlies the MH walls. It is defined by two long walls, running roughly in a west–east direction. *Wall 6* (Notebook 1931, 45–51; 1932, 10–11, 24) is 0.63–0.68 m thick and is preserved to a length of 10.40 and a height of 1.16 m. Its foundation is made of three rows of large stones and forms an indentation at the level of the floor (Figure 1.3).[7] The wall is constructed of stones held together by clay mortar and its east end forms an *anta* 0.95 m thick (approximately 0.30 m thicker than the

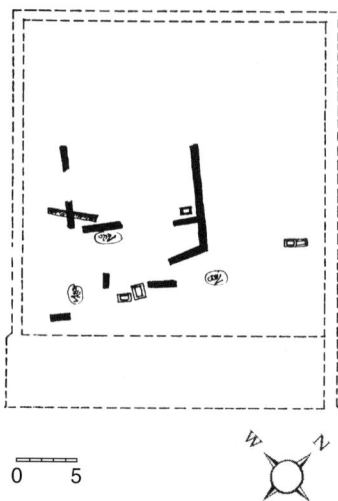

Figure 1.2 Plan of the Middle Helladic walls under the Peisistrateian Telesterion (based on an unpublished drawing by I. Travlos)

wall) and built of stones placed in clay mortar (Figure 1.5, B); LH IIIA1 sherds are wedged in between the stones. The south/external face of the anta is rather crudely made, with stones protruding from the line of the wall, and was presumably covered by a thick layer of plaster. The north/internal face of the anta is smoother, made of smaller and more regular stones placed in horizontal rows; presumably it would have been covered also with a thick layer of plaster. In fact, next to the wall was found a small fragment of a fresco with a representation of an eye looking towards the right, bordered by a vertical band. The east end of the anta is carefully made of large flat stones placed in horizontal rows and sitting on a large block of black Eleusinian stone (h. 1 m, w. 0.83 m, th. 0.55 m), whose face had been artificially smoothed; the block is conical with an almost rectangular section and one of its corners has been chiseled away, giving it an irregular polygonal shape. It rests on a layer of flat stones. In the narrow (0.20–0.25 m) space between the anta and the base of the adjacent Kimonian column V_6, there is a flight of three steps (Figure 1.5, A). The two lower steps, measuring 0.72×0.20 and 0.72×0.25 m, are constructed of large blocks of Eleusinian stone, whereas the third is aligned with the floor of the vestibule (see p. 6), made of a layer of small stones; a flat upright stone and a large fragment of a slab (0.80×0.75 m) were found next to wall 6 and, according to Mylonas, could have been part of a stone seat. The floor of the main room was made of a layer of packed earth, pebbles and lime, and sloped gently from west to east; its thickness ranged from 0.04 m in the central part to 0.08 m near the entrance. One part of the floor, measuring 0.60×0.85 m, was found near

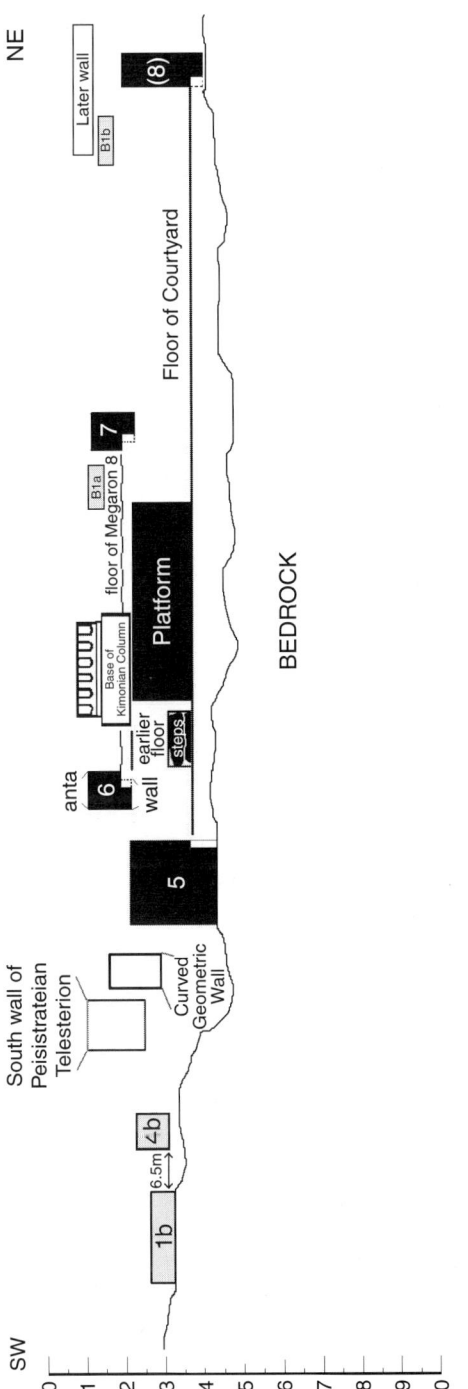

Figure 1.3 Schematic section (SW–NE) at the Telesterion (*cf.* Figure 1.1)

the base of wall 6, at an elevation of −1.50 m from the surface, overlaying an earlier pebble floor (Notebook 1931, 51). Another part of it, of unrecorded dimensions, was discovered near the western end of wall 6 at an elevation of −1.46 m. The bulk of the pottery found on the later floor dates to LH IIIA1–IIIA2, although LH IIA and IIB sherds were also found on and under the level of this floor. At a distance of 2.20 m from the east wall of the room (wall 6a) a base of a column, which would have supported the roof, was found (Kourouniotes 1933, 2). A second column base was restored approximately 2 m to the northwest of the first one (Mylonas 1961, 35).

Wall 7 (Notebook 1932, 23–25) is preserved to a length of 9.70 m and is 0.65 m thick. In some places it is made of large stones placed in a double row and the space in-between is filled with small stones and clay. In other places, relatively large flat stones are placed horizontally in the wall, spanning its entire width (Figure 1.4). Smaller stones, sherds, and carbonized remains of wood are wedged in the spaces between and under the stones of each row. This wall also ends in an anta, constructed in a similar manner as the anta of wall 6, although the ending block of the face (h. 0.70 m, max. w. 0.94 m, th. 0.50 m) has a round irregular shape. This block rests on an artificial fill, 0.43 m thick. The sherds wedged between the stones of the wall are LH IIIA1. A staircase was originally placed immediately to the south of the anta of wall 7, in symmetry with the flight of steps of wall 6, but it was dismantled when room B1 (see p. 11) was built; the slabs used for the steps of this staircase were incorporated into the west part of wall B1a (Figure 1.1).

Walls 6 and 7 are connected by a partly preserved cross wall (*wall 6a*), which divided the building into two rooms, a short vestibule and a main room (Notebook 1932, 12–13, 19–22). This cross wall sat on an earlier MH wall, slightly diagonally oriented, and its upper course connected it also with the later extension to Megaron B (B1/B2/B3). The vestibule was 2 m deep from the cross wall to the east end of the platform and accessed through the two flights of steps. Its floor was 1.25 m higher than the level of the court in front of the anta. The floor was partly made of a large (l. 1.1 m, w. 0.96 m, th. 0.20 m) rectangular slab of amygdalite stone, whose western end was irregular and covered by a layer of packed earth and small pebbles. The south end of the slab sat on a narrow wall built parallel to the wall of the anta; it formed one side of a drain that ran towards the south and connected with the drain that exited under wall 5 (see p. 8). The opening of the entrance from the vestibule to the main room was 1.30 m wide and would

Figure 1.4 Plan of wall 7 (based on G. Mylonas, Notebook 1932, 24)

Figure 1.5 View of the steps (A), the anta of wall 6 (B) and the platform (C) from the SE (photo in the General Archive of the Athens Archaeological Society)

have been made of at least one step, as the floor of the main room was 0.30 m higher than that of the vestibule.

The back (west) wall of the room has not been preserved, but its precise location can be surmised on the basis of the following (Notebook 1932, 26):

- The west end of wall 7, made up of small stones, seems to turn towards the south (the change in direction is visible under the foundation of the Roman Telesterion).
- Part of the floor of the main room is preserved in the west end of wall 7 (Figure 1.1). The floor has an elliptical outline, which can be explained only if we accept that wall 7 turned towards the south.
- Crossing wall 7, in the place where the west wall of the main room would have been, there are three oblong stones in a row, aligned in a west–east direction (Figure 1.1). These stones appear to have belonged to a wall running in a north–south direction, following a practice that is common in Megaron B: large oblong stones are placed perpendicular to the direction of the wall and span its entire width, whereas smaller stones are parallel to the direction of the wall (cf. the similar construction of wall 7 itself, in Figure 1.4).
- Further back to the west, the bedrock rises sharply and does not leave enough space for an additional room, unless there were several steps leading up. This is not likely, though, as the entire area was not leveled until Kimon.

In front of the vestibule, between the two flights of steps, there is a raised *platform* (Figures 1.3, 1.5C, 1.6) 1.10 m above the surface of the first step: the thickness of the steps is not recorded, but assuming that each step would have been 0.20–0.30 m thick, the floor of the platform would have been approximately 1.30 to 1.40 m from the courtyard. The platform is a Π-shaped construction made up of three walls: the south wall is 0.65 m thick and 2.50 m long, the north wall is 0.60 m thick and 2.46 m long, and the east wall, vertical to the slope of the hill, is 1.60 m thick and 2.80 m long. These walls are made of medium-size stones, placed rather irregularly in horizontal rows; the area enclosed by these three walls was filled with soil and stones and formed a raised platform, extending to a length of 2 m from the external surface of the south anta and 1.30 m beyond the lowest step. The sherds wedged in the walls of the platform are LH IIIA1.

In the past, the purpose of this platform has been debated. Mylonas suggested that it could have been used both as a retaining wall for Megaron B and as an altar, but Darcque (1981) maintains that it only served to support Megaron B. A careful analysis of the architectural elements of the platform suggests that it was much more than a simple retaining wall. If retaining Megaron B were the only function that the builders had in mind, there would have been no need for a complex Π-shaped construction; the simplest and most effective way to support Megaron B would have been to build one sturdy retaining wall, spanning the *entire* width of Megaron B, either on or close to wall 6a. More importantly, the platform is 2.80 m wide,[8] whereas Megaron B is 5.90 m wide: in reality, the platform spans only *half* of the width of Megaron B (Figures 1.3, 1.6). Therefore, as much as the platform may have partially supported the building, it is evident that it also served a non-structural purpose. The elevation of the platform (1.30–1.40 m from the level of the courtyard in front of it) could indicate that it was used for an activity that was meant to be seen from the court below, which would not preclude its use as an altar. This possibility will be further discussed in the Conclusion.

Megaron B was enclosed by a wall, of which only two sections survive. The first section, called *wall 5* (Notebook 1932, 6–7), lies at a distance of

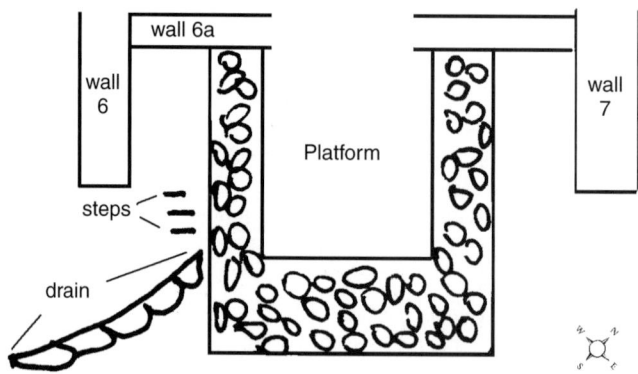

Figure 1.6 Plan of the platform and the east end of Megaron B (based on Mylonas, Notebook 1932, 20)

1.15 m to the south of wall 6. It is a long wall running roughly west–east, 0.84 m thick at its east end and 0.60 m thick at its west end, preserved to a length of 19 m and a height of 1.50–1.70 m. Its east part is founded on the bedrock, but its west part sits on an artificial fill because of the slope of the ground. Its lower course is constructed with large flat stones, averaging 0.50 m in length and 0.23 m in width. The wall is formed by two rows of relatively large stones placed in clay, forming an even façade, with the space in between filled with small stones and clay. The three lower rows (which constitute the foundation of the wall) are 0.17–0.20 m narrower than the socle, forming an indentation at the height of the floor of the courtyard (Figure 1.3). At this point the north side of the wall sits on the rock.

At a distance of 5.35 m from its east end, and for a length of 4.30 m, wall 5 almost triples in width to 1.80 m (Figure 1.7). The thickened part would originally have been rectangular, as one of its original blocks, 0.40 m wide (marked as "v" in Mylonas' notebooks) seems to have been pushed inwards. The external side of the thickened part lies on a thin (0.07 m) deposit, which in turn sits on the bedrock. Its foundation is made of five large Eleusinian stones, the largest of which measures 0.75 × 0.70 m. These stones, the wider side of which faces towards the external face of the wall, were meant to provide additional support to the wall. Although the thickened part of wall 5 is taken by Mylonas to be a small "tower," it may also have a practical explanation. At that spot, the bedrock falls sharply: at the west end of this "tower" the bedrock is found at an elevation of −3.10 m and at the east end at −4.05 m, a difference of 1 m over a length of 4 m; this drop would have

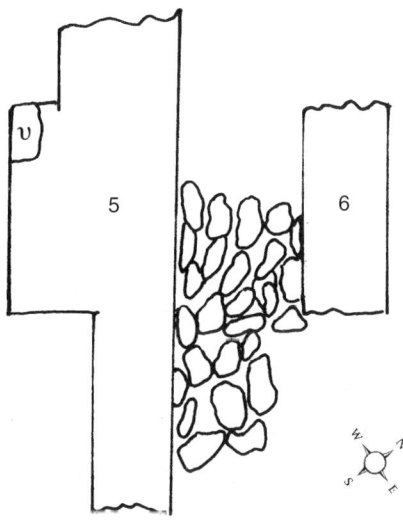

Figure 1.7 Plan of the "tower" of wall 7 and the paved courtyard (based on Mylonas, Notebook 1932, 6)

required extra support for the wall. The wall continues beyond the base of the Archaic Telesterion, but towards the west its width diminishes from 0.80–0.85 m to 0.65–0.70 m. The sherds found wedged in the east side of the wall, to the south of the thickened part, are LH IIIA1–IIIA2 (Notebook 1931, 13). The extension of this wall towards the east, as well as the point where it would have turned towards the north, is unknown. It is possible that the wall turned under the foundation of the Peisistrateian stoa to extend towards the north and then turned towards the west to meet wall 8, thus enclosing the courtyard.

The other preserved section of the enclosure wall is *wall 8*. This wall runs parallel to wall 5 and lies at a distance of 16 m to the east. It is 0.80–0.90 m thick, preserved to a length of 14 m, and founded on the bedrock. By the north foundation of wall 5 and the south foundation of wall 8 were found slabs and flat stones forming a paved area which formed the floor of the courtyard; the rest of the courtyard was covered with a layer of packed earth (Notebook 1932, 4, 17, 38). Wall 8 belongs to the same structure as wall 5, because:

- the two walls have the same direction and their foundations are at the same depth;
- walls 5 and 8 are, respectively, the south and north end of the paved courtyard as indicated by the end of the paved area;
- their construction technique is identical (Notebook 1932, 51), including the *indentation* at the height of the floor of the courtyard (Figure 1.3).

Accordingly, wall 8 seems to have been the north section of a peribolos enclosing the courtyard and Megaron B. An opening roughly in the middle of wall 8, to which a paved road leads from the northeast, permits the suggestion that a gateway would have led into the courtyard.

Two connecting drains were found to the west and south of Megaron B. The first starts at the corner formed by the north edge of the lowest step next to the south anta of wall 6 and the foundation of the south side of the platform (Figure 1.6), and runs towards the south; this drain is uncovered and has one side lined up with small stones. It connects with the second drain, which also runs towards the south and exits under wall 5 at a distance of 1.90 m from its east end (Notebook 1931, 15–16; 1932, 2–4, 17–19). The walls of the second drain are carefully made of three layers of stones, reaching a height of 0.43 m at the east and 0.52 m at the west end (Figure 1.8a). The width of the drain on the external side is 0.46 m in the base and 0.38 m at the top (i.e. the drain is a little narrower towards the top). The opening of the drain is covered with two large slabs (w. 0.30–0.40 m, h. 0.15–0.20 m, l. 0.75–0.80 m) at a distance of 0.15 m from each other, and irregular stones

Figure 1.8 Section (a) and top view (b) of the drain (based on Mylonas, Notebook 1932, 2–3)

between the two slabs (Figure 1.8b). The floor of the drain is formed mainly by the bedrock, and also by a layer of small stones placed on a thin fill. The exit of the drain under wall 5 is well preserved, made up of two parallel rows of small stones that form a smooth façade.

An important find was brought to light on July 18, 1931, inside the second drain and at a distance of 2.40 m from the south wall of the Peisistrateian Telesterion (immediately to the north of wall 5 and inside the courtyard):

> In the upper layer [of the drain], immediately beneath the large slab that covers the opening, we found small fragments of mudbricks. Under this layer, inside the fill, we found carbonized remains mixed with Late Helladic sherds. In the south part, at a depth of 1.15 m there was a layer of pebbles and large stones, under which we found a concentration of ashes mixed with animal bones and fragments from Late Helladic flat round vases ["ἀρτόσχημα"].
>
> (Notebook 1931, 15–16)

The find group has been identified in the Eleusis museum and consists of eighteen burned bones of sheep, goats or pigs, fragments of flat round alabastra, goblet stems and rims, and coarse jar fragments dating to LH III A1 (Cosmopoulos, in preparation). Because of the summary way in which the excavation was published, this find did not make its way into the published reports; yet, as we shall see below (p. 17), it has significant impact on the issue of the function of Megaron B.

Units B1/B2/B3

Immediately to the northeast of Megaron B a complex of three rooms was found, oriented roughly from north to south (Figure 1.1). These rooms (B1, B2, B3) seem to have been an extension of Megaron B (Notebook 1932, 29–38; Mylonas and Kourouniotes 1933, 276–277; Mylonas 1961, 37–38).

Room B1 measures 7 × 4.40 m and is preserved in its entirety. Its *south* wall (B1a in Figure 1.1) is built directly on the north side of the platform

Figure 1.9 Section of the anta of the east part of B1a (not to scale, based on Mylonas, Notebook 1932, 30)

(Figure 1.3) and is divided into two halves (east and west) by a doorway leading onto the platform. The east half is preserved in its entire length (1.45 m). Its foundation is built of large stones, placed perpendicularly to the direction of the wall, and is 0.78 m thick, but the upper rows are narrower (0.65 m). Its face is made of large flat stones, held in place by small stones used as wedges. It ends in an anta made of large regular stones forming a criss-cross pattern (Figure 1.9). The west half is not as well preserved as the east one. It is preserved to a length of 1.46 m, a height of 1.30 m, and is 0.60–0.65 m thick. It continues the line of the internal cross wall of Megaron B (6a in Figure 1.1), and it seems that when this connection was made the shared wall was continued beyond the anta and in this way partially blocked the opening of the door of Megaron B. The *west* wall of B1 is preserved to a height of 0.60 m. It is founded on an artificial fill, 1.10 m thick. In its north end there seems to be an opening to the west, possibly accessing another room, but the wall at that point is destroyed by the Peisistratean column and the case remains uncertain. The *east* wall is preserved to a height of 1.40 m and is 0.60 m wide. It is founded on a MH deposit, 0.50 m thick (remains of MH walls were discerned under its south corner, see Figure 1.2). It was carefully made of stones placed in irregular horizontal rows, wedged in place by small stones. The lower course protruded from the line of the wall and formed an indentation at the level of the floor. The *north* wall is preserved to a height of 1.25 m and is 0.60–0.65 m thick. It was built on an artificial fill, 0.50 m thick, and constructed with large stones placed in irregular horizontal rows. The west end of this wall was not well preserved, but the base of a staircase leading up from room B1 into room B2 survived: the staircase was 1.45 m wide and rested on a layer of large stones, some of which were smooth and regular. It was aligned with the entrance of wall 8 (north section of the enclosure wall), which lies at a distance of 1.25 m to the north. The space between the staircase of room B1 and wall 8 was paved with pebbles.

In the interior of room B1, and near its east wall, part of the floor was found. It was made of a layer of packed earth 0.05 m thick and another layer of loosely placed pebbles 0.08 m thick. A threshold in front of its entrance would have facilitated access to the platform. Access to the interior of room

B1 would have been provided from the platform. Built into the west part of wall B1a there were three slabs that appear to have been the steps of a staircase that would have led from the courtyard up to the platform; this staircase would have flanked the north side of the platform in symmetry with the staircase between wall 5 and the south side of the platform. It appears to have been dismantled when room B1 was built and its slabs were incorporated into the west part of wall B1a.

Rooms B2 and B3 are partially preserved. Room B2 was excavated by Philios, whereas the largest part of B3 lay under the floor of the Peisistrateian prostoon and could only be excavated by means of tunnels. Only its width could be established with certainty, which was 5.75 m. It was accessed from room B1 through a doorway, 1.05 m wide. Part of its floor was preserved, made of packed earth and small pebbles. The pottery from the floor dates to the LH IIIB1–IIIB2 periods.

Walls to the south of Megaron B and the problem of the peribolos

A number of Mycenaean walls dated to LH IIIB1–IIIB2 were found in the area of the Roman Telesterion, but to the southwest of the Peisistrateian Telesterion (Figure 1.1, walls 1–4). Of these, wall 3 is relevant to the stratigraphy of Megaron B. One of Darcque's major arguments against the religious function of Megaron B concerns the existence of an enclosure wall. On the basis of a discrepancy between two plans published by Kourouniotes and Mylonas in 1933, Darcque suggested that the plan published in *AJA* had been retouched to make it appear that walls 5 and 8 were contemporary, whereas in the plan published in the *ArchDelt* wall 5 appears contemporary with wall 3. Thus, in the *ArchDelt* plan, walls 3 and 5 are grouped together and dubbed "Mycenaean A," whereas in the *AJA* plan wall 3 has been dubbed "Mycenaean B" and disassociated from wall 5, which is called "Mycenaean A." The difference is crucial, given the fact that the west section of the enclosure wall has not been preserved: if walls 3 and 5 belonged to the same building, there would be no enclosure wall surrounding Megaron B, thus one of the main arguments for a religious function of Megaron B would collapse.

According to the excavation notebooks, wall 3 (Notebook 1932, 56–62) is founded on a deposit 0.60 m thick (same as wall 4b in Figure 1.3). It runs roughly from east to west and is preserved to its entire length, which is 8.75 m. It is constructed of irregular stones placed in mortar, has an average thickness of 0.55 m and is preserved to a height of 0.86 m. Although it is *almost* parallel to wall 5, it is narrower (0.50 m as opposed to the 0.60–0.80 m of wall 5) and, more importantly, is constructed in a different manner: not only is it founded on a thick deposit, whereas wall 5 is founded directly on the bedrock, but it does not have one of the most distinct constructional features of wall 5, the indentation at the height of the floor of the courtyard. Furthermore, the pottery associated with wall 3 is LH IIIB1–IIIB2, whereas the sherds wedged into wall 5 are LH IIIA1. Given the differences between walls 3 and 5 and the arguments presented above, wall 5 clearly belongs to the same structure as wall 8 and *not* with wall 3, rendering Darcque's thesis untenable.

The analysis of the architectural elements and the stratigraphy of the Mycenaean remains under the Telesterion allows us to reconstruct in detail the architectural development of these remains and to define their character. The earliest building under the Telesterion dates to the MH period. It is possible that LH I pottery was found in the excavations, but has not been identified. The earliest identifiable pottery dates to LH IIA and comes from deposits on and under the floor of Megaron B and the courtyard, possibly suggesting that the building was first erected in LH II. The walls of Megaron B and of the courtyard were built (or, quite possibly, underwent repairs) in LH IIIA1–IIIA2 (as indicated by the sherds wedged in them). The lack of any indications for destruction or abandonment of the building during LH IIIA–IIIB, and the continuation of the use of the entrance to the main room of Megaron B after the construction of B1, suggests that the building was in use throughout those periods. As far as we can tell, the extension B1/B2/B3 was added in LH IIIB1, at which time the walls to the south of the peribolos were constructed.

Megaron B in context

How do the architectural features of Megaron B compare to those of other Mycenaean buildings? At Eleusis itself, the most complete examples of Mycenaean domestic architecture come from the south slope (Mylonas 1932a, 29–36; 1932b, 108–109), where two buildings, Houses H and I, were partially preserved. The construction manner of these houses is similar to that of Megaron B: foundations are made of a double row of stones, the space between which is filled with smaller stones and clay; larger blocks are used at the ends of the walls to form antae; the superstructures are made of mudbrick; and the floors are made of packed earth and pebbles, covered with a thin layer of clay and lime. In plan, however, these houses are more complex than Megaron B, as they have an open vestibule, a large central room, and a small back chamber. Although House H opened into a courtyard there were no signs of an enclosure wall and it seems that the courtyard was shared by the house(s) to the east of House H. The size of House I cannot be established, but House H was 11.80 m long – longer than Megaron B. These houses date to LH I and II, therefore they could be contemporary with the earliest phase of Megaron B. Other Mycenaean walls, discovered on the east slope under the Roman Telesterion but outside the Peisistrateian Telesterion (Figure 1.1, walls 1–4) and on the top of the hill (Mylonas 1936, 429), are not preserved sufficiently well to allow the reconstruction of additional house plans. The houses excavated by Mylonas and Travlos (1952, 56–57) to the east of the Telesterion date to LH IIIB and do not allow useful comparisons. Consequently, on present evidence, except for the enclosure wall and the platform, Megaron B does not have any unusual features that would set it aside from the LH houses at Eleusis.

The same holds true if we compare Megaron B with Mycenaean domestic architecture beyond Eleusis (Mylonas-Shear 1968; Darcque 1980; Hiesel 1990; Whittaker 1997). In general, Mycenaean residential units are freestanding rectangular houses, with one to three rooms arranged along the long axis of the building and the entrance in one of their short sides; posts are used for internal support on the central axis and antae are not uncommon. Sometimes houses will share open courtyards. The plan and size of Megaron B present nothing unusual and find parallels in residential units at Aghios Kosmas (Houses S and T), Eutresis (Houses BB and V), Krisa (House E, second phase), and Korakou (House O) (Mylonas-Shear 1968, 479–480). The only architectural features of Megaron B that are unparalleled in Mycenaean domestic architecture are the peribolos wall and the raised platform. These two features clearly give a special character to the building complex; but could they be interpreted as religious?

The identification of Mycenaean cult places presents many difficulties, which relate both to our own methodological inadequacies and the nature of the material. On the one hand, scholars working on Mycenaean religion have to cope with the lack of a universally accepted methodological framework and of a standard definition of "cult places" and their characteristics. For example, how can a cult site be recognized in the archaeological record? Traditionally, such recognitions are based on certain distinct architectural features (such as hearths, columns, altars, and benches) and the objects associated with them. In most cases these objects are not unusual or exotic, but plain everyday objects, ranging from kylikes and cooking vases to clay figurines, beads, and stone tools. Less often are found rhyta, stone vases, offering tables, spindlewhorls, and exotic items such as scarabs, ivory pieces, sealstones, and seashells (Whittaker 1997, 145, 275–276, table 6; cf. Wright 1994, 62; Shelmerdine 1997, 577–578). Because of the fragmented and uneven character of the archaeological material (Hägg 1968; Mylonas 1977), the criteria applied for the definition of cult places have been subjective (discussion in Renfrew 1985; Wright 1994). Furthermore, the known Mycenaean cult buildings present a low degree of uniformity and standardization (Rutkowski 1986, 169–199; Albers 1994; Whittaker 1997, 17; Shelmerdine 1997, 570–577) and allow the definition of only three (very) broad types, as distinguished by Whittaker (1997, 25–26): (a) one small room without interior platforms or posts, but opening up to a relatively small courtyard where a platform that could have been used as an altar stood; (b) a large main room and a forehall, the main room having had a platform or hearth; and (c) a complex with several small rooms with platforms.

The religious rituals performed in Mycenaean cult places are even more elusive than the places themselves. The ritual that is most commonly attested is libations, for which kylikes and drinking vessels seem to have been used (Marinatos 1988; Hägg 1990, 183; Wright 1995, 346; Shelmerdine 1997, 588–589). Ceremonial feasting is likely to have occurred in cult places as well, given the fragments of cooking vases found at Phylakopi, Mycenae, Tsoungiza and Methana, and the reference to ritual meals in the Linear B tablets (Palaima 1989; Killen 1994; Godart 1999). On the other hand, the issue of the nature of animal sacrifices is not clear; although evidence for slaughtering of sacrificial animals without burning is widespread (Mylonas 1977; see also the references in Whittaker 1997, 147), burned sacrifices are rare (Bergquist 1988). In fact, only recently have archaeologists and zoo-archaeologists been in a position to recognize burned sacrifices in Mycenaean cult places. So far the evidence is restricted to Epidauros-Mt Kynortion (Lambrinoudakis 1981), Methana (Hamilakis, forthcoming), Pylos (Isaakidou *et al.* 2002) and Mycenae (Albarella, personal communication). How does this evidence for early Mycenaean cult fit with the evidence from Eleusis?

Religious activity in Megaron B

Any attempt to compare the evidence from Megaron B with Mycenaean religious architecture and practices stumbles first and foremost upon chronological difficulties. Almost all securely dated Mycenaean cult places belong to the LH IIIB and IIIC periods,[9] leaving us with only two sites that were contemporary with Megaron B. The first is the LH I/II sanctuary on Mt Kynortion, at the sanctuary of Apollo Maleatas in Epidauros. Here an open-air sanctuary was found, including a 10.5 m long terrace supporting an altar in the form of a Greek letter Π – interestingly enough situated right underneath the Archaic and Classical altars. This LH altar contained ashes, burned animal bones, coarse and fine pottery fragments, human and animal figurines, and other objects, and opened up to a paved courtyard immediately to the west (Lambrinoudakis 1977, 193, pl. 120; 1981, 59, 62; Rutter 1993, 794). Another early cult place could be identified in a building at Methana, which was constructed in LH IIIA1 and destroyed in LH IIIB2. This is a complex of four rooms arranged from north to south; room A includes stone platforms, one of which has three steps in the east side, a hearth in the southeast corner, and a number of kylikes, clay figurines, a rhyton, and animal bones (Konsolaki 1991, 1995; Hamilakis, forthcoming). Finally, a large LH IIIA2 (early) deposit containing animal bones, fragments of bowls, kylikes, and other vases, as well as small figurines and a large "Lady of Phylakopi"-type figure, was found at Tsoungiza (Wright 1994, 69–70 with earlier references).

As mentioned in the beginning of this chapter, the arguments for a religious function of Megaron B rely on indirect evidence. So far in our discussion we have confirmed that an enclosure wall did indeed surround Megaron B, units B1/B2/B3 and the courtyard, thus providing to the complex an isolation unusual for Mycenaean architecture. How can this feature be reconciled with the lack of indications for cult activities? The detailed analysis of the excavation records offers important clues that can help us to illuminate this point. The first clue is the remains of fire, ashes, animal bones, and squat alabastra, discovered in 1931 in the drain (*supra*, pp. 10–11). The pottery dates to LH IIB–LH IIIA1, which gives us a general time-frame during the life of Megaron B. The next question is where these remains came from. The drain in which they were found connects with the drain that begins under the platform of Megaron B and slopes southwards towards wall 5; the remains of ashes and bones were found near the base of wall 5, under a layer of sand of the sort that water carries as it flows through the drain. Consequently, these remains appear to have been washed down from the platform into the drain and then carried inside the drain by the flowing waters a few meters to the south.

How are these remains to be interpreted? Given the combination of burned animal bones with ashes and fragments of vases like alabastra and goblets, the possibility of a ritual involving burned animal sacrifices (burned bones) and libations (goblets) on the platform of Megaron B is not only reasonable and probable but consistent with the evidence from Epidauros and Methana.[10] The only problem with this interpretation is the small size of the find. Ritual deposits (such as the ones at Mycenae, Tsoungiza, and Pylos) are substantial and often found in a pit or a specially made deposit. On the other hand, at Eleusis the disturbance of the Mycenaean levels by later construction is incomparably much more severe than in any other site with LH ritual deposits. The fact that only a small part of the remnants of a ritual should survive is not surprising.

One serious problem with this interpretation is the lack of figurines from Megaron B, given the fact that figurines are considered by many scholars the most conspicuous artifacts related to cult practices (Tzonou 2002). There is, however, evidence to suggest that the archaeological landscape of Megaron B may have not been as barren of cult objects as originally thought: a large number of Mycenaean figurines were indeed found in the vicinity of Megaron B, but were not published because they came from disturbed deposits. Two groups of Mycenaean figurines were found in a disturbed deposit to the southwest of Megaron B and, interestingly enough, close to the exit of the drain under wall 5. The first group consists of five figurines, two broken and three intact, from an elevation of −0.30 m and the second of an undisclosed number of figurines from an elevation of −0.60 m (Notebook 1931, 24, 31). A third group of "numerous figurines" ("*pleista eidolia*") was found in a mixed layer inside the courtyard to the south of Megaron B (Notebook 1931, 39).

Although we do not have details about these figurines (until now it has been possible to identify only a few at the Eleusis museum (Cosmopoulos in preparation)), their mere presence is important, as they form an integral part of the systems of activities that were taking place in Megaron B and the courtyard in the LH II and IIIA periods. This thesis is based on anthropological theory, which suggests that each human activity (in our case a ritual) is not isolated but part of a system of activities (see, e.g., Rapoport 1990; Tzonou 2002), which includes also the various depositional stages of the objects involved with the activity. Within this framework, not only primary but also secondary and tertiary deposits are valuable in the interpretation of the archaeological record (Schiffer 1987), as long as they can be related to the original context; objects recovered from disturbed deposits should not be ignored, but studied as parts of the post-activity processes. In our case, although a direct connection to the original context cannot be made, the spatial proximity of the discarded figurines to Megaron B is unquestionable and suggests that these figurines originated in the only building that dominates that spot and the only building from which some kind of activity is attested (i.e. Megaron B). Indeed, the possibility that these figurines were votive offerings discarded from Megaron B or from the courtyard supports the religious function of Megaron B, especially since two of the three figurine findgroups were found near the exit of the drain, after perhaps having been thrown in the drain.

If the platform can be explained as a locus for religious ritual(s), one has to wonder about the function of the courtyard and the peribolos wall. The floor of the platform is approximately 1.30–1.60 m above the level of the courtyard, the floor of which gently slopes towards the east. As the platform faces east, as well, it is reasonable to assume that the sacrifices were meant to be visible by those standing or sitting in the courtyard. The peribolos wall, then, could be explained in terms of the need for privacy of the occupants of Megaron B and the events that took place on the platform and in the courtyard.

This arrangement parallels closely that of the LH I/II sanctuary at Mt Kynortion, where the platform is Π-shaped and viewable from a paved courtyard and leads to the conclusion that the complex of Eleusis served a similar function. At the same time, the domestic and everyday objects found at Megaron B would also indicate its use as a residence, in which case the building would have served a double, residential and cultic, purpose.

Conclusion

The detailed study of the unpublished excavation records has shown that:

(a) doubts about the existence of an enclosure wall around Megaron B should be dismissed: a peribolos did indeed surround the building and its extension;
(b) the raised platform in front of Megaron B was not a simple retaining work, but served a non-structural function;

(c) remnants of what appears to have been one or more sacrificial pyre(s) could have originated on this platform, suggesting that the platform was used as an altar, which is consistent with the other known early Mycenaean sanctuary at Epidauros;

(d) a large number of LH figurines found in the immediate periphery of Megaron B could indicate ritual activity.

The picture that emerges from the above is that a ritual involving libations, animal sacrifices, and offering of votive (?) figurines could indeed have occurred on the platform of Megaron B. The ritual could have been attended by people in the courtyard and its privacy could have been afforded by the peribolos. This ritual could have started during or after the LH IIB period (on the basis of the sherds found in the drain) and could have continued at least as late as the LH IIIB (when the extension B1/B2/B3 is dated).

In general, it is accepted that Mycenaean religious architecture grew out of local domestic architecture and found its inspiration largely in residential buildings, possibly developed from shrines in the houses of prominent leaders (Rutkowski 1986; Whittaker 1997, 136). Therefore, we may consider the possibility that in Megaron B we have a building used both as a residence and as a family shrine. Its architectural development can be reconstructed as follows: a simple rectangular building in late MH/early LH, Megaron B with its platform and peribolos was built in LH II/IIIA1, and the extension B1/B2/B3 in LH IIIB1. These changes indicate a progressively increasing complexity and may suggest an initially unstructured and informal cult, which with the passage of time became more formalized.[11] Such a development fits well with our knowledge about the evolution of Mycenaean religion. Wright (1994) discerns an early (LH I/II) stage in the development of Mycenaean religion, when cult is unstructured and focuses on non-formalized rituals with underdeveloped and non-standardized symbolism. Furthermore, he suggests that "the formalization of ritual practice and its codification and monumentalization are directly related to the scale of sociopolitical complexity" (Wright 1994, 74), which explains the increasing trend for formalization, monumentalization, and institutionalization of Mycenaean religion in the palatial period. The progressive expansion of the architectural space of Megaron B and the increasing complexity of its premises could very well have been an expression of the same trend.

The fact that Megaron B was also used as a residence brings us back to Travlos' suggestion that it was the house of an important family; the new evidence presented here suggests that the residential function of Megaron B was complemented by another function, involving rituals with animal sacrifices and libations.

All this does not beg the question of continuity of cult to the Dark Age. The religious character of Megaron B should, in fact, be disassociated from the more general problem of religious continuity at Eleusis. On present evidence, cult activity in Megaron B should be considered certain; whether or not this was the precursor of the later cult remains an open question.

Notes

*This paper stems from the Eleusis Archaeological Project, which I have undertaken on behalf of the Athens Archaeological Society (Cosmopoulos 1993, 1998; Cosmopoulos et al. 1999). The purpose of the project is the study and publication of the Bronze Age finds from the old excavations at Eleusis, as well as those from a new stratigraphic excavation in the northwest slope of the Eleusinian hill (Cosmopoulos 1994a, 1994b, 1995a, 1995b, 1995c, 1995d, 1996a, 1996b). I would like to thank the Board of the Athens Archaeological Society and the Third Ephoreia of Antiquities for permission to study the material. Funding for the project has been provided by the Social Sciences and Humanities Research Council of Canada, the Institute for Aegean Prehistory, the University of Manitoba, the Shelby White–Leon Levy Program for Archaeological Publications, and the Hellenic Government-Karakas Foundation Chair in Greek Studies at the University of Missouri-St. Louis. The notebooks and plans from the old excavations at Eleusis are now in the General Archive and the Travlos Archive of the Athens Archaeological Society. I would like to thank the archaeologists Ioanna Ninou and Elena Papanikolaou for their help in locating and accessing these records. The drawings from the Notebooks have been inked, scanned, and retouched electronically. I am grateful to Professor James Wright and Cynthia Shelmerdine for reading drafts of this chapter and offering valuable advice. Needless to say, I remain solely responsible for all errors or omissions. Special thanks are due to Ms. Popi Papaggeli for facilitating greatly my work at the Eleusis museum. Abbreviations used in this chapter: EH (Early Helladic), MH (Middle Helladic), LH (Late Helladic).

1 It is unknown whether the original suggestion was made by Kourouniotes or Mylonas. It is expressed for the first time in Kourouniotes' 1931 excavation notebook, but Mylonas was in charge of the Bronze Age excavation that year, so it is possible that the original idea was his.

2 Desborough (1964, 43, 114–115), Hägg (1968, 46–47), Vermeule (1972, 287; 1974, 142–143), Dietrich (1974, 224–225), Rutkowski (1986, 189–191). Although Clinton (1993, 114) and Kokkou-Vyridi (1999, 24) express reservations, they still consider Megaron B a religious building.

3 Darcque's arguments were expressed first in his dissertation (Darcque 1980) and then elaborated in his 1981 BCH article. Darcque is followed by Hope-Simpson (1981, 46), Rolley (1983, 113), Whittaker (1997, 14–15), Mazarakis-Ainian (1997, 149) and Binder (1998).

4 The term *megaron* is used here for convenience, as this is how the building has become known. For the ambiguity of the term see Darcque (1980, 70; 1990) and Werner (1993, 3–5).

5 Sporadic Early Helladic sherds have been found in various locations under the Telesterion, always in disturbed deposits and never associated with architecture (Notebook 1931, 16). A stratified EH II deposit was found in 1995 in the stratigraphic excavation conducted by the present writer in the southwest slope of the hill, immediately to the north of the area excavated by Mylonas in the 1930s (Cosmopoulos 1996a).

6 As is pointed out below, characteristic LH I sherds have not been recognized in the material from the Telesterion, but this does not mean that some Grey and/or Yellow Minyan and some late matt-painted sherds could not date to LH I.

7 Unless otherwise indicated, all elevation measurements are taken from the level of the base of column IV_6 of the Kimonian Telesterion.

8 The measurement is the one recorded in the notebooks (Notebook 1932, 20).
9 See Shelmerdine (1997, 570–577) for a useful summary with references.
10 As the bones were burned, it does not seem likely that they were the remains of a feast. On the other hand, they could not have been burned refuse either, because in that case the sherds found mixed with them would have been burned as well, which is not the case.
11 Hägg (1981, 36) considers Megaron B an expression of "official" cult, because of its formal architectural features, especially the peribolos wall. As tempting as this suggestion is, given the paucity of the evidence from Eleusis, I hesitate to take a position on this matter. For the general question of "popular" vs. "official" Mycenaean cult, see Hägg (1981, 1995), Kilian (1992), Shelmerdine (1997, 577).

References

Albers, G., 1994: *Spätmykenische Stadtheiligtümer. Systematische Analyse und vergleichende Auswertung der archäologische Befunde.* BAR International Series 596, London.

Bergquist, B., 1988: "The archaeology of sacrifice: Minoan–Mycenaean versus Greek," in R. Hägg, N. Marinatos, and G.C. Nordquist (eds), *Early Greek Cult Practice* (Swedish Institute at Athens, Stockholm), 21–34.

Binder, J., 1998: "The early history of the Demeter and Kore sanctuary at Eleusis," in R. Hägg (ed.), *Ancient Greek Cult Practice from the Archaeological Evidence. Proceedings of the Fourth International Seminar on Ancient Greek Cult, organised by the Swedish Institute at Athens, 22–24 October 1993* (Skrifter utgivna av Svenska Institutet i Athen, Acta Instituti Atheniensis Regni Sueciae, XV, Stockholm), 131–139.

Clinton, K., 1993: "The Sanctuary of Demeter and Kore at Eleusis," in Marinatos and Hägg (eds) 1993, 110–124.

Cosmopoulos, M.B., 1993: "Eleusis in the Bronze Age: The Early and Middle Helladic Pottery." 94th Meeting of the Archaeological Institute of America, New Orleans, 27–30 December 1992. Abstract published in *AJA* 97 (1993), 344–345.

Cosmopoulos, M.B., 1994a: "Anaskafe Eleusinas 1994," *Prakt* 1994, 45–60.

Cosmopoulos, M.B., 1994b: "Eleusina," *Ergon* 1994, 25–26.

Cosmopoulos, M.B., 1995a: "The University of Manitoba excavation at Eleusis, 1994 season," *ÉchCl* 14 (1995), 75–94.

Cosmopoulos, M.B., 1995b: "Anaskafe Eleusinas 1995," *Prakt* 1995, 33–49.

Cosmopoulos, M.B., 1995c: "Eleusina," *Ergon* 1995, 24.

Cosmopoulos, M.B., 1995d: "The University of Manitoba Excavations at Eleusis," Archaeological Institute of America, 96th Annual Meeting, Atlanta, 27–30 December 1994. Abstract published in *AJA* 99 (1995), 341.

Cosmopoulos, M.B., 1996a: "Recherches sur la stratigraphie préhistorique d'Eleusis," *ÉchCl* 15 (1996), 1–26.

Cosmopoulos, M.B., 1996b: "New excavations in the ancient sanctuary of Eleusis," Annual Meeting of the Classical Association of the Canadian West, Winnipeg, 16 March 1996.

Cosmopoulos, M.B., 1998: "Eleusi nell'età del Bronzo Medio," in R.de Marinis, A.-M. Bietti-Sestieri, R. Peroni, and Carlo Peretto (eds): *Proceedings of the XIII International Congress of Prehistoric and Protohistoric Sciences, Forli, Italy, 8–14 September 1996.* Vol. 4 (Forli), 195–200.

Cosmopoulos, M.B., in preparation: *The Bronze Age Pottery from Eleusis.* Library of the Athens Archaeological Society, Athens.

Cosmopoulos, M.B., V. Kilikoglou, I. Whitbread, and E. Kiriazi, 1999: "Physicochemical analyses of Bronze Age pottery from Eleusis," in P. Betancourt, V. Karageorghis, W.D. Niemeier, and R. Laffineur (eds), *Meletemata. Studies in Aegean Archaeology Presented to Malcolm H. Wiener.* (Aegaeum 20, Annales d'archéologie égéenne de l'Université de Liège et UT-Pasp, Liège), 131–137.
Darcque, P., 1980: "L'Architecture Domestique Mycénienne." Thèse de IIIe Cycle, École des Hautes Études en Sciences Sociales, Paris.
Darcque, P., 1981: "Les vestiges Mycéniens découverts sous le Télestérion d'Éleusis." *BCH* CV, 593–605.
Darcque, P., 1990: "Pour l'abandon du term 'megaron'," in P. Darcque and R. Treuil (eds), *L'habitat égéen préhistorique. Actes de la table ronde internationale organisée par le Centre National de la Recherche Scientifique* (Athènes, 23–25 juin 1987, BCH Supplement XIX), 21–31.
Desborough, V.R. d'A., 1964: *The Last Mycenaeans and their Successors.* Clarendon Press, Oxford.
Dietrich, B.C., 1974: *The Origins of Greek Religion.* De Gruyter, Berlin and New York.
Godart, L., 1999: "Les sacrifices d'animaux dans les textes mycéniens," in S. Deger-Jalkotzy, S. Hiller, O. Panagl, and G. Nightingale (eds), *Floreant Studia Mycenea: Akten des 10 mykenologischen Kolloquiums 1995* (Salzburg, Österreichische Akademie der Wissenschaften), 249–254.
Hägg, R., 1968: "Mykenische Kultstätten im archäologischen Material," *OpAth* 8, 39–60.
Hägg, R., 1981: "Official and popular cults in Mycenaean Greece," in Hägg and Marinatos (eds) 1981, 35–39.
Hägg, R., 1990: "The role of libations in Mycenaean ceremony and cult," in R. Hägg and G. Nordquist (eds), *Celebrations of Death and Divinity in the Bronze Age Argolid. Proceedings of the Sixth International Symposium at the Swedish Institute at Athens, 11–13 June 1988* (Skrifter Utgivna av Svenska Institutet i Athen, Stockholm), 177–184.
Hägg, R., 1995: "State and religion in Mycenaean Greece," in R. Laffineur and W.-D. Niemeier (eds), *Politeia. Society and State in the Aegean Bronze Age. Proceedings of the 5th International Aegean Conference, Heidelberg, 10–13 April 1994* (Aegaeum 12, Liège 1995), 387–391.
Hägg, R. and N. Marinatos (eds), 1981: *Sanctuaries and Cults in the Aegean Bronze Age. Proceedings of the First International Symposium at the Swedish Institute at Athens, 12–13 May 1980* (Skrifter Utgivna av Svenska Institutet i Athen, Stockholm).
Hägg, R. and N. Marinatos (eds), 1994: *Placing the Gods. Sanctuaries and Sacred Space in Ancient Greece.* Oxford, Clarendon Press.
Hamilakis, Y., forthcoming: "Animal sacrifice and Mycenaean societies: preliminary thoughts on the zooarchaeological evidence from the sanctuary at Ag. Konstantinos, Methana," in E. Konsolaki (ed.), *Proceedings of the First International Congress on the History and Archaeology of the Argo-Saronic Gulf, Poros.*
Hiesel, G., 1990: *Späthelladische Hausarchitektur. Studien zur Architekturgeschichte des griechischen Festlands in der späten Bronzezeit.* Mainz.
Hope-Simpson, R., 1981: *Mycenaean Greece.* Noyes Press, Noyes, N.J.
Isaakidou, V., P. Halstead, J. Davis, and S. Stocker, 2002: "Burnt animal sacrifice in Late Bronze Age Greece: new evidence from the Mycenaean 'Palace of Nestor' at Pylos," *Antiquity* 76, 86–92.
Kilian, K., 1992: "Mykenische Heiligtümer der Peloponnes," in H. Froning, T.

Hölscher, and H. Mielsch (eds), *Kotinos: Festschrift für Erika Simon* (P. von Zabern, Mainz am Rhein), 10–25.

Killen, J.T., 1994: "Thebes sealings, Knossos tablets, and Mycenaean state banquets," *BICS* 39, 67–84.

Kokkou-Vyridi, K., 1999: *Proimes pyres thysion sto Telesterio tes Eleusinos.* Library of the Athens Archaeological Society 185, Athens.

Konsolaki, E., 1991: "Methana-Ayios Konstantinos," *ArchDelt* 46, 71–74.

Konsolaki, E., 1995: "The Mycenaean Sanctuary at Methana," *BICS* 40, 242.

Kourouniotes, K., 1930–1931: "Hai teleutaiai anaskafai tes Eleusinos. Anaskafe en to Telesterio," *ArchDelt* 13 (1930–1931), Parartema, 17–30.

Kourouniotes, K., 1931–1932: "Anaskafe Eleusinos kata to 1933," *ArchDelt* 14 (1931–1932), Parartema, 1–30.

Kourouniotes, K., 1933–1935: "Anaskafe Eleusinos 1934," *ArchDelt* 15 (1933–1935), Parartema, 1–48.

Kourouniotes, K., 1935: "Das eleusinische Heiligtum von den Anfängen bis zur vorperikleischen Zeit," *Archiv für Religionswissenschaft* 32, 52–78.

Lambrinoudakis, V., 1977: "Anaskafe sto Iero tou Apollonos Maleata," *Prakt*, 187–194.

Lambrinoudakis, V., 1981: "Remains of the Mycenaean period in the Sanctuary of Apollo Maleatas," in Hägg and Marinatos (eds), 1981, 59–65.

Marinatos, N., 1988: "The imagery of sacrifice: Minoan and Greek," in R. Hägg, N. Marinatos, and G.C. Nordquist (eds), *Early Greek Cult Practice* (Swedish Institute at Athens, Stockholm), 9–19.

Marinatos, N. and R. Hägg (eds), 1993: *Greek Sanctuaries. New Approaches.* Routledge, London and New York.

Mazarakis-Ainian, A., 1997: *From Rulers' Dwellings to Temples. Architecture, Religion, and Society in Early Iron Age Greece (1100–700 BC).* SIMA CXXI, Jonsered.

Mylonas, G.E., 1932a: *Proistorike Eleusis.* Athens.

Mylonas, G.E., 1932b: "Eleusis in the Bronze Age," *AJA* 36, 104–117.

Mylonas, G.E., 1936: "Eleusiniaka," *AJA* 40, 415–431.

Mylonas, G.E., 1961: *Eleusis and the Eleusinian Mysteries.* Princeton University Press, Princeton.

Mylonas, G.E., 1977: *Mycenaean Religion. Temples, Altars, and Temenea.* Publications of the Academy of Athens 39. Athens.

Mylonas, G.E. and K. Kourouniotes, 1933: "Excavations at Eleusis, 1932," *AJA* 37, 271–286.

Mylonas, G.E. and I. Travlos, 1952: "Anaskafai en Eleusini," *Prakt* 1952, 53–72.

Mylonas-Shear, I., 1968: "Mycenaean Domestic Architecture." Ph.D. diss., Bryn Mawr College.

Nilsson, M.P., 1950: *The Minoan–Mycenaean Religion and its Survival in Greek Religion.* Second edition, Lund.

Palaima, T.G., 1989: "Perspectives on the Pylos oxen tablets: textual and archaeological evidence for the use and management of oxen in Late Bronze Age Messenia (and Crete)," *Studia Mycenaea 1988 (Ziva Antica* Monograph 7, Skopje), 85–124.

Philios, D., 1884: "Ekthesis peri ton en Eleusini anaskafon," *Prakt*, 64–87.

Rapoport, A., 1990: "Systems of activities and systems of settings," in S. Kent (ed.), *Domestic Architecture and the Use of Space. An Interdisciplinary Cross-cultural Study* (Cambridge University Press, London), 9–20.

Renfrew, C., 1985: *The Archaeology of Cult: the Sanctuary at Phylakopi*, BSA Suppl. 18, London.

Rolley, C., 1983: "Les grand sanctuaires panhelléniques," in R. Hägg (ed.), *The Greek Renaissance of the Eighth Century BC. Tradition and Innovation. Proceedings of the Second International Symposium at the Swedish Institute in Athens, 1–5 June, 1981* (Skrifter Utgivna av Svenska Institutet i Athen, XXX, Stockholm 1983), 109–114.

Rutkowski, B., 1986: *The Cult Places of the Aegean.* Yale University Press, New Haven.

Rutter, J.B., 1993: "Review of Aegean prehistory II: The prepalatial Bronze Age of the southern and central Greek mainland," *AJA* 97, 745–797.

Schiffer, M.B., 1987: *Formation Processes of the Archaeological Record.* University of New Mexico Press, Albuquerque.

Shelmerdine, C., 1997: "Review of Aegean prehistory VI: The palatial Bronze Age of the southern and central Greek mainland," *AJA* 101, 537–585.

Travlos, I., 1970: "Die Anfänge des Heiligtums von Eleusis," in E. Melas, *Tempel und Stätten der Götter Griechenlands* (Köln), 55–73.

Travlos, I., 1983: "E Athena kai e Eleusina ston 8o kai 7o aiona," *Annuario della Scuola Archeologica di Atene* LXI, 323–338.

Tzonou, I., 2002: "A contextual analysis of mycenaean terracotta figurines." Ph.D. diss., University of Cincinnati.

Vermeule, E.T., 1972: *Greece in the Bronze Age.* Harvard University Press, Harvard.

Vermeule, E.T., 1974: "Götterkult," *Archaeologia Homerica*, vols. III–V.

Werner, K., 1993: *The Megaron during the Aegean and Anatolian Bronze Age.* SIMA CVIII, Jonsered.

Whittaker, H., 1997: *Mycenaean Cult Buildings. A Study of their Architecture and Function in the Context of the Aegean and the Eastern Mediterranean.* Monographs from the Norwegian Institute at Athens, vol. 1. Bergen.

Wright, J.C., 1994: "The spatial configuration of belief: The archaeology of Mycenaean religion," in Hägg and Marinatos (eds), 1994, 37–78.

Wright, J.C., 1995: "The archaeological correlates of religion: Case studies in the Aegean," in R. Laffineur and W.-D. Niemeier (eds), *Politeia. Society and State in the Aegean Bronze Age. Proceedings of the 5th International Aegean Conference, Heidelberg, 10–13 April 1994* (Aegaeum 12, Liège 1995), 341–348.

2

FESTIVAL AND MYSTERIES

Aspects of the Eleusinian cult[1]

Christiane Sourvinou-Inwood

The attempted reconstruction of the basic lines of the Eleusinian Mysteries is especially vulnerable to the intrusion of culturally determined assumptions. To minimize this vulnerability we should not confront the data directly, or structure their reading through the filters of earlier discussions, which entails the deployment of modern assumptions. Instead, we should try to set in place some basic parameters for the reconstruction of the most elementary aspects of the nexus; that is, reconstruct some of the essential parameters that had shaped it and had also shaped the ways in which participants in the culture had made sense of its ritual elements. This can be done by artificially reconstructing a basic skeleton of "stable points" reflecting clearly established ancient realities. Then we should attempt to reconstruct the results of the interactions between those parameters, in a process very roughly comparable to that of pinpointing the location of a radio transmission through triangulation – though (because of the nature of our phenomena and our limitations of access) we are trying to recreate fluid contours, not locate accurately definite positions. For example, the setting in place of the parameters that Demeter and Kore were the central deities in the cult, and that the cult had an eschatological dimension, entails that it had also implicated the "Queen of the Underworld" persona of Kore. This judgement may be not unaffected by modern assumptions but it is not far off the ancient reality and is supported by other evidence. It may also appear obvious, but since we do not share the ancient religious and cultural assumptions we need strategies to minimize the effect of culturally determined judgements, and processes of this kind allow us to construct – more tentatively the further away we move from firmly established facts – a somewhat less culturally determined approximation of the most basic lines of the Mysteries, and to some extent the even more basic lines of the associated perceptions and beliefs.

I have tried to reconstruct a few "stable points" for the Mysteries in an earlier essay,[2] where I investigated the different sets of evidence separately. Thus I tried to limit the intrusion of assumptions by preventing cross-contamination and unconscious adjustments to make the different parts of the evidence fit, and also to construct the opportunity for cross-checks, so that the convergence of the results of the independent studies provided some validation. I will summarize my conclusions, for they set in place some basic parameters for the reconstruction of the Mysteries and their perceptions, and will also help to place in context the aspects of the festival I am exploring here. First, the Eleusinian cult had a double nature: it was an integral part of Athenian polis religion and at the same time a restricted cult accessible through initiation by individual choice, which led to membership of a category *mystai* to which Athenians and non-Athenians had access (the latter since the "Peisistrateian" phase in the sixth century). Second, Eleusis had been part of Athens from the beginning and was not incorporated later; the Eleusinian cult was, from the beginning,[3] an important agricultural, "central polis" cult – in which the worshipping group encompassed the whole polis – located in the periphery; it was ritually and mythologically connected with the centre and helped articulate symbolically polis territory, the integration of the periphery. Its agricultural and poliadic aspects are correlative with Eleusis' location in an especially fertile area and at the live frontier with Megara.[4] Third, the nature of the cult changed in the early sixth century, when an eschatological facet was introduced, and the reshaped cult became mysteric, based on individual choice and promising a happy afterlife.

Evidence that became available after my article was published provides some confirmation. If my reconstruction of the early history of the cult is right there should be a correlative situation in the City Eleusinion involving, first, a phase of use before the "Solonian" phase of the Eleusis sanctuary (usually thought by the supporters of the incorporation theory to mark the Athenian takeover), and second, a significant change contemporary with the "Solonian" phase at Eleusis. This is indeed the situation at the City Eleusinion (though the beginning of the early phase is uncertain). Its recent publication (Miles 1998) has shown that it had been a sanctuary of Demeter, with an open-air shrine, at least as early as the mid-seventh century, and possibly earlier (Miles 1998, 16–18; there is eighth-century material in both seventh-century deposits: Miles 1998, 17); and that in the first half of the sixth century the upper terrace was enclosed by a finely built wall, contemporary with the "Solonian" Telesterion at Eleusis (Miles 1998, 25–28). The fact that there is a fit between the main lines of the history of the City Eleusinion and the expectations about its history generated by my reconstruction of the Eleusinian cult does not necessarily prove that my reconstruction is right; in theory it could be argued that before the early sixth century this had simply been a Demeter sanctuary unconnected with Eleusis. But this is unlikely, and it is not simply my own bias that makes it seem so: Miles (1998, 21–23) also thinks that the link with Eleusis is likely to have existed at least by the seventh century. The City Eleusinion, then, supports the view that the Eleusinian cult had been part of Athenian religion from the beginning.⁵ As regards my conclusion that there had been a change in the nature of the cult in the "Solonian" phase, the evidence can only show that there were also changes in the city sanctuary at that time. The enclosure of the upper terrace by a peribolos may be simply an embellishment (Miles 1998, 28) and cannot be assumed to show a change in the nature of the cult. On the other hand, though the enclosure of a sacred space with a peribolos was by no means limited to restricted, let alone mysteric, cults, the change would certainly be consistent with a cult that had changed from a "normal" cult to a mysteric one.

The conclusion of my analyses of the Eleusinian sanctuary, that the cult became mysteric and eschatological in the early sixth century, had converged with the conclusions of my analysis of the cult. According to these, first, the mysteric elements were intertwined with a schema "agricultural and poliadic central polis cult located in the periphery", which articulated the Mysteries; and second, there were dissonances between the Mysteries' identity as a central polis cult and their nature as a restricted cult accessible through individual initiation by choice, which were symbolically "resolved" (and so also articulated) in the *pais aph' hestias*, in whose person the whole Athenian polis was symbolically initiated. These dissonances would make sense as the result of a shift in which a cult structured by the "central polis cult" schema acquired a facet of individual mysteric initiation aiming at a happy afterlife. These conclusions also converged with the readings of traditions which indicate that something involving the Mysteries was believed to have happened in the early sixth century. First, there was a fifth-century tradition that Solon had passed laws on the Mysteries (Andoc. 1.111); this does not necessarily mean that such laws were Solonian, only that they were perceived to be ancient; nor does legislative activity entail that there had been change in the cult. But the fact that fifth-century Athenian perceptions placed an important phase in the history of the Mysteries at about the time when archaeological evidence shows that something important had happened to this cult cannot be assumed to be coincidental, especially since other fragments of evidence also point in the same direction. A tradition about the crisis provoked by the Kyloneion *agos*, and the responses to it, had crystallized around the figure of Epimenides, usually in association with Solon; it describes circumstances conducive to the change suggested here, and one of its strands connects Epimenides with the Eleusinian Mysteries; whatever the date of that tradition, it indicates a perception that the Eleusinian cult had come into play in the course of the cultic foundations and reforms that constituted the response to the *agos* which tradition crystallized into the figure of "Epimenides". The very least that this tradition indicates is a perception that the Mysteries "fit" the perceived nature of the responses to the crisis, and therefore that my suggestion that the circumstances surrounding the *agos* and the responses to it were conducive to the transformation of the Eleusinian cult into the Mysteries is not a culturally determined perception. At the maximum end, it offers support for my reconstruction, for the fact that different types of evidence point in the same direction, some more tentatively than others, suggests that the presumption should be against a coincidental convergence between later invention and my conclusions; while individual convergences may be each capable of being explained away separately as coincidental, only the hypothesis that the Eleusinian cult was transformed into the Mysteries in the early sixth century can account for all convergences without postulating a series of independent coincidences. The thesis that the Eleusinian cult acquired an eschatological component in the early sixth century is in harmony with the conclusion of my investigations of social attitudes to death (Sourvinou-Inwood 1981, 1983, 1995) that there was a shift in these attitudes in the Archaic period, from an acceptance of a familiar (hateful but not frightening) death, to the appearance of attitudes of greater anxiety and a more individual perception of one's death, conducive to the creation of eschatologies involving a happy afterlife and, above all, of reassuring religious responses, of which the Mysteries is an important instance.

In this chapter I am aiming at reconstructing a few further "stable (or quasi-stable) points", parameters that helped to shape the festival. The evidence is scarce and problematic; it comes from mostly late sources, often of questionable reliability, as we often do not know how well-informed the relevant writers were – and in any case their particular filters had shaped their perceptions of what had taken place (let alone of what it had meant) and their articulations of what they had perceived, in texts written with particular aims and biases. But it is necessary to attempt such reconstructions; for the purist option of not doing so would result not only in the vacuum being implicitly filled by orthodoxies derived from earlier reconstructions, which are often less methodologically aware, but also in assumptions derived from those orthodoxies seeping into other discourses where their questionable origin is not apparent. The late date of the sources is, for my purposes here, less of an insurmountable problem than may appear. Though we cannot unproblematically use evidence from late periods for reconstructing earlier practices, implicitly assuming that there had been no change, the presumption here, I suggest, should be that the basic schema of the ritual had not changed. For at the very centre of the Mysteries was the belief that these rites had been revealed by Demeter.[6] Such divine revelation of ritual is extraordinarily rare in Greek religion, and created certain constraints on fundamental change and the construction of change-supporting mythopoea. Because the Mysteries were believed to have been based on divine revelation, changes would have taken place only within certain parameters, and are unlikely to have included the main lines of what happened at the festival – though the associated beliefs and perceptions would have been changing through the centuries.[7] As for the use of sources, clearly, if different and unconnected texts refer to a particular element as being part of the ritual (ideally in different ways, or referring to different aspects), they are likely to be reflecting ritual reality. Of course, we need to try to reconstruct the filters through which the later writers perceived and described the elements of the ritual, but such operations are also vulnerable to cultural determination. In any case, we need to try to minimize and control the danger of manufacturing culturally determined constructs by deploying the strategy of comparing the tentatively reconstructed rites to other Greek rituals, to determine whether there are close parallels that indicate that the reconstructed rites fit Greek ritual logic and schemata, which would give support to the validity of the reconstructions.

Several authors mention a "sacred drama", the representation of the story of Demeter and Persephone by priestly personnel impersonating the deities.[8] The most explicit reference is in Tertullian (*Ad Nationes* II.7): after saying that pagan religion puts faith in the poets and arranges in some cases its very rituals in accordance with the poems, Tertullian asks: "Why is the priestess of Ceres abducted, if it is not because Ceres suffered the same thing?" This formulation clearly refers to a ritual performance involving *mimesis*, in which a myth was acted out, and in which the person Tertullian refers to as "the priestess of Ceres" is abducted, from which he deduces that Demeter had herself been abducted. The priestess was in fact a joint priestess of Demeter and Kore, and his deduction was wrong; the reality he is distorting may have been that the priestess of Demeter and Kore had impersonated Kore; in which case perhaps the *hierophantis* of Demeter had impersonated Demeter. Clinton (1992, 131) suggests that the two goddesses were impersonated by their *hierophantides*. Mylonas' view (1961, 310–311) that both roles were taken by the priestess of Demeter is unlikely, for the two goddesses' reunion would have been a climactic moment. Tertullian's claim that a mimetic ritual had taken place is not wrong, for this is also reported by others. Clement of Alexandria, born a pagan and well acquainted with Athenian culture, says (*Protreptikos* 2.12) that Demeter and Persephone have become the heroines of a *drama mystikon*; and their wanderings, and rape and grief, Eleusis celebrates with torches. The selection of the expression *drama mystikon* testifies to the perception that the Mysteries had included a ritual enactment. Gregory Nazianzenos differentiates Christianity from pagan Mysteries as follows (*Oration* 39.4): "Nor have we any abduction of some maiden nor does Demeter wander, nor brings in besides (*epeisagei*) Keleous and Triptolemous and Dragons, and some things she does while others she suffers (*ta men poiei, ta de paschei*). For I am ashamed to bring the nocturnal ceremony (*teleten*) into daylight and to make indecency into a *mysterion*. Eleusis knows these things, and so do those who were spectators of the things about which silence is kept and which are indeed worthy of silence." That Gregory was referring to a ritual enactment is indicated by the use of the formulations *epeisagei* and *ta men poiei, ta de paschei*, and the fact that he uses the latter expression because he does not want to set out what happened in the *telete* and present indecency as a *mysterion* – for this makes clear that those things were part of a nocturnal *telete*, a *mysterion* at Eleusis, and involved things that were seen, not simply a story being heard. There was also, we shall see, a reference to the sacred drama in Lactantius. Aristides (19 p. 422 Dindorf) in his *Eleusinios*, written in response to the sanctuary's partial destruction by the Kostovoks at AD 170, addresses Demeter as follows: *O Demeter, he palai men autothi ten Koren heures, nyn de soi zetein ho neos leipetai*. There are clearly three time-frames: first, now, after the destruction; second, the mythological past, the time of the reunion of Demeter and Kore at Eleusis; this is presented as Demeter "finding" Kore, to match the mention of the search, which in the "now" frame is presented as something which had belonged to the third frame, the time in-between, the normality now lost. In this normality Demeter was searching for Kore in the temple (see also Deubner 1969, 84); this cannot mean that she was perceived to have been searching for Kore in the temple, which would have been absurd; it can only mean that Demeter was represented as searching in the temple, that the enactment of Demeter's search for Kore in the sacred drama had taken place in the temple. Proklos' reference to laments by Kore and Demeter in connection with Mysteria and *teletai* (Kern 1922, 209, 227–228) may or may not pertain to the Eleusinian drama (Clinton 1992, 85, thinks it does).

The sacred drama would be representing something very close to the *Homeric Hymn to Demeter*,[9] so it would have enacted Demeter's arrival at Eleusis, her withdrawal, her reunion with Kore and the establishment of the new order after the crisis: Kore's life between Hades and Olympos, the re-establishment of normality in agriculture and the foundation of the Mysteries by Demeter.

In the *Epitome of the Divine Institutes* Lactantius mentions a rite of Isis in which her priests and attendants, in imitation of Isis, lament and search for Osiris and then find him, and celebratory rites replace the mournful ones, adding: "The mystery of Ceres also resembles these, the mystery in which torches are lighted, and Proserpina is searched for through the night; and when she has been found, the whole rite ends with congratulations and the throwing about of torches" (*Div. Inst. Epit.* 23). In the main work, written long before its epitome (see Preface to *Epit.*), Lactantius said (*Div. Inst.* 1.21) that, as Osiris is searched for with the wailing of Isis, so in the Eleusinian rites Proserpina is abducted to have an incestuous marriage with her uncle; and because Ceres had searched for her in Sicily with torches lighted from Aetna, "her sacred rites are celebrated with the throwing of torches". Clearly, the statement that Persephone is abducted in an Eleusinian ritual is another reference to the sacred drama. The *Epitome* passage draws an intelligible parallel; *Div. Inst.* 1.21 does not, for a search for Osiris does not have much in common with the abduction and incestuous marriage it is compared to; this seems to be a stream of consciousness comparison, in which the Eleusinian rite that was perceived to be comparable to the search for Osiris is not mentioned. This passage taken on its own suggests that the assumptions that shaped Lactantius' selections had included the knowledge that the Eleusinian

Mysteries included a search for Persephone, which at some point involved the throwing of torches; and that the central similarity (which is not set out) was between the two searches – though there was also a parallel between the searchers for Osiris imitating Isis' wailing and the searchers for Persephone imitating Demeter searching with torches lighted from Aetna. The *Epitome* confirms this hypothesis – to put it differently, when Lactantius came to write the *Epitome* he tightened up his formulations and made his text less lurid, but clear to those who did not share the knowledge that had shaped his selections: he describes a ritual search for Kore, at night by people carrying torches. The fact that this search is compared to a ritual which involved a search by religious functionaries, not one priestess impersonating a goddess, suggests that the Eleusinian search was not part of the sacred drama. The view that the search was a separate rite, not part of the sacred drama, is strongly supported by the fact that the myth, and so the sacred drama, does not, and cannot, involve Kore being found: she was brought back by Hermes. Furthermore, the drama's main lines would have had to resemble those of the myth in the Homeric hymn, in which the appearance of Kore was not the end of the story – it had to be followed by the establishment of the new order, of the world as it now is. So this appearance could not have been the end of the rite, as it is in Lactantius' search. "Finding" Kore, "finding a deity and celebrating this discovery", belongs to a different type of rite, a ritual search, a rite performed in certain Greek festivals I shall consider in a moment.

In the *Epitome* Lactantius says that when Kore was found the rite ended with rejoicing and the throwing about of torches – clearly by those who had searched for her. In *Div. Inst.* 1.21 he explains the throwing of torches as an imitation of Demeter's experiences in her search for Kore.[10] This would be an instance of the initiates re-enacting some of Demeter's experiences, as they did when fasting and drinking the *kykeon* (Clement of Alexandria, *Protr.* 2.21.2; cf. Richardson 1974, 22–23, 165–166; Mylonas 1961, 258–259, 294–295). On my reconstruction, this search was separate from the sacred drama, in the same way that the initiates' fasting and drinking the *kykeon* was separate from any re-enactment of Demeter's actions in the sacred drama. If this is right, the Mysteries had included a ritual search by initiates, which had been perceived as an imitation of Demeter's search, a part of the initiates' undergoing some of Demeter's experiences. But there is not an exact coincidence between the myth and the ritual, certainly not as far as the finding of Kore is concerned. Demeter had not "found" Kore; Hermes had brought her back from Hades. Correlatively with this, in Greek eyes this rite was not a simple commemoration: a rite involving priestly personnel and worshippers searching for a deity would have been perceived also as a search for a deity, a rite that characterizes also other festivals, in some of which at least the search also had a commemorative function.

Ritual searches took different forms in different festivals.[11] At the Tonaia in Samos a search for Hera's statue re-enacted a mythological search. A search on a mountain sacred to Dionysos, Mount Larysion, above Migonion, involved the discovery (*aneuriskousi*) of a ripe bunch of grapes during a festival of Dionysos at the beginning of the spring – given the season a miraculous find that suggested the advent of the god. At the Agrionia in Chaironeia the women searched for Dionysos "as if he had run away", and then stopped and said that he had fled to the Muses and was hidden with them. At least some ritual searches were part of advent festivals. Advent festivals[12] (and what we may call advent segments in more complex festivals) were focused on a deity's arrival and presence. Demeter, Persephone, Dionysos, and Apollo are the main deities involved in such rituals. There was a general perception that deities were present in their festivals, but in advent festivals the arrival and presence of the deity was focused on, and ritually enacted, in different ways. At the City Dionysia Dionysos' statue was moved to a shrine in the Academy and then brought back, received and entertained, in a ritual re-enacting the cult's first reception, which also gave concrete expression to the god's arrival in the present (Sourvinou-Inwood 2002, II.1; 1994, 269–290). In the Elean festival Thyia Dionysos was invoked by women, by name and by the invocation *axie taure*; in response a bull, the animal destined for sacrifice, presumably appeared; certainly in this festival there was a miraculous appearance of wine, which mysteriously filled empty jars placed by the priests in a sealed building.[13] This miraculous filling up of the pots, and perhaps also the appearance of the bull, were signs of the god's presence. As in the search on Mount Larysion, then, there was an enacted discovery, a ritually manipulated miracle which was a sign of the divine advent and presence.

We cannot assume that Lactantius had reliable knowledge concerning the Mysteries or that his information on the search is accurate. But it is not methodologically justifiable to reject it without reason. The fact that in the *Epitome* he tightened up his formulation and described the rite which had been implied in his earlier text, which shows that he had a firm grasp of the ritual he was referring to, suggests that he is not reporting or copying something vaguely perceived and thus easily distorted. Most importantly, the fact that what he described corresponds to a rite included in other Greek festivals, festivals of a type that characterizes Persephone, provides some support for the view that the Mysteries had included a search for Persephone. In addition, the fact that what Lactantius described also corresponds to a relationship between the actions and experiences of the initiates and those of Demeter that is attested for other parts of the initiation, the initiates' imitation of Demeter's actions and experiences in the myth, adds further support to the conclusion that the Mysteries had included a search for Kore.

Apollodoros of Athens (*FGrH* 244 F 110b), a reliable source on Athenian religion, said that in Athens the hierophant sounded a gong while Kore was being invoked (*epikaloumenes*). The expression, which denotes the invocation of a deity, and the fact that the hierophant performed a ritual act in *propria persona*, makes it clear that this was an actual solemn invocation – not part of the sacred drama. The context of the fragment (Schol. Theokr. 2.35–36; cf. Theokr. 2.36) and Apollodoros' comments connect the sounding of bronze with Hekate, death and the dead, eclipses of the moon and purifications. This suggests that the persona of Persephone as Queen of the Underworld was implicated – whatever other aspects may have been involved. The fact that Kore alone was invoked was not because Kore was summoned from Hades, for, we shall see, she had not been in Hades in Boedromion. A solemn invocation of Kore alone would make excellent ritual sense as part of the search: after it had run its course, and before the deity was "found", the invocation would have taken place, with the hierophant sounding a gong. Solemn invocations, though common and by no means limited to advent festivals – let alone to ritual searches – nevertheless had a special place in both, since both focused on the deity's arrival, which was the objective of an invocation.

Plutarch's fragment 178 (Sandbach), for which a connection with the search has been claimed,[14] states that at the moment of death the *psyche* ... *paschei pathos* like that suffered by those being initiated into great mysteries; at first there are wanderings and walkings in circles, and frightening marches through the darkness; then, before the end, all the terrible things, shivering, quivering, sweating and amazement; and then wonderful light comes to meet you and you are received by pure places and meadows (*edexanto*), with voices (*phonas*) and dances and the solemnities of holy *akousmata* and sacred *phasmata*... The initiates wander free there and consort with holy and pure men. In order to reconstruct the main lines of the mysteric experiences deployed to construct this image of the afterlife (the assumptions shared by writer and readers) we should try to construct some (quasi-) stable points by determining what, if any, echoes the mysteric correlative to the *psyche*'s experience would have evoked for the initiates. The notion that pure places and meadows receive the *psyche* in the afterlife as they *edexanto* the initiates in the Mysteries would have evoked the Telesterion, which was associated with the notion of receiving the initiates: Aristophanes (*Clouds* 302–304) speaks of the Telesterion as the *mystodokos domos*, the initiates' receiving house. That the Telesterion is the mysteric correlative of the holy meadows is also shown by the association of these meadows with elements which in the Mysteries were located in the Telesterion: *phonai* would have evoked the hierophant's voice coming from inside the Anaktoron – the expression *hai ex anaktorou phonai* was a synonym of *hierophantia* (Philostr., *Soph.* 600.20; cf. Clinton 1974, 40, 46); *phasmata* occurs, in close association with the notions *myoumenoi ... kai epopteuontes*, in a Platonic passage (*Phaedr.* 250C) that deploys (in complex ways) assumptions, including language, based on the Eleusinian Mysteries (Burkert 1987, 92–93); *akousmata hiera* corresponds, and may have been an expression referring to the *aporrheta* things said by the hierophant ([Lys.], *Against Andok.* 51) inside the Telesterion. If it is right that the mysteric correlative of the meadows is the Telesterion, it would follow that the wanderings in the dark had taken place before the initiates entered the Telesterion. Were these wanderings part of the search for Persephone?

The fact that, according to Lactantius (*Div. Inst. Epit.* 23, *Div. Inst.* 1.21), the finding of Kore was celebrated with the throwing of torches does not mean that the searchers were carrying lighted torches throughout, and that the wanderings in the dark could not have been part of the search. On the contrary, an alternation of darkness and light within the search would fit the alternation of darkness and light that characterized the Mysteries, and indeed structured the succession of rites described by Plutarch, where light comes to meet the initiates, which suggests torch-bearing figures (religious personnel) meeting the initiates who were in the darkness. This is exactly the situation in Lucian's dialogue *Kataplous* 22: two men who have reached Hades' outer reaches comment on the darkness, and one adds "tell me, for of course you have been initiated in the Eleusinian Mysteries, do you not think that things here are similar to those there?"; the other replies "You are right; *idou goun* a torch-bearing female figure is approaching . . ." Wanderings in the dark and being met by torch-bearing figures fit the search for Kore – with perhaps the initiates lighting torches (comparably to the candle-lighting at the announcement of the resurrection in the Greek Easter service) and throwing them in celebration when Kore was found. These two passages suggest that the initiation included a part perceived to be mimicking the shade's descent to Hades. But it cannot be excluded that this perception may have been constructed by the writers who articulate it, or their predecessors, and not been part of the mysteric discourse. If it had been part of the mysteric discourse, how would it fit the hypothesis that the wandering was part of the search for Persephone? It would fit the fact that Persephone's persona as Queen of the Underworld was implicated in the invocation, but would it fit a search?

The search of which we have refractions was part of the mysteric initiation; any "simple" search that may have been part of the pre-mysteric ritual would have been open to a mysteric reinterpretation, at the cult's mysteric reshaping, or subsequently. If Plutarch's wanderings had been part of the search it would follow that this search had been reinterpreted (at some point) so that it was both a ritual search for a deity and at the same time a *mimesis* of the shade's descent to Hades.[15] But was this reinterpretation part of the mysteric discourse? Leaving aside all other considerations, the fact that the mysteric ritual's ultimate goal was the achievement of a happy afterlife in Hades makes it more likely than not that the search for Persephone was given an eschatological reinterpretation when the festival became the Mysteries. This likelihood is further increased by the fact that Persephone's Underworld persona had been involved in the invocation and thus the search, which shows that the Mysteries' ritual search was connected with the eschatological sphere. In these circumstances it would, I suggest, be perverse to doubt that Plutarch was refracting an eschatological reinterpretation of the search that was part of the mysteric discourse.

What of the "finding" of Kore? We can, I submit, reconstruct the possible outcomes of this search on the basis of the ritual schemata structuring comparable rites. It seems that in Greek religion a ritual search culminated either in some form of "giving up", as at the Agrionia at Chaironeia, or in the "finding" of the deity. The search in the Mysteries, we know, had ended with the finding of Kore. What evidence there is on searches and on modalities of divine presence in Greek rituals suggests that the finding of a deity had taken one of two forms: the finding of the statue, or the finding of something else closely connected with the deity which was in some way miraculous. Both are modalities for articulating the notion of the divine advent and presence, as in the miraculous appearance of wine in the Thyia and the arrival of the statue at the City Dionysia. I suggest that the "finding" of Kore in the Mysteries consisted of the miraculous appearance of something connected with her which was perceived to be a sign of her advent; that, as with the miraculous discovery of the ripe grapes at the beginning of the spring on Mount Larysion, the advent of Kore was ritually enacted through the miraculous finding of an unseasonable ear of corn.

The Eleusinian cult was closely connected with corn and both Demeter and Kore were iconographically characterized by ears of corn. The relationship between Kore and the ear of corn is comparable to that between Dionysos and grapes and wine – the two signs of the god's presence in his advent festivals, to which the ear of corn would be comparable if my reconstruction is right. Not only are grapes and wine, on the one hand, and ears of corn, on the other, common attributes of each deity, but also the relationships are such that allegorical thought has created comparable identifications. Dionysos was identified with grapes and wine (e.g.: Diodoros 3.62.2–7, 9; Plut., *Mor.* 377D). Kore, as Burkert (1987, 80) put it, "became grain, or, in a more refined way, the 'life breath' which is transported and killed in the grain". This is Kleanthes' formulation (fr. 547 [ap. *Plut.* Mor. 377D]; cf. Plut., *Mor.* 367C). According to Augustin (*Civ.* 7.20), Varro discussed the Eleusinian Mysteries, in which there were many rites, all relevant to the invention of corn, which Ceres discovered; Persephone, whom Ceres lost because Orcus abducted her, represented the fertility of the seeds which had once failed and was restored. Cicero (*De natura deorum* 2.66) says that Persephone is thought to be the seed of the produce and they imagine that she was hidden and searched for by her mother. Cornutus (28,54,12–14) interpreted the rape myth as signifying the seeds' disappearance into the earth for part of the year.[16] Such allegorical interpretations were constructed out of a relationship between Kore and corn in the perceptions articulating, and articulated in, Greek rituals that was comparable to that between Dionysos and grapes and wine, both of which functioned as signs of his advent. This helps support the view that the ear of corn had played a comparable role at the culmination of the search for Kore in the Mysteries.

My reconstruction, in which the finding of Kore consisted of the finding of an ear of corn, partly coincides with a rite described in a late text: [pseudo-?] Hippolytos (*Refutation of All Heresies* 5.8.39–40) attributes to a Naassene Gnostic the information that the Mysteries included a rite in which an ear of corn was displayed. The text mentions "a green ear of corn reaped" in connection with the Phrygians, and then says that when the Athenians initiate people into the Eleusinian rites they display to the *epopteuousi* (those who are watching), the great, marvellous, and most perfect *epoptikon mysterion*: an ear of corn reaped in silence (or: they display in silence ... a reaped ear of corn); and this ear of corn is for the Athenians the perfect great radiance from that which cannot be portrayed, as the hierophant cries out at night at Eleusis beneath a huge fire "the Mistress has given birth to a holy son, Brimo to Brimos". I cannot consider Brimo here, but I will discuss below the problem that may arise from the fact that the text seems to place this rite in the *epopteia* – though we cannot be totally certain that *epopteuousi* and *epoptikon* were used to signify "*epopteia*" as opposed to "initiation".

The reliability of this text has been questioned. It is true that the filters through which the material deployed had been perceived and articulated were syncretic and (variedly) Christian, and so were conducive to distortion; the question is whether its skeleton, the basic information that an ear of corn was displayed in the Mysteries, which corresponds to the rite which I suggested was the culmination of the search for Kore, does reflect the ancient ritual reality. Mylonas argued (1961, 275, cf. 305–306) that Hippolytos attributed to the Eleusinian Mysteries what had belonged to the Phrygian Mysteries; this a priori position is much less plausible than the notion that the two cults are mentioned together at this point precisely because they both involved the reaped ear of corn. The Eleusinian cult and its goddesses were closely associated with corn, and, we saw, there was a connection between Kore and the ear of corn comparable to that between Dionysos and grapes and wine. A rite involving an ear of corn, then, belongs most naturally in the ritual of the Mysteries, and the notion that Hippolytos wrongly ascribed a Phrygian rite to Eleusis seems an implausible special pleading. Mylonas then argued (1961, 275–276) that ears of corn were represented on the lesser Propylaea and an old law ordered the initiates to bring handfuls of agricultural produce, which "surely" had included ears of corn; if the ear of corn was such a great mystery, how is it that it is freely shown on monuments and was brought by the initiates? It is possible that the information that an ear of corn had been displayed in the Mysteries had been right, whereas Hippolytos' perception that it had been a great mystery had been wrong. Most importantly, if the ear of corn had been perceived to be a *mysterion*, it was a *mysterion* in context; it was not the existence of the ear of corn that was the mystery – how could it have been? It was its appearance at a particular place and time, as part of a particular ritual, ascribed a particular meaning and significance by the context. Mylonas also argued (1961, 276) that Tertullian's statement (*Valentin.* 1) that the phallos was the central symbol of the Eleusinian *epopteia* casts doubt on Hippolytos' assertion. In theory both writers may have been partly right, and the ear of corn and the phallos could both have been central symbols of the *epopteia*; but whether one or neither of them were right, their disagreement cannot throw any light on the validity of the basic information that an ear of corn had been displayed in the Mysteries, at the *epopteia*, or in another part of the Mysteries.

Clearly, then, Mylonas' arguments against the view that an ear of corn was displayed at the Mysteries are invalid. It does not necessarily follow that this view is right, but the fact that the display of an ear of corn described by Hippolytos coincides with a rite, the finding and displaying of an unseasonable ear of corn, reconstructed on the basis of the ritual schemata structuring comparable festivals as one of the two most likely rites bringing closure to the search for Kore, is, I submit, significant; each of these, the text and the reconstruction, supports the validity of the other. What, then, of the fact that Hippolytos seems to say (though, we saw, this is not certain) that this rite was part of the *epopteia*? In my reconstruction it would have been part of the main initiation, a rite constructed when the Mysteries were created out of the redeployment, and perhaps reinterpretation, of a search for the goddess that had been part of the pre-mysteric ritual, comparable to other searches for deities in other festivals. There are at least two explanations that can account for this divergence without affecting the validity of my reconstruction. First, Hippolytos may have been wrong about the rite's place in the festival, which he clearly did not contemplate as an articulated structure but as a collection of rites and beliefs from which to pick material. Alternatively, the pre-mysteric ritual search may have been redeployed twice, perhaps in different versions, once in the main initiation ritual and once in the *epopteia*.

In my reconstruction, the ear of corn was the sign of the divine advent at the end of the search. This was its meaning in the pre-mysteric ritual; further semantic layers were probably added when the mysteric ritual and discourse were created,[17] but this central meaning had not been discarded, otherwise it would not have been possible for Lactantius to speak of the finding of Kore. In Hippolytos the ear of corn was a kind of radiant reflection of the divine that cannot be portrayed. This can be seen as a transformation, a reinterpetation through Christian filters, of the ear of corn's identity as the sign of the divine advent. Thus, Hippolytos' account can be seen as resulting from an interpretation of (perhaps a mysteric reinterpretation of) the notion that the ear of corn was the sign of Kore's advent.[18]

Ritual searches took place in the open air and it is in an outside space, not in a cult building, that we would expect the ear of corn to have been "found" – as Dionysos' grapes were. It is therefore likely that the search for, and the invocation and "finding" of, Kore had taken place outside, before the initiates entered the Telesterion. This coincides with the structuring of the echoes of the Mysteries in the Plutarch fragment, where (what is probably) the search is presented as taking place before the rites inside the Telesterion.[19]

A common advent schema, we saw, involved the removal of a statue from, and its return to, its usual location, which re-enacted the mythical arrival of the deity, or of the cult, and helped articulate the deity's advent in the present. Sacred things, *ta hiera*, were removed from, and eventually returned to their usual place also in the Mysteries, but we do not know what they were and whether they had included a (small) statue of Demeter – and perhaps of Kore.[20] If they had, their movement would have been similar to that of statues in other festivals. I argued (1997, 144–150) that this movement of the *hiera* to Athens and back was structured by, and expressed, meanings pertaining to the cult's territorial/poliadic aspects and helped place the territory under Demeter's protection. Those meanings were created by the specific forms of the movement; but, whether or not the *hiera* had included a statue, the basic schema of removing them from, and returning them to, their normal place also had a function comparable to that involved in the removal and return of the deity's statue elsewhere: it allowed the ritual enactment of and gave concrete manifestation to the deity's advent in the present. Since Demeter revealed secret rites to the Eleusinian princes (*HomHymDem*. 474–476), and a central part of the Eleusinian secret rites involved the showing of the *hiera* (for this function defined the hierophant),[21] she must have been believed to have given the *hiera* to the princes when she founded the Mysteries. In any case, the *hiera* were the cult's most sacred things, so they were the objects that came closest to giving it a physical expression, a role which in other cults was fulfilled by the statue. Hence, while in other cults the arrival of the deity and/or cult, and through this the deity's advent in the present, was represented through the arrival of the statue, in the Mysteries it was represented through the arrival of the *hiera* given by the goddess in a symbolic re-enactment of the cult's first arrival at Eleusis.

The movement of the *hiera* and their ceremonial arrival at Eleusis is the second advent festival schema structuring the Mysteries, the first in terms of the ritual's syntax; it articulates the advent of Demeter, while the search articulates that of Kore. This does not entail that the goddesses came from different places, or even that they had not both been (in some way) "there" from the beginning (cf. Eur., *Ion* 1074–1086); these schemata, which articulate the deities' arrival and presence, are the ritual correlatives to the myth: Demeter arrived first in her search for Kore, Kore was eventually brought to Eleusis by Hermes. In the myth Kore came from Hades, but I will argue that in the ritual she did not. According to the *Homeric Hymn* (398–403) Kore returned annually to the upper world in the spring. The same perception is reflected in cult, at least in the one case in which it is possible to be certain – a festival in Syracuse.[22] Diodoros (5.4.4–7) mentions the festival *Kores Katagoge*, celebrated when the fruit of the grain was about to reach ripeness, about May, which is undoubtedly the same festival as that which he describes at 5.4.2 (cf. 4.23.4), a Kore festival at the spring Kyane: Plouton abducted Kore near Syracuse and, having split the earth, descended into Hades with her; Kyane rushed forth at that point. Every year the Syracusans celebrated a festival there, in which the public sacrifices involved sinking bulls into the pool. Since Kyane was a passage between the upper world and Hades, created by Hades during Persephone's abduction, this rite is connected with Persephone's movement between the two worlds. This, then, was an advent festival, as is indicated by its name (see Burkert 1988, 84–85), celebrating Kore's return from Hades, which took place during the festival. If in the Syracusan calendar Kore returned to the upper world in May, in the perceptions articulated in, and articulating, that calendar she stayed in Hades for half a year (as she does in some late sources: e.g. Ovid, *Met.* 5.565–567; Hyg., *Fab.* 146), not one-third of the year as in the *Homeric Hymn* (398–403, 445–447, 463–465; see also Apollodoros 1.5.3), which reflected Athenian perceptions. Variations in the precise time of Kore's return from, and descent to, Hades in different places are likely, but a major divergence as to which part of the year she spent in Hades, autumn/winter or spring/summer, is extremely unlikely, especially given the radiation of her Panhellenic persona. On any reckoning, then, Kore would not have been perceived to be in Hades in the middle of Boedromion, least of all in Athens where she was believed to spend two-thirds of the year in the upper world.

A combination of advent and mysteries occurs in the Koragia in Mantineia (*IG* V.2 265; cf. also *IG* V.2 266; Jost 1985, 346–349; this volume 145), another advent festival for Kore, in which the statue was removed from the temple, taken to the house of the priest or priestess and eventually returned to the temple which on that day was open to the worshippers. The festival included a procession, sacrifices, the offering of a peplos, and a part referred to as *mystika ta arrheta*, and *arrheta mysteria*. In Laconia a *xoanon* of Kore was brought up (*anagousin*; cf. Hesych., s.v. *koragein: to anagein ten Koren*) on stated days from Helos to a sanctuary of Demeter Eleusinia in Therai (Paus. 3.20.4, 7; cf. Nilsson 1906, 334–335). The minimum that can be established by these parallels is that the combination of advent festivals with mysteries and things Eleusinian was perceived as compatible in Greek religious mentality. These parallels may conceivably indicate more; given the prestige and radiation of the Eleusinian Mysteries it is not inconceivable that cults in which Demeter had the epithet Eleusinia, or which involved mysteries, could have been influenced by – and even in very broad terms reflected – the Eleusinian cult. But even the minimum that is established with certainty offers support for the basic lines of the reconstruction offered here: that divine advent is a major facet in the festival of the Mysteries.

The "public" section of the Mysteries was articulated by Demeter's advent ritual. One segment of the initiatory part inside the Eleusinian sanctuary was structured by Kore's advent ritual and another by the sacred drama (which, on Aristides' testimony, took place inside the Telesterion), which was also a third advent schema; for its re-enactment of Demeter's arrival, epiphany and withdrawal, Kore's return and the cult's foundation (like the simpler, schematic re-enactments involving the movement of a statue) gave a concrete expression to the goddesses' presence in the festival.

The drama represented the most terrible crisis imaginable, the crops' failure to grow, which threatened mankind's survival; but it also showed that the crisis was overcome and the present order established, which ensures that catastrophe will not occur: Demeter protects the crops and, correlatively, she receives worship through this cult she herself founded. This order, and the cult of which the drama is part, established a guarantee of Demeter's protection (see Sourvinou-Inwood 1990, 306–307 on this notion of divine "guarantee"). In Greek ritual mentality, in which New Year dissolution followed by the restoration of normality brought renewal (Burkert 1983, 142–143), the temporary "suspension" of the cult when the *hiera* were taken to Athens and the re-enactment of its arrival when they returned, and then the re-enactment in the drama of the crisis and of the establishment of the present order which ended it, brought about a renewal of this order, a renewal of the guarantee of Demeter's protection. The renewal of Demeter's guarantee took place in Boedromion, before the beginning of the agricultural year. This is a significant time; it is not necessary to imagine that the festival had been moved from the time just before sowing, as Brumfield (1981, 214–215, 231) thought. For this renewal is most appropriately located before the beginning of the new agricultural year, on which Demeter's renewed (and so strongest) blessings were thus bestowed.

The Mysteries involved strong emotional experiences, and so a strong emotional involvement with the ritual and the deities (see Plut., *Mor.* 47A, 943C; Burkert 1987, 89–95, 109–110, 113–114). In such a context the representation in the sacred drama of the construction of the relationship with the deities that ensures the security of the crops and a happy afterlife would have involved an intense religious experience, especially when the representation of the cult's foundation by Demeter (inevitably) zoomed the drama, and the past in which this foundation took place, to the here and now, fused that world with the world of the initiates – in the (perceived) presence of the two goddesses. This intense religious experience would have connected the initiates to the deities. Besides the benefit of the experience itself, this connection would also have sealed the effects of the ritual: at the level of the community (experienced by its individual members, as well as articulated by, and on behalf of, the polis) it would have sealed the renewal of the guarantee of Demeter's protection of the crops; at the level of the individual it would have sealed the forging of a relationship (in the framework of polis religion) between each initiate and the two goddesses; this privileged access to Persephone, the Queen of the Underworld, ensured a better lot in the afterlife.

To sum up, I hope to have shown that divine advent was a major facet of the festival of the Mysteries. It helped articulate the concerns about, and bring about positive results for, agriculture, poliadic ideology and eschatology. In its pre-mysteric form this had been an advent festival, structured through the interacting schemata "advent festival" and "agricultural and poliadic central polis cult located in the periphery"; it annually renewed the relationship between Demeter and her worshippers, and the guarantee of the goddess's protection, just before the beginning of the agricultural year.[23] Then the festival was reshaped to serve eschatological concerns through the overarching schema "initiation", which here took the form of individual initiation based on choice, aiming at the achievement through ritual of a higher "status" after death, that of initiate entitled to a happy afterlife. This overarching schema transformed the meanings of the festival's constituent elements. Advent schemata – and the schema "agricultural and poliadic central polis cult located in the periphery" – continued to structure segments of the festival, but they (or, at least, some of them) now had forms and meanings that also contributed to the cult's initiatory structure and/or eschatological aims – for example, the meanings of the search for Persephone were expanded to encompass the initiatory-eschatological dimension.

Appendix: Refocusing Eleusis – a response

Kennell (1997) claimed that my article on Eleusis has a blatantly fallacious methodology and invalid arguments, and that I am ignorant of fundamental aspects of the evidence (besides having "a less-than-firm grasp of English idiom"). If he were right the validity of my conclusions would be undermined; I will therefore respond to his (forensically skilful) criticisms and take the opportunity to refocus some of my arguments.

Kennell comments:

> Although she purports to examine three sets of evidence (archeology, literary texts, and epigraphy), it is no surprise when they all converge to support her view that Eleusis was part of the Athenian state from the beginning of the polis. How much more interesting it would have been if they had not converged, and new ways of assessing the evidence had to be devised.

This shows a fundamental misconception of the very nature of the object of the enquiry, which was the reconstruction of events that had either happened or not happened: either the Eleusinian cult had been part of Athenian religion from the beginning or it had not; either the eschatological dimension had been part of the cult from the beginning, or it had been a subsequent development. These are determinable facts, and I was trying to determine them, reconstruct (the main lines of) what had happened. Therefore, if the conclusions of the separate analyses had not converged, those conclusions would have been wrong. For this is not a question of reconstructing beliefs, or the readings of a text or myth, in which converging results may suggest that ambivalences and multivocalities were suppressed. When it comes to attempts at reconstructing something that had actually happened, whatever ways of assessing the evidence one adopts, the results should converge, or the analyses are wrong.

Kennell continues:

> Despite S.-I.'s claims to "rigour" in order to avoid "fallacious assumptions and unconscious adjustments to make the different parts of the evidence fit" (p. 132), the article is rife with just these failings. Perhaps the most blatant occurs when S.-I. tries to support her contention that the main entrance route to the sanctuary in the eighth and seventh centuries BC was from the north, at the end of the Sacred Way that led from Athens... As an "independent argument", she states that the geometric temple of Demeter in the sanctuary and a contemporary apsidal temple found under the later temple of Artemis Propylaia in the forecourt to the east seem to have been roughly aligned along the same axis and were oriented towards the Sacred Way. In fact, so little remains of the apses of both buildings that it is quite impossible to determine anything of either's orientation. (She hints at this in endnote 8.) Nothing daunted, S.-I. fills another page with arguments based on this assertion, even adducing a parallel for such alignment with the sanctuary of Athena Pronaia at Delphi.

Now the reality. I set out two separate and independent archaeological arguments. The first (which Kennell ignored) pertained to the organization of space inside the city wall and aimed at reconstructing the direction from which the stairway giving access to the temple was approached; it indicated a north–south ceremonial route to the temple, which suggested that the main approach to the city and sanctuary was at the north. The second argument concerned the area around the sanctuary's north entrance and aimed at reconstructing the direction from which the city and sanctuary were ceremonially entered. An eighth-century road under the Little Propylaia, where the "Peisistrateian North Pylon" had stood at the sanctuary's main entrance, was, there can be no doubt given the topography, the last stretch of a road from Athens to Eleusis. An eighth-century road from Athens to Eleusis leading to the sanctuary from the north suggests that the sanctuary's main entrance was at the north from the beginning. I did not make the claim that the road alone shows this, because I believe that, provided the argument is not circular, it is more rigorous to take account of as many fragments of evidence as possible, however problematic their reading. Kennell believes my argument is circular, but he does not seem to realize what this argument is. I said of the apsidal building under the Artemis Propylaia temple that the fact that "It would seem to have been very roughly on the same axis as that of Demeter may conceivably suggest that the two were not unrelated" and then suggested that this supports the view that the sanctuary's main entrance was at the north in the eighth century — since a temple of Artemis Propylaia would be situated before the sanctuary's main entrance. What Kennell failed to understand is that the notion that the two eighth-century buildings were related was an argument for the identification of the apsidal building as the Artemis Propylaia temple: my alignment argument offered *further* support to a thesis, which Travlos (1988, 92) assumed was right, that this was the eighth-century Artemis Propylaia temple. As for my "even" adducing the sanctuary of Athena Pronaia as a parallel, I mentioned its relationship to the sanctuary of Apollo to show that temples and sanctuaries could be related in this way in the eighth century, which supports further the identification of the eighth-century Artemis Propylaia temple. It is clear, I hope, that far from piling hypothesis upon assertion to support a dubious proposition as part of my distortion of the evidence to make the different parts fit, I used the alignment argument to give further support to an established view. The fact that each of the two independent archaeological arguments concluded that in the eighth and seventh centuries the sanctuary's main entrance had been at the north removes the one archaeological argument used to support the notion that Eleusis had been independent: the claim that the main entrance had been at the south and only moved to the north in the sixth century when Eleusis became part of Athens.

Kennell also claims that I use late evidence illegitimately:

> In considering the textual and epigraphical evidence, S.-I.'s rigor does not evidently extend to taking into account the disparate dates of the texts she uses to illuminate the sanctuary in the early archaic period... Plutarch's *Moralia*, Aristophanes' *Clouds*, and inscriptions ranging from the fifth century BC to the third century AD are pressed into service without regard for the possibility that the information they provide may be chronologically conditioned. To S.-I., the participation of the ephebes is one of the indicators that the Mysteries were part of the Athenian polis religion and, by implication, in conformity at least with her view that Athens always controlled Eleusis. Had she looked further, she would have seen that the participation of the ephebes in the procession rests on a single inscription, IG II/III2 1078, a decree dated to about AD 220... In consequence, to retroject the information from this third century AD document to the classical period, let alone to the archaic, is methodologically unjustifiable. The participation of Athenian ephebes in the processions beginning under the Roman Empire tells us nothing about the antiquity of the connection between Eleusis and Athens.

I will consider each indictment separately.

Contrary to Kennell's claim, I did not use *Clouds* and Plutarch in my study of the textual and epigraphical evidence, but in a strategy that tested the conclusions of my investigation of the sanctuary's "Solonian" phase, according to which this phase had involved radical changes that implicated the cult building and its relationship to outside space and were different in nature from changes in other sanctuaries, suggesting changes in the nature of the cult; since the basic spatial arrangements that began then continued into the fifth century and beyond – with changes only in the size and monumentality of individual elements – those arrangements reflect the cultic needs of the Mysteries as we know them; since they result from changes in a sanctuary that had not until then appeared different from other sanctuaries, this suggests that the cult had not begun as a mysteric cult but was transformed into one in the early sixth century. I tried to test the validity of this conclusion through a form of model testing; this strategy has serious flaws (Sourvinou-Inwood 1995, 413–422), but in this case these are minimized, because it was not a constructed model that was tested but the conclusion of an analysis, and, most importantly, because the danger that the model will implicitly structure the data, thus validating itself, is radically minimized by the fact that the testing involved one simple question to which the answer can be either "yes" or "no". To put it in cruder terms than I did in the paper: if I were right that there had been such a change in the cult, reflected in a spatial arrangement that continued into the classical period and beyond, there should be later evidence showing that the area in front of the entrance of the Telesterion had some role in the Mysteries (since the increase in its size and change in its shape and relationship to the temple was a major change of the "Solonian" phase). Is there such evidence? Yes. *Clouds* 302–304 establishes that in the fifth century the Mysteries included a ceremonial opening of the gates of the Telesterion to display its interior to the *mystai*, who therefore were outside the Telesterion; so the area in front of its entrance had a role in the Mysteries. Since this is established for the fifth century it is legitimate to use *Mor.* 81 D–E for more information – about Plutarch's time at least.

As for the ephebes, far from being ignorant of the late date of the evidence I commented (n.38 after "the role of the ephebes"): "Whenever this began, and whoever may have preceded them in the role of receiving the *hiera*." I mentioned them as one of the manifestations of the fact that the Mysteries were part of polis religion; I did *not* use them in the argument that Eleusis had been part of Athens from the beginning – or in any reconstruction of archaic history. They do not carry much weight even with regard to the relationship between the Mysteries and Athenian religion, of which there are many manifestations attested for the classical period (see now also Cavanaugh 1996, 211–216), with the role of the *archon basileus* generally believed to have been rooted in the early archaic world. So why mention the ephebes? Because I believe that their introduction, at whatever date, shows the continuing strength of the perception of the Mysteries as part of Athenian religion.

Clearly, then, Kennell radically misunderstood and (venomously, as well as radically) misrepresented my methodology and arguments and even my use of the evidence – the ways in which data and arguments relate to specific conclusions.

Notes

1 I am very grateful to Professor Robert Parker for many discussions on Eleusinian matters.
2 Sourvinou-Inwood (1997, 132–164).
3 Whether or not Binder (1998, 131–139) is right to downdate the beginning of the Eleusinian sanctuary to "the seventh century, certainly no earlier than the late Geometric period" does not affect my argument; first, because the late eighth century is where I am inclined to situate the cult; second, because I am not envisaging the formation and crystallization of the Athenian polis as an overnight operation. Space prevents me from discussing Binder's article; I will only say that, whereas I agree that some of the dates given have been too high, and that cultic pyre A and the terrace belong to a single project, if, as it seems, the term "ex-apsidal temple" implies the rejection of the reading that makes the curving Geometric wall part of the apsidal temple, I strongly disagree (see on this identification Mylonas 1961, 58–59); Travlos' change of mind on this is part of his whole argument about dates, which she rightly rejects; Binder's view that there was no Geometric city wall also presents great difficulties.
4 See Sourvinou-Inwood (1997, 154–155, 157). On L'Homme-Wéry 1996, see Clinton (2001, 168–170).
5 Clinton's thesis (1996, 111–125) that the Thesmophoria of Melite took place in the City Eleusinion, which had begun as a local Thesmophorion, if right, might have diminished the force of the validation. But there are, I believe, serious objections to this thesis, not least the fact that the function of the City Eleusinion as the physical manifestation of the presence of the Eleusinian cult at the centre, articulating its identity as a central polis cult, makes it extremely implausible that it should have taken over, and been housed in, the sanctuary of a sub-polis local community.
6 There are two basic versions of the foundation of the Mysteries. In *HomHymDem*. 473–482, the Mysteries had been revealed by Demeter to Eleusinian heroes, including an Eleusinian Eumolpos. This stresses the divine authority of the rite. In the second (Sourvinou-Inwood 1997, 143–144 with bibliography, 156, 157, 159) the Mysteries were founded by someone connected with Thrace or Orphic poetry or both, a Eumolpos of Thracian origin or his homonymous descendant or Orpheus; this was a "historical" myth expressing certain perceptions about the cult's beginning and nature (Sourvinou-Inwood 1997, 156, 157, 159). It is the first that was central to the cult.
7 For example, the ethical dimension is absent from the programmatic statement in *HomHymDem*. 480–482; it is present in the fifth century in Aristophanes (*Frogs* 456–459). Other aspects of the cult also changed, for example, there was at least some expansion in the number of sacred officials.
8 See also on this Mylonas (1961, 261–264), Clinton (1992, 84–95). Cf. also Richardson (1974, 24–26, 162).
9 On the status of the *Homeric Hymn to Demeter* with regard to the Eleusinian Mysteries, see esp. the masterly discussion in Parker (1991, 1–17).
10 On Demeter and torches: *HomHymDem*. 47–48; 59–61; Richardson (1974, 162 40ff., 165, 171 59–61). On initiates manipulating torches in the Mysteries cf. (shaking the torches): Aristophanes (*Frogs*, 340–344); Statius (*Silvae* 4.8.50–51) probably did not refer directly to the Eleusinian Mysteries (Coleman 1988, 217–218, 50, 51).

11 Tonaia: Menodotos (*FGrH* 541 F 1). See Burkert (1979, 129–130; 1985, 134–135; 1997, 24), Graf (1985, 93–96). Agrionia: Plutarch (*Moralia* 716F–717A), Nilsson (1906, 274), Schachter (1981, 173–174; 1986, 146), Bonnechere (1994, 197–199). On the Mount Larysion rite: Pausanias (3.22.2), Parker (1988, 100), Henrichs (1978, 145–146).
12 On which see Burkert (1988, 81–87); cf. Burkert (1985, 134–135; 1997, 24).
13 Paus. (6.26.1–2), Plut. (*Aetia gr.* 299A), Theopompos (*FGrH* 115 F 277). Nilsson (1906, 291–293), Detienne (1986, 84–88), Bérard (1976, 68–73), Mitsopoulos-Leon (1984, 275–290), Versnel (1990, 138–139 and bibl. in n.168).
14 Mylonas (1961, 264–266) thinks we cannot be certain that the passage pertained to the Eleusinian Mysteries. I will argue that it did. Clinton (1992, 85–90) takes the passage to be relevant to the search, and sets out a reconstruction in which the search is part of the sacred drama. My different reconstruction of a few (relatively) stable points agrees with his in considering the Telesterion to be the mysteric correlative of the holy meadows. But Clinton (1992, 89, 126–132) revived the theory that the Anaktoron is to be identified with the Telesterion. Mylonas (1961, 85–87) had already argued against this, and I do not find Clinton's reformulation more convincing. I cannot set out a systematic critique here. Some of the arguments Clinton adduces have already been criticized by Mylonas, such as on his testimonion 5 (Mylonas 1961, 86) – to which we may add that what would have been perceived as impiety would have been erecting a throne for a *hetaira* by the Anaktoron, inside the Telesterion, where thrones of priestly personnel are in "normal" Greek temples, not outside the Telesterion; even if she was in a good position to see the hierophant emerging from the Telesterion, this was hardly worth much compared to the things that would have gone on inside, hardly worth alienating public opinion for. Second, the fact that according to *IG* II2 3764 an *hierophanties* is said to have revealed the *teletai* of the goddesses *par' anaktora Deous* (a description that Clinton himself [1974, 89] correctly translates as "beside the anaktora of D") entails that the Anaktoron was a structure inside the Telesterion; for if it had meant "by the Telesterion" the revelation would have taken place outside, which is in conflict with what we know of the cult. The revelation of the *teletai* would have taken place inside the Telesterion. Then, besides some inconclusive testimonia (such as his no.7, *IG* II2 1552a), which seem to me to point against Clinton's theory rather than in its favour, most of the arguments adduced to support it disappear once it is realized that they are based on a misreading of tropes, the mistaking of, above all, *pars pro toto* metonymies, aimed at stressing proximity to the most sacred part of the complex, for literal language. Also, in my view, the fragment of Aelian (fr. 10) which says that only the hierophant was permitted to enter the Anaktoron, which would be consistent with the Anaktoron being a structure inside the Telesterion but not with it being the same as the Telesterion cannot convincingly be interpreted to mean that this prohibition only pertained to part of the ceremony. It is true that the text is not wholly secure, but in its present state it points in the same direction as a lot of other evidence: against the identification of the Anaktoron with the Telesterion.

Clinton's response to these views (see this volume, p. 73 n.40) does not engage with the specific arguments concerning, above all, the throne/impiety question, which pertains to the important issue of Greek religious mentality – or indeed that involving Aelian. As to whether the *pars pro toto* metonymies are unlikely, all I can say is that the distinction between literal language and metonymic tropes is unstable, and so in a way the Telesterion, which on my interpretation contained, but was not the same as, the Anaktoron, was also Demeter's anaktoron. And lest I am accused of importing such complex use of language in a context that did not encourage it, in the reflections of Eleusinian language, I simply remind the reader of the fact that *hai ex anaktorou phonai* was a synonym of hierophantia (Philostr., *Soph.* 600.20; cf. Clinton 1974, 40, 46).

15 If those wanderings and the other experiences mentioned had been part of the search for Kore that search would have been a confusing experience. Richardson (1974, 25) objected to the notion that a search was part of the Mysteries that "we can hardly believe" that "vast crowds, of perhaps thousands of initiates, roamed about the sanctuary searching for Core". Clinton (1992, 85 n.118) thinks it is very unlikely that the *mystai* were more than a few hundred. Cavanaugh (1996, 211) calculated that in 408/7 about 2,200 people had been initiated. I suggest that any confusion that may have arisen had been part of the experience.

16 On modern interpretations of Kore as the corn maiden see Richardson (1974, 284–285), Brumfield (1981, 211–214, 230–231).

17 The mysteric reinterpretation is beyond my scope here. See Burkert (1987, 80–81, 100).

18 It could in theory be argued that an Alexandrian syncretic rite in Epiphanios (*Panarium* 51.22; see Fraser 1972, 2.336–338 with bibl.; Burkert 1987, 37–38, 148 n.46 with bibl.; cf. Mylonas 1961, 302–303) involved the finding of Kore's statue and reflected an Eleusinian rite, in which case the Eleusinian Mysteries would have included a finding of Kore's statue. But (even leaving aside the rite's date, 6 January, the fact that it is not said to be part of a wider festival, and the fact that it is not clear whether there had been Eleusinian-type Mysteries in Alexandria at all (Burkert 1987, 37–38, 147 n.44)) such hypothesis would be wrong, for this rite involved not the finding of the statue, but its removal from its usual place and its return, a common advent schema, since a statue was taken by torch-bearing worshippers from an underground *sekos* for the performance of a ritual and returned there.

19 Clinton's objections (see this volume, p. 73, n.40 and p. 74, n.55) are not valid. My argument is that there were *two* distinct rituals: on the one hand the sacred drama that takes place inside the Telesterion and involves the reunion of Demeter and Kore, and on the other the ritual search which takes place outside and culminates in the finding of the ear of corn.

20 Iakkchos' statue, which was carried in the procession, had a different function. On the notion of two processions, one escorting the *hiera*, the second the initiates' procession led by Iakkchos, see now Graf (1996, 62–63).

21 Clinton (1974, 46–47), Mylonas (1961, 273–274), Richardson (1974, 302–303, 474–476). See [Lys.] (*Andoc.* 51), Plut. (*Alc.* 22.4); cf. Plut. (*Mor.* 81E).

22 According to Brumfield (1981, 235–236), in Athens the Antheia, Chloaia and Lesser Mysteries in Anthesterion reinforce the view that the *Hymn* suggests that Kore goes to Hades in the autumn and returns in early spring.

23 It had not been a Thesmophoria-type festival, for Thesmophoria did not involve an advent and excluded men; the Mysteries included (transformations of) material also deployed in the Thesmophoria (e.g. the women's fasting in imitation of Demeter: Plut., *Mor.* 378E), but such redeployments are common; it is the structuring schemata that indicate, or exclude, a direct relationship.

References

Bérard, C., 1976: "*Axie taure*", in, *Mélanges d'histoire ancienne et d'archéologie, offerts à Paul Collart*. Cahiers d'archéologie romande de la Bibliothèque historique Lausanne. Bibliothèque historique vaudoise. Lausanne.

Binder, J., 1998: "The early history of the Demeter and Kore sanctuary at Eleusis", in R. Hägg (ed.), *Ancient Greek Cult Practice from the Archaeological Evidence. Proceedings of the Fourth International Seminar on Ancient Greek Cult, Organized by the Swedish Institute at Athens, 22–24 October 1993* (Svenska Institutet i Athen, Stockholm), 131–139.

Bonnechere, P., 1994: *Le sacrifice humain en Grèce ancienne. Kernos* Supplement 3 Athens, Centre International d'Étude de la Religion grecque antique, Liège.
Brumfield, A.C., 1981: *The Attic Festivals of Demeter and their Relation to the Agricultural Year.* Arno Press, Salem.
Burkert, W., 1979: *Structure and History in Greek Mythology and Ritual.* University of California Press, Berkeley.
Burkert, W., 1983: *Homo Necans. The Anthropology of Ancient Greek Sacrificial Ritual and Myth* (2nd edition). University of California Press, Berkeley, Los Angeles, London.
Burkert, W., 1985: *Greek Religion. Archaic and Classical* (2nd edition). Blackwell, Oxford.
Burkert, W., 1987: *Ancient Mystery Cults.* Harvard University Press, Cambridge, Mass.
Burkert, W., 1988: "*Katagogia-Anagogia* and the goddess of Knossos", in R. Hägg, N. Marinatos, and G.C. Nordquist (eds), *Early Greek Cult Practice. Proceedings of the Fifth International Symposium at the Swedish Institute at Athens, 26–29 June 1986.* (Svenska Institutet i Athen, Stockholm), 81–88.
Burkert, W., 1997: "From epiphany to cult statue: early Greek *theos*", in A.B. Lloyd (ed.), *What is a God? Studies in the Nature of Greek Divinity* (Duckworth, London), 15–34.
Cavanaugh, M.B., 1996: *Eleusis and Athens, Documents in Finance, Religion and Politics in the Fifth Century BC.* American Philological Association. American Classical Studies 35. Scholars, Atlanta.
Clinton, K., 1974: *The Sacred Officials of the Eleusinian Mysteries.* The American Philosophical Society, Philadelphia.
Clinton, K., 1992: *Myth and Cult. The Iconography of the Eleusinian Mysteries.* Svenska Institutet i Athen, Stockholm.
Clinton, K., 1996: "The Thesmophorion in central Athens and the celebration of the Thesmophoria in Attica", in R. Hägg (ed.), *The Role of Religion in the Early Greek Polis. Proceedings of the Third International Seminar on Ancient Greek Cult Organized by the Swedish Institute at Athens, 16–18 October 1992* (Svenska Institutet i Athen, Stockholm), 111–125.
Clinton, K., 2001: Review of L.M. L'Homme-Wéry: *La perspective éleusinienne dans la politique de Solon* (Bibliothèque de la Fac. de Philosophie et Lettres de l'université de Liège, Droz, Geneva, 1996), in *Gnomon* 73, 2001, 168–170.
Coleman, K.M., 1988: *Statius. Silvae IV.* Clarendon Press. Oxford.
Detienne, M., 1986: *Dionysos à ciel ouvert.* Hachette, Paris.
Deubner, L., 1969: *Attische Feste* (3rd edition). Georg Olms, Hildesheim, New York.
Fraser, P.M., 1972: *Ptolemaic Alexandria.* Clarendon Press, Oxford.
Graf, F., 1985: *Nordionische Kulte.* Schweizerisches Institut in Rom, Rome.
Graf, F., 1996: "Pompai in Greece. Some considerations about space and ritual in the Greek polis", in R. Hägg (ed.), *The Role of Religion in the Early Greek Polis. Proceedings of the Third International Seminar on Ancient Greek Cult Organized by the Swedish Institute at Athens, 16–18 October 1992* (Svenska Institutet i Athen, Stockholm), 55–65.
Henrichs, A., 1978: "Greek Maenadism from Olympias to Messalina", *HSCP* 82, 121–160.
Jost, M., 1985: *Sanctuaires et cultes d'Arcadie.* Librairie philosophique J. Vrin, Paris.
Kennell, N.M., 1997: Review of Mark Golden and Peter Toohey (eds), *Inventing Ancient Culture: Historicism, Periodization, and the Ancient World* (Routledge, London and New York 1997), *Bryn Mawr Classical Review* 8, 1.1b.

Kern, O., 1922: *Orphicorum Fragmenta*. Weidmann, Berlin.
L'Homme-Wéry, L.M., 1996: *La perspective éleusinienne dans la politique de Solon*. Bibliothèque de la Fac. de Philosophie et Lettres de l'université de Liège. Droz, Geneva.
Miles, M.M., 1998: *The Athenian Agora: Results of Excavations Conducted by the American School of Classical Studies at Athens: Vol. XXXI, The City Eleusinion*. The American School of Classical Studies, Princeton.
Mitsopoulos-Leon, V., 1984: "Zur Verehrung des Dionysos in Elis. Nochmals: *AXIE TAURE* und die sechzehn heiligen Frauen", *AM* 99, 275–290.
Mylonas, G.E., 1961: *Eleusis and the Eleusinian Mysteries*. Princeton University Press, Princeton and Routledge, London.
Nilsson, M.P., 1906: *Griechische Feste von religiöser Bedeutung mit Ausschluss der attischen*. Teubner, Leipzig.
Parker, R., 1988: "Demeter, Dionysus and the Spartan pantheon", in R. Hägg, N. Marinatos, and G. Nordquist (eds), *Early Greek Cult Practice. Proceedings of the Fifth International Symposium at the Swedish Institute at Athens, 26–29 June, 1986* (Svenska Institutet i Athen, Stockholm), 99–103.
Parker, R., 1991: "The *Hymn to Demeter* and the *Homeric Hymns*", *Greece and Rome* 38, 1–17.
Richardson, N.J., 1974: *The Homeric Hymn to Demeter*. Clarendon Press, Oxford.
Schachter, A., 1981: *Cults of Boeotia*, vol. 1. Institute of Classical Studies, London.
Schachter, A., 1986: *Cults of Boeotia*, vol. 2. Institute of Classical Studies, London.
Sourvinou-Inwood, C., 1981: "To die and enter the House of Hades: Homer, before and after", in J. Whaley (ed.), *Mirrors of Mortality. Studies in the Social History of Death* (Europa Publications, London), 15–39.
Sourvinou-Inwood, C., 1983: "A trauma in flux: Death in the eighth century and after", in R. Hägg (ed.), *The Greek Renaissance of the Eighth Century BC: Tradition and Innovation* (Svenska Institutet i Athen, Stockholm), 33–48.
Sourvinou-Inwood, C., 1990: "What is polis religion?", in O. Murray and S. Price (eds), *The Greek City from Homer to Alexander* (Clarendon Press, Oxford), 295–322 [="What is polis religion?", in R. Buxton (ed.), *Oxford Readings in Greek Religion* (Oxford University Press, Oxford), 13–37].
Sourvinou-Inwood, C., 1994: "Something to do with Athens: Tragedy and ritual", in R. Osborne and S. Hornblower (eds), *Ritual, Finance, Politics. Athenian Democratic Accounts presented to David Lewis* (Clarendon Press, Oxford), 269–290.
Sourvinou-Inwood, C., 1995: *"Reading" Greek Death. To the End of the Classical Period*. Clarendon Press, Oxford.
Sourvinou-Inwood, C., 1997: "Reconstructing change: Ideology and ritual at Eleusis", in M. Golden, and P. Toohey (eds), *Inventing Ancient Culture. Historicism, Periodization and the Ancient World* (Routledge, London), 132–164.
Sourvinou-Inwood, C., 2002: *Tragedy and Athenian Religion*. Lanham, Md., Rowman and Littlefield (in press).
Travlos, J., 1988: *Bildlexikon zur Topographie des Antiken Attika*. Ernst Wasmuth, Tübingen.
Versnel, H.S., 1990: *Inconsistencies in Greek and Roman Religion 1. Ter Unus. Isis, Dionysos, Hermes. Three Studies in Henotheism*. Brill, Leiden.

3

STAGES OF INITIATION IN THE ELEUSINIAN AND SAMOTHRACIAN MYSTERIES*

Kevin Clinton

The terminology of initiation in ancient authors and inscriptions is not easy to understand, largely because no single text or readily discernible combination of texts elucidates it completely. It is therefore not surprising to find significant diversity in modern interpretations. The subject, however, has not received as comprehensive a treatment as it deserves. The present study aims at examining the terminology of initiation in mystery cults primarily in the classical and early Hellenistic periods, to see whether it is used consistently. If the terminology is consistent across the various cults, we may then be in a position to ascertain more precisely the nature and arrangement of the main rituals in the Eleusinian and Samothracian Mysteria.

First-time participants in the Mysteria at Eleusis were called *mystai*, and those who participated in the rite a year later were called *epoptai* (ἐπόπται, "viewers"). The same terms were used for first-time and second-time participants at Samothrace, though there the interval between these stages, as we shall see, could have been much shorter. Since this combination of terms, *mystai* and *epoptai*, occurs, to my knowledge, only at Eleusis and Samothrace, and since the Eleusinian Mysteries are attested considerably earlier than the Samothracian, it is surely justified to assume that the Samothracian terminology imitated the Eleusinian.[1]

The term used for the initiate, namely *mystes* (μύστης), is derived from the verb μύω, "to close (the lips or, more usually, the eyes), and means the one 'who keeps silence or closes the eyes'," as Dowden (1980, 414) emphasized. In the context of the Mysteria it is much more likely that it indicates the one who is closed with respect to the eyes; evidence from other mystery cults shows that it was the practice for an initiate to be blinded; the term expresses the opposite of *epoptes* (ἐπόπτης, "viewer"):[2] the first stage is characterized mainly by ritual blindness (when the initiate is led by a mystagogue), the second stage by sight. In Greek usage, the Mysteria, then, are the festival of the *mystai* (Clinton 1992, 86). So, for example, in the Mysteria at Andania the first-time initiates are called *protomystai* (πρωτόμυσται) and they were led by *mystagogoi* (μυσταγωγοί).³

Eleusinian terminology in the literary and inscriptional evidence

At Eleusis three stages can actually be formulated, though the first two may not have been regarded in the classical period as distinct "stages": (1) a preliminary initiation, (2) the festival proper of the Mysteria at which the main participants were the *mystai*, and (3) when the Mysteria were celebrated a year later, the *mystai* of the preceding year could attend as *epoptai*, together with the *mystai* of the current year. Though the existence of the preliminary initiation has recently been questioned, the evidence for it is relatively abundant, even if its precise nature needs clarification.⁴ It was called *myesis* (μύησις), and was conducted by a member of the Eumolpidai or Kerykes at some moment before the start of the festival, either in the Eleusinian sanctuary or the Athenian Eleusinion.⁵ Modern scholars have applied the ancient terms *myesis, telete, epopteia* to the three grades. Although Roussel (1930, 52, n.1) regarded the German terms *Einweihung* and *Weihe* as particularly apt designations for the first two stages, Dowden (1980) challenged the aptness of calling the first stage "preliminary initiation" and of restricting use of the term *telete* to the second "grade." The difficulty becomes most apparent, he pointed out, in Plutarch's description of the initiation of Demetrius Poliorcetes (*Demetr.* 26.1):

> Τότε δ' οὖν ἀναζευγνύων εἰς τὰς Ἀθήνας ἔγραψεν, ὅτι βούλεται παραγενόμενος εὐθὺς μυηθῆναι καὶ τὴν τελετὴν ἅπασαν ἀπὸ τῶν μικρῶν ἄχρι τῶν ἐποπτικῶν παραλαβεῖν. τοῦτο δ' οὐ θεμιτὸν ἦν, οὐδὲ γεγονὸς πρότερον, ἀλλὰ τὰ μικρὰ τοῦ Ἀνθεστηριῶνος ἐτελοῦντο, τὰ δὲ μεγάλα τοῦ Βοηδρομιῶνος· ἐπώπτευον δὲ τοὐλάχιστον ἀπὸ τῶν μεγάλων ἐνιαυτὸν διαλείποντες. ἀναγνωσθέντων δὲ τῶν γραμμάτων, μόνος ἐτόλμησεν ἀντειπεῖν Πυθόδωρος ὁ δᾳδοῦχος, ἐπέρανε δ' οὐδέν· ἀλλὰ Στρατοκλέους γνώμην εἰπόντος, Ἀνθεστηριῶνα τὸν Μουνυχιῶνα ψηφισαμένους καλεῖν καὶ νομίζειν, ἐτέλουν τῷ Δημητρίῳ τὰ πρὸς Ἄγραν· καὶ μετὰ ταῦτα πάλιν ἐξ Ἀνθεστηριῶνος ὁ Μουνυχιὼν γενόμενος Βοηδρομιὼν ἐδέξατο τὴν λοιπὴν τελετήν, ἅμα καὶ τὴν ἐποπτείαν τοῦ Δημητρίου προσεπιλαβόντος.

At that time as he was moving his quarters to Athens he wrote that he wished upon arrival to be initiated immediately and to receive the entire *telete* from the Lesser Mysteries to the *epoptika*. This was unlawful, nor had it happened before: the Lesser were celebrated in Anthesterion, the Greater in Boedromion, and people participated as *epoptai* after at least an interval of a year. When his letter was read, only Pythodoros the daduch dared to oppose it, but accomplished nothing. Upon the motion of Stratokles, they voted to call Mounychion Anthesterion, and performed the (Lesser) Mysteria at Agra for Demetrius, and after this Mounychion, again changed, from Anthesterion to Boedromion, got the rest of the *telete*, as Demetrius received at the same time even the *epopteia*.

As Dowden observed, the Greater Mysteria and the *epoptika* (or *epopteia*) were both called *telete*. To be precise, at the Greater Mysteria there was only a single *telete* for both *mystai* and *epoptai*, but the special experience of the *epoptai* at this *telete* was referred to as *epoptika* (or *epopteia*). The Lesser Mysteria were a *telete* as well. Although Dowden saw in the verb *myethenai* (μυηθῆναι) reference to the preliminary rite, the *myesis*, this is at first sight not completely clear. The καὶ following μυηθῆναι may express apposition; i.e. following καὶ the entire process of μυηθῆναι may be specified: reception of the entire *telete*, from the Lesser Mysteria through the *epoptika*.[6] In fact, this interpretation seems to be confirmed by the following list of the rites which Demetrius actually received (Lesser Mysteria through *epoptika*), among which *myesis* is not mentioned. Its omission, however, may be due to the fact that, unlike the Lesser and Greater Mysteria, it did not require changing the name of a month. At any rate, from a strictly grammatical point of view (use of καί), the passage does not appear to offer a certain reference to the preliminary *myesis*. We are left, then, with the task of determining from other evidence the precise meaning of μυηθῆναι and τελετή.

Use of the passive verb μυεῖσθαι/μυηθῆναι to refer to the main festival of the Mysteria is actually quite old. We find it as early as Herodotus (8.65.4) and again in Aristophanes' *Peace*:

Εἰς χοιρίδιόν μοί νυν δάνεισον τρεῖς δραχμάς·
δεῖ γὰρ μυηθῆναί με πρὶν τεθνηκέναι.

(374–375)

Now lend me three drachmas for a piglet,
for I must be initiated before I die.

Trygaeus must have the main festival of the Mysteria in mind, with its well-known promise of a happier afterlife (mere preliminary *myesis* would be insufficient for this purpose). It was this rite, too, which indeed required a piglet; preliminary *myesis* required a different victim: a ewe.[7] Pringsheim (1905, 46), who was the first to identify the *myesis* as a preliminary ceremony, noted the ambiguity of the verb. The more narrow, technical sense of the verb (to perform the preliminary ceremony of *myesis*), occurs fairly consistently in inscriptions (for both passive and active forms of the verb, see n.4), except in the Roman period when even active forms of the verb occasionally occur to indicate the main ceremony of the Mysteria (see Clinton 1989, 1502, n.9; forthcoming, nos. 454, 503 [=*IG* II² 3575, 3620]; the absence of this use in classical inscriptions may simply be accidental). Thus the context is crucial for determining the precise meaning of the verb.

The term *telete*, which Plutarch used for both the Lesser and Greater Mysteria (including the celebration of the latter as *epoptika*), is more difficult. Though it frequently refers to initiations, and is often taken by modern scholars as a certain indication of initiation, it actually had a broader meaning.[8] Diotima's description in Plato's *Symposium* of the *daimonion* (δαιμόνιον), the region of the δαίμονες ("spirits") that lies between men and gods, provides perhaps the best illustration of its broader sense:

Ἑρμηνεῦον καὶ διαπορθμεῦον θεοῖς τὰ παρ' ἀνθρώπων καὶ ἀνθρώποις τὰ παρὰ θεῶν, τῶν μὲν τὰς δεήσεις καὶ θυσίας, τῶν δὲ τὰς ἐπιτάξεις τε καὶ ἀμοιβὰς τῶν θυσιῶν, ἐν μέσῳ δὲ ὂν ἀμφοτέρων συμπληροῖ, ὥστε τὸ πᾶν αὐτὸ αὑτῷ συνδεδέσθαι. διὰ τούτου καὶ ἡ μαντικὴ πᾶσα χωρεῖ καὶ ἡ τῶν ἱερέων τέχνη τῶν τε περὶ τὰς θυσίας καὶ τελετὰς καὶ τὰς ἐπῳδὰς καὶ τὴν μαντείαν πᾶσαν καὶ γοητείαν. θεὸς δὲ ἀνθρώπῳ οὐ μείγνυται, ἀλλὰ διὰ τούτου πᾶσά ἐστιν ἡ ὁμιλία καὶ ἡ διάλεκτος θεοῖς πρὸς ἀνθρώπους, καὶ ἐγρηγορόσι καὶ καθεύδουσι·

(202e–203a)

[The function of the *daimonion* is] to interpret and convey messages to the gods from men and to men from the gods, prayers and sacrifices from the one, and commands and rewards from the other. Being of an intermediate nature, it bridges the gap between them, and prevents the universe from falling into two separate halves. Through this class of being come all divination and the skill of priests in sacrifices and rites (*teletai*) and spells and every kind of divination and wizardry. God does not deal directly with man; it is by means of this *daimonion* that all the intercourse and communication of gods with men, both in waking life and in sleep, is carried on.[9]

Religious acts destined for the gods, and passing therefore through the *daimonion*, are divided into five categories: sacrifices (θυσίαι), *teletai* (τελεταί), spells (ἐπῳδαί), divination (μαντεία), wizardry (γοητεία). Purifications (καθαρμοί), which are not sacrifices and were elsewhere distinguished by Plato from *teletai* (*Leg.* 815c, *Phdr.* 244e), are not listed here, presumably because they are not destined for the gods.[10] Excluded from τελεταί, then, are θυσίαι, ἐπῳδαί, μαντεία, and γοητεία. The natural inference is that *teletai* are more complex than simple sacrifices (the distinction between sacrifices and *teletai* occurs also at *Leg.* 738c: θυσίας τελεταῖς συμμείκτους).

Pindar uses *telete* for the festivals Theoxenia at Acragas (*Ol.* 3.41) and the Panathenaia at Athens (*Pyth.* 9.97), Euripides for the Choes (*I.T.* 959–960), Aristophanes for the Mysteria, Dipolieia, and Adonia (*Pax* 420) and evidently – perhaps in jest – even for sacrifice (*Pax* 413).[11] Prose usage, too, was certainly not restricted to mystery cults or initiations. Herodotus refers to the Thesmophoria, which were neither Mysteria nor an initiation, as Demeter's *telete* (2.171.2–3).[12] The Scythian king, Scyles, was initiated into Bacchic cult (Διονύσωι Βακχείωι τελεσθῆναι), which Herodotus called a *telete* (4.79): this is a good example of the verb (τελεσθῆναι) and noun (*telete*) being used to indicate initiation, but there is no sign that this was a mystery cult (Scyles was not called *mystes*, and the cult was not called *mysteria*; we shall return to this question on p. 55). The reference to *telete* in a decree cited by [Dem.] *In Neaeram* 104 must include cults that had nothing to do with initiation:

Ἱπποκράτης εἶπεν, Πλαταιέας εἶναι Ἀθηναίους ἀπὸ τῆσδε τῆς ἡμέρας, ἐπιτίμους καθάπερ οἱ ἄλλοι Ἀθηναῖοι, καὶ μετεῖναι αὐτοῖς ὧνπερ Ἀθηναίοις μέτεστι πάντων, καὶ ἱερῶν καὶ ὁσίων, πλὴν εἴ τις ἱερωσύνη ἢ τελετή ἐστιν ἐκ γένους, μηδὲ τῶν ἐννέα ἀρχόντων, τοῖς δ' ἐκ τούτων.

Hippokrates proposed that the Plataeans be Athenian (citizens) from this day forward, and have the same rights as the other Athenians, and have a share of whatever Athenians have a share of, both sacred and secular matters, except if a priesthood or *telete* belongs to a clan (*genos*), nor are they eligible to be one of the nine archons, but their descendants are to have this right.

A Plataean will not have the right to become a priest of a cult controlled by a *genos* or participate in such a cult; such cults included many that did not involve initiation.[13]

In the post-classical period, as has been claimed, the meaning of *telete* narrowed to indicate only initiation.[14] However, while it is true that this more narrow usage predominates,[15] it is not universal. An Athenian ephebic decree of the first century BC, though fragmentary, mentions that the ephebes took part in all the *teletai* that tradition called for ([τ]ῶν τε τελετῶν ἁπασ[ῶν ὧ]ν πάτριον ἦν, *IG* II² 1042.c.14); these ought to include non-initiatory cults, since the only initiation in which the ephebes took part occurred at the Eleusinian Mysteria.[16] At Ephesus in (apparently) the second century BC the κοινὸν τῶν Ἀφροδισιαστῶν ("association of the Aphrodisiasts") in honoring a benefactor had the announcement made ἐν ταῖς τε[λεταῖς] ἐν ἁπάσαις ταῖς ἡμέραις αἷς ἄν [α...], i.e. at public moments in several rites, all of which are unlikely to have been initiatory (Knibbe *et al.* 1993, 125–126, no. 17).

It should be clear from the foregoing that *telete* did not include all rituals (Plato distinguished it from sacrifice among others) nor was it limited to mystery cult and initiation. In accordance with its etymology, *telete* emphasizes "performance" (Waanders 1983, 13). From Plato we infer that it implied more significant performance than sacrifice. In some *teletai* the participants performed the ritual acts, as at the Thesmophoria; in other cases ritual acts were performed by and on the participants, as at the Mysteria.

To return for a moment to Bacchic initiation, briefly mentioned on p. 54 with regard to Scyles, the Scythian king, it should be noted that it was not necessarily a mystery cult, according to classical usage of the term *mysteria*. A mystery cult (1) presupposes *mystai* as described above, (2) normally requires that they undergo a death-like experience or at least an experience of suffering, and (3) holds forth a promise of prosperity in this life and usually also in the afterlife.[17] In the maenadic cult reflected in Euripides' *Bacchae* nothing is said about the afterlife; the initiates normally do not suffer; and there is no mention of *mysteria* or *mystai*. The participants are Bacchai, not *mystai*. In the case of Scyles it is significant that he is not called a *mystes* but is described simply as βακχεύων (νῦν οὗτος ὁ δαίμων καὶ τὸν ὑμέτερον βασιλέα λελάβηκε, καὶ βακχεύει τε καὶ ὑπὸ τοῦ θεοῦ μαίνεται: "Now this god has seized your king too, and he behaves like a *Bakchos* and is being driven mad by the god" [Hdt. 4.79.4]. As the process was called Διονύσωι Βακχείωι τελεσθῆναι, Scyles could presumably also be referred to as τετελεσμένος, though Herodotus happens not to have used the term here.[18]

What appears to be a fairly precise use of the terminology of initiation in mystery cult occurs at Plato, *Phaedo* 69c:

> καὶ κινδυνεύουσι καὶ οἱ τὰς τελετὰς ἡμῖν οὗτοι καταστήσαντες οὐ φαῦλοί τινες εἶναι, ἀλλὰ τῷ ὄντι πάλαι αἰνίττεσθαι ὅτι ὃς ἂν ἀμύητος καὶ ἀτέλεστος εἰς Ἅιδου ἀφίκηται ἐν βορβόρῳ κείσεται, ὁ δὲ κεκαθαρμένος τε καὶ τετελεσμένος ἐκεῖσε ἀφικόμενος μετὰ θεῶν οἰκήσει. εἰσὶν γὰρ δή, [ὡς] φασιν οἱ περὶ τὰς τελετάς, "ναρθηκοφόροι μὲν πολλοί, βάκχοι δέ τε παῦροι·" οὗτοι δ' εἰσὶν κατὰ τὴν ἐμὴν δόξαν οὐκ ἄλλοι ἢ οἱ πεφιλοσοφηκότες ὀρθῶς.

And it seems that also those who established the *teletai* for us are not incompetent but in fact have all along been speaking in riddles (in saying) that whoever arrives in Hades as uninitiate (*amyetos*) and non-participant in the *telete* (*atelestos*) will lie in mud, but he who has been *both* purified (*kekatharmenos*) *and* has participated in the *telete* (*tetelesmenos*), upon arrival there, will dwell with gods. For indeed, those concerned with *teletai* say, "Many are the thyrsos-bearers, but the *bakchoi* are few." In my opinion these are none other than those who have done philosophy in the right way.

The specification "for us" in the subject "those who established the *teletai* for us" can, to an Athenian audience, hardly not refer to the Eleusinian Mysteria.[19] The phrase *amyetos kai atelestos* may at first sight appear to be simply descriptive of a person who has not been initiated in the Mysteria, and so it has been understood by many modern readers. But the opposite formulation, *ho de kekatharmenos te kai tetelesmenos*, implies two separate procedures, purification (*katharmos*) and *telete*; a purification, as we have seen, is to be distinguished from a *telete*. Therefore the preceding negation of *kekatharmenos te kai tetelesmenos*, namely *amyetos kai atelestos*, should refer to non-participation in the same two procedures, purification (*katharmos*) and *telete*. In the case of the Eleusinian Mysteria it is hard to see what else these two procedures might be but preliminary *myesis* (μύησις) and *telete*: the term *amyetos*, referring here to a procedure prior to the *telete*, most naturally indicates a person who has not undergone the preliminary *myesis*;[20] and *atelestos* is a person who has not proceeded to completion of initiation by participating in the *telete*. Both formulations (*amyetos kai atelestos/kekatharmenos te kai tetelesmenos*), then, ought to apply to the procedures in the Eleusinian Mysteria, and presumably to other mystery cults as well. The following maxim – ναρθηκοφόροι μὲν πολλοί, βάκχοι δέ τε παῦροι – refers of course to Bacchic initiation (not to a mystery cult), i.e. to the completion of it, experiencing possession by the god, as opposed to mere parading with a thyrsos; it parallels the preceding description of initiation in a mystery cult in that it reinforces the point that in order for the process to be done correctly (ὀρθῶς) it must be carried through to completion, as in philosophy (cf. Burkert 1987, 112). With regard to the Eleusinian Mysteria, since *kekatharmenos* is the opposite of *amyetos*, this passage implies that the preliminary *myesis* was a purification.[21]

We might think that Plato could have produced a more exact correspondence to *amyetos* (not having undergone preliminary *myesis*) *kai atelestos* (not having undergone the *telete*) by expressing the opposite as *memyemenos kai tetelesmenos*.[22] However, the only time the perfect participle *memyemenos* occurs in the epigraphical record it refers, as we should expect, to those who have undergone the main rite (*telete*) of the Mysteria as *mystai*, not to those who have merely completed the preliminary *myesis*: the law on the Mysteria of ca. 360 BC contrasts μεμυημένους καὶ ἐπωπτευκότας (the context is fragmentary, but there can be no doubt about the meaning).[23] This coincides with the terminology in Plato's *Phaedrus*, used of initiates experiencing the Mysteries:

ὁλόκληρα δὲ καὶ ἁπλᾶ καὶ ἀτρεμῆ καὶ εὐδαίμονα φάσματα μυούμενοί τε καὶ ἐποπτεύοντες ἐν αὐγῇ καθαρᾷ, καθαροὶ ὄντες κτλ.

(250ψ)

Being *mystai* and *epoptai* of whole, simple, unchanging, and blissful images in a pure light, being pure ourselves...

It is not hard to understand why the verb μυεῖσθαι is used of those partaking of the *telete* for the first time: they are *mystai*, whose experience as *mystai* began with the preliminary *myesis* and continues in the *telete*; they are, throughout, *myoumenoi*.[24] Once they have completed the *telete*, they are "initiated," *memyemenoi*. A year later, if they participate again, they are no longer *myoumenoi* but *epopteuontes*.[25]

In the trial of Andocides the jurors consist only of *memyemenoi* (Andoc. 29); some of them surely must also have experienced the *epoptika*, but the only necessary qualification to be juror was participation in the *telete* as *mystes*.

Decrees found at the Kabeirion on Lemnos were passed at a meeting of the δῆμος τῶν τετελεσμένων (Accame 1941–1943, 75–105, nos. 2–4, 7, 11). The inscriptions contain no mention of the term *mystes*, and if it is indeed true that the participants in the cult were not called *mystai*, then it seems that we are obliged to infer that although there was a *telete* in the Kabeirion, it did not constitute a mystery cult (i.e. was not called Mysteria).[26]

Still unresolved, however, is the difference between the use of the passive verbs μυεῖσθαι and τελεῖσθαι in the context of mystery cult. The former, as we have seen, can apply to both the preliminary *myesis* and the activity of the *mystes* in the *telete*; the latter has a wider application, to initiation in general, or, more precisely, to the performance of a ritual action on someone; that is, it is not limited to mystery cults. In the case of the Eleusinian Mysteria sometimes initiates are called μυούμενοι (or μεμυημένοι or μυηθέντες), sometimes τελούμενοι (or τετελεσμένοι). A Hellenistic decree found in the City Eleusinion sheds some light (Agora I 3844, ed. J.H. Oliver, *Hesperia* 10, 1941, pp. 65–72, no. 31; Sokolowski 1962, 15 [=*SEG* XXI 496]). Lines 19–21 read:[27]

[- - - - τ]ῶν μυσταγωγῶν ἐ[κ]κλησ[ία - - - - - - - - - - - - - - - οἱ πάρε]-
20 [δροι τοῦ βασι]λέως καὶ οἱ ἐπιμεληταὶ τῶν μυστηρίων [- - - - -]
[- - - - - - -]ως, λειτουργείτωσαν δὲ τοῖς τελο[υμένοις - - - - - - - - -].

[- - - - - - - - -] assembly of the mystagogues [- - - - the assis]-
[tants of the Bas]ileus and the Epimeletai of the Mysteria [- - - -]
[-], but they are to serve the *teloumenoi* (those undergoing the *telete*) [-]

Elsewhere in this fragmentary document, which preserves regulations mainly concerning processions, initiates are called *mystai*. The sense of the verb in line 21 ("they [sc. the officials] are to minister to") suggests that its dative object should be all initiates, both *mystai* and *epoptai*; hence the participle *teloumenoi* here must refer to initiates of both grades. This confirms what the preceding analysis was leading us towards: in the context of the *telete*, the verb *myeisthai* is used in reference only to the lower grade of initiation, that of the *mystai*, whereas *teleisthai* is used of initiates of either grade.[28] At *Phaedrus* 250c, then, μυούμενοί τε καὶ ἐποπτεύοντες ἐν αὐγῇ καθαρᾷ, καθαροὶ ὄντες κτλ. describes initiates of both grades, while *Phaedrus* 249c refers to either grade:

τοῖς δὲ δὴ τοιούτοις ἀνὴρ ὑπομνήμασιν ὀρθῶς χρώμενος, τελέους ἀεὶ τελετὰς τελούμενος, τέλεος ὄντως μόνος γίγνεται·

Thus if a man uses such reminders correctly, by being always initiated (τελούμενος) in perfect *teletai*, he alone becomes truly perfect (τέλεος).

This helps to explain why in the expression *kekatharmenos te kai tetelesmenos* (*Phaedo* 69c), *tetelesmenos* is used as the second term rather than *memyemenos*: *tetelesmenos* is less restrictive; it can refer to simple *mystai* or to those who went beyond the stage of the *mystai* and took part in the *epopteia*.[29]

In the light of the use of *myeisthai* we can reconsider the initiation of Demetrius Poliorcetes: βούλεται παραγενόμενος εὐθὺς μυηθῆναι καὶ τὴν τελετὴν ἅπασαν ἀπὸ τῶν μικρῶν ἄχρι τῶν ἐποπτικῶν παραλαβεῖν ("he wished upon arrival to be initiated immediately and to receive the entire *telete* from the Lesser Mysteria to the *epoptika*"). The use of καὶ here should not indicate apposition, for μυηθῆναι, as we have just seen, should not refer to those who have completed both grades of the *telete*: it should not include the *epoptika*. Thus μυηθῆναι here ought to refer to the preliminary *myesis*. The passage can then be seen to correspond quite well to the order of the stages given by Clement of Alexandria, *Strom.* 5.70.7–71.1, namely purification, Lesser Mysteria, Greater Mysteria (that is, purification, or *myesis*, took place before the Greater Mysteria, or before the Lesser Mysteria if one participated in them):

οὐκ ἀπεικότως ἄρα καὶ τῶν μυστηρίων τῶν παρ' Ἕλλησιν ἄρχει μὲν τὰ καθάρσια, καθάπερ καὶ τοῖς βαρβάροις τὸ λουτρόν. μετὰ ταῦτα δ' ἐστὶ τὰ μικρὰ μυστήρια διδασκαλίας τινὰ ὑπόθεσιν ἔχοντα καὶ προπαρασκευῆς τῶν μελλόντων, τὰ δὲ μεγάλα περὶ τῶν συμπάντων, οὗ μανθάνειν ⟨οὐκ⟩έτι ὑπολείπεται, ἐποπτεύειν δὲ καὶ περινοεῖν τήν τε φύσιν καὶ τὰ πράγματα[30]

Not unreasonably do the Mysteria of the Greeks begin with purification, just as those of the barbarians also begin with bathing. After this there are the Lesser Mysteria, which have a function of teaching and preparation for the Mysteria to come, but the Greater (Mysteria) concern everything, where it is no longer a matter of learning but contemplating (ἐποπτεύειν) and pondering nature and concrete realities.

STAGES OF INITIATION IN THE MYSTERIES

It corresponds also to the stages as listed by Theon of Smyrna (14.20–22), namely purification (*katharsis*), *telete* (μετὰ δὲ τὴν κάθαρσιν δευτέρα ἐστὶν ἡ τῆς τελετῆς παράδοσις), *epopteia*.[31]

In Plato's *Symposium* Diotima, according to Socrates, momentarily stops her instruction of him in matters of Eros at a critical point, and plays upon mystery terminology to describe the progress of her instruction up to this moment:

Ταῦτα μὲν οὖν τὰ ἐρωτικὰ ἴσως, ὦ Σώκρατες, κἂν σὺ μυηθείης· τὰ δὲ τέλεα καὶ ἐποπτικά, ὧν ἕνεκα καὶ ταῦτά ἐστιν, ἐάν τις ὀρθῶς μετίῃ, οὐκ οἶδ' εἰ οἷός τ' ἂν εἴης.

(210α)

In these love matters (*erotika*) perhaps even you, Socrates, might be initiated (*myetheieis*); but the perfect (*telea*) and *epoptic* matters, for the sake of which also the former exist if one pursues correctly, I do not know whether you would be able [to attain].

The mystery context would be completely transparent if *erotika* were replaced with *mystika*, serving as a reference to preliminary *myesis*. But it is clear enough: Socrates could receive the preliminary *myesis* (κἂν σὺ μυηθείης), but it remains to be seen whether he is capable of experiencing the *telete* (τέλεα/τέλη)[32] and *epoptika*.

The passage in the *Phaedo* (*amyetos* vs. *kekatharmenos*), as we have seen, implies that the preliminary *myesis* involved purification, and this is reinforced by the statements of Clement of Alexandria and Theon of Smyrna. For a possible illustration of this rite we may turn to two Roman works of art, the Lovatelli Urn and the Torre Nova Sarcophagus. Although they only indirectly and imprecisely reflect Eleusinian imagery, each shows three roughly corresponding scenes: Demeter seated at the left (on the sarcophagus flanked by a figure who looks like Iakchos or Eubouleus and by fragmentary female figures; on the urn by Kore and by the initiate Heracles), in the center a seated Heracles as initiate, hooded (on the sarcophagus flanked on the left by a woman with downturned torches; on the urn by a woman holding a winnowing fan over his head), and on the right an altar scene (on the sarcophagus a priest and Heracles pour libations onto the flames; on the urn a priest seems to be pouring a libation on a piglet held by Heracles).[33] Similar scenes on Campana revetments that come from a building on or near the Palatine suggest that all these Roman scenes are derived from a local cult that must have been modeled in some respects after the Eleusinian Mysteria.[34] The downturned torches and the winnowing fan are emblematic of a rite of purification, in this case the purification of Heracles.[35] The fact that he is hooded suggests that he is becoming a *mystes*, and that this scene reflects the Eleusinian *myesis*.[36] What also characterizes the rite as the

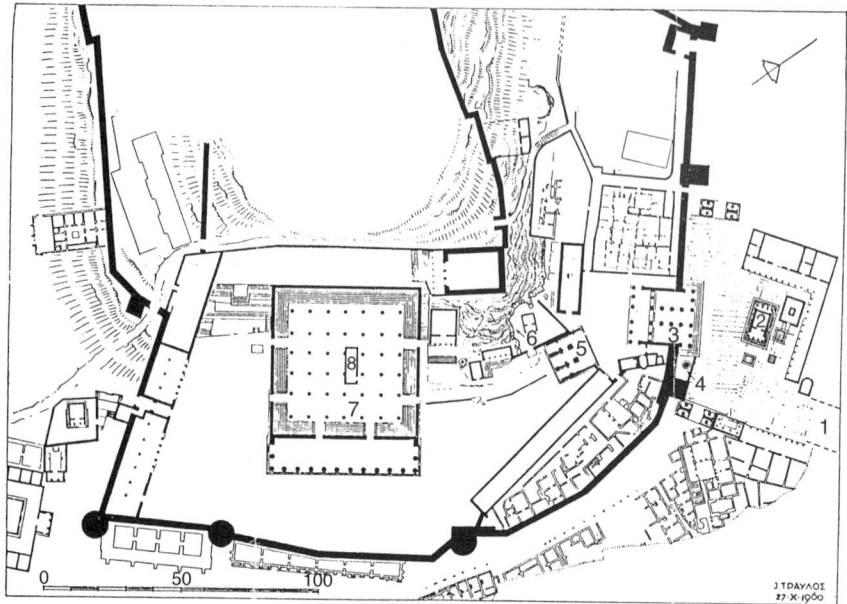

Figure 3.1 Plan of the sanctuary at Eleusis
1. Sacred Way. 2. Temple of Artemis and Poseidon. 3. Greater Propylaea. 4. Callichoron Well. 5. Lesser Propylaea. 6. Mirthless Rock. 7. Periclean Anaktoron. 7. Interior structure.

Source: Mylonas, G.E.: *Eleusis and the Aleusinian Mysteries*. Copyright ©1961 by PUP. Reprinted by permission of Princeton University Press.

Eleusinian *myesis* is the fact that the ceremony is performed on an individual, which was the rule for *myesis* (as opposed to the *telete*).[37]

The Eleusinian preliminary *myesis* took place within certain periods in advance of the Lesser and Greater Mysteria, and the initiate apparently had the option of receiving it either in the Eleusinian sanctuary or in the City Eleusinion.[38] Having completed this rite, the candidate was now a *mystes*, no longer *amyetos*. His sponsor, a member of the Eumolpidai or Kerykes, performed it, ἐμύησε, i.e. completed the process of making him a *mystes* (Andoc. 132, with MacDowell 1962, 156, following Makkink 1932, 10). Now and during the rest of the rite, the *telete*, he was μυούμενος, undergoing the experience of a *mystes*; at the end of the *telete* he was "initiated as *mystes*" (μεμυημένος/μυηθείς). A year later he could be ἐποπτεύων, participating as *epoptes*; at the end, he was "one who has completed the *epopteia*" (ἐπωπτευκών). While undergoing either rite he could be called, less specifically, "the one being initiated," τελούμενος, and at the end, "initiated" τετελεσμένος (neither of these terms designates initiation specifically in a Mystery cult).

Samothrace

At Samothrace, the fact that the cult was called Mysteria and its terminology imitated the Eleusinian suggests the existence of preliminary *myesis*. Unlike the situation at Athens, where the Eleusinian sanctuary was situated ca. 21 kilometers from the center of the city, in Samothrace there was no significant separation between sanctuary and city, hence no need for more than a single venue for preliminary *myesis*, which presumably took place somewhere in or in close proximity to the sanctuary. A likely spot, to which we shall return on pp. 64–65, lies on the Eastern Hill just inside the later Propylon (Figure 3.2, no. 26) – a peculiar circular area surrounded by steps (Figure 3.2, no. 25).

Beyond this area the path ("Sacred Way") leads to the heart of the sanctuary, to the building now called the Hall of the Choral Dancers (formerly "Temenos"). This marble building (Figure 3.2, no. 17), the largest in the sanctuary, with an interior space of ca. 20×24 m, lies approximately in the center of the sanctuary.[39] Its frieze of approximately 800 choral dancers surrounds the entire building. In view of its size, centrality, frieze, marble construction, and early date (constructed ca. 340 BC, it predates the other two major marble buildings in the center of the sanctuary, the "Hieron" in its present form [Figure 3.2, no. 15] and the Rotunda of Arsinoe [Figure 3.2, no. 20]), there can hardly be any doubt that it is the hall in which initiation of the *mystai* took place (i.e. the Anaktoron, or Telesterion).[40] This fact suggests that we take a fresh look at the interpretation of some of the other buildings in the sanctuary.

In the building that has previously been called the "Anaktoron" (Figure 3.2, no. 23) there is no demonstrable cult installation.[41] It certainly was a place of assembly, as the supports for seating demonstrate, but its quality (limestone coated with stucco) and peripheral position do not suggest that it was a cult building, or at least not a cult building of similar importance as the Hall of the Choral Dancers.[42] The prohibition inscription that was found within it (*Deorum sacra qui non acceperunt non intrant*/ἀμύητον μὴ εἰσιέναι: "The uninitiate may not enter") was not found *in situ*, and was almost certainly set up outside the building, at a border of the sanctuary or a point within beyond which the unitiate was not allowed.[43] A similar setting, at an entrance to the sanctuary, should be assumed for the other prohibition inscription (ἀμύητον μὴ εἰσιέναι εἰς τὸ ἱερόν: Fraser [1960, 117–118, no. 62]; its width is probably original). It was not found *in situ* but among marble debris near the building called by K. Lehmann "Hieron."[44] This inscription was Lehmann's only evidence for calling this building "Hieron," but as Fraser pointed out, the technical name of the building could not be τὸ ἱερόν ("the holy place" which would ordinarily signify "the sanctuary"): although a building could be referred to as "the holy place" that could not be its technical name.[45] The inscription presumably was placed at a boundary of

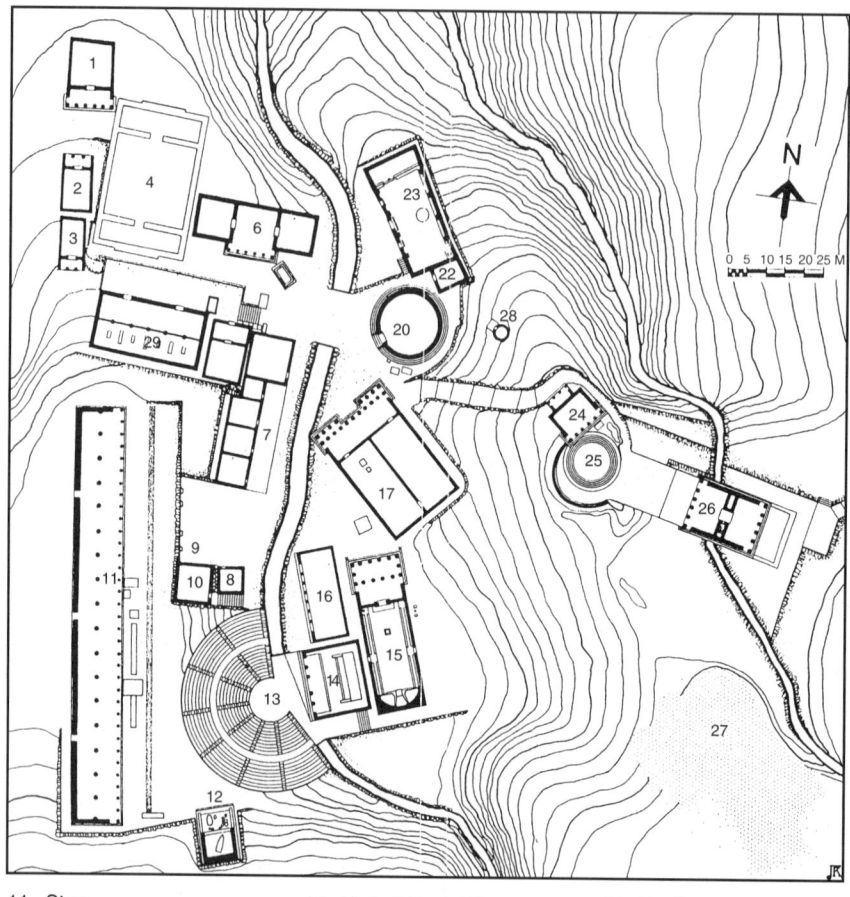

11 Stoa	17 Hall of Choral Dancers	24 Dedication of Philip III
12 Nike Monument	19 Sacred Rock	and Alexander IV
13 Theater	20 Rotunda of Arsinoe II	25 Theatral area
14 Altar Court	21 Orthostate Structure	26 Propylon of Ptolemy II
15 Hieron	22 Sacristy	27 Southern Nekropolis
16 Hall of Votive Gifts	23 Anaktoron	28 Doric Rotunda

Figure 3.2 Plan of the sanctuary at Samothrace

the sanctuary to prohibit the *amyetoi*, those who had not undergone preliminary *myesis*, from entering. Only those who had undergone *myesis* and were therefore *mystai* could enter τὸ ἱερόν, the sanctuary.[46]

What form did preliminary *myesis* take at Samothrace? Given the similarity of the Eleusinian and Samothracian stages of initiation (*mystai/epoptai*), the Samothracian preliminary ritual should, like Eleusinian *myesis*, involve purification. Sixty years ago A.D. Nock (1941) proposed that the preliminary *myesis* at Samothrace took the form of the Korybantic rite of θρόνωσις (*thronosis*, "enthronement"). As we know from Plato (*Euthydem.* 277d), *thronosis* could be preliminary to *telete*:

ἴσως γὰρ οὐκ αἰσθάνῃ οἷον ποιεῖτον τὼ ξένω περὶ σέ· ποιεῖτον δὲ ταὐτὸν ὅπερ οἱ ἐν τῇ τελετῇ τῶν Κορυβάντων, ὅταν τὴν θρόνωσιν ποιῶσιν περὶ τοῦτον ὃν ἂν μέλλωσι τελεῖν. καὶ γὰρ ἐκεῖ χορεία τίς ἐστι καὶ παιδιά, εἰ ἄρα καὶ τετέλεσαι· καὶ νῦν τούτω οὐδὲν ἄλλο ἢ χορεύετον περὶ σὲ καὶ οἷον ὀρχεῖσθον παίζοντε, ὡς μετὰ τοῦτο τελοῦντε.

Perhaps you do not perceive what sort of thing the two guests are doing around you. They are doing the same thing that those at the *telete* of the Korybantes do when they perform the *thronosis* around the person for whom they are going to perform the *telete*. For indeed there is dancing and playfulness there (i.e. in the *thronosis*), as you know if in fact you too have experienced the *telete*. And now these two are just performing a choral dance about you and as it were dancing playfully in order to perform the *telete* (for you) afterwards.

The connection between *thronosis* and a great mystery cult is made explicit by Dio Chrysostom (*Or.* 12.33) in a comparison of the cosmos with a "mystic recess":

If one would bring a man, Greek or barbarian, for initiation into a mystic recess (μυστικόν τινα μυχόν), overwhelming by its beauty and size, so that he would behold many mystic views and hear many sounds of the kind, with darkness and light appearing in sudden changes and other innumerable things happening, and even, as they do in the so-called enthronment ceremony – they have the initiands sit down, and they dance around them (ἐν τῷ καλουμένῳ θρονισμῷ καθίσαντες τοὺς μυουμένους οἱ τελοῦντες κύκλῳ περιχορεύειν) – if all this were happening, would it be possible that such a man should experience just nothing in his soul, that he should not come to surmise that there is some wiser insight and plan in all that is going on, even if he came from the utmost barbary?[47]

Dio does not present *thronismos* as a culminating ceremony in an initiation but mentions it simply as another rite that can take place during an initiation, a rite that entails a psychic experience leading to "wider insight." *Thronosis*, like Eleusinian preliminary *myesis*, was a purificatory ritual (Linforth 1946, 121–162; cf. Ustinova 1992–1998, 503–520; Graf, this volume, 244). It could take place before the *telete* of the Korybantes, as illustrated by Plato in *Euthydem.* 277d (see p. 62, this volume). Several ancient authors identify the Great Gods of Samothrace with the Korybantes (for a list of passages see Hemberg 1950, 304). For example, Diodorus (3.55.9):

> the Mother of the Gods, well pleased with the island, settled on it certain other people, and also her own sons, who are known by the name of Corybantes – who their father was is handed down in their initiation as a matter not to be divulged (ἐν ἀπορρήτῳ κατὰ τὴν τελετήν); and she taught the mysteries which are now celebrated on the island, and ordained by law that the sacred area should enjoy the right of sanctuary.
>
> (Lewis 1959, no. 31)

Strabo (10.3.19):

> Further, some call the Corybantes sons of Cronus, but others say that they are sons of Zeus and Calliope and are the same as the Cabiri, and that these went off to Samothrace, ... and that their doings are mystical.
>
> (Lewis 1959, no. 163)

Strabo (10.3.7):

> But, roughly speaking and in general, they represent them all [Corybantes and similar figures] as a kind of inspired people and as subject to Bacchic frenzy, and, in the guise of ministers, as inspiring terror at the celebration of the sacred rites by means of war-dances, accompanied by uproar and noise and cymbals and drums and arms, and also by flute and outcry; and consequently these rites are in a way regarded as having a common relationship, I mean these and those of the Samothracians and those in Lemnos and several other places, because the divine attendants are called the same.
>
> (Lewis 1959, no. 214)

Nock's hypothesis is therefore very attractive, although the remains which he assumed might be the site of the ceremony have proved not to be ancient (see n.41).

Since in the rite of *thronosis* ministrants circled a seated initiand in a wild, ecstatic dance to the accompaniment of loud music, a circular area would be an appropriate setting. Such a site, as mentioned above, was excavated many years after Nock's article appeared: on the Eastern Hill a spectacular circular area (Figure 3.2, no. 25) of approximately 9 meters in diameter, paved with flagstones and completely surrounded by five steps, upon which spectators must have stood to watch whatever took place within the circle (for the structure and its date see McCredie 1968, 216–234 and 1979, 6–8;

Lehmann 1998, 96–97). This architectural complex was created apparently in the fifth century BC, and, until the Propylon of Ptolemy II was erected in 285–281, would have been the first significant structure which the initiand confronted at the sanctuary. The event that took place within it must have been a ritual, and would have occurred just before the initiate proceeded down the path leading to the center of the sanctuary. Whatever stood in the center of the circle has long since disappeared.[48] It is unlikely to have been an altar, as altars are not usually set in a circular sunken area surrounded by steps.[49] The circular area is reminiscent of an *orchestra*, a space for dancing, observed by spectators standing on the steps. The initiand(s) could have sat in the center, presumably blindfolded, while ministrants of the cult danced around him (them) in a wild and noisy dance, while others (among them perhaps *epoptai*), looked on.[50] Such a *thronosis* could have served as the preliminary *myesis* (*thronosis* is preliminary to the *telete* according to Plato, *Euthydem.* 277d), the rite that formally made the candidate a *mystes* and thereby eligible to take part in the *telete* within the Anaktoron (Hall of Choral Dancers, Figure 3.2, no. 17). In the absence of specific literary or epigraphical evidence regarding the theatral area, however, this can be no more than a hypothesis. In any case, it is highly probable that before taking part in the *telete* the candidate had undergone preliminary *myesis* and had become a *mystes*, thus was no longer *amyetos*.

At or just beyond the theatral area, there would have stood a prohibition inscription proclaiming ἀμύητον μὴ εἰσιέναι ("The uninitiate may not enter").[51] Mystagogues are not explicity attested for the Samothracian mysteries, but the veiled initiates must have been guided, if not by persons designated as *mystagogoi*, then in any case by officials appointed for this purpose. It is possible that there were men called "Holy Ones" (*hieroi*), as at Andania, from whom mystagogues were drawn.[52] According to scholia to Apollonius of Rhodes the initiates were said to have girded themselves with purple fillets (ταινίαι), explicitly about the waist according to one scholion (Scholia Laurentiana, *Argon.* 1.917–918; scholia Parasina, *Argon.* 1.918 = Lewis 1959, nos. 229g–h); but it is conceivable that these fillets were used first as blindfolds. Fillets were used as blindfolds in the Mithraic mysteries.[53]

At Eleusis an interval of a year had to pass before a *mystes* could take part in the Mysteria as an *epoptes*. It has been suggested that at Samothrace a *mystes* could become an *epoptes* on the same day (Lehmann 1998, 38–39; Cole 1984, 27; 1989, 1572). This is not so clear. In the one inscription in which the same three *mystai* are listed also as *epoptai* (Fraser 1960, no. 36), the names of the latter, though carved by the same hand, are an addition to the original list, so that it is possible that they experienced the *epopteia* at a later time.[54]

It is often thought that the *epoptika* at Eleusis took place on the day after the climactic rite that the *mystai* experienced on Boedromion 21. The passage in the *Phaedrus* quoted above (p. 56), however, implies that the *mystai* and *epoptai* were experiencing this rite at the same moment: ὁλόκληρα δὲ καὶ ἁπλᾶ καὶ ἀτρεμῆ καὶ εὐδαίμονα φάσματα μυούμενοί τε καὶ ἐποπτεύοντες ἐν αὐγῇ καθαρᾷ, καθαροὶ ὄντες κτλ. (250c). Moreover, it is clear that at this point the *mystai* no longer lacked sight. When did they regain it? Logically, of course, they needed to regain it at least just before they saw the climactic vision, at the end of their experience of a quasi-death, such as was described by Plutarch, *On the Soul*, fr. 178 (Sandbach):

> Then [at the point of death] it [i.e., the soul] suffers something like what those who participate in the great initiations (τελεταί) suffer. Hence even the word "dying" (τελευτᾶν) is like the word "to be initiated" (τελεῖσθαι), and the act (of dying) is like the act (of being initiated). First of all there are wanderings and wearisome rushings about and certain journeys fearful and unending (ἀτέλεστοι) through the darkness, and then before the very end (τέλος) all the terrors – fright and trembling and sweating and amazement. But then one encounters an extraordinary light, and pure regions and meadows offer welcome, with voices and dances and majesties of sacred sounds and holy sights; in which now the completely initiated one (παντελὴς ... μεμυημένος) becoming free and set loose enjoys the rite, crowned, and consorts with holy and pure men.

The *mystes* remained blindfolded as he or she wandered through the darkness, helped by a mystagogue, and experienced all the terrors of the route. But finally the veil was removed and the initiate experienced the extraordinary vision. It is hard to imagine who the "holy and pure men" might be but the *epoptai* (in the actual rite; whereas in the vision of the underworld in Aristophanes' *Frogs* they are the deceased initiates, to whom Plutarch's account simultaneously refers). While the initiate wandered, blinded and frightened, through the darkness, the *epoptai* were able to watch.

One goal of the *mystai* at Eleusis was apparently to find Kore. According to Lactantius, *Div. Inst. Epit.* 23:

> His etiam Cereris simile mysterium est, in quo facibus accensis per noctem Proserpina inquiritur, et ea inventa ritus omnis gratulatione ac taedarum iactatione finitur.

> with lit torches Persephone is sought through the night, and when she is found the entire rite ends in rejoicing and the display of torches.

Of course the *mystai* only succeed in "finding" her when she finally reveals herself to them, presumably in the midst of the extraordinary light within the Telesterion (Figure 3.1, no. 7).[55] Before that moment, as the blinded *mystai* search for Kore, the *epoptai* who are waiting outside the Telesterion could see her, together with her mother, emerging from the cave precinct (Figure 3.1, no. 6) where she arose from the underworld, but the *epoptai* waiting within the Telesterion would see mother and daughter only as they enter the building. The light that blazed forth from within the Telesterion came, I imagine, from the torches that were suddenly lit by the hundreds, perhaps thousands, of these *epoptai* standing on the steps that line the walls of the Telesterion. It was at that moment that the *mystai* entered and beheld the image of the reunited goddesses.

At Samothrace too the *mystai* evidently wandered in the dark in search of a goddess. From a statement of Ephorus (*FGrH* 70 F 120) we learn that the goddess for whom the initiates searched was Harmonia:

> Ἔφορος δὲ Ἠλέκτρας τῆς Ἄτλαντος αὐτὴν εἶναι λέγει, Κάδμου δὲ παραπλέοντος τὴν Σαμοθράκην ἁρπάσαι αὐτήν, τὴν δὲ εἰς τιμὴν τῆς μητρὸς ὀνομάσαι τὰς Ἠλέκτρας πύλας. καὶ νῦν ἔτι ἐν τῇ Σαμοθρᾴκῃ ζητοῦσιν αὐτὴν ἐν ταῖς ἑορταῖς.

> Ephorus says that she (sc. Harmonia) was the child of Electra daughter of Atlas, that Cadmus carried her off when he sailed by Samothrace, and that she named the gates of Electra in honor of her mother. And even now in Samothrace they search for her in their festivals.[56]

The great Hall of Choral Dancers (Figure 3.2, no. 17), situated in the center of the sanctuary and most probably to be identified as the Telesterion, is decorated with a frieze of choral dancers and musicians which surrounds the entire building. The frieze should reflect the rite that was enacted within. P.W. Lehmann has shown that the dance can be interpreted as a wedding dance.[57] According to Samothracian legend this should be the wedding of Cadmus and Harmonia. Diodorus Siculus (5.48.4–50.1) described it at some length:

> And after this Cadmus, the son of Agenor, came in the course of his quest for Europa to the Samothracians, and after having participated in the initiation he married Harmonia, who was the sister of Iasion and not, as the Greeks recount in their mythologies, the daughter of Ares.
> This wedding of Cadmus and Harmonia was the first, we are told, for which the gods provided the marriage feast, and Demeter (enamored of Iasion) presented the fruit of the grain, Hermes a lyre, Athena the renowned necklace and a robe and flutes, and Electra the sacred rites of the Great Mother of the gods, as she is called, together with cymbals and kettledrums and the ecstatic revelers of

her ritual; and Apollo played on the cithara and the Muses on their flutes, and the rest of the gods spoke them fair and gave the pair their aid in the celebration of the wedding.[58]

Unlike the ritual at Eleusis, at Samothrace no information about an abduction to the underworld is preserved, nor is there a hint in any account describing Harmonia's abduction by Cadmus that her mother missed her and searched for her. The happy outcome of the search for Harmonia therefore was apparently not the reunion of mother and daughter, as at Eleusis, but the union of a divine bride and divine groom, identified in local myth with Harmonia and Cadmus. The "Greek" account, to which Diodorus alluded in the passage just quoted, has the wedding of Cadmus and Harmonia take place at Thebes – Diodorus in fact briefly recounted the "Greek" version earlier in his work (4.2.1; cf. [Apollod.], *Bibl.* 3.4.2) – and it seems logical to infer that local Samothracian mythography appropriated the central figures of the "Greek" version but set their wedding in Samothrace, the appropriation presumably inspired by the similar name of one of the Samothracian gods, namely Kadmilos/Kasmilos.[59] This is not the place to discuss the difficult question of the names of the Samothracian Kabeiroi or Great Gods, especially as given by Mnaseas – Axieros, Axiokersa, Axiokersos (apparently pre-Greek names in origin).[60] The scholion in which the quotation from Mnaseas appears goes on to mention that the god "Kasmilos, who is added as a fourth, is Hermes." In a certain sense Kadmilos/Kasmilos would parallel the figure of Cadmus of Samothracian myth: the scholion indicates he is not one of the central Theoi Megaloi; in the myth Cadmus is not a Samothracian but an outsider (a foreigner, he was passing by). This happens to be true also of the status of Kasmilos on Imbros: an invocation of the local gods in an inscription distinguishes Kasmilos from the Theoi Megaloi.[61]

What is striking in the myths that have come down to us about the gods of Samothrace is the role of sexual union. Varro assigns to Samothrace the union of Earth and Sky, who are, he says, *Dei Magni* (*Ling.* 5.10.57–58 = Lewis 1959, no. 175). The reason that the god Kasmilos could be identified with Hermes was probably the fact that both shared some salient characteristic, most likely ithyphallicism.[62] A glimpse of this Hermes may be seen, as Burkert (1993, 182) noted, in the "first Hermes" in a list of various Hermai given by the sceptic in Cicero's *De Natura Deorum* (3.56):

Mercurius unus Caelo patre Die matre natus, cuius obscenius excitata natura traditur quod aspectu Proserpinae commotus sit.

First Mercury [Hermes], son of Sky and Day, whose nature was aroused in a rather obscene way, according to tradition, because he was moved by the sight of Proserpina [Persephone] (on the passage cf. Pease 1958, 1107–1109).

If "Hermes" is understood as Cadmus and Persephone as Harmonia, we may have here an echo of the Samothracian myth of Cadmus and Harmonia.

Cadmus's abduction of Harmonia, mentioned by a couple of sources,[63] is most fully described in the scholion to Euripides (*Phoen.* 7), which gave us the fragment of Ephorus quoted above (see p. 67):

Δημαγόρας δὲ ἀπὸ Λιβύης ἐλθοῦσαν τὴν Ἠλέκτραν οἰκῆσαι τὴν Σαμοθράκην· ἔνθα συγγενομένη Διὶ ἐτέκνωσεν Ἠετίωνα Δάρδανον Ἁρμονίαν. τὸν δὲ Κάδμον παραπλέοντα ἐπὶ ζήτησιν τῆς ἀδελφῆς μετὰ Θάσου μυηθῆναί τε καὶ μυούμενον ἰδεῖν τὴν Ἁρμονίαν, προνοίᾳ δὲ Ἀθηνᾶς ἁρπάσαι αὐτήν.

Demagoras recounts that Electra came from Libya and settled in Samothrace, where she bore to Zeus Eétion, Dardanus, and Harmonia; that Cadmus, sailing by with Thasos in quest of his sister, was initiated and while being initiated saw Harmonia, and with Athena's assistance carried her off.[64]

If the dramatization of the abduction myth parallels that of Kore at Eleusis, then only its ending was represented in the rite.[65] Accordingly, at the beginning of the *telete*, the abduction of "Harmonia" had already taken place. The initiates, after undergoing the preliminary rite in the theatral area and proceeding to the center of the sanctuary, were faced with the sad fact that "Harmonia" had been abducted, and they began their search for the young goddess in the mystic night. This in fact corresponds rather well to the information given by Ephorus: first abduction and then a search. She was "found," as at Eleusis, when she revealed herself, here in Samothrace making her appearance not in reunion with her mother but evidently in the company of "Cadmus." This happy event presumably culminated in the initiates' celebration of the joyful wedding.

There must have been much more than that, for the initiates gained the favor of two essential Kabeiroi/Theoi Megaloi, namely the two gods who were often equated with the Dioscuri. In myth this pair should be Dardanus and Iasion/Eétion, the two brothers of Harmonia who are most closely associated with the Mysteria. What role they played in the rite is not at all clear. If we recall that they were savior gods who came to the rescue of people in peril, especially initiates in peril at sea, it may be reasonable to speculate that in the cult they performed their salvific function by bringing back "Harmonia," and they then made an epiphany with her and presumably also "Cadmus."[66] (In this connection we may recall that the very similar Dioscuri retrieved their sister, Helen, after she was abducted by Theseus.) Since Cadmus was "sailing by" when he abducted Harmonia, in this myth he most likely carried her off by sea, and it would be logical to assume that she was at sea when her brothers saved her and brought her back to Samothrace. This would also be consistent with the well-known role of the Great Gods – saving people in peril at sea. If this is correct, then an *anodos* from the earth would be unlikely. In any case, however her return was dramatically represented, we do at least know that the initiates searched for her.

To search in the dark for the goddess will have been a terrifying experience for the blindfolded *mystai*, while the *epoptai* were able to watch all the while. Finally, both the *mystai*, their vision restored, and the *epoptai* could take delight in the spectacle of a divine wedding, with its magnificent dance, and all its attendant blessings.[67]

Notes

*I am very grateful to James R. McCredie, director of the excavations in Samothrace conducted by the Institute of Fine Arts of New York University for the American School of Classical Studies, for facilitating my study of the Sanctuary of the Great Gods and its cult, and to Bonna Daix Wescoat for discussion of her work on the monuments on the Eastern Hill and for her helpful comments on an earlier draft. I, of course, am solely responsible for the views expressed here. Figure 3.1 was drawn by J. Travlos and published as *ArchDelt* 16, 1960, p. 49. fig. 4, but the labels are my own. Figure 3.2 was drawn by J. Kurtich and published as Plan IV in Lehmann (1998).

1 Farnell (1915, 631) assumed considerable Eleusinian influence.
2 See Clinton (1992, 86). On blinded initiates in Dionysiac cult see Matz (1964, 1405, pl. 8). Chantraine (1974, 728, s.v. μύω) commented, "le μύστης est proprement celui qui ferme les yeux, ce qui n'apparait pas très naturel...," but apparently without taking into account the practice of covering the initiates' eyes.
3 Sokolowski (1969, 65.14, 149–150). They presumably had undergone *myesis* or an equivalent rite. *Myesis* is not mentioned in the law (*diagramma*), but the beginning of the law, undoubtedly on another stele, is not preserved; it would have contained the qualifications for *mystai* and the *Hieroi* and *Hierai*, among other matters. But we do learn that there was significant income from the purification (*katharmos*, line 50); it is possible that the *myesis* was simply called *katharmos*; on the purificatory nature of *myesis* see pp. 55–60.
4 For a full discussion of the evidence for preliminary initiation (*myesis*) see the Introduction to the second volume of my edition of Eleusinian inscriptions, now being published by the Archaeological Society at Athens (Clinton, forthcoming). For partial discussion see the reference below, n.39.
5 *IG* I³ 6.C.43–46 (=Clinton, forthcoming, no. 19), where the restorations should be μυομ]έ.νος/[μυομένος]. Note that in this document the terms *mystai* and *epoptai* indicate "*mystai*-to-be" and "*epoptai*-to-be," so used clearly on Face B of pilgrims who are merely on their way to Eleusis.
6 On this use of *kai* see Denniston (1966, 291, s.v. καί, I (5)).
7 See Clinton (1988, 69–70). Other early examples: Pl. (*Meno* 76e), where *myethenai* must indicate the *telete*, in the context of Meno's departure πρὸ τῶν μυστηρίων; Ar. (*Ran*. 456), μεμυήμεθ(α), used of initiates in the underworld.
8 *Telete* as certain or probable indication of initiation and mystery cult: e.g. Seaford (1997, 41, 157–158) (while acknowledging a broader sense). For the other extreme, that *telete* merely indicates a rite, see e.g. Graf (1997, 97).
9 Trans. W. Hamilton, *The Symposium by Plato*, Baltimore, 1951, p. 81, with slight modification.

10 For the evidence that purifications are technically not sacrifices (*thysiai*) see Clinton, "Pigs in Greek Rituals," in *International Seminar: "Greek Sacrificial Ritual, Olympian and Chthonian," Göteborg, 25–27 April 1997* (ed. R. Hägg, forthcoming).
11 On the meaning of *telete* in the Classical period Zijderveld (1934) provides a very good collection of data, but with analysis deficient in some respects; see also Kern (1934, cols. 393–397), Waanders (1983, 156–159), Sfameni Gasparro (1987, 137–152).
12 On the Thesmophoria as containing *mysteria* see below, n.14.
13 On the cults controlled by *gene* see now Parker (1996, 284–318).
14 So, e.g., Kern (1934). The meaning of *mysteria*, on the other hand, broadened, and could mean simply "secrets": Nock (1952, 184–189), Nilsson (1961, 367–372), who emphasizes the degeneration of the term into mere metaphor; for further bibliography see Herrmann (1996, 339–340, n.75); for *mysteria* in the sphere of magic see Graf (1997, 97–98). The germ of this development can be seen in Plato, *Tht.* 155e–156a, where philosophical *mysteria* can be "told," but not to the ἀμύητοι ("uninitiated"); cf. *Symp.* 210a. So Strabo (10.3.9), for example, could use the term "mystic" to distinguish cults that were conducted in secret (μυστικῶς) from those that were not, and the scholion to Lucian, 275 Rabe, could refer to the Thesmophoria as containing *mysteria*.
15 Cf. especially Ath. 2.40d (*telete* defined as a festival with μυστικὴ παράδοσις).
16 For the cults in which they participated see Pélékidis (1962, 211–255).
17 Burkert (1987, 12) in defining "mysteries" emphasizes the third characteristic. On the experience at Eleusis, see ibid., pp. 90–93; Clinton (1992, 84–90). By the time of the Roman period, however, the term *mysteria* could refer simply to a secret cult; cf. n.14.
18 Heraclitus, 14 DK, distinguishes *mystai* from *bakchoi*, putting both in a reprehensible category of religious practitioners.
19 For a list of various identifications by scholars of the mystery cult(s) in this passage see Graf (1974, 100–101, n.30), who notes the significance of "to us" as indicative of a reference to the Eleusinian Mysteries (following von Wilamowitz-Moellendorff 1955, 58, n.2 and Boyancé 1937, 21–22).
20 Very rarely *amyetos* indicates a person who has merely completed the preliminary *myesis*. Diog. Laert. (2.101) reports an instance where *amyetos* apparently refers to such a person: Theodoros, the atheist philosopher, pointed out to a hierophant that he was committing impiety since he revealed the Mysteries to *amyetoi*. It is easy enough to see how Theodoros can make this charge: he who is οὐ μεμυημένος (not having completed initiation in the *telete*) can be termed *amyetos*. But *amyetos* should normally mean "uninitiated," i.e. a person who has not taken part in initiation at all.
21 A similar pattern is observable in the (apparently) Sabazian rites led by the mother of Aeschines: a complex purificatory ritual at night, followed by the "maenadic" marching of *thiasoi* in the daytime *telete* (Dem., *De Cor.* 259–260); but there is no mention of *myesis* or *mystai*, so that we cannot be sure whether it was a mystery cult (Demosthenes' description is bound to be incomplete). In the rites that lie behind the so called "Bacchic-Orphic" Golden Tablets, only once is the technical term of the participants given, namely μύσται καὶ βάκχοι in the Hipponion Tablet (*SEG* XXVI 1139 = XL 824); they were not just *Bacchoi* like the *Bacchae* in Euripides' play who participate in the maenadic *telete*, but they were also *mystai*, participants in a mystery cult, of which there is no sign in Euripides' play. Many if not all of the holders of the other Golden Tablets may also have been μύσται καὶ βάκχοι, despite the absence of a title.
22 So, for example, Aristid., *Eleusinios* 12, *amyetoi* vs. *memyemenoi*.
23 *SEG* XXX 61.A.47. So too Ar. (*Ran.* 456), an example of the perfect indicative (see n.7), naturally refers to those who have completed the *telete*.

24 For use of the present participle for those undergoing preliminary *myesis*, see n.5.
25 Inasmuch as the experience of the *mystai* began in the preliminary *myesis* and continued in the *telete*, the question arises whether their experience in the *telete* can be indicated by a single noun, just as that of the *epoptai* can be expressed by *epoptika* (or *epopteia*). If the participle μυούμενοι can be used of them as participants in the preliminary *myesis*, and they are also μυούμενοι in the *telete*, it seems logical that *myesis* should also be the correct term for their experience in the *telete*. However, so far as I know, the noun *myesis* does not occur in an Athenian author before Sopater, though it is not infrequent among non-Athenian writers, including Plutarch, and generally (perhaps always) indicates the experience in the *telete*. In inscriptions it occurs three times (*IG* II² 1673.62, 1672.207, and *SEG* XXI 494.27), the context in each case indicating the preliminary *myesis*. In a Pergamene document of the second century BC, *OGI* 764.7–9 (recent discussion in Wörrle 2000, 558), *myesis* fairly clearly refers to the ritual during the *telete*.
26 The only reference to the cult as *"mysteria"* occurs, to my knowledge, in a fragment of Accius' *Philocteta*, quoted by Varro (*Ling.* 7.11): "celsa Cabirum delubra,... mysteria." But this does not necessarily mean that "Mysteria" was the local term. The restoration of [μυ]ηθῶ in *SEG* XII 399.12 is far from certain; see Robert and Robert (1953, no. 162).
27 In line 21 Oliver restored τελ[εσι, Sokolowski τελ[ουμένοις. The latter must be correct: I was able to read part of the omicron after lamda.
28 A similar use occurs in the Mysteria at Andania; cf. Sokolowski (1969, 65.14: τῶν δὲ τελουμένων οἱ πρωτόμυσται). Unfortunately the term for those who have come to the τελετά (line 3) for a second time does not occur in this document.
29 It can of course refer to those who were not initiated in a mystery cult, but that use is not relevant here (*amyetos* points to mystery cult).
30 Cf. *Strom.* 7.27.6: purification, then Mysteria.
31 Cf. Riedweg (1987, 5–8). Proclus (*Theol. Plat.* 4 p. 77.9–10) calls the three stages *telete, myesis, epopteia* (in this order), a mistake that appears also in Hermias of Alexandria (*In Phaedr.* p. 178.14–19), but there *telete* is explained as a purificatory προπαρασκευή. (The error may have arisen from misinterpretation of a phrase such as ἐν τελετῇ καὶ μυήσει, which Plutarch [*De def. or.* 422c] used, apparently as a kind of hendiadys.) Interestingly, Hermias relates μύησις to μύειν τοὺς ὀφθαλμούς.
32 The term τέλη (*tele*) is found in poetry for τελετή (*telete*); cf., e.g., Soph., *OC* 1050, and fr. 837 Radt. It seems best to regard initiation in *erotika* as an allusion to preliminary *myesis* (so also apparently Burkert 1987, 92) rather than to the Lesser Mysteria (as it is interpreted by several translators and by Riedweg 1987, 5–8), because the language suggests an event *before* the *telete*, and the Lesser Mysteria were a *telete*, whereas the preliminary *myesis* was not.
33 For a recent full discussion see Kinney (1994, 64–96). On the lack of concord with Eleusinian iconography, Clinton (1992, 137–138, no. 6, with bibliography).
34 The best preserved example of the type: Museo Nazionale Romano 4357/4358, discussed by Kinney (1994, 79, pl. 8d); for the finding place see von Rohden and Winnefeld (1911, 7–8, 261–262, 15*).
35 See now Kinney (1994, 80–86).
36 It was so understood by Pringsheim (to whom only the urn was available) and Roussel; and I allowed for this possibility in Clinton (1992, 137–138), while pointing out the non-Eleusinian characteristics of the iconography of both scenes. On the connection with the *myesis* see also Deubner (1932, 77–78); on purificatory aspects and the aetiology, Parker (1983, 284–285); Burkert (1983, 266–268) called the ceremony *thronosis*, but this is incorrect (although *thronosis* may have been used in other cases of *myesis* [see pp. 62–65]), as R.G. Edmonds recently demonstrated in a paper, "To Sit in Solemn Silence? Thronosis in Ritual, Myth, and Iconography,"

given at the annual meeting of the American Philological Association in 2001 at San Diego.
37 *IG* I³ 6.C.26–30; Clinton (1974, 11–12). The individual purification would strongly militate against associating this scene with the Lesser Mysteria, which, though reputed to include purification, involved initiation *en masse*.
38 On the time see Agora I 3844, ed. J.H. Oliver, *Hesperia* 10, 1941, pp. 65–72, no. 31; Sokolowski (1962, 15 [=*SEG* XXI 496], line 26), with my commentary, "The Epidauria and the Arrival of Asclepius in Athens," in R. Hägg (ed.), *Ancient Greek Cult Practice from the Epigraphical Evidence*, Stockholm, 1994, p. 26, n.29; on the place, above, n.5.
39 For a description of the building see Lehmann (1998, 73–78); on its function, ibid. (35).
40 On the equivalence of the terms "Anaktoron" and "Telesterion," see Clinton (1992, 126–132). Sourvinou-Inwood (this volume, p. 46, n.14) disputes the equivalence, but the fact remains that there is not a single unambiguous reference in a sound text to "Anaktoron" as meaning "interior structure" (such as Figure 3.1, no. 6) or "inner sanctum." In my treatment just cited I discussed several unambiguous passages in which "Anaktoron" must indicate the entire Telesterion (she interprets these passages as metonymies, but this is very unlikely in some cases); indeed, some passages mention initiates *entering* the Anaktoron. On the whole matter the reader will need to consult my treatment and consider all the evidence discussed there (including, p. 127, the passage in Aelian). On a specific matter raised by Sourvinou-Inwood: the erection by Demetrios of a *thronos* for a private individual, in this case a hetaira, next to the Telesterion (Ath. 167f) was regarded as an offensive act; Hegesander did not describe it as an act of impiety (as it surely would have been, had it occurred within the Telesterion) but bracketed it with erecting a platform for her on which she could watch the Panathenaic procession. In a forthcoming article I shall discuss physical aspects of the interior structure in the Eleusinian Telesterion. With regard to the Anaktoron at Samothrace no one has argued that it is an inner sanctum.
41 For a description of the building see Lehmann (1998, 56–61). The installation in the center of the building which Lehmann took to be a wooden platform, and Nock interpreted as the site of *thronosis*, further investigation has shown to be the remnants of a lime kiln, as Professor McCredie has informed me (already reported by Burkert 1993, 186). The "bothros" in the southeastern corner, composed of smaller stones than the walls against which it is set, gives the impression that it may not be an ancient construction; I will present the details in a later publication.
42 Its predecessor, the "Proto-Anaktoron," is later than the Rotunda of Arsinoe, which was constructed after 289 BC; the predecessor of the "Proto-Anaktoron," the "Orthostate Structure," was constructed in the first half of the fourth century; no earlier structure was found. For the chronology of the "Anaktoron" and its predecessors, see McCredie (1979, 27–35).
43 Fraser (1960, 118–121, no. 63). It was logical for K. Lehmann to associate it with the building in which it was found, but my own study of the circumstances of its finding, which I will present in another publication, has led me to the conclusion that it was not set up originally, as Lehmann believed, next to the spot where it was found. Furthermore, there would have been in principle no reason to place an inscription on a massive stone block such as this within a building (its lower rough-picked half shows that it was meant to be placed well into the ground, which was hardly necessary within a building); here a simple painted board or thin plaque would have sufficed.
44 Lehmann (1953, 14–15). According to my inspection, the base that the excavators assigned to it, Block 523, held a much wider stele.
45 Lehmann (1953, n.77a), cited the Thesmophorion in Delos as a parallel for this use

of *hieron* (*BCH* 59, 1935, p. 388), but the Thesmophorion was a sanctuary in its own right; Fraser (1960, 117–118) cited Hdt. 7.72.3 to illustrate that τὸ ἱερόν could not serve as the technical name of a building.

46 So too in Pl. (*Tht.* 155e–156a), *mysteria* (here philosophical) cannot be accessible to the *amyetoi*; see above, n.4. At Andania there was a similar prohibition against entry into an area demarcated by the Sacred Men; Sokolowski (1969, 65.36–37): μηδὲ παρερπέτω μηθεὶς ἀμύητος εἰς τὸν τόπον ὅν κα περιστεμματώσωντι. The *amyetoi* are presumably those who have not undergone *myesis* (see above, n.3), although here the possibility cannot be excluded that it refers to those who have not completed initiation at the *telete*.

47 Trans. Burkert (1987, 89–90).

48 The pavement in this area has also disappeared. McCredie (1968, 219) explained that the pavement was "removed and the fill beneath it excavated by robbers who hoped to find treasure under whatever object stood there."

49 A possible connection between the area in the center and a round base found in the vicinity in 1939 (fragments of its base molding were found in the debris of his own excavation of the circular area) was made by McCredie (1968, 219), which he regarded as "speculative." The base was found "at a point nearly facing the northern bridge pillar of the Ptolemaion on the East slope of the central sanctuary" (Excavation Diary 1939, pp. 6–7). Judging from the dowel holes in its upper surface it looks like a member in a monumental dedicatory base rather than an altar. Cole (1984, 26; 1989, 1574) suggested that instruction (the *praefatio sacrorum* mentioned by Livy, 45.5) was delivered here to the initiands; this is possible, but surely so elaborate an architectural setting was designed primarily for a function specifically suited to it, namely dance; instruction could have been an additional use.

50 One unpublished list of initiates can be estimated to contain around ninety names; in such cases the preliminary rite may have had to be performed on several initiands at a time.

51 At the time the circular area was constructed, toward the end of the fifth century BC, it was possible to exit at the level of the floor of the circle in the direction of the sanctuary, but this exit was later filled in and the area was occupied by two successive rectangular buildings, the second an elegant Doric structure in marble (Figure 3.2, no. 24), hexastyle, prostyle, dedicated by Philip III Arrhidaios and Alexander IV, therefore between 323 and 316 BC; for a description of these structures see McCredie (1968, 221–230) and Lehmann (1998, 97–99). Apparently it was not possible to leave the circular area through this building to reach the path to the central sanctuary; one had to go around it.

52 Andania: Sokolowski (1969, 65.145–150). Possible "Holy Woman" at Samothrace: Clinton and Karadima-Matsa (forthcoming).

53 Wall paintings of blindfolded initiates in the Mithraeum at Capua Vetere, illustrated by Merkelbach (1984, 136, figs. 29–30). Literary evidence: Pseudo-Augustine (Ambrosiaster), *Quaestiones Veteris et Novi Testamenti* 113.11.

54 I owe this observation to Nora Dimitrova.

55 Sourvinou-Inwood (this volume, pp. 31–38) argues that the initiates' search for Kore ended in the finding of an ear of grain; this constituted the "finding of Kore." Of course in the myth as told in the *Homeric Hymn to Demeter* and in other sources (though not all) Demeter did not go down to Hades and actually "find" Kore; Kore returned to her, and in that sense she was "found." This clearly is the sense that Aristides had in mind when he said that after Demeter "*found* Kore she established the Mysteria" (*Eleusinios* 3 Humbel: τὴν κόρην εὑροῦσαν ποιῆσαι τὰ μυστήρια). The initiates, in "finding Kore," imitated Demeter; that is, as Demeter "found" Kore when Kore returned, the initiates "found" Kore in the same way. Aristides' later statement, "O Demeter, who formerly found Kore right there (sc. at Eleusis), now it

remains for you to find the temple" (*Eleusinios* 11 Humbel: ὦ Δήμητερ, ἢ πάλαι μὲν αὐτόθι τὴν Κόρην εὗρες, νῦν δέ σοι ὁ νεὼς ζητεῖν λείπεται); the connection of the "temple" with the search implies a connection, there too, with the finding; see commentary of Humbel (1994, 139–140).

56 Quoted in a scholion to Euripides (*Phoen.* 7), trans. Lewis 1959, no. 75, with slight modification. Ephorus refers to a plurality of festivals, but we need not assume that he had in mind any other festival but the Mysteria, which were in fact celebrated several times in the course of the year.

57 Lehmann (1998, 35) and Lehmann and Spittle (1982, 220–233). The suggestion that the wedding of Cadmus and Harmonia was represented in the rite was made earlier by Rubensohn (1892, 133) and Kern (1919, 1428–1429).

58 *FGrH* 548 F 1 (=Lewis 1959, no. 142).

59 Kadmilos: Nonnus, *Dion.* 4.87–89 (=Lewis 1959, no. 165). Kasmilos: Scholia Ap. Rhod., *Argon.* 1.917 (=Lewis 1959, no. 150–150a); Varro, *Ling.* 7.3.34 (=Lewis 1959, no. 164, with notes). Cf. Hemberg (1950, 95–96). Wedding of Cadmus and Harmonia: Steph. Byz., s.v. Δάρδανος (=Lewis 1959, no. 65); Nonnus, *Dion.* 3.124–179, 4.4–15 (=Lewis 1959, no. 67); Scholia Ap. Rhod., *Argon.* 1.915–916 (=Lewis 1959, nos. 70–70a); Ephorus, *FGrH* 70 F 120 (=Lewis 1959, no. 75).

60 Mnaseas, *FGrH* 546 F 1b (from Scholia to Ap. Rhod., *Argon.* 1.917 (=Lewis 1959, nos. 150–150a); on the names cf. Burkert (1993, 186–187) and Hemberg (1950, 82–96).

61 *IG* XII.8 74.1–5: Θεοὶ Μεγάλοι Θεοὶ Δυνατοὶ ἰσχυρροὶ καὶ Καδμεῖλε ἄναξ. Beschi (1994, 23–50, esp. 36, 40–41, 48) argues that Kadmilos was original to Lemnos and was adopted from there by the Samothracians. A. Hoffmann, "Dionysos and Kadmilos on a Curse Tablet from Antioch," APA Annual Meeting, Dallas, 1999, reports his presence on a curse tablet in the company of "Arxieros," "Arxierissa," Persephone, and Zeus.

62 On the ithyphallic "Hermes" in the Samothracian Mysteria see especially Burkert (1993, 181–182), with discussion of the sources, including Callimachus (fr. 199 Pfeiffer). The ithyphallic images which according to Hippolytus (*Haer.* 5.9.7–9 [=Lewis 1959, no. 148]), were set up "in the Anaktoron" Lehmann (*AJA* 43, 1939, p. 138 and *AJA* 44, 1940, p. 336 [followed by Lewis]) identified with the two Great Gods whose masculine images Varro (*Ling.* 5.10.57–58) says were set up "*ante portas*" (presumably gates of the sanctuary or the city); but Lehmann's hypothesis requires "portas" to be interior doors, which is hardly likely. Hippolytus' description implies that the two statues in the Anaktoron (they are "of the primal man") are identical; in this connection it is interesting that the Hall of Choral Dancers had two doors, and its interior space was divided into two parts. Varro gives names to other Samothracian gods whom he mentions but not to the two "masculine" (presumably therefore ithyphallic) images set up *ante portas*; they too may represent duplicate images.

63 Scholia Laurentina Ap. Rhod., *Argon.* 1.916 (=Lewis 1959, no. 70) (ἣν ἠγάγετο Κάδμος); Ephorus (above, n.56) (ἁρπάσαι αὐτήν).

64 Trans. Lewis (1959, no. 75), with slight modification. Diodorus (5.48.5) also mentioned that in the myth the marriage occurred after Cadmus' initiation.

65 On the myth at Eleusis, see Clinton (1992, 78–90).

66 Anodos scenes in fifth-century painting are tantalizing, especially one where the goddess rising out of the earth is greeted by an ithyphallic Pan and Hermes (pelike from Rhodes, 12.454, *ARV*² 1218.2 [Bérard 1974, fig. 63], its possible relevance noted by Burkert 1993, 182), another in which she is greeted by satyrs and is accompanied by a figure who is similar to Eleusinian Eubouleus (volute crater from Spina, Ferrara 3031, *ARV*² 612.1 (Clinton 1992, 72, fig. 42); corresponding figures in Samothracian myth might be an ithyphallic "Cadmus" and the two Kabeiroi/Theoi Megaloi, Dardanus and Iasion. But such an anodos may be foreign to the Samothracian cult.

67 Bonnechere, this volume (p. 180) in his discussion of Hadrian's demes of Antinoupolis raises the question of the significance of those in the tribe *Sab(e)inios*, namely *Harmonieus, Gamelieus, Heraieus, {Phy}talieus, Trophonieus*. Though an association with Eleusis has sometimes been suggested, the first two deme-names point rather to Harmonia's marriage at Samothrace. Marriage could appear to be the theme that connects these two names and *Heraieus*, perhaps also *{Phy}talieus*, but the restoration is uncertain.

References

Accame, S., 1941–1943: "Iscrizioni del Cabirio di Lemno," *ASAtene* 3–5, 75–105.
Boyancé, P., 1937: *Le culte des Muses chez les philosophes grecs*. De Boccard, Paris.
Bérard, C., 1974: Anodoi. *Essai sur l'imagerie des passages chthoniens*. Neuchâtel.
Beschi, L., 1994: "I Tirreni di Lemno alla luce dei recenti dati di scavo," in *Atti del XXXIII Convegno di studi sulla Magna Grecia* (Bardi Editore, Taranto), 23–50.
Burkert, W., 1983: *Homo Necans: The Anthropology of Ancient Greek Sacrificial Ritual and Myth*. University of California Press, Berkeley.
Burkert, W., 1987: *Ancient Mystery Cults*. Harvard University Press, Cambridge, Mass.
Burkert, W., 1993: "Concordia discors: the literary and the archaeological evidence on the sanctuary of Samothrace," in N. Marinatos and R. Hägg (eds), *Greek Sanctuaries: New Approaches* (Routledge, London and New York), 178–191.
Chantraine, P., 1974: *Dictionnaire étymologique de la langue grecque*, III. Klincksieck, Paris.
Clinton, K., 1974: *The Sacred Officials of the Eleusinian Mysteries*. Transactions of the American Philological Society 64.3. American Philological Society, Philadelphia.
Clinton, K., 1988: "Sacrifice at the Eleusinian Mysteries," in R. Hägg, N. Marinatos, and G.C. Nordquist (eds), *Early Greek Cult Practice, Proceedings of the Fifth International Symposium of the Swedish Institute in Athens* (Svenska Institutet i Athen, Stockholm), 69–80.
Clinton, K., 1989: "The Eleusinian Mysteries: Roman initiates and benefactors, second century BC to AD 267," *Aufstieg und Niedergang der römischen Welt* 18.2, 1499–1539 (De Gruyter, Berlin).
Clinton, K., 1992: *Myth and Cult: The Iconography of the Eleusinian Mysteries. The Martin Nilsson lectures on Greek religion, delivered 19–21 November 1990 at the Swedish Institute at Athens*. Skrifter Utgivna av Svenska Institutet i Athen. Vol. 8, xi. Stockholm.
Clinton, forthcoming: *Eleusinian Inscriptions*. Athens Archaeological Society, Athens.
Clinton, K. and Ch. Karadima-Matsa, 2002: "Korrane, a holy woman in Samothrace." *ZPE*, 138, 87–92.
Cole, S.G., 1984: *Theoi Megaloi: The Cult of the Great Gods at Samothrace*. Brill, Leiden.
Cole, S.G., 1989: "The Mysteries of Samothrace during the Roman period," *Aufstieg und Niedergang der römischen Welt* 18.2, 1564–1598.
Denniston, J.D., 1966: *The Greek Particles*. Clarendon Press, Oxford.
Deubner, L., 1932: *Attische Feste*. H. Keller, Berlin.
Dowden, K., 1980: "Grades in the Eleusinian Mysteries," *RHR* 197, 409–427.
Farnell, L.R., 1915: "Kabeiroi," in J. Hastings (ed.), *Encyclopedia of Religion and Ethics*, VII, 628–632. C. Scribner's Sons, New York.

Fraser, P.M., 1960: *Samothrace, Excavations Conducted by the Institute of Fine Arts of New York University. 2.1, The Inscriptions on Stone.* Routledge & Kegan Paul, London.
Graf, F., 1974: *Eleusis und die orphische Dichtung Athens in vorhellenistischer Zeit.* De Gruyter, Berlin.
Graf, F., 1997: *Magic in the Ancient World.* Harvard University Press, Cambridge, Mass.
Hemberg, B., 1950: *Die Kabiren.* Almquist Wiksells, Uppsala.
Herrmann, P., 1996: "Mystenvereine in Sardis," *Chiron* 26, 339–340.
Humbel, A., 1994: *Ailios Aristeides, Klage über Eleusis (Oratio 22).* Verlag der Österreichischen Akademie der Wissenschaften, Vienna.
Kern, O., 1919: "Kabeiros, Kabeiroi," *RE* 10, cols. 1428–1429.
Kern, O., 1934: "Telete," *RE* V.A.1, cols. 393–397.
Kinney, D., 1994: "The Iconography of the ivory diptych Nicomachorum-Symmachorum," *JAC* 37, 64–96.
Knibbe, D., H. Engelmann, and B. Iplikçioglu, 1993: "Neue Inschriften aus Ephesus XII," *ÖJh* 62, 124–130.
Lehmann, K., 1953: "Samothrace: Sixth preliminary report," *Hesperia* 22, 1953, 1–24.
Lehmann, K., 1998: *Samothrace: A Guide to the Excavations and the Museum* (6th edition, rev. J.R. McCredie). Institute of Fine Arts, New York University, Thessaloniki.
Lehmann, P.W. and D. Spittle, 1982: *Samothrace, Excavations Conducted by the Institute of Fine Arts of New York University, 5.1, The Temenos.* Princeton University Press, Princeton.
Lewis, N., 1959: *Samothrace, Excavations Conducted by the Institute of Fine Arts of New York University, 1, The Ancient Literary Sources.* Routledge & Kegan Paul, London.
Linforth, I.M., 1946: *The Corybantic Rites in Plato.* University of California Publications in Classical Philology 13.5, 121–162.
MacDowell, D., 1962: *Andokides*, On the Mysteries. Oxford University Press, Oxford.
Makkink, A.D.J., 1932: *Andokides' Eerste Rede.* H.J. Paris, Amsterdam.
Matz, F., 1964: ΔΙΟΝΥΣΙΑΚΗ ΤΕΛΕΤΗ, *Archäologische Untersuchungen zum Dionysoskult in hellenistischer und römischer Zeit.* Abhandlungen der Akademie Mainz, Wiesbaden.
McCredie, J.R., 1968: "Samothrace: Preliminary report on the campaigns of 1965–1967," *Hesperia* 37, 216–234.
McCredie, J.R., 1979: "Samothrace: Supplementary investigations, 1968–1977," *Hesperia* 48, 1–44.
Merkelbach, R., 1984: *Mithras.* Hain, Königstein i.T.
Nilsson, M.P., 1961: *Geschichte der griechischen Religion*, II. Handbuch der Altertumswissenschaft, V, 2, 2, Munich.
Nock, A.D., 1941: "A Cabiric rite," *AJA* 45, 377–381.
Nock, A.D., 1952: "Hellenistic Mysteries and Christian sacraments," *Mnemosyne* 5, 177–213.
Parker, R., 1983: *Miasma: Pollution and Purification in early Greek Religion.* Oxford University Press, Oxford.
Parker, R., 1996: *Athenian Religion: A History.* Oxford University Press, Oxford.

Pease, A.S., 1958: *M. Tulli Ciceronis de Natura Deorum*. Harvard University Press, Cambridge, Mass.

Pélékidis, C., 1962: *Histoire de l'éphébie attique des origines à 31 avant Jésus-Christ*. École française d'Athènes. Travaux et mémoires des anciens membres étrangers de l'École et de divers savants, 13, Paris.

Pringsheim, G.H., 1905: *Archäologische Beiträge zur Geschichte des eleusinischen Kults*. Diss, Bonn and Munich.

Riedweg, C., 1987: *Mysterienterminologie bei Platon, Philon und Klement von Alexandrien*. W. de Gruyter, Berlin.

Robert, J. and L. Robert, 1953: *Bulletin épigraphique* 1953 (in *REG* 66), 81–180.

Roussel, P., 1930: "L'Initiation préalable et le symbole Éleusinien," *BCH* 54, 51–74.

Rubensohn, O., 1892: *Die Mysterienheiligtümer in Eleusis und Samothrake*. R. Gaertner's Verlagsbuchhandlung, Berlin.

Seaford, R. (ed.), 1997: *Euripides, Bacchae*. Aris & Phillips, Warminster.

Sfameni Gasparro, G., 1987: "Ancora sul termine ΤΕΛΕΤΗ," in *Filologia e forme litterarie, Studi offerti a Francesco della Corte* (Quattro Venti, Urbino), 137–152.

Sokolowski, F., 1962: *Lois sacrées des Cités grecques, Supplément*. De Boccard, Paris.

Sokolowski, F., 1969: *Lois sacrées des Cités grecques*. De Boccard, Paris.

Ustinova, Y., 1992–1998: "Corybantism: The nature and role of an ecstatic cult in the Greek polis," *Horos* 10–12, 503–520.

von Rohden, H. and H. Winnefeld, 1911: "Architektonische römische Tonreliefs der Kaiserzeit," in R. Kekulé von Stradonitz, *Die antiken Terrakoten* 4. W. Spemann, Berlin/Stuttgart.

von Wilamowitz-Moellendorff, U., 1955: *Der Glaube der Hellenen*, II2. Hrsg. v. Günther Klaffenbach, Berlin.

Waanders, F.M.J., 1983: *The History of Τέλος and Τελέω in Ancient Greek*. Grüner, Amsterdam.

Wörrle, M., 2000: "Pergamon um 133 v. Chr.," *Chiron* 30, 543–576.

Zijderveld, C., 1934: "Τελετή: Bijdrage tot de de kennis der religieuze terminologie in het Grieksch." Ph.D. Diss. University of Utrecht.

4

"IN THE SANCTUARY OF THE SAMOTHRACIAN GODS"

Myth, politics, and mystery cult at Ilion

Mark L. Lawall

The phrase in the chapter comes from a now lost inscription, a fragment of which was found by Schliemann's excavation on the citadel at Ilion. Two other fragments were found at Çiplak, a town two kilometers from Ilion with many stones reused from the site (Cook 1973, 106). Together the three fragments record an agreement between Ilion and Scamandreia, possibly to be dated ca. 100 BC (Frisch 1975, no. 63). The stele was to be erected, as the phrase in our title makes clear, "in the sanctuary of the Samothracian Gods." This inscription has played a key role in the proposal that there was such a sanctuary at Ilion (Cole 1984, 65, n.527; Cohen 1996, 202; Rose 1998, 87; cf. Robert and Robert 1964, 189–190).

Figure 4.1 View of the southern area of the West Sanctuary: Upper and Lower Sanctuaries (neg. Troia 97/43-11)

Figure 4.2 View of the northern area of the West Sanctuary: Temple A (foreground), the Late Hellenistic Building and its predecessors (neg. Troia 94/124-10)

A likely candidate for this sanctuary has been studied by a joint University of Tübingen – University of Cincinnati project, which uncovered an extensive sanctuary complex on the west side of the Troy VI citadel wall. These discoveries expanded the cult area exposed by Carl Blegen's excavations (Blegen *et al.* 1958, 259–263, 274–279, figs. 363, 369–379). This area is now referred to as the West Sanctuary.[1] In preliminary reports, C. Brian Rose developed the hypothesis that this was Ilion's sanctuary of the Samothracian Gods, which, he argued, also included cults of Cybele and Dardanos (Rose 1998, 87–90). Study of the West Sanctuary is in progress, and the present volume offers the opportunity to explore how archaeological and textual research affects our understanding of this section of post-Bronze Age

Ilion even at this preliminary stage.[2] I begin, therefore, with a summary of the excavation results in the West Sanctuary followed by the textual evidence for cultic activity at Ilion. These archaeological and textual data set the stage for further discussion of the history of the West Sanctuary.

Both Rose's preliminary presentation and the additional considerations presented below raise the importance of interaction among three factors: local (or appropriated) mythology, political and economic interests, and the embellishment of sacred sites. How these factors interact in the particular setting of the West Sanctuary over nearly eleven centuries of activity cannot be considered fully here. Nevertheless it is possible to consider the dynamic situation of the Hellenistic period. This case study demonstrates clearly the significance of all three factors while highlighting the importance of historical setting for the interpretation of cult.

Archaeology of the West Sanctuary (Figures 4.1–4.3)[3]

Blegen's excavations between 1935 and 1938 uncovered a series of altars within two adjacent precincts (Upper and Lower sanctuaries) at the southern area and an impressive grandstand along the east side of what is now referred to as the West Sanctuary. Otherwise, much of the West Sanctuary remained unexplored until the present Tübingen–Cincinnati excavations. The lengthy and complex history of ritual activity in this area starts perhaps as early as the eighth century BC and continues through the third century AD.

Archaic (Figure 4.4)

The earliest post-Bronze Age remains in the West Sanctuary consist of Protogeometric and Geometric buildings, Late Geometric caches of pottery, including a tall stand with lattice-work support and a grey-ware thymiaterion, and fibulae (Rose 1995, 89–93; 1997, 82–83; 1998, 74; Lenz et al. 1998, 194, 196, 197; Koppenhöffer 1997, 309, fig. 4; Blegen et al. 1958, 273–274). While ritual function of the early buildings is not always clear, these artifacts may be interpreted as votive material.

More securely ritual architecture in the West Sanctuary appears in the early seventh century BC. Altar A is a J-shaped altar surrounded by a series of pavements and low, curving walls (Blegen et al. 1958, 259–262; Rose 1995, 88). Although Blegen published the finds from this area without reference to the precise stratigraphy, more recent excavation near the outermost of the terraces recovered a stratified sequence beginning in the early seventh century. Even if the current form of Altar A does not date so early, the earliest terraces likely supported cult activity.

Just north of the Upper Sanctuary, Blegen's team uncovered a series of 28 stone-paved, small circles, ca. 2 m diameter (Blegen et al. 1958, 274–279; Rose 1995, 89). Recent excavations have uncovered further examples.

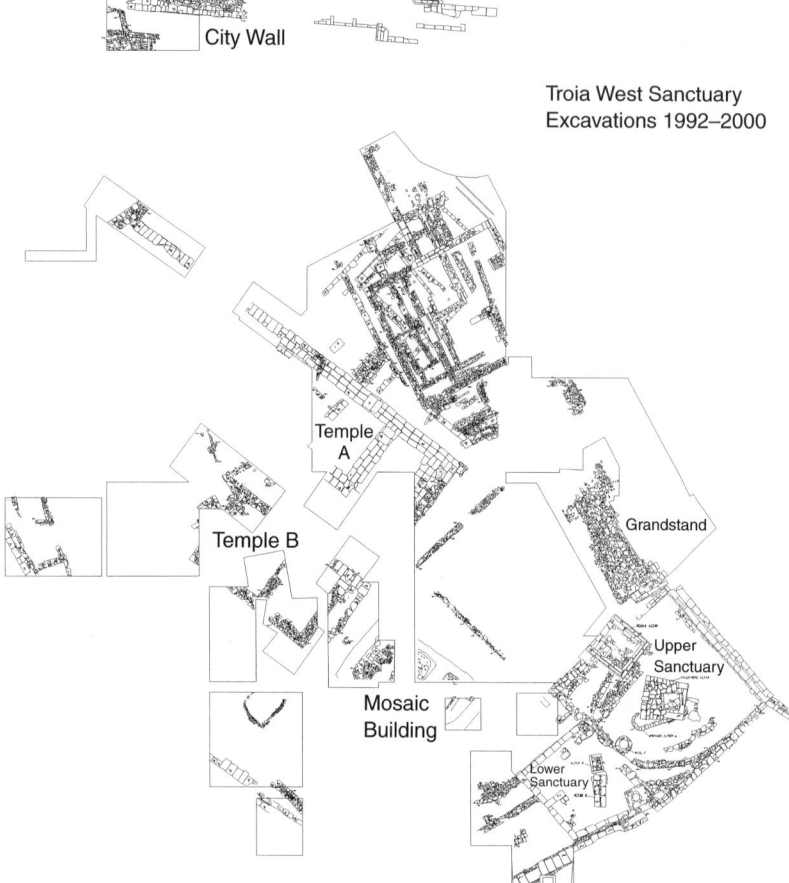

Figure 4.3 State plan of excavations in the West Sanctuary 1992–2000. Prepared by Elizabeth Riorden *et al.* and John Wallrodt

Blegen reports pottery, similar to the early seventh-century finds near the terrace walls, as the earliest diagnostic material associated with these circles.

Also in the first half of the seventh century, a two-room building was constructed at the north end of the West Sanctuary area (Rose 1997, 80–82; 1998, 74). This building is attested by preserved floors, post holes, and one stone base for a column. The lines of the outer walls are not preserved. The eastern room included two hearths, and so is presumably the back room. The same orientation and plan is repeated in subsequent archaic buildings with better-preserved ritual artifacts on this same spot; late Geometric votive deposits were found not far away. This earliest building has been labeled Archaic Cult Building 1.

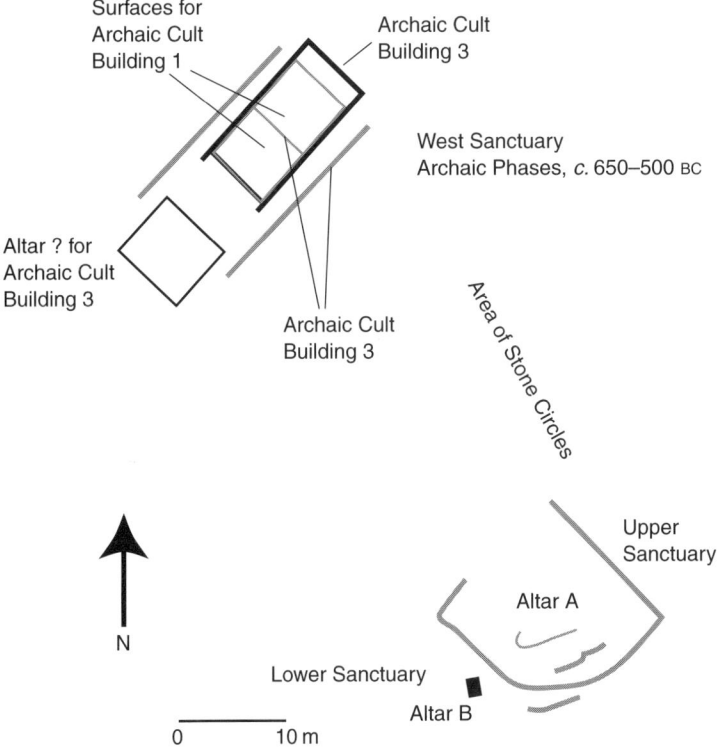

Figure 4.4 Archaic West Sanctuary. Prepared by the author

This building is replaced in the late seventh–early sixth century by a more substantially preserved, one- or two-room building, Archaic Cult Building 2. The narrow stone socles of this building were founded upon a heavily walled, paved terrace (Rose 1997, 79–81; 1998, 74). A male quadruped figurine (horse or bull?: Menadier, pers. comm.) and a large greyware krater were found on the floor, encouraging a cultic interpretation of the structure.

Archaic Cult Building 3 was then built around the middle of the sixth century (Rose 1995, 85–87; 1997, 78–79, 85–86; 1998, 73–74). The cella can be reconstructed as measuring roughly 8 m × 13 m (Rose 1997, 78), fronted by a shallow porch. Remains possibly belonging to a large altar are found at the western end of the building. An Aeolic capital, found nearby in a late Hellenistic context, may have decorated this building, along with a terracotta disc acroterion. Although certainly a temple, to judge from the reconstructed plan and altar, there were no identifiable votive offerings directly associated with this building.

Also near the middle of the sixth century, to the south, just west of Altar

A, a second altar (Blegen's Altar B, the Lower Sanctuary; see Blegen *et al.* 1958, 262–263, 268–273) was installed, surrounded by an extensive surface. Altar A was likely still in use at this time, though the evidence is not so clear.

The Archaic phase of the West Sanctuary closed ca. 500 BC. The latest Archaic Cult Building was destroyed sometime at the very end of the sixth century or early fifth century.

Classical

The dearth of remains from Classical Ilion is an often heard refrain (e.g. Blegen *et al.* 1958, 248; Rose 1995, 93; 1997, 86). Excavations in the West Sanctuary have made some progress in clarifying the nature of this "Classical Gap." There is no Classical architecture; however, relatively rich dumps of Classical pottery do appear and help define areas of activity between ca. 500 and 300 BC.

Most of the Classical pottery has been found in the robbing trench of a long, north–south running terrace wall along the east side of the area (Rose 1994, 84–86). The fill of this trench is datable between ca. 440 and 390 BC, with the majority datable to the very latest fifth and earliest fourth century. The fill is largely devoid of cooking and other plainware vessels and seems, therefore, to derive from ritual activity. This activity, however, probably occurred farther up the slope of the citadel (K. Lynch, pers. comm.).

The open area between the Archaic Cult Building area and the precincts of Altars A and B also included Classical finds, mostly datable to the fourth century. Neither the area of the Archaic Cult Building nor the Altar B precinct revealed much Classical pottery. This absence is particularly noticeable near Altar B where datable finds in stratified fills jump from the late Archaic to Hellenistic.

Ritual activity in the fifth and much of the fourth century seems to have occurred higher on the citadel, no longer within the West Sanctuary.

Early Hellenistic (Figure 4.5)

The first indication of renewed construction and activity in the West Sanctuary is a large multi-room building at the north end of the area, the Early Hellenistic Building (Rose 1994, 82–84; 1995, 96–97; 1998, 76–79). This building had at least two large rooms entered from a wide porch or hall. The walls were constructed of rough fieldstones; the interior was painted in imitation of drafted-margin revetment. The construction date of the building, based on pottery from the foundation trenches and leveling fills, falls within the first quarter of the third century. Rare figurines from contexts associated with the use of the building in its original form suggest the possibility of ritual function. And yet the activity debris within the building also includes

MYTH, POLITICS, AND MYSTERY CULT AT ILION

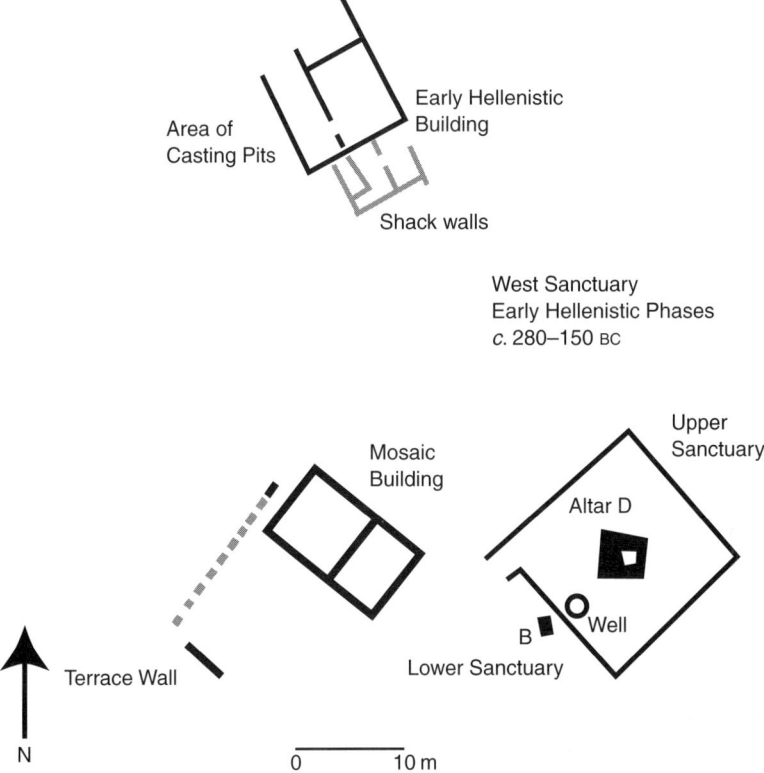

Figure 4.5 Early Hellenistic West Sanctuary. Prepared by the author

remains of a more industrial nature – murex shell, slag, burnt patches. The plan recalls both secular and sacred public buildings (e.g., prytaneia, so-called priest's houses, and dining halls; see Graf, this volume p. 251), on dining as part of ritual), but the Early Hellenistic Building's original function remains uncertain.

It is important to note at this point, however, that there is no clear evidence of early third-century ritual activity elsewhere in the West Sanctuary. The Hellenistic Altar (D), two wells, and a square precinct wall, excavated by Blegen in the Upper Sanctuary, are of uncertain Hellenistic date (Blegen *et al.* 1958 303–304). The Upper Sanctuary's precinct wall, the propylon, perhaps the digging of the second well, and perhaps the marble cladding of Altar D date to the mid-second century (see below). The Upper Sanctuary's earlier Hellenistic phase might therefore date within the third century, but any further precision is not possible. Archaic Altar B may have been in use throughout this period, but fills raising the ground level in the area seem more like periodic dumps of debris rather than gradual

85

accumulations. Blegen's excavation did find poorly preserved stones resting on the top surface of Altar B, and he took these as evidence for a Hellenistic raising of the height to accommodate the rising ground level (Blegen *et al.* 1958, 263). The only preserved Hellenistic activity level was set down in the mid-second century when a second altar was installed beside Altar B, along with a precinct wall (see below).

Activity in the West Sanctuary increased considerably in the third quarter of the third century. South of the Early Hellenistic Building and just northwest of the Lower Sanctuary, a deep-pronaos temple facing south was constructed – the Mosaic Building (Figure 4.6) (Rose 1995, 94–95; 1998, 85–86). The building measures ca. 8.5 × 13 m, with the pronaos comprising one-third of the building. The cella floor rests 0.10–0.15 m higher than the pronaos floor. The name of this building comes from the heavily damaged pebble mosaic pavement of the cella and pronaos. In the cella the design of the mosaic may be reconstructed as follows. The outermost rectangular border features a running spiral design; within this another rectangular border may have a combined floral and animal motifs; these borders surround a circular emblema with some sort of figural design. A heavy, cut-stone footing for a cult-statue base or offering table (M. Basedow, pers.

Figure 4.6 Mosaic Building: rear of the cella with torch base in foreground, remains of pebble mosaic (right); robbing trench of north wall (center); foundations of Temple B (left) (neg. Troia 97/166-27)

comm.) was set near the back wall of the cella. Beside these foundations is a small stone set into the floor with a hole cut into its top surface. This is likely the stand for a torch. The walls were decorated with painted plaster imitating drafted-margin revetment with a stucco Ionic molding.

The ground for the Mosaic Building was supported by a massive terrace wall, also of the mid-late third century, preserved along the southwest side of the West Sanctuary area. This wall runs just east of a late second-century terrace wall and threshold block, discussed below (Rose 2000, 55–58).

The first half of the Hellenistic period in the sanctuary ends with the destruction of both the Mosaic Building and the Early Hellenistic Building. Pottery from destruction contexts from both buildings dates to the middle of the second century. Why did these buildings collapse? A possible explanation comes from a puzzling feature of the Mosaic Building. Wall plaster there was found scattered over the excavated area of the building, but the walls themselves were completely removed. The plaster must have shaken off the walls; the walls were too unstable to remain; the wall blocks and the cult base were removed; the fallen debris was left on the floor of the Mosaic Building. An earthquake could have caused such damage to the Mosaic Building while at the same time ending the usefulness of the Early Hellenistic Building.[4] Such an earthquake could have also damaged the Upper Sanctuary (around Altar D). Blegen identified a second phase of the high precinct wall and a second well replacing Well F. While precise evidence for the date of the new precinct wall and the new well is unavailable (Blegen *et al.* 1958, 303–304), pottery from under the propylon dates to the mid-second century (Rose 1999, 50) implying a renovation of the gateway, at least, at this time.

Late Hellenistic (Figure 4.7)[5]

The same types of pottery that helped determine the date of the destruction of the Mosaic Building appear in the construction fills for a temple, Temple B, of similar plan just to the northwest (Rose 1998, 86–87). The cella is similar in size, and there are similar proportions between the pronaos and cella in each building (2:3). Only the rubble fill of the foundations is preserved, so it is unknown whether the interior decoration, too, mimicked that of the Mosaic Building. The proximity to the Mosaic Building, the similarity of plan, and the closeness of date between the destruction of the Mosaic Building and the construction of Temple B all suggest that Temple B was intended to replace the Mosaic Building.

Temple B, like the Mosaic Building, is also supported by a heavy terrace wall to the west (the stretch of wall preserved in section x7, see Rose 2000, 55–58). This wall angled to the southeast to meet the older Mosaic Building Terrace wall where that wall had turned up slope toward the back of the Mosaic Building. The juncture of the two terrace walls now became the entrance to the Sanctuary area from the west.

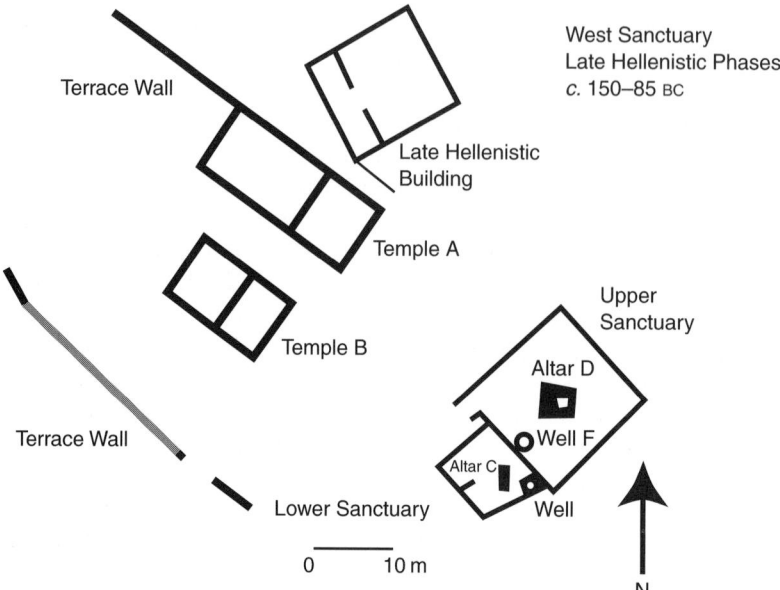

Figure 4.7 Late Hellenistic West Sanctuary. Prepared by the author

Near the middle of the second century, too, a precinct wall was constructed around the area of the Lower Sanctuary and a narrow, elongated altar (Altar C: Blegen *et al.* 1958, 306) was added beside the Archaic Altar B (Rose 1995, 93). Accumulated Archaic and earlier Hellenistic fill was leveled over the surrounding precinct, and the underpinnings of this surface included the chipped stone from dressing the new precinct walls and the altar itself. This new surface seems to date to the middle of the second century. Unfortunately, it is not possible to know if this renewed activity predates or post-dates the proposed mid-century earthquake.

At roughly the same time as the construction of Temple B, bronze-casting pits and one furnace structure were cut directly in front of the porch of the Early Hellenistic Building (Rose 1998, 79–85). The furnace and eight casting pits are datable after ca. 225 BC. Since the pits were cut directly in front of the Early Hellenistic Building they should post-date the damage to that building in the mid-second century. There are, however, another five, stratigraphically earlier casting pits exhibiting somewhat different design. There was no clear evidence for the absolute dates of these earlier pits, and they might not be much earlier than the later examples.

Also in the mid-second century, adjacent to the Early Hellenistic Building, a series of poorly founded fieldstone walls were built abutting the building's south wall (Rose 1994, 83–84; 1995, 96–97). In association with these walls and within the Early Hellenistic Building itself, various traces of industrial activity were found, including pigments, plant remains from dye production, and small ovens.[6] The construction, furnishing, and perhaps further upkeep of the Temple B, constructed at roughly the same time, could explain these activities.

Near the end of the second century two further buildings were added to the West Sanctuary. The earlier of the two buildings (though not earlier by many years) is Temple A, facing southeast, parallel to Temple B, and just west of the site of the Early Hellenistic Building (Rose 1994, 80–82; 1995, 95; 1998, 90–92). At ca. 20×10 m this is the largest building in the West Sanctuary. Little of the superstructure is preserved apart from a large marble floral acroterion. The foundation trenches and adjacent working surfaces include pottery datable very late in the second century. There is a substantial terrace wall extending north from, and bonded to, the foundations of Temple A. A further stretch of late second-century terrace wall was built just west of the old Mosaic Building terrace wall. This new wall reinforcing the southern terrace was then joined to the wall supporting Temple B by a wide threshold and gate clearly aligned to lead visitors up the hill in front of Temples B and A.

The second major late second-century construction, the Late Hellenistic Building, was built over the southern end of the Early Hellenistic Building (Rose 1993, 100–104; 1994, 76–80). This roughly square building, 11.5×9.5 m, had one large room opening at the west to a relatively deep, wide porch; there were windows in the north and south walls. This building had a well-cut marble threshold, ashlar masonry walls in local limestone, and rubble foundations. Nearly the same pottery types appear in the construction fills for the Late Hellenistic Building as had been found with construction contexts of Temple A.

This late second-century flurry of activity in the West Sanctuary came to a sudden end in 85 BC when the Roman quaestor C. Flavius Fimbria sacked Troy during the Mithridatic wars (Strabo 13.1.27). The impact of this attack is clearly visible in the thick layer of burnt debris over the floor of the Late Hellenistic Building (Rose 1993, 100–104); the walls are cracked and discolored from the fire; amphoras and other pottery on the floor were nearly vitrified (Hayes 1995); and the bones of one unfortunate man were found on the floor. Temples A and B were also damaged, but Temple A survived sufficiently well to be rebuilt (see below); Temple B was completely destroyed.

Roman (Figure 4.8)

When Blegen's team described the Roman period activity around the Upper Sanctuary and the long grandstand bordering the West Sanctuary along its eastern side, the dominant assumption was that Augustus' refurbishing of

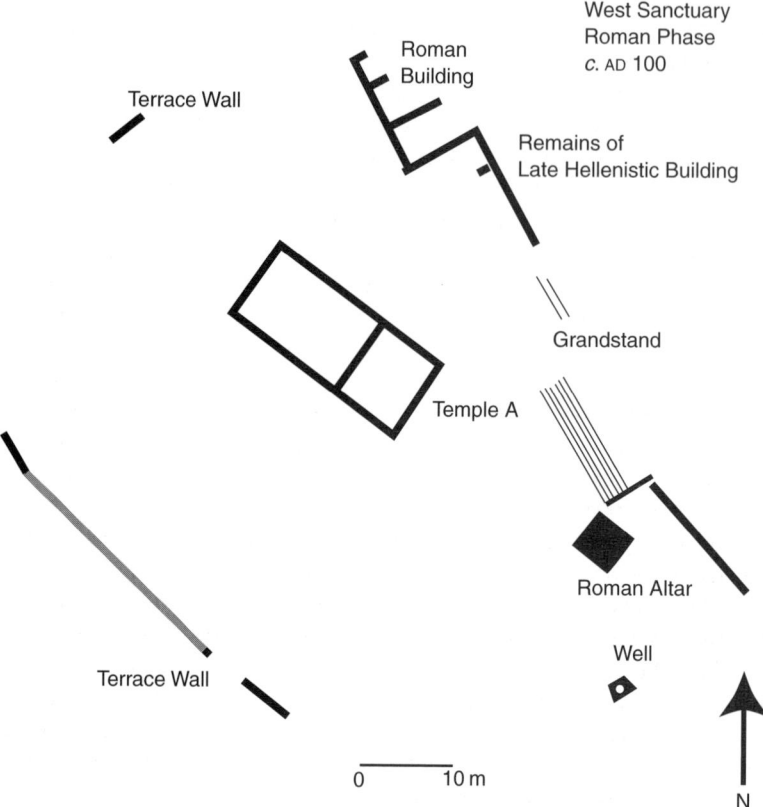

Figure 4.8 Roman West Sanctuary. Prepared by the author

the Athena temple carried over to a general renovation of the city (Blegen *et al.* 1958, 304; Thompson 1963, 4; Rose 1992, 44–45). The current excavations have confirmed Augustan period activity in the area of the West Sanctuary, but it now appears that much of the work was only completed later in first century AD.

In the West Sanctuary, the only building to be fully carried over from the Hellenistic period was Temple A (Rose 1994, 80–81; 1997, 92). The porch was reinforced and extended to the south. Mortar in the renovated section includes marble fragments that are likely part of the earlier Hellenistic temples (Basedow, pers. comm.). Strata including marble chips in front of the porch of Temple A, overlying burnt debris to be associated with the Fimbrian sack, and early Roman pottery in fills related to the new porch construction add further evidence for the restoration of Temple A very late in the first century AD or early in the second century AD.

The wide open area south of Temple A, an area that had been terraced down to the much lower level of the southern precincts, was raised roughly 1.5 m and was leveled with a stone pavement (Rose 1999, 50–51). While there is much Fimbrian destruction debris in this fill, there is also plenty of Augustan and later first century AD pottery and coins. The filling and paving process seems to have been completed around AD 100.

The east side of this area was defined by a large grandstand, first exposed by Blegen's excavations. Blegen placed this grandstand as part of the Augustan rebuilding (Blegen et al. 1958, 304, 306). Although the latest pottery in its construction fills is Augustan (Rose 1993, 98), the later pottery and coins associated with other parts of the Roman renovations should place the grandstand, too, in the early second century AD. The grandstand is not oriented to the axis of Temple A. Instead the orientation is closer to that of the Late Hellenistic Building. The north and east walls of this building were still visible; however, an earlier boundary of the sanctuary area below the grandstand – rather than the ruined Late Hellenistic Building – may have determined the orientation of the grandstand.

At the southern end of the paved area, straddling the earlier precinct wall for the Upper Sanctuary, is the Roman Altar. The altar was discovered by Blegen's team and restored with marble step blocks found nearby. These blocks, Blegen proposed, came from the earlier Hellenistic Altar D (Blegen et al. 1958, 304), and indeed mismatched clamp cuttings clearly indicate the blocks' reuse. The Roman Altar is oriented to Temple A. The northern and southern areas were unified in this fashion for the first time. Again, Blegen proposed an Augustan date for this altar; no new dating evidence is available, but a post-Augustan date seems likely.

Also in the first century AD, a small building of uncertain function and poorly preserved plan was built abutting the north wall of the Late Hellenistic Building (Rose 1997, 92). The area of the Late Hellenistic Building itself was filled in, creating a slope from the east wall down toward Temple A. The east wall was buttressed during the second century AD, by which time it was acting simply as a terrace wall (Rose 1994, 80). Finally, sometime between ca. AD 50 and 150, the terrace wall north of Temple A was substantially robbed of its upper courses and a new terrace wall, this one oriented roughly east to west, was built north of Temple A (Rose 1998, 92).

In AD 267 the Herulians sacked Ilion (Jordanes, Getica 20.108; Rose 1992, 44), and activity in the West Sanctuary seems to have declined about the same time. Indeed, there may have been much stone robbing in the northern part of the site even before the Herulian attack (Rose 1994, 80; 1995, 98). Two successive earthquakes ca. AD 500 considerably damaged remaining walls (Rose 1997, 98–99; 1998, 97; 1999, 45; 2000, 60). In the Byzantine period there was renewed occupation, but no church has been found in this formerly sacred area (Rose 1999, 51–52; 2000, 57–58; for the late history of Ilion, see Sage 2000, 218–220).

Cults at Ilion

Further study and interpretation of these remains in the West Sanctuary depend on the identity of the cults worshipped there. One starting point for such a study is the textual evidence for cults at Ilion. This evidence comes largely from inscriptions and a few passing references in literary sources. The range of cults indicated by this evidence, however, attests to a varied and dynamic religious sphere. The relevant epigraphic and literary testimonia tend to date from the end of the fourth century BC through the second century AD.

The dominant cult was that of Athena Ilias. Xerxes' sacrifice to Athena Ilias, attested by Herodotus (7.43.1–2), is the earliest literary evidence for ritual at the site. This cult was the focus not only of a large temple and temenos on the citadel at Ilion but also of a koinon of ten cities, sacred lands, and a Panathenaic festival (Dörpfeld 1902, 208–227; Frisch 1975, *passim*; Cook 1973, 364; Robert 1966, 18–43, 89–93; Bellinger 1961, 3; Brückner 1902, 577–579; Goethert and Schlief 1962; Rose 1992, 45–46; 1997, 96–101; 1998, 97–99). Nearly all statues and decrees mentioned in the textual record are designated to be set up in this sanctuary, and Athena is the pre-eminent figure on Ilian coinage through the Hellenistic period (Bellinger 1961). Athena is the only Olympian for whom a named sanctuary site is attested.

Athena was not, however, the only Olympian deity worshipped at Ilion. Alexander the Great offered sacrifices to Priam at an altar to Zeus Herkeios (of the courtyard) (Arrian, *Anabasis* 1.11.8; Frisch 1975, no. 144). Zeus Polieus is mentioned in one inscription, and Dörpfeld's excavation recovered an over life-size head of Zeus on the Acropolis (Frisch 1975 no. 52.24; Winnefeld 1902, 438–439, fig. 54). Apollo appears primarily as the patron divinity of the Seleucid dynasty (Frisch 1975, nos. 31, 32), though there is one reference to Ilian Apollo on a statue base dedicated by the Mytileneans (Frisch 1975, no. 230).

Cults outside the Olympian mainstream are quite common. A priest of Dionysos and a Greater Dionysiac festival appear in the epigraphic record (Frisch 1975, nos. 25, 152, 154). Frequent, and surprisingly early, references appear to a priest τῶν πάντων θεῶν ("of all the gods"). This priesthood is not commonly attested in the Greek world, though the cult itself was quite widespread, especially in the second century BC and later (Frisch 1975, nos. 32, 35, 52, 59; for lists of other attested cults, see Ziegler 1949, 707–727). There is one extant dedication to Demeter and Kore (Frisch 1975, no. 153). A cult of the Trojan hero Hector emerges in the Roman period and figures prominently on Ilion's coinage after ca. AD 161 (Frisch 1975, no. 142; Bellinger 1961, T135, T147, T150, etc.; Sage 2000, 216–217). Strabo mentions that the Ilians sacrificed to Achilles, Patroclus, Antilochus, and Ajax – but not in Ilion itself (13.1 32; for Achilles, see Sage 2000, 216; Rose 1999,

61–63; 2000, 65–66). Cults of selected Hellenistic dynasts were also present at Ilion (Seleucus I: see Frisch 1975, no. 31 with reference to an altar in the agora; Antiochus I: see Frisch 1975, nos. 32, 36, and possibly nos. 26 and 35; in general see Price 1984, 23–40). And finally, there are three inscriptions referring to the Samothracian Gods (Frisch 1975, nos. 44, 63; Cohen 1996).[7] Two are dedications by women, one of whom is from Pergamon. The other inscription (part of which is quoted in the title) refers to a sanctuary of the Samothracian Gods. The significance of this cult will be considered below, but here it suffices to note that Athena and the Samothracian gods are the only cults for which a sanctuary (ἱερόν) is attested.

Indeed, so far as the testimonia indicate, there are only two specifically named sanctuaries at Ilion. One of these, the Athena sanctuary, has been identified with certainty by the presence of the temple. While there may well have been more than two named sanctuaries, this scarcity of ἱερά in our sources raises the possibility of more than one divinity having been worshipped at either sanctuary area. This is a common practice at other sites (e.g., Lebedeev 1996; Rigsby 1996, 185–186; Couilloud-Le Dinahet 1991; Chapouthier 1935). At the West Sanctuary at Ilion, the extensive ritual facilities and the range of dedications present also suggest multiple cults. The fact that the Athena sanctuary, of the two named sanctuaries, has already been identified raises the further possibility that the West Sanctuary should be identified as the Sanctuary of the Samothracian Gods.

Samothracian gods, Cybele, and Dardanos

In 1998, following the 1997 excavation season, Rose proposed the identification of the West Sanctuary with the Samothracian Gods, coexisting with worship of Dardanos and Cybele. His case depended on various elements of the archaeological and textual records. The following summary adds further evidence to the case first outlined by Rose.

A mystery cult

Rose's argument for the West Sanctuary being associated with a mystery cult began by noting the focus on interior or enclosed spaces. The worn mosaic floor of the Mosaic Building, along with that building's painted walls, cult table or statue base, and torch base, all indicate indoor activity (Rose 1998, 87). Interior wall painting and/or mosaic decoration is not at all common in Greek temples, but examples are often associated with mystery and hero cults.[8] The high wall preserved at the northeast corner of the Upper Sanctuary temenos also implies a more cut-off space, which, though open to the sky, meant rituals around the altar would be difficult to observe. Although the height of the Lower Sanctuary temenos is not preserved, it too could have been quite high on the basis of the depth and thickness of the preserved foundations and the buttressing spur wall (Rose 1998, 87). Torch bases – the one inside the Mosaic Building, one outside the same building, and one outside Temple A – recall torch bases at the Samothrace Hieron (Lehmann 1969, v. 2, 55, fig. 365) and at the Sanctuary of Demeter and Kore at Corinth (Bookidis and Stroud 1997, 201). A very similar, pierced stone was found in front of the Demeter Temple at Pergamon, but that stone has been identified as an anchor block for tethering sacrificial animals (Kasper 1972, 84, figs. 19–20; Bohtz 1981, 51).[9]

A further architectural feature supporting the presence of mystery cult in the West Sanctuary is the first-century grandstand constructed between Temple A and the Roman Altar. Grandstands or theatrical areas are found at other mystery cult sites: the Kabeirion at Thebes (Heyder and Mallwitz 1978, 25–28), the Sanctuary of the Great Gods on Samothrace (Lehmann 1998, 91; for another area for performance and seating at Samothrace see Clinton, this volume, p. 64), Demeter at Pergamon (Radt 1999, 180–181, figs. 126, 127; Bohtz 1981, 57–58), and Despoina at Lykosoura (Dickens 1905–1906, fig. 3). At Eleusis there is seating both inside and just outside the Telesterion (Mylonas 1961, fig. 4, nos. 29, 53). Indeed, the grandstand at Ilion could have taken as its inspiration the very similar layout of the Demeter Sanctuary at Pergamon. Though much earlier in construction, the Demeter Sanctuary would have been well known to both Ilians and perhaps Roman benefactors in the first century AD.

The Samothracian Gods

Mystery-cult worship at Ilion is attested through the cult of the Samothracian Gods and, possibly, through a dedication to Demeter and Kore. As noted above, the Samothracian Gods receive one of only two attested, named sanctuaries at Ilion, and two dedications to the Samothracian Gods come from Ilion. While Demeter and Kore do receive one extant dedication (Frisch 1975, no. 153), there is no attested sanctuary of Demeter. The epigraphic evidence suggests that if there was a mystery-related sanctuary at Ilion, it was likely associated with the Samothracian Gods.

Elements of the architectural ensemble and the associated finds at the West Sanctuary support the identification of this mystery cult with the cult of the Samothracian Gods. The Mosaic Building's wall painting and torch base, as well as the torch base along the east side of Temple A, recall the Hieron at Samothrace (Lehmann 1969, v. 1, 138–142, 204–212; v. 2, 55, fig. 365). High-walled hypaethral precincts, such as the Upper and Lower Sanctuaries, are paralleled by the Altar Court on Samothrace (Lehmann and Spittle 1964; Lehmann 1998, 89–91). The Early Hellenistic Building and the Late Hellenistic Building, each with its broad porch and large interior spaces, bear some resemblance to the main building of the Sanctuary of the Samothracian Gods on Delos (Chapouthier 1935) and to the Hall of the

Votive Gifts and the Anaktoron at Samothrace (Lehmann 1962; 1998, 86–87, 56–61). The Delos Sanctuary, however, does not include the more temple-like buildings (Mosaic Building and Temples A and B) found at Ilion.

Alongside the architectural evidence, further support for a Samothracian cult here comes from a graffito on a third century BC West Slope kantharos lip reading Μελίτηι τρία. Rose (1998, 87–88, fig. 13; and 1999, 50, with correction to reading) pointed out that "Melite" could refer either to the island of Samothrace (Strabo 10.3.19) or to a person's name (e.g., Fraser and Matthews 1987, 304). The presence of the τρία following "Melite" suggests a reading of "three [things, possibly ποτήρια (cups)] to Melite." If Melite were to be read as a person's name, it seems more likely that the name would refer to the owner of the three (cups?) and would read Μελίτης. The dedication of three objects "to Samothrace" fits the preserved syntax of the graffito.[10]

The placement of the West Sanctuary also encourages a connection with Samothrace. The location, on the west side of the citadel, is in view of Samothrace (Rose 1998, 87) and is positioned along a likely route from port cities to Ilion's Agora. The association between the Samothracian Gods and safety in sea travel makes this location particularly appropriate (for the connection to safety at sea, see Cole 1984, 61–66).

The possibility that the West Sanctuary was dedicated to the Samothracian Gods raises the further possibility that this cult was equated with the Kabeiroi in Ilion as it was on Delos (Chapouthier 1935) and, as some have argued, on Samothrace itself (Daumas 1997; Burkert 1993, 181; Graf 1999, 126–127; cf. Cole 1984, 1–2; the ancient debate is found in Strabo 10.3.19–21; see also Schachter, this volume p. 112). Kabeiric worship is certainly common in the region of Ilion, with attestations at Lemnos, Imbros, Pergamon, and Birytis; Pherekydes, indeed, noted the frequency of Kabeiric worship near Ilion (*FGrH* 3 F47, cited by Graf 1999, 124; Strabo 10.3.21). The only direct evidence at the West Sanctuary for a blending of Kabeiric and Samothracian worship comes in the form of two representations of a double axe, both from second-century BC contexts: one miniature iron axe (Rose 1994, 78, fig. 5), and an unusual votive relief with a double axe shown alongside a grape cluster (unpublished SS56, from near the south end of Temple B). The double-axe motif, however, is not limited to the Kabeiroi,[11] so Kabeiric worship remains only a possibility.

Cybele

As noted above, it seems quite likely that multiple cults shared the West Sanctuary, even if its ancient name was the Sanctuary of the Samothracian Gods. Worship of Cybele has been proposed somewhere in the area since the earliest German excavations; the Blegen excavations narrowed the focus to the area of the Upper Sanctuary; and recent excavations have added further evidence in favor of Cybele. It may be noted, however, that Cybele remains unattested in epigraphic evidence from Ilion. Cybele is, however, closely associated with Ilion, the Troad, and Samothrace in literary sources and on coinage (e.g., Diodorus 5.49, Dionysius of Halicarnassus, 1.68–69; Vergil, *Aeneid* 3.102–120; 7, 139; 10, 252–255; Ovid, *Fasti* 4.249–250 and 263–264 [referring to Mt Ida]; and generally see Vermaseren 1977, 24–25; Rose 1998, 89 with references to Cybele on coins from Samothrace; Roller 1999, esp. 178, 270–271, and 299–303).

The attribution of the West Sanctuary area to Cybele was earlier proposed by Thompson on the basis of remains of wild animal sacrifices and terracotta figurines of Cybele (Figure 4.9) and Attis (Thompson 1963, 59–60).

Figure 4.9 Terracotta figurine of Cybele from the West Sanctuary (neg. Troia 93/156-0)

Blegen's excavations recovered lion (or tiger) and bear bones near the Upper Sanctuary (Blegen et al. 1958, 263; Thompson 1963, 59, n.20), and recent excavations brought to light further examples (Rose 1994, n.19; Fabis, pers. comm.). Recent excavations also recovered a marble lion's paw fragment (Rose 1993, 100, n.15), which is of sufficient size to have come from a cult statue. The terracotta figurines include many related to Cybele (Winnefeld 1902, 440–441; Thompson 1963, 77–84; Miller 1991, esp. 45–46; Rose 1993, 98). The figurines appear in association with late Classical/early Hellenistic pottery dumps (Menadier, pers. comm.) and so worship may predate the later third-century architectural embellishment of the West Sanctuary. Worship of Cybele clearly existed beyond the West Sanctuary, as attested by stone and terracotta images elsewhere on the site (e.g., Rose 1995, 99, fig. 23; Thompson 1963, 77, 80). Nevertheless, the faunal remains and the terracotta figurines in the West Sanctuary area point toward Cybele worship.

Indeed, the plan of the Mosaic Building (and its replacement Temple B) resembles the Pergamene Cybele temple at Mamurt Kale (Conze and Schazmann 1911) and the temple of Magna Mater in Rome (Pensabene 1982, 1988; Roller 1999, 271–278; Romanelli 1963; Huelsen 1895, 3–28). The Pergamene temple, built by Philetairos, is slightly smaller than the Mosaic Building (7 × 11.15 m compared with 8.5 × 13 m); but the proportions of the euthynteria are quite similar (0.63 and 0.65 m respectively). Both buildings feature a higher cella floor. Both buildings share an unusually deep pronaos, but the Mamurt Kale pronaos is roughly half the length of the building so it is larger in proportion. At the back of the cella at Mamurt Kale is a deeply founded "throne" of cut stone. The foundations at the back of the Mosaic Building are similar in plan and similarly well-founded, though on a smaller scale.

The temple of Magna Mater on the Palatine, first built between 204 and 191, and rebuilt in 111 BC, similarly had a heavy, well-built cult base at the back of the cella. Here, too, there is a deep pronaos (perhaps a colonnaded porch, see Huelsen 1895, 10–11; however no trace of the stylobate survives). The cella and pronaos are the same depth (12.73 m each: Romanelli 1963, fig. 14), and the cella also had a mosaic floor (Romanelli 1963, 239).

Dardanos

Alongside the terracottas often associated with Cybele, another major class of finds in the West Sanctuary is a series of clay plaques (Figure 4.10) showing a male rider, sometimes accompanied by a snake and standing female figure (Winnefeld 1902, 442–444, fig. 57; Thompson 1963, 108–116; Miller 1991, 48–49; Barr 1996; Rose 1998, 88, fig. 14). Rose sought an heroic identity for this rider and proposed Dardanos, whose great-grandson, Ilos, founded the city of Ilion itself. The iconographic connection between the plaques and Dardanos depends on a Caracallan coin found in

Figure 4.10 Terracotta rider plaque from the West Sanctuary (neg. Troia 94/150-28)

the West Sanctuary, as well as earlier coins – all of the city of Dardanos. On the reverse of the Caracallan issue is a rider in travelling cloak carrying the Palladion; an earlier Hellenistic issue shows the rider on the obverse and the Palladion on the reverse.[12] These Hellenistic and Roman images of Dardanos as rider led Rose to suggest that the horseman plaques served a hero-cult of Dardanos.

Rose's case is further supported by a reference in Lykophron's *Alexandra* (line 72) to a grave of Dardanos at Ilion. The explanation as to why Dardanos would be considered buried at Ilion instead of his own city-foundation, Dardanos (Cook 1973, 57–60), might stem from Lykophron's possible activity at Pergamon in the early second century BC and his desire to strengthen Pergamon's ancestral connection to Rome via Ilion (see below) (Kosmetatou 2000). In other words, Hellenistic Ilion may have claimed such a grave even in the face of more plausible locations.

Myths of Dardanos bring together the two other proposed cults in the West Sanctuary. Dardanos introduced the Samothracian cult to the region and brought the Palladion and images of the Samothracian Gods from

Samothrace to the Troad (Strabo 7, figs. 49, 50; Dionysius of Halicarnassus 1.68.4–1.69.1). Cybele married Dardanos' brother Iasion and bore a son Corybas (Diodorus 5.49.2); Dardanos, Cybele, and Corybas then established a cult of Cybele in Phrygia on Mt Ida (Diodorus 5.49.2; cf. Dionysius of Halicarnassos 1.61.4). A cult of Dardanos, therefore, would fit very easily into a sanctuary with worship of Cybele and the Samothracian Gods. Further examples of the idea of a rider-hero, though not necessarily Dardanos, accompanying worship of Cybele come from second- and third-century AD stone reliefs showing Cybele in the company of a rider (Metropoulou 1996, 142–143; Oppermann 1981, 513–514). Another case of Cybele worship accompanied by terracotta rider plaques appears at Hellenistic Kyme (Papadopoulos 2000, 418).

The proposed connection between the rider on the plaques and Dardanos has been disputed and requires certain qualifications. Barr notes that the rider on the plaques does not carry the Palladion (1996, 135). Other numismatic images, furthermore, show Dardanos without horse, though again with the Palladion (Kahil 1986, 353). It should be noted, too, that rider plaques are found at many other sites without such an immediate connection, if any, to Dardanos (Papadopoulos 2000, 418; e.g., armed rider plaques from Messene: Themelis 1998, 162–165; "rider reliefs" from Corinth of a somewhat different form: Davidson 1952, nos. 308–319). Indeed, even at Ilion there may have been multiple "identities" for this rider since many plaques have appeared outside the West Sanctuary (Winnefeld 1902, 443 and Dörpfeld 1902, 229 for plaques on the east side of the Athena temenos area; Thompson 1963, 56; Miller 1991, 48). A generic, "heroic" reference is clear in grave stelai showing a similar rider, where the deceased is referred to as hero (ἥρως) (Schwertheim 1980, 167, no. 410 among others; Thompson 1963, 108, n.221 refers to "innumerable examples" of terracotta horseman plaques from cemeteries in Boeotia). The "heroic" plaques could serve multiple personae depending on context. Nevertheless, a general reference to "hero" through the imagery of the plaques may have been sufficient to indicate Dardanos for the worshippers in the West Sanctuary. Within the physical setting of a Sanctuary of the Samothracian Gods and alongside worship of Cybele at Ilion no other hero seems so appropriate as Dardanos.

Epigraphic evidence first encouraged the search for a sanctuary for the Samothracian Gods at Ilion. Elements of the archaeological evidence fit such an interpretation. The accompanying archaeological evidence in favor of the addition of Cybele and Dardanos to the sanctuary then leads back to other textual evidence, which has been used here to suggest an appropriate packet of divinities for the West Sanctuary: Samothracian Gods, Cybele, and Dardanos.

Historical context

The combination of archaeological and textual evidence can be taken further, now, into the interaction between cult activity and political interests. If the attribution of the West Sanctuary to this packet of divinities is correct, then the archaeologically attested physical embellishment of the West Sanctuary in the late third and second centuries BC fits well with the textually attested Ilian strategy for survival, and even profit, among the Hellenistic powers (including Rome). The people of Ilion had seen, at least as early as 480 BC, how important their past, and especially cults associated with their past, could be for ensuring their security. Cities of a similar size, without such a famous past, could hardly have received such attention from Persian satraps, Greek kings and warlords, and ambitious Romans (Sage 2000; Vermeule 1995). Ilion's strategy for survival emphasized cultic connections to successive, apparently dominant powers – first the Seleucids, then Pergamon, and finally Rome.

Seleucid dynasty

Around 281 BC the Ilians saw the advantages of welcoming a cult of Seleucus I, his ancestor Apollo, and shortly thereafter, Antiochus I; increased territory was the result (Frisch 1975, no. 33). During the reign of Antiochus II, Ilion parlayed her heroic past – and especially her connection to Samothrace – into political influence: Ilion, Samothrace, Sardis, Didyma, and Ephesos were designated as sites for the erection of stelai carrying a royal decree (Dittenberger 1903, 225.25–30). This instance stands at the head of a series of inscriptions being published both at Ilion and Samothrace (or sites with Samothracian cults) (Frisch 1975, nos. 45, 63; Dittenberger 1903, no. 335).[13] During the reign of Seleucus II – perhaps during the troubled times of the uprising of Antiochus Hierax (242–227 BC) – Ilion was relieved of paying tribute to the Seleucids. The privilege was granted through the intercession of Rome apparently already claiming Trojan ancestry.[14] The Ilians cannot help but have noticed the potential political influence of their local mythology; the resulting privileges would have been a substantive economic windfall for the city.

The date of construction of the Mosaic Building, the first temple in the West Sanctuary, and the major terrace/temenos wall to the east depends on similarity of the pottery assemblage there with the pottery in construction fills of Ilion's city wall, which is itself thought to date within the third quarter of the third century during Hierax's revolt (Rose 1997, 93–96; Aylward 1999, 175; Berlin 1999, 147; Tekkök 2001). If the episode involving Rome occurred before or during this uprising, then any architectural reference to cults with ties to Ilion's Homeric (and pre-Homeric) past and her connection to Samothrace would have made a fitting nod to the importance of Ilion's ancestral, and obviously profitable, connection to Rome.

Pergamon

The other major Hellenistic dynasty with potential interests in Ilion, namely Pergamon, was slower to take an active interest in Ilion. Instead, Early Hellenistic architecture and cult at Pergamon seem to seek a position in the broader regional koine. Philetairos' Temple of Meter (Cybele) at Mamurt Kale emphasized Phrygian identity (cf. Roller 1999, 210–212). Cybele worship at the site of Kapikaya may have started about the same time, though no architecture can be dated to the Hellenistic period (Nohlen and Radt 1978). The urban temple to Cybele, the Megalesion (Varro, *de lingua latina* 6.15), has been identified with a square peristyle building just outside the southeast, Philetairean gate (Ohlemutz 1940, 183–184; Radt 1999, 247–248); this temple, too, should date to the third century BC. Philetairos' elaboration of the Demeter Sanctuary at Pergamon depended heavily on stylistic influence from Samothrace (Hoepfner 1997, 34). Finally, the Temple of Athena at Pergamon has been linked to both the Assos temple and the Temple of Athena at Ilion (Hoepfner 1997, 30–34, and 46–48 for further similarities between Pergamene and Ilian architecture). This early identity-establishing activity on the part of Philetairos indicates key elements of a northern Aegean/north Asia Minor religious koine. While Ilion, between the Athena temple and the West Sanctuary, fully participated in this koine, the Attalids did little initially to promote Pergamon's connection to the Trojan cycle (Hansen 1947, 9, 14; Heres 1997, 83).

Once the early period of good relations between Pergamon and the Seleucids ended, especially after the death of Antiochus Hierax, Pergamon made many different attempts to establish a link with Ilion. In the late third through second centuries what had been a broad northern koine was redefined as a cultic reference to Ilion's influential past. Although connections between Ilion and Pergamon were not stable in the late third century, Attalid expressions of favor toward Ilion (and vice versa) commonly appear. Ilion established an Attalid tribe (Frisch 1975, nos. 31, 121), perhaps in the reign of Attalos I, and Attalid rulers bestowed various gifts on Ilion (Attalos I: Polybius 5.78; Attalos II: Welles 1934, no. 62). The Pergamene Aristarche, daughter of Mikythos, made a dedication to the Samothracian Gods at Ilion on behalf of Ptolemy IV and Arsinoe (209–205 BC) (Frisch 1975, no. 44). Pergamon was at the time allied with the Ptolemies against Philip V; Ilion, again with reference to Samothrace, became the third-party – but hardly neutral – place for the expression of this alliance.

Rome, Pergamon, and Ilion

Attalid use of Ilion to strengthen political alliances, and Ilion's apparent interest in benefiting from this role, is most clear in Attalid relations with Rome. Cybele was the first divinity that Pergamon used to promote her ties with Rome. In 205 BC, Rome was instructed by the Sibyl and by Delphi to bring the cult image of Cybele to Rome for success against Hannibal (Thomas 1984; Gruen 1990; Takács 1996; Roller 1999, 263–285). Gruen has argued that it was in Rome's interest at the end of the first Macedonian war to improve her status in the Aegean and that it was likewise in Pergamon's interest to emphasize her ties to Rome (Gruen 1990, 29–32). Ilion was the linchpin.

Cybele was associated with Ilion's ancestors, Dardanos and his family, who had in turn been closely connected to Samothrace. Romans had already recognized these connections with activities on Samothrace in 211 BC (Cole 1989, 1570). This and other events of the end of the third century make clear that Rome had embraced the set of myths linking Troy, Samothrace, Aeneas and Rome (Takács 1996; Gruen 1992, 46–48; Bömer 1964). The contrast with Pergamon's cult of Cybele could not be greater: it had no such ancient connections. The Pergamene cult of Cybele, however, could be connected to Ilion and from there to Rome. At the same time as the transferral of Cybele from Pergamon to Rome (initiated in 205, completed in 204), Ilion was able to parlay her ancient connection to Rome into a political role as signatory to the Peace of Phoenice ending the First Macedonian War (despite having played no role in the preceding hostilities) (Livy 29.12.14; Gruen 1990, 31–33; 1992, 48). Ilion's later economic and territorial benefits from the settlement at Apamea in 188 BC likewise resulted only from the city's influential ancestral connection to Rome. Livy noted that Ilion's rewards stemmed "not from any recent accomplishment but from memory of their origins (38.39.10)" (Gruen 1992, 49).

The West Sanctuary at Ilion, thus, held the keys to Ilian influence – Samothrace, Cybele, and Dardanos. These cults, both individually and collectively, created links between Ilion and Pergamon and Ilion and Rome. Precisely at the time of great activity in the West Sanctuary, the late third and early second centuries BC, these three cities actively sought to tie Ilion's legendary past to the current struggles among the Hellenistic powers.

Ilion continued to use the West Sanctuary to bolster foreign interests throughout the second century even after Pergamon had been willed to Rome. The massive Temple A and the accompanying Late Hellenistic Building were built after Attalos III's bequest and Aristonicus' short-lived challenge (Gruen 1986, 595–603). Though the West Sanctuary never eclipsed the Athena Sanctuary in importance or splendor, the importance of its upkeep must have been clear to Ilion. Athena Ilias, while of great renown, had little connection to Rome. The cults of the West Sanctuary, by contrast, had direct connections to Rome. Rome had taken in both Cybele and the Samothracian Gods (in the form of the Penates [Dionysius of Halicarnassus 1.69.4]; see Rose 1998, 89; Cole 1989, 1588–1596) right along with embracing the idea of Ilion as their mother city and Cybele as a Trojan (more than Phrygian) goddess (Wiseman 1984; Rose 1998, 89; Galinsky

1969; Gruen 1990, 13; 1992, 26–29; Roller 1999, 287–320). The West Sanctuary provided the physical manifestation of the connection between Ilion and Rome. The lingering importance of the sanctuary is clear: Temple A was refurbished after the sack by Fimbria in 85 BC and continued to receive attention at least until the third century AD.

Problems in the archaeology of cult at Ilion

This interaction between Ilion's political interests and the embellishments of the West Sanctuary highlights the potential importance of cult in the overall historical development of any city. At the same time the legendary background of these cults and the city itself could never have been far from the foreground. This latter topic, however, is only one of many that could be considered in terms of the archaeological record of the West Sanctuary. Although there is not room here to consider all such further topics, it seems appropriate to draw attention to some additional concerns as study of the West Sanctuary proceeds.

Continuity of cult

With such a long history of activity in the area of the West Sanctuary, a natural issue for consideration is whether there is evidence for continuity either in the general identity of the space as "sacred" or in the specific cults proposed for the Hellenistic and Roman periods, as just discussed. And moving even earlier, is there any indication of Bronze Age to Iron Age continuity of cult in this area? This latter question is currently the most difficult to consider since the very complex Bronze Age stratigraphy in this area remains to be sorted out. Nevertheless, some observations on Early Iron Age through Roman continuity are possible.

Activity from the late eighth century BC through the third century AD is marked by a number of significant breaks and shifts of activity. The eighth-century votive caches may be seen as evidence of cultic activity preceding, and essentially associated with, the seventh- and sixth-century Archaic remains. Continuity of activity in this case is especially clear with the sequence of the three Archaic Cult Buildings and the Archaic development of the Upper and Lower Sanctuaries. For the fifth and fourth centuries, however, there is no evidence of continued ritual activity at any of these earlier areas. Ritual seems to have moved to the east, higher on the citadel. From the early third century, when activity in the West Sanctuary resumes, the number, types, and placements of buildings change often. The Upper and Lower Sanctuary areas, however, return to being foci of cult; and the area of the Archaic temples, while no longer a temple site, returns to use as a building site.

Among the associated finds, too, there are points of both continuity and discontinuity between the Archaic and Hellenistic periods. Botanical remains show a greater proportion of domesticated plants in the Archaic contexts (ca. 60 percent) compared with the Hellenistic (ca. 30 percent) (Riehl, pers. comm.). The faunal remains include ca. 60 percent domesticates in the Archaic period as compared to ca. 90 percent domesticates in Hellenistic contexts. Among the domesticates, however, proportions of cow to sheep to pig remain essentially constant, and large wild carnivores are present – though quite rare – in both phases (Fabis 1999, 244). Around Altar B in the Archaic period the ceramic assemblage is dominated by equal numbers of small cups and bowls (Aslan, pers. comm.); there is no such dominance of a particular pair of forms apparent yet in later periods. Figurines around Archaic Altar B suggest worship of a female deity in both Archaic and Hellenistic periods (Menadier, pers. comm.; Blegen 1939, figs. 18, 22).

While there is clear evidence of continued perception of this area as "sacred" even across the Classical hiatus in activity, there are significant changes in the material manifestation of ritual. Whether these changes require the interpretation of differences in specific cults being worshipped between the Archaic and Hellenistic periods remains to be determined. Worship of both Cybele and the Samothracian Gods may have begun in the region during the seventh century BC (Roller 1999, 121–141; Cole 1984, 10–11), so long-term continuity remains a possibility. The evident continuity of sacred place, however, is important in itself and deserves further consideration.

Sanctuary placement

Two quite striking features of the current topography of the West Sanctuary are its position overlooking the plains north and west of the site out to the northeast Aegean beyond and its position along the massive Bronze Age period VI citadel wall. As noted above, the view of Samothrace from the West Sanctuary may have played a role in its identification with the Samothracian Gods. The visibility and position of the ancient fortification wall brings to mind discussions of Geometric and Hellenistic hero cults at other visible Bronze Age monuments (Basedow and Menadier, pers. comm.; Alcock 1991, 1994; Antonaccio 1993).

The most direct association between the West Sanctuary and the Citadel wall comes with the placement of the early Archaic stone circles along its façade. Similar circles, though perhaps of earlier date, are encountered near Bronze Age tombs and early Iron Age buildings (Antonaccio 1993, 50–51). Other, later elements of the West Sanctuary seem more separated from the wall, either cut off by a precinct wall or facing in the opposite direction. The locations of the earliest activity at the site may have been inspired by the remains of the ancient citadel; however, while the sacred nature of the area was thus established, the original point of inspiration seems to have lost importance. By contrast, ritual activity near Bronze Age monuments elsewhere, which often continued or reappeared in the Hellenistic period, maintained a closer connection to the monument in question (Alcock 1991, 1994).

These and other topics will certainly receive more attention as research toward the final publication of the West Sanctuary continues. Indeed, even the attribution of the sanctuary to worship of the Samothracian Gods, Cybele, and Dardanos remains open to questions. Were all three cults active at the site throughout its history? Was the Mosaic Building, with parallels both to the worship of the Samothracian Gods and to the worship of Cybele, intended for the one cult's practice instead of others in the group? This question raises the more fundamental issue of which architectural elements are most important in a given setting for identification of cult.

The specific identification of a cult of Dardanos is especially difficult. While we know Homeric heroes received sacrifice by Ilians, hero-worship in the Hellenistic period was much diluted. Hero-worship differed little at this time from a cult of family ancestors (Price 1984, 35–36; Hughes 1999), and cult places could be private houses (e.g., Papadopoulos 2000, 142). It is not surprising, then, that horse-and-rider plaques are so widespread across the site. At the same time, even within one sacred space, the votive intent of a plaque may have been the worship of a family ancestor in the context of the greater divinity such as Cybele or the Samothracian Gods (or Athena in the case of the rider plaques found on the citadel itself).

Thus far, however, the triad of cults – Samothracian Gods, Cybele, and Dardanos – fits well with both the archaeological and textual evidence. The Hellenistic history of the site in its broader political context draws attention to the potential impact of "secular," political and economic concerns on choices of religious activity. It seems that the West Sanctuary received architectural elaboration starting in the third quarter of the third century BC, thanks in large part to its role as the physical setting of Ilion's connection first to other Hellenistic dynasties and then, and perhaps most importantly, to Rome. This line of exploration can be moved earlier to consider the Archaic development of the West Sanctuary. Could the sequence of Archaic Cult Buildings similarly play a role in Ilion's negotiation among the intersecting Phrygian, Lydian, later Achaemenid, and Greek interests in the general region of the Troad?

Notes

1 This sanctuary area of Troia has received various designations over the past century. The current label replaces "sanctuary" in the preliminary reports in *Studia Troica*. The West Sanctuary includes the Upper and Lower Sanctuaries from Carl Blegen's excavations. Readers should be aware, too, that labels for different structures within the West Sanctuary have changed over the course of research, but these changes should be clear in the phase plans (Figures 4.4, 4.5, 4.7, 4.8).

2 I thank Michael Cosmopoulos for the invitation to write this chapter. I serve as coordinator for publication of the West Sanctuary with the brief of publishing the transport amphoras and the historical overview of the area. I am indebted to the ongoing assistance and advice I have received from my colleagues working toward the final publication: Carolyn Aslan (Archaic pottery), Maureen Basedow (architecture and stratigraphy), Marian Fabis (animal bones), Blanche Menadier (small finds), Kathleen Lynch (Classical pottery), Stella Miller-Collett (architectural terracottas and wall painting), Kathleen Quinn (Byzantine period), Simone Riehl (botanical remains), and Billur Tekkök (Hellenistic and Roman pottery). The evidence presented here depended as much on their work as my own. Nevertheless, given that our research is ongoing, there remain many points of debate within the group, and the conclusions here may not reflect all opinions. The usual caveat that the author bears all responsibility for errors cannot be overemphasized here. Manfred Korfmann, Troy excavation director, and Brian Rose, head of post-Bronze Age excavations, have provided all manner of encouragement for the research in the West Sanctuary, and I am grateful to both of them. John Wallrodt, Susan Wallrodt, and Sinan Ünlusoy provided immeasurable logistical support.

3 In the following summary there are places where my interpretation differs from that presented in preliminary reports, and I have added elements that were not mentioned in earlier reports. I wish to emphasize that Maureen Basedow is responsible for publication of the architecture and stratigraphy. There are various points where she and I disagree (e.g., the reconstruction of Archaic Cult Building 3, the phases of activity in the Lower Sanctuary, and in other details). The full explication of these points will appear in the final publication. The preliminary summary here, which represents my current understanding of the excavations, will be superseded by the final publication.

4 Perhaps Demetrios of Skepsis' description of Ilion's houses as lacking rooftiles (Strabo 13.1.27) has some relation to these two destructions. Demetrios' visit is supposed to have occurred "κατ' ἐκείνου τοῦ καιροῦ" ("around that time"), referring to events of 192–189 BC, in Demetrios' youth. Moving Demetrios' visit somewhat later into the second century, and considering the potential flexibility of the dates suggested by the pottery, it may be possible to reconcile Demetrios' observation and the archaeological evidence.

5 The later Hellenistic and Roman pottery has received preliminary publication in Tekkök-Biçken (1996).

6 The various kinds of evidence for industrial activity have been noted by Basedow, Riehl, and Tekkök (pers. comm.).

7 Note that Frisch no. 44, a dedication by Aristarche to the Samothracian Gods, was found at Sestos, not Ilion. For the argument in favor of the stone's original position in Ilion, see Robert and Robert (1964, 188–190, no. 272).

8 For wall painting at the Hieron at Samothrace, see Lehmann (1969, v. 1, 138–142, 204–212) and Barbet (1985, 13–14); for a mosaic and possible remains of a foundation layer of stucco for interior wall painting at the Temple of Despoina at Lykosoura, see Lehmann (1964); wall painting at the heroon at Kalydon, see Dyggve et al. (1934, 314, 391). For wall painting in the Aegean area, see Andreou (1988). For Hellenistic mosaics, see Salzmann (1982) and Dunbabin (1999). An exception to the association between interior decoration and mystery or hero worship is the Temple of Athena at Assos, which has a pebble mosaic floor dated to the second half of the third century BC, see Salzmann (1982, no. 150, pl. 84.3, 4). Mosaics appear in pronaoi of more mainstream Olympian cults: the Temple of Zeus at Olympia (Salzmann 1982, nos. 138–139) and the Temple of Apollo Karneios on Thera (Salzmann 1982, no. 171). For Early Hellenistic wall painting and mosaics in Turkey, see Bingöl (1997, 68–97).

9 For further discussion of torches and the cult of Demeter, see Sourvinou-Inwood, this volume, p. 31.
10 The use of the dative to indicate possession is attested, but never common, in graffiti; see for example Lang (1976, 27).
11 Rose (1994, 78, n.11) emphasizes the ambiguity in the double-axe image; for double-axe imagery associated with Kabeiric worship, see Bruneau (1970, 382), Chapouthier (1935, 81–82, fig. 104), and Rose (1998, 90, n.97) emphasizing the potential conflation of Kabeiroi and the Samothracian Gods.
12 Rose (1993, 104–105, figs. 8–9; 1998, 88) and Miller (1991, 48, n.35). For the Hellenistic (fourth century) example, see Mannsperger (1989, no. 2577). Another Hellenistic example shows a very similar petasos and cloak as seen on many plaques from Ilion (Mannsperger 1989, 2590; cf. Barr 1996, fig. 31).
13 A copy of Frisch 1975, no. 63 is also found at Samothrace; see Cole (1984, 24).
14 Suetonius, *Life of Claudius* 25.3; Gruen (1992, 46, n.186) argues in favor of the general accuracy of the reference (also cited by Brückner 1902, 584). For epigraphic evidence of relations between Ilion and Seleucus II(?), see Frisch (1975, no. 35).

References

Alcock, S.E., 1991: "Tomb cult and the post-classical polis," *AJA* 95, 447–467.
Alcock, S.E., 1994: "The heroic past in a Hellenistic present," *EchCl* 36 n.s. 13, 221–234.
Andreou, A., 1988: *Griechische Wanddekoration*. Ph.D. dissertation Johannes Gutenberg-Universität zu Mainz (Michelstadt: Neuthor-Verlag, 1989), Mainz.
Antonaccio, C., 1993: "The Archaeology of Ancestors," in C. Dougherty and L. Kurke (eds), *Cultural Poetics in Archaic Greece* (Cambridge University Press, Cambridge), 46–70.
Aylward, W., 1999: "Studies in Hellenistic Ilion: The houses in the lower city," *Studia Troica* 9, 160–186.
Barbet, A., 1985: *La peinture murale romaine*. Picard, Paris.
Barr, A.E., 1996: "Horse and rider plaques at Ilion. A preliminary study of the Hellenistic hero cult in Asia Minor," *Studia Troica* 6, 133–157.
Bellinger, A.R., 1961: *Troy. The Coins*. Supplementary Monograph 2. Princeton University Press, Princeton.
Berlin, A.M., 1999: "Studies in Hellenistic Ilion: The lower city. Stratified assemblages and chronology," *Studia Troica* 9, 73–157.
Bingöl, O., 1997: *Malerei und Mosaik der Antike in der Türkei*. Kulturegeschichte der Antiken Welt 67. P. von Zabern, Mainz am Rhein.
Blegen, C.W., 1939: "Excavations at Troy, 1938," *AJA* 43, 204–228.
Blegen, C.W., C.G. Boulter, J.L. Caskey, and M. Rawson, 1958: *Troy IV. Settlements VIIa, VIIb and VIII*. Princeton University Press, Princeton.
Bohtz, C.H., 1981: *Das Demeter-Heiligtum*. Altertümer von Pergamon 13. W. de Gruyter, Berlin.
Bömer, F., 1964: "Kybele in Rom: Die Geschichte ihres Kults als politisches Phänomen," *RM* 71, 130–151.
Bookidis, N. and R.S. Stroud, 1997: *Corinth XVIII.iii. The Sanctuary of Demeter and Kore: Topography and Architecture*. The American School of Classical Studies, Princeton.
Brückner, A., 1902: "IX. Abschnitt. Geschichte von Troja und Ilion," in Dörpfeld 1902.

Bruneau, Ph., 1970: *Recherches sur les cultes de Délos a l'époque hellénistique et a l'époque impériale*. Bibliothêque des Écoles Françaises d'Athènes et de Rome 217. De Boccard, Paris.

Burkert, W., 1993: "Concordia discors: The literary and the archaeological evidence on the Sanctuary of Samothrace," in N. Marinatos and R. Hägg (eds), *Greek Sanctuaries: New Approaches* (Routledge, London), 178–191.

Chapouthier, F., 1935: *Le sanctuaire des dieux de Samothrace*. Exploration archéologique de Délos 16. De Boccard, Paris.

Cohen, G.M., 1996: "A dedication to the Samothracian Gods," *Studia Troica* 6, 201–207.

Cole, S.G., 1984: *Theoi Megaloi: The Cult of the Great Gods at Samothrace*. E.J. Brill, Leiden.

Cole, S.G., 1989: "The Mysteries of Samothrace during the Roman period," *ANRW* 2.18.2, 1564–1598 (W. de Gruyter, Berlin–New York).

Conze, A. and P. Schazmann, 1911: *Mamurt-Kaleh: ein Tempel der Göttermutter unweit Pergamon. JdI* Erg 9. G. Reimer, Berlin.

Cook, J.M., 1973: *The Troad. An Archaeological and Topographical Study*. Clarendon Press, Oxford.

Couilloud-Le Dinahet, M.-Th., 1991: "Autels monolithes et monolithoides de Délos," in R. Étienne and M.-Th. Le Dinahet (eds), *L'Espace sacrificiel dans les civilisations Méditerranéennes de l'Antiquité* (Actes du colloque tenu à la Maison de l'Orient, Lyon, 4–7 juin 1988, de Boccard, Paris), 109–120.

Daumas, M., 1997: "Des Cabires thébains aux Grands Dieux de Samothrace: Aspects d'une recherche sur un culte a mystères," *RA* 1, 201–209.

Davidson, G., 1952: *Corinth XII. The Minor Objects*. The American School of Classical Studies at Athens, Princeton.

Dickens, G., 1905–1906: "Damophon of Mesene," *BSA* 12, 109–136.

Dittenberger, W., 1903: *Orientis Graeci Inscriptiones Selectae. Supplementum Sylloges Inscriptionum Graecarum*. S. Hirzel, Leipzig.

Dörpfeld, W., 1902: *Troja und Ilion. Ergebnisse der Ausgrabungen in der vorhistorischen und historischen Schichten von Ilion 1870–1894*. Beck and Barth, Athens [reprint edn Otto Zeller, Osnabrück, 1968].

Dunbabin, K.M., 1999: *Mosaics of the Greek and Roman World*. Cambridge University Press, Cambridge.

Dyggve, E., F. Poulson, and K.A. Rhomaios, 1934: *Das Heroon von Kalydon*. Kongelige Danske Videnskabernes Selskab, Skrifter, Historik og Filolosofisk Afdeling, 7 Raeke IV, 4. Levin and Munksgaard, Copenhagen.

Fabis, M., 1999: "Studies in Hellenistic Ilion: The archaeofaunal remains of C29, w28, and y28/29, lower city," *Studia Troica* 9, 237–252.

Fraser, P.M. and E. Matthews, 1987: *A Lexicon of Greek Personal Names*. Vol. 1: *The Aegean Islands, Cyprus, Cyrenaica*. Oxford University Press, Oxford.

Frisch, P., 1975: *Die Inschriften von Ilion*. Inschriften Griechischen Städte aus Kleinasien 3. Habelt, Bonn.

Galinsky, K., 1969: *Aeneas, Sicily, and Rome*. Princeton University Press, Princeton, N.J.

Goethert, F.W. and H. Schlief, 1962: *Der Athenatempel von Ilion*. W. de Gruyter, Berlin.

Graf, F., 1999: "Kabeiroi," in H. Cancik and H. Schneider (eds), *Der neue Pauly: Enzyklopädie der Antike* v.6, 123–127. J.B. Metzler, Stuttgart.

Gruen, E.S., 1986: *The Hellenistic World and the Coming of Rome*. University of California Press, Berkeley.
Gruen, E.S., 1990: *Studies in Greek Culture and Roman Policy*. E.J. Brill, Leiden.
Gruen, E.S., 1992: *Culture and National Identity in Republican Rome*. Cornell University Press, Ithaca, N.Y.
Hansen, E.V., 1947: *The Attalids of Pergamon*. Cornell University Press, Ithaca, N.Y.
Hayes, J.W., 1995: "Two kraters 'After the Antique' from the Fimbrian destruction in Troia," *Studia Troica* 5, 177–183.
Heres, H., 1997: "The myth of Telephos in Pergamon," in R. Dreyfus and E. Schraudolph (eds), *Pergamon. The Telephus Frieze from the Great Altar*. Vol. 2 (Fine Arts Museums of San Francisco, San Francisco), 83–108.
Heyder, W. and A. Mallwitz, 1978: *Die Bauten im Kabirenheiligtum bei Theben II*. Kabirenheiligtum bei Theben 2. W. de Gruyter, Berlin.
Hoepfner, W. 1997: "The architecture of Pergamon," in R. Dreyfus and E. Schraudolph (eds), *Pergamon. The Telephus Frieze from the Great Altar*. Vol. 2 (Fine Arts Museums of San Francisco, San Francisco), 23–57.
Huelsen, Chr., 1895: "Untersuchungen zur Topographie des Palatins," *RM* 10, 3–37.
Hughes, D.D., 1999: "Hero cult, heroic honors, heroic dead: Some developments in the Hellenistic and Roman periods," in R. Hägg (ed.), *Ancient Greek Hero Cult. Proceedings of the Fifth International Seminar on Ancient Greek Cult, April 21–23, 1995* (Svenska Institutet i Athen. P. Åströms Forlag, Stockholm), 167–175.
Kahil, L., 1986: "Dardanos," *LIMC* III.1, 352–353.
Kasper, S., 1972: "Zum großen Altar der Demeterterrasse in Pergamon," in E. Boehringer (ed.), *Gesammelte Aufsätze. Pergamenische Forschungen* 1 (W. de Gruyter, Berlin), 69–93.
Koppenhöffer, D., 1997: "Troia VII – Versuch einer Zussamenschau einschliesslich der Ergebnisse des Jahres 1995," *Studia Troica* 7, 295–353.
Kosmetatou, E., 2000: "Lycophron's 'Alexandra' reconsidered: The Attalid connection," *Hermes* 128, 32–53.
Lang, M., 1976: *The Athenian Agora 21. Graffiti and Dipinti*. The American School of Classical Studies at Athens, Princeton.
Lebedeev, A., 1996: "The devotion of Xanthippos: Magic and Mystery cults in Olbia," *ZPE* 112, 279–283.
Lehmann, K., 1962: *Samothrace 4.1. The Hall of the Votive Gifts*. Pantheon Books, New York.
Lehmann, K., 1998: *Samothrace, A Guide to the Excavations and the Museum*. Sixth rev. edn. Thessaloniki.
Lehmann, K. and D. Spittle, 1964: *Samothrace 4.2. The Altar Court*. Pantheon Books, New York.
Lehmann, P.W., 1964: "The technique of the mosaic at Lykosoura," in L.F. Sandler (ed.), *Essays in Memory of Karl Lehmann* (J.J. Augustin, Locust Valley, N.Y.), 190–197.
Lehmann, P.W., 1969: *Samothrace 3.1–3. The Hieron*. Princeton University Press, Princeton.
Lenz, D., F. Ruppenstein, M. Baumann, and R. Catling, 1998: "Protogeometric pottery at Troia," *Studia Troica* 8, 189–222.
Mannsperger, D., 1989: *Sylloge Nummorum Graecorum*. Deutschland. Münzsammlung

der Universität Tübingen. 4. Heft. Mysien–Ionien, nr. 2174–3106. Hirmer, Munich.

Miller, S.G., 1991: "Terracotta figurines: New finds at Ilion, 1988–1989," *Studia Troica* 1, 39–68.

Metropoulou, E., 1996: "The goddess Cybele in funerary banquets and with an equestrian hero," in E.N. Lane (ed.), *Cybele, Attis, and Related Cults. Essays in Memory of M.J. Vermaseren* (E.J. Brill, Leiden), 135–161.

Mylonas, G.E., 1961: *Eleusis and the Eleusinian Mysteries*. Princeton University Press, Princeton.

Nohlen, K. and W. Radt (eds), 1978: *Kapikaya. Ein Felsheiligtum bei Pergamon*. Altertümer von Pergamon 12. W. de Gruyter, Berlin.

Ohlemutz, E., 1940: *Die Kulte und Heiligtümer der Götter in Pergamon*. Würzburg.

Oppermann, M., 1981: "Thrakische und danubische Reitergötter und ihre Beziehungen zu orientalischen Kulten," in M.J. Vermaseren (ed.), *Die orientalischen Religionen in Römerreich. Études préliminaires aux religions orientales dans l'empire romain* 93 (E.J. Brill, Leiden), 520–530.

Papadopoulos, J.K., 2000: "A Toronaian horseman-hero and some of his Trojan mates," in P. Adam-Veleni (ed.), *Mneme. Iouilias Vokotopoulou* (Thessaloniki), 411–421.

Pensabene, P., 1982: "Nuove indagini nell'area del Tempio di Cibele sul Palatino," in U. Bianchi and M.J. Vermaseren (eds), *La soteriologia dei culti orientali nell'impero Romano. Atti del Colloquio Internazionale, Roma 24–28 Settembre 1979*. EPRO 92 (E.J. Brill, Leiden), 68–108.

Pensabene, P., 1988: "Scavi nell'area del Tempio della Vittoria e del Santuario della Magna Mater sul Palatino," *Archeologia Laziale* 9, 54–67.

Price, S.R.F., 1984: *Rituals and Power: The Roman Imperial Cult in Asia Minor*. Cambridge University Press, Cambridge.

Radt, W., 1999: *Pergamon, Geschichte und Bauten einer Antiken Metropole*. Primus Verlag, Darmstadt.

Rigsby, K.J., 1996: *Asylia. Territorial Inviolability in the Hellenistic World*. University of California Press, Berkeley.

Robert, J. and L. Robert, 1964: "Bulletin Épigraphique," *REG* 77, 127–259.

Robert, L., 1966: *Monnaies antiques en Troade. Hautes études numismatiques* 1. Droz and Minard, Geneva and Paris.

Roller, L.E., 1999: *In Search of God the Mother: The Cult of Anatolian Cybele*. University of California Press, Berkeley.

Romanelli, P., 1963: "Lo scavo al tempio della Magna Mater sul Palatino e nelle sue adiacenze," *MonAnt* 46, 201–330.

Rose, C.B., 1992: "The 1991 post-Bronze Age excavations at Troia," *Studia Troica* 2, 43–60.

Rose, C.B., 1993: "The 1992 post-Bronze Age excavations at Troia," *Studia Troica* 3, 97–116.

Rose, C.B., 1994: "The 1993 post-Bronze Age excavations at Troia," *Studia Troica* 4, 75–104.

Rose, C.B., 1995: "The 1994 post-Bronze Age excavations at Troia," *Studia Troica* 5, 81–105.

Rose, C.B., 1997: "The 1996 post-Bronze Age excavations at Troia," *Studia Troica* 7, 73–110.

Rose, C.B., 1998: "The 1997 post-Bronze Age excavations at Troia," *Studia Troica* 8, 71–113.
Rose, C.B., 1999: "The 1998 post-Bronze Age excavations at Troia," *Studia Troica* 9, 35–71.
Rose, C.B., 2000: "The 1999 post-Bronze Age excavations at Troia," *Studia Troica* 10, 53–71.
Sage, M., 2000: "Roman visitors to Ilion in the Roman Imperial and Late Antique period: The symbolic functions of a landscape," *Studia Troica* 10, 211–231.
Salzmann, D., 1982: *Untersuchungen zu den antiken Kieselmosaiken.* Archäologische Forschungen 10. Gebr. Mann, Berlin.
Schwertheim, E., 1980: Die Inschriften von Kyzikos und Umgebung Teil 1. Grabtexte. Habelt, Bonn.
Takács, S.A., 1996: "Magna Deum Mater Idaea, Cybele, and Catullus' *Attis*," in E.N. Lane (ed.), *Cybele, Attis, and Related Cults. Essays in Memory of M.J. Vermaseren* (E.J. Brill, Leiden), 367–386.
Tekkök, B., 2001: "The city wall of Ilion, new evidence for dating," *Studia Troica* 10, 85–95.
Tekkök-Biçken, B., 1996: "The Hellenistic and Roman Pottery from Troia: The Second Century BC to the Sixth Century AD." Ph.D. dissertation, University of Missouri-Columbia.
Themelis, P.G., 1998: "The Sanctuary of Demeter and the Dioscouri at Messene," in R. Hägg (ed.), *Ancient Greek Cult Practice from the Archaeological Evidence. Proceedings of the Fourth International Seminar on Ancient Greek Cult, October 22–24, 1993* (Svenska Institutet i Athen, P. Åströms Forlag, Stockholm), 157–186.
Thomas, G., 1984: "Magna Mater and Attis," *ANRW* 2.17.3, 1500–1535 (W. de Gruyter, Berlin–New York).
Thompson, D.B., 1963: *Troy. The Terracotta Figurines of the Hellenistic Period.* Supplementary Monograph 3. Princeton University Press, Princeton.
Vermaseren, M.J., 1977: *Cybele and Attis.* Thames and Hudson, London.
Vermeule, C.C., 1995: "Neon Ilium and Ilium Novum: Kings, soldiers, citizens and tourists at Classical Troy," in J.B. Carter and S.P. Morris (eds), *The Ages of Homer. A Tribute to Emily Townsend Vermeule* (University of Texas Press, Austin), 467–482.
Welles, C.B., 1934: *Royal Correspondence in the Hellenistic Period.* Yale University Press, New Haven, Conn.
Winnefeld, H., 1902: "V. Abschnitt. Die Bildwerke aus Marmor und Thon," in Dörpfeld 1902, 429–446.
Wiseman, T.P., 1984: "Cybele, Virgil and Augustus," in T. Woodman and D. West (eds), *Poetry and Politics in the Age of Augustus* (Cambridge University Press, Cambridge), 117–128.
Ziegler, K., 1949: "Pantheion," *RE* v. 18B, 697–747.

5

EVOLUTIONS OF A MYSTERY CULT

The Theban Kabiroi[1]

Albert Schachter

Kabeiroi sit uneasily in the Greek pantheon. As their title shows, they were not originally Greek. Their nature was never fully understood by Greek commentators, and from the earliest times they were confused with the Great Gods of Samothrace (there is no evidence *in situ* for Kabeiroi at Samothrace, only the word of learned outsiders like Stesimbrotos, Herodotos, and Mnaseas). So it is not surprising that at the two Greek sanctuaries of Kabeiroi about which we know anything, Lemnos and Thebes, attempts were made to integrate them into the local religious environment. At Lemnos there were three Kabeiroi and three Kabeirid nymphs, and the Kabeiroi were associated at an early date with the principal deity of the island, Hephaistos. At Thebes, there were two Kabiroi (possibly because divine and semi-divine male pairs were common in Boiotia), who were also associated – but only in a casual, unsystematic way – with Dionysos and his circle, or with Hermes and Pan.[2]

Inevitably any attempt to understand this cult will meet with only partial success. We cannot expect to get to the heart of an ancient mystery cult. All we can hope to do is to try to comprehend the information we do have, avoiding as well as we can the temptation to read too much into it and to impose modern concepts on ancient practices. The evidence – inscriptions, votive offerings, pottery, architectural remains, literature – is not easy to interpret. On the other hand, it does cover a long period of time and is copious and varied enough to allow the careful investigator to make some progress towards a reconstruction.

We do not know who it was who introduced the Kabiroi to Thebes, but we can make some guesses. They were probably Greek. There need not have been many of them, perhaps only a family group, who settled in the countryside west of Thebes. They may have come in the eighth or seventh century, possibly in the same small wave of migration which brought Hesiod's father from Kyme in Aiolis to Askra (not far away from the

Kabirion as the crow flies) and others to the region of Teumessos on the eastern fringes of Theban territory. Eventually they, and the land they lived on, were incorporated into the polis of Thebes, but the Kabirion and its mystery seem to have been their own property until late in the fourth century BC. Even after the cult was taken over by the polis, it remained a fairly local operation. For example, proper names derived from Kabiros come from a very restricted area. Only one is known from the Classical period, the Theban Kabirichos, the unfortunate polemarch slain with his pro-Spartan colleagues late in 379 BC (Schachter 1986, 78, and n.2); even names current in the Hellenistic and Roman periods come almost exclusively from Boiotia and its near neighbours. Most of the coins found on the site were from Boiotia and adjacent regions. This is not to say that initiation was ever restricted to local people: the geographical distribution of names derived from the Kabiroi during the Hellenistic and Roman periods covers all of Boiotia, and the discovery of Kabirion-ware vases in the Thespian polyandrion – the mass grave of Thespian hoplites killed at the battle of Delion in 424 BC – shows that it was open in the Classical period at least to members of the hoplite class. In the Hellenistic period again, when the cult was operated by the polis of Thebes, one of the women who made a dedication at the sanctuary was identified as a Thespian, and an Aitolian from Melitea dedicated a statue. The Kabirion seems to have resembled Eleusis and Samothrace in being open to all comers.[3]

The literary sources are late and consist of a short poem attributed to one Diodoros (Anth. Palat. 6, 245), and the following passages by Pausanias:[4]

> When one has gone on for 25 stades from here [i.e. the deserted western suburbs of Thebes], there is a grove of Demeter Kabeiria and Kore: those who have been initiated are permitted to enter. The sanctuary of the Kabeiroi is about seven stades away from this grove. With regard to who the Kabeiroi are, and the nature of the rites performed for them and the Mother, I must be excused by men of good will if I keep silent. But nothing hinders me from revealing at least what the Thebans say was the origin of the rites. For once upon a time, they say, there was a city in this place, and men named Kabeiraians, and Demeter came to know Prometheus, one of the Kabeiraians, and Aitnaios son of Prometheus, and entrusted something to them. It seemed to me impious to write down what this thing was, and what happened to it: suffice it to say that the celebration of the mystery is a gift of Demeter to the Kabeiraians.
>
> At the time of the expedition of the Epigonoi and the capture of Thebes, the Kabeiraioi were uprooted by the Argives, and the celebration of the mystery lapsed for a time. Later on, they say, Pelarge, daughter of Potneus, and her husband Isthmiades established the ritual, to begin with at the same place, but then transferred it to the

so-called Alexiarous. But because Pelarge had performed initiations outside the ancient boundaries, Telondes and those of the clan of Kabeiritai who were left, returned to the Kabeiraia. They were required, in accordance with an oracle from Dodona, to establish various rites in honour of Pelarge, including the sacrifice of a beast bearing another in its womb.

The wrath which emanates from the Kabeiroi cannot be avoided by men, as has been made clear on many occasions. For some laymen had the temerity to perform the Theban rites in the same way at Naupaktos, and punishment came upon them soon thereafter. And again, when some members of Xerxes' army who had been left in Boiotia with Mardonios, slipped into the sanctuary, possibly in the hope of plunder, but more, I think, through impiety, they were immediately driven mad and perished by throwing themselves off cliffs and into the sea. And when Alexander, victorious in battle, was setting fire to Thebes itself and the whole of the Thebais, some men from Macedonia who had come into the sanctuary of the Kabeiroi, as being in enemy territory, were struck by thunder and lightning and killed. This is how revered this sanctuary has been from the very beginning.

(Pansanias 9, 25, 5–10)

Elsewhere, in writing about the Mysteries of Andania in Messenia, Pausanias refers to the Athenian Methapos, who had reorganized the Mysteries there, as having also established the celebration of the Mysteries of the Kabeiroi for the Thebans (4, 1, 7).

Pausanias wrote much of his work during the reign of Marcus Aurelius (AD 161–180). This was a time when renewed interest in the glorious past of Hellas was at its highest point. Sanctuaries which had previously fallen into disuse were open once again, and rituals and festivals which had lapsed were being practised and celebrated anew. Many of those which Pausanias describes had been revived fairly recently. So it was, too, with the Kabirion and its cult. It is hardly to be expected, therefore, that there would have been consistency any more than there was continuity of activity. A close look at the architectural development of the sanctuary, and the variations over time in what went on there, will make this clear.

The sanctuary[5]

The Kabirion is about six kilometres west of Thebes, in the low range of hills south of the Teneric Plain. In the Plain, at a point about eight kilometres west of Thebes and three north-west of the Kabirion valley, a cemetery with graves of the Late Archaic and Classical periods reveals the existence in the neighbourhood of a substantial settlement: this could have been the city about which Pausanias was told, but which had disappeared by his day. The sanctuary of Demeter Kabeiria and Kore has not been found, but it must have been between Thebes and the Kabirion.[6]

The Kabirion valley is bordered on the west by a stream running north into the Teneric Plain. Originally this valley was bisected by a second stream coming from the east and flowing into the south–north stream. The northern slope of the valley forms an irregular amphitheatre. Roughly in the middle of the slope, and about half-way up it, is an outcropping of natural rock (Figure 5.1). In the earlier stages of the sanctuary's life building was restricted to the southern, more open, side of the stream. The main way into the valley throughout antiquity was at the north-west corner, beside the south–north stream.

The site was probably chosen because of the natural rock formation. Such formations seem to have been a central feature of mystery sanctuaries: for example the Mirthless Rock at Eleusis, and the various rock altars at Samothrace. At Eleusis the Rock was where Demeter sat and mourned the loss of her daughter. Just as a stream of water issuing from the earth could inspire those who drank from it with the ability to transmit the will of the gods, so a rock, emerging from the earth, might be thought to provide a direct connection with the gods underground. It is noteworthy that the Kabirion rock formation remained unaltered and untouched throughout the history of the sanctuary. There never was an enclosed telesterion; rather, initiation seems to have taken place out of doors, at the amphitheatre and

Figure 5.1 Rock formation (September 2000, author's photograph)

around the rock. Since this was a mystery cult, the audience would have been composed of initiates, and perhaps initiands, unless the latter were part of the show.[7]

Originally the sanctuary was aligned north–south, with the Rock Formation as the apex of an irregular triangle completed by the "Lower Tholos" (12) and the "Middle Tholos" (18) on the southern side of the east–west stream (Figure 5.2). Near Tholos (12) was a rectangular building (2), while abutting Tholos (18) were another round building (28), and what seems to have been an apsidal building (29). Not far away to the east of this cluster was another tholos (M125). The earliest buildings on the site – the tholoi 12 and 18 – were put up at a period of Theban prosperity and power, in the

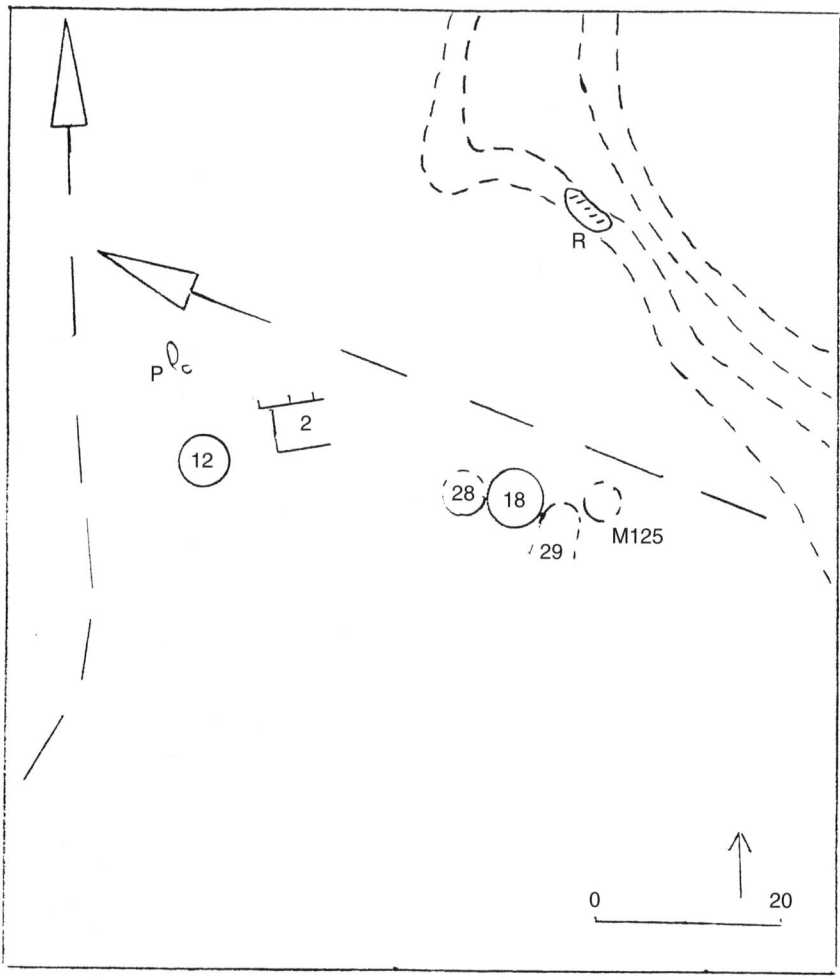

Figure 5.2 Theban Kabirion: to the end of the fourth century BC

years before the Persian Wars. The domestic family-oriented origins of the cult are reflected in the haphazard way in which the earliest buildings on the site were grouped. North of the Lower Tholos were a pair of sacrificial pits (P), presumably the first call for people entering the sanctuary. There are no signs of any formal barrier to the site: a stone inscribed in epichoric characters ΝΤΟΣ (possibly for *entos*) may have been part of a boundary marker (Schachter 1986, 99, n.1).

The second phase of the Kabirion's life began late in the fourth century BC (Figure 5.3). At this time the natural cavea was banked up and extended to the east and south; the waters of the east–west stream were channelled underground, and what appear to have been sacrificial pits were dug on the

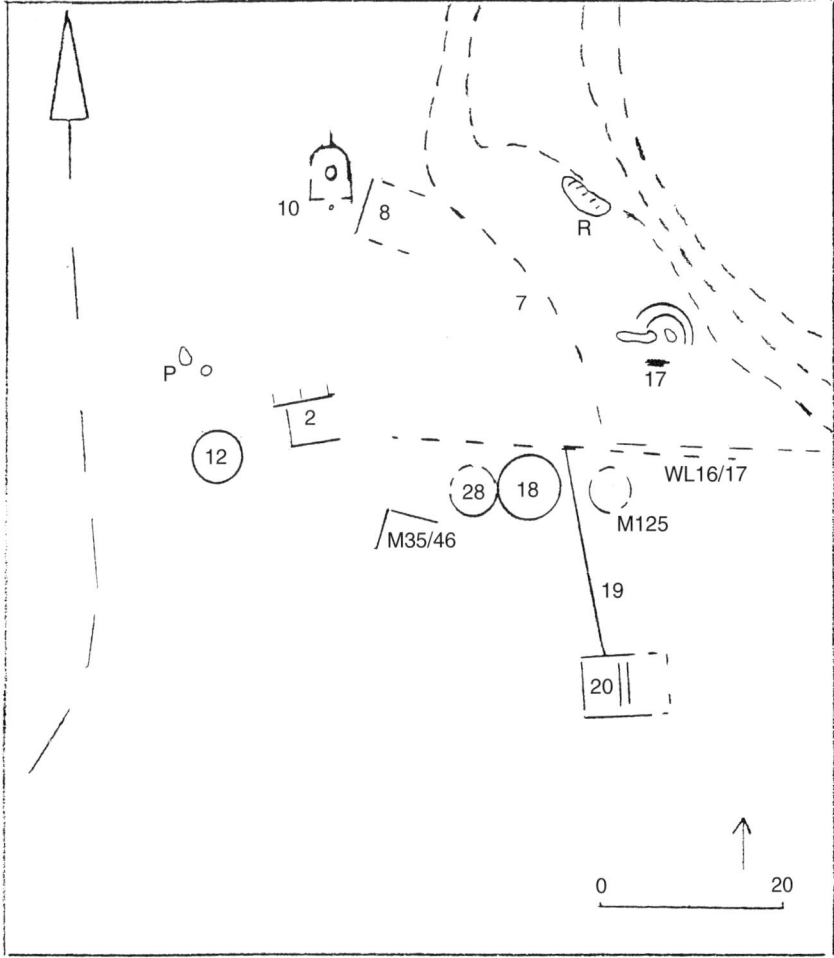

Figure 5.3 Theban Kabirion: late fourth/early third century BC

new embankment more or less directly opposite the older sacrificial pits at the western end of the sanctuary (17). It is pottery found at these pits which dates the whole operation to within the last two decades of the fourth century BC. Contemporary with the pits is the channel 19.1, with whose construction the apsidal building (29: see Figure 5.2) was destroyed: the latter contains pottery going down to *c.* 300 BC. It is difficult not to associate this activity with the restoration of Thebes which began in 315, and which was aided by contributions from a number of Greek states, including, probably, the people of Samothrace and various Macedonian monarchs (Schachter 1986, 80, and n.6). Some of this money might well have found its way to the Kabirion. The finds at (17) and (29) together provide a reasonable estimate for the end of the first phase and the beginning of the second.

This, however, was just the beginning. Only a generation later, in the latter part of the second quarter of the third century, the whole sanctuary was rebuilt (Figure 5.4): the cavea was extended to the south and the alignment of the sanctuary shifted 90 degrees from a north–south to an east–west axis. A new underground pipe (WL6/7) was laid to take the waters coming from the east and south, entailing the demolition of the Middle Tholos (18: see Figure 5.3). Almost everything at the bottom of the valley was razed, and a low ovoid terrace wall (3) was built and filled with earth and debris from the old buildings to provide a base for two new structures, a rectangular podium (5.1) towards the east and a circular or apsidal building towards the west (1.1), just east of the old sacrificial pits which marked the main entrance to the sanctuary. A complicated entry complex (11) was erected at the north-west corner of the valley, and the southern half of the valley was bounded by a portico, the "Southern Stoa" (23). The only building which survived from the Classical period was the Lower Tholos (12), but it was now sealed off completely.

This was a major undertaking, and inscriptions make it clear that it was the polis of Thebes which was responsible for it. One of these, from the second quarter of the third century, records the dedication of a *prothyron* – part of the entry complex, no doubt – from the proceeds of the Mysteries. From this, and two other inscriptions of the third century, we learn that there was a college of two priests, whose office was hereditary, and who served for life; there was also a college of Kabiriarchai (aided by a secretary), whose number varied from three to two, and it is clear that they were public rather than hieratic officials. One of the inscriptions lists twelve paragogeies. These have been identified with mystagogoi, but they may have been appointed to collect a *paragogion*, or entrance fee, from initiands. Indeed entrance tokens to the Kabirion have been found, which could have been handed over at the entry. Another inscription is a list of supplementary dedications for three archon years. The dedicators are mostly women (one man is a banker, leaving a deposit for safekeeping), and may include a pair of freed slaves.[8]

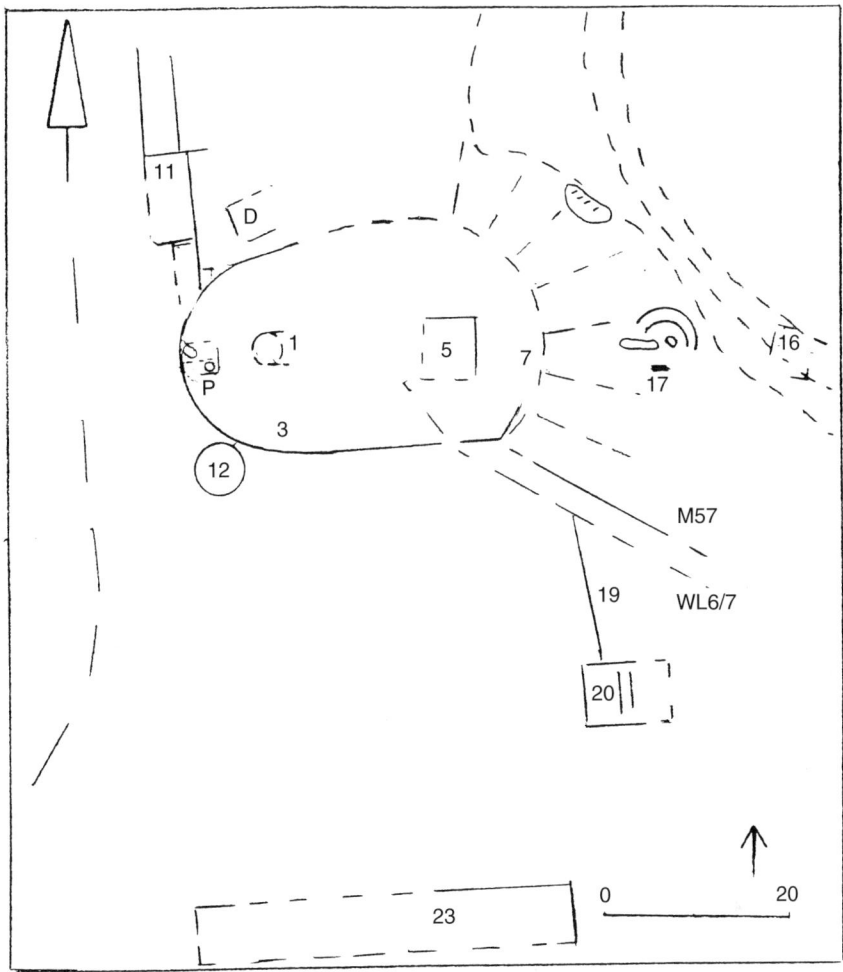

Figure 5.4 Theban Kabirion: second quarter, third century BC

Later on another portico, the "Western Stoa" (13) was put up. This had the effect of putting the Lower Tholos (12) outside the sanctuary proper, and it may have been pulled down at this time, if not before. The round or apsidal building in the new central area (1.1) was replaced by the first of a succession of rectangular buildings opening to the east. This, we can deduce from a later inscription, was called the *Anaktoron* (1.2). A late Hellenistic inscription – in koine, therefore to be dated soon after the dissolution of the Boiotian confederacy in 171 BC – records the dedication of a *dutes*, a cistern or well, from the proceeds of the god (*IG* 7, 2477, and see Schachter 1986, 85, n.1) (Figure 5.5).

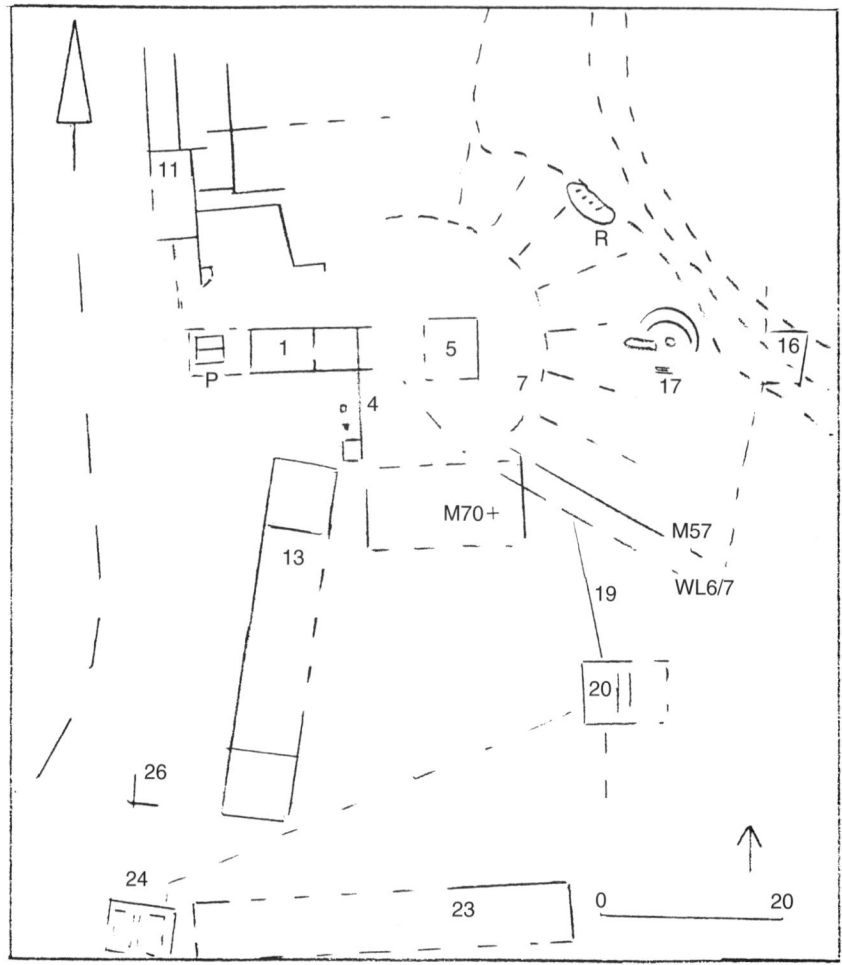

Figure 5.5 Theban Kabirion: late Hellenistic

The next big change at the Kabirion happened when Hellas was part of the Roman Empire: a new cavea was erected, probably during the second half of the first century BC at a time when Thebes and its neighbours were prospering (Figure 5.6). These halcyon days ended in the middle of the first century AD, a period of general recession, but there was a recovery in the second half of the century, when a new *anaktoron* was built, continuing into the second century, when a series of *oikoi* (dining rooms?) were built along the back of the Western Stoa (13). When Pausanias came by, the sanctuary was still flourishing, and it seems to have continued to do so for about a century and a half afterwards.[9]

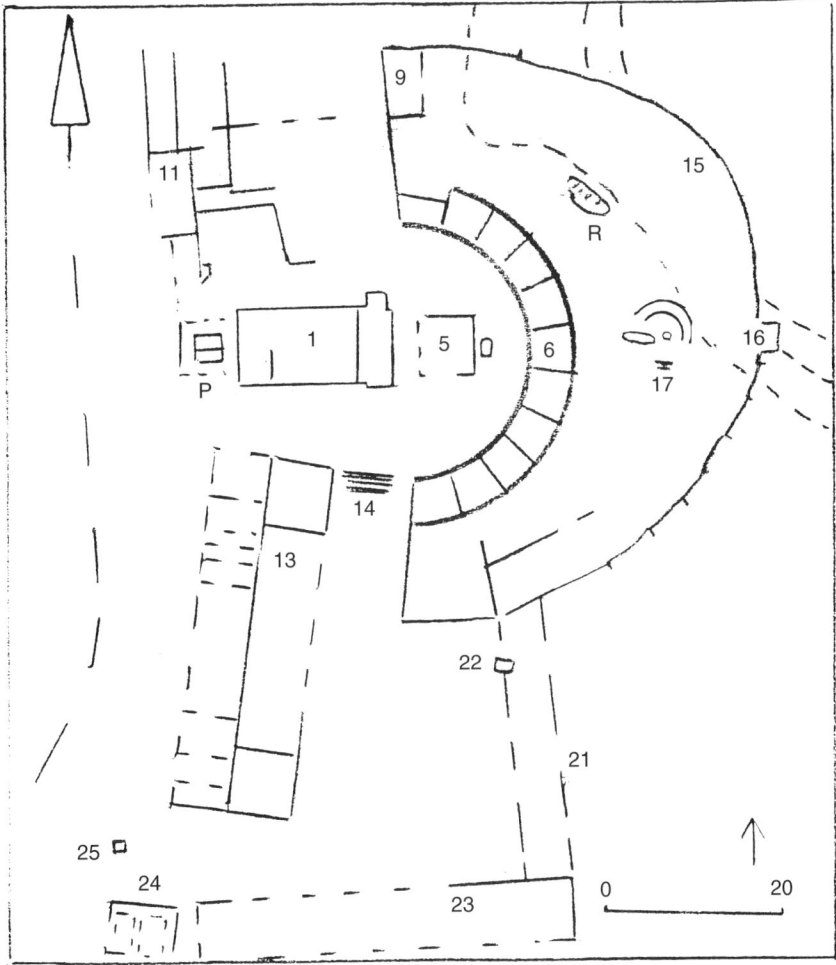

Figure 5.6 Theban Kabirion: Roman

The cult

Most of the evidence for the cult comes from the Late Archaic and Classical periods. From the former there are some 562 lead and bronze statuettes, 534 representing bulls. From the Classical period there are hundreds of terracotta figurines of animals and humans (mostly boys); the remains of hundreds of black glaze vases and dishes; Kabirion-ware drinking vessels, many with scenes painted on them, and the foundations of several buildings. From both periods there are several hundred votive graffiti, mostly on potsherds.

The cult complex at the Kabirion consisted of the Kabiroi – Kabiros and his son Pais (invoked singly or together) – a mother goddess, and her consort. A substantial minority of the dedications were made by women. Most of the dedications were made to Kabiros, who was obviously the senior figure, and the inhabitant, according to a poem incised on fragments of a black glaze vase of early fifth century date, of a *naos kalos* (*CEG* 1, 330). This may have been the Middle Tholos (18), which was put up early in the fifth century, and whose foundations were carefully preserved when its superstructure was pulled down in the second quarter of the third century BC.

Although the Kabiroi were gods in a mystery cult, they were nevertheless accessible in the sense that they could be openly addressed, by title if not by name: "Kabiros" and "Pais" mean "Lord" and "Son". Harder to reach were the other two gods of the cult. In fact the existence of the goddess can be inferred only from the presence of her consort. Inside the Lower Tholos (12), a large tub was found. It dates from the beginning of the fifth century, and had been buried with its upper lip about 30 cm below the floor of the second tholos on the site, which was erected late in the fifth century. The position of the tub is at the centre of the first building on the site, off-centre in relation to the second building. At some point a hole was made near the bottom of the tub, which seems to have been used for liquid offerings, possibly when it was buried. Once buried, of course, it was no longer meant to be seen. On the rim of the tub was incised ΤΟΘΑΜΑΚΟ, that is, *to thamako*, which G. Klaffenbach associated with the gloss in Kyrillos s.v. *thamakes: symbios*. By the time of Kyrillos, *symbios*, which in earlier times had meant "companion" or "partner", had come to mean "spouse"; *ho *thamakos*, therefore, would have meant the "husband", and *to thamako* "property of the husband" (Schachter 1986, 76, 94, and n.2) (Figures 5.7 and 5.8).

The existence of a secret "Husband" means that there was also a secret "Wife". She would have been the goddess called "Meter" (Mother) in the second century AD; if she must be given a particular place in the sanctuary to inhabit, the Rock Formation on the northern slope seems a likely choice.

As time went on, the **thamakos* gradually faded from the scene, a process aided perhaps by the concealment of his title. We can see this by following the changes to the Lower Tholos (12), which was marginalized in stages, first late in the fourth century, when its entrance was shifted from the south-east to the south-west quadrant, and then, less than half a century later, when its new doorway was blocked off entirely, until it was finally put effectively outside the sanctuary when the Western Stoa (13) was built. People seem to have forgotten about the **thamakos*, a case, one might say, of "out of sight, out of mind".

There was no fixed iconography for the Kabiroi, any more than there was for other purely local gods. It is understandable that worshippers, and through them artists when seeking to depict these gods, would have fixed on characteristics which they shared with more widely known gods, whose iconography was fixed. Thus, in Boiotia, for example, Amphiaraos and Tro-

Figure 5.7 Large tub found in Lower Tholos (12) (Heimberg 1982, pla. 47)

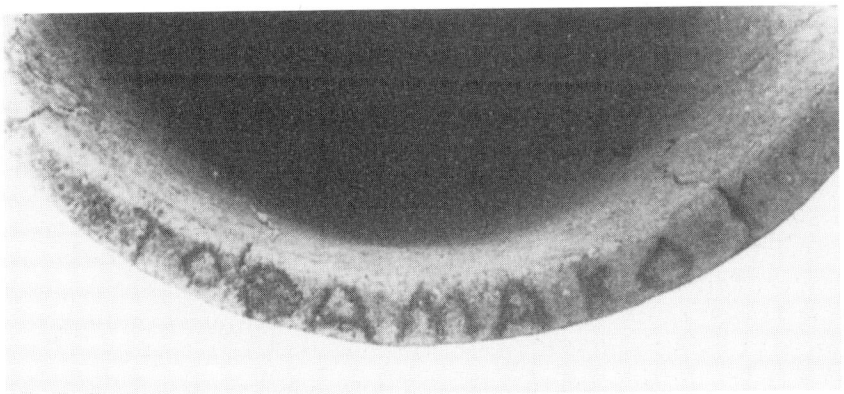

Figure 5.8 Name incised on the tub from the Lower Tholos (Heimberg 1982, pla. 53.1)

phonios were depicted as Asklepios, because of the association of the one with healing and the other with snakes (and the brothers Amphion and Zethos could be called Dioskouroi). The Kabiroi would have been envisaged by some of their worshippers as the patrons of herdsmen – as they seem to have been from the beginnings of this cult – while others focused on Kabiros as the patron of vegetation and chose Dionysos as his model. It is

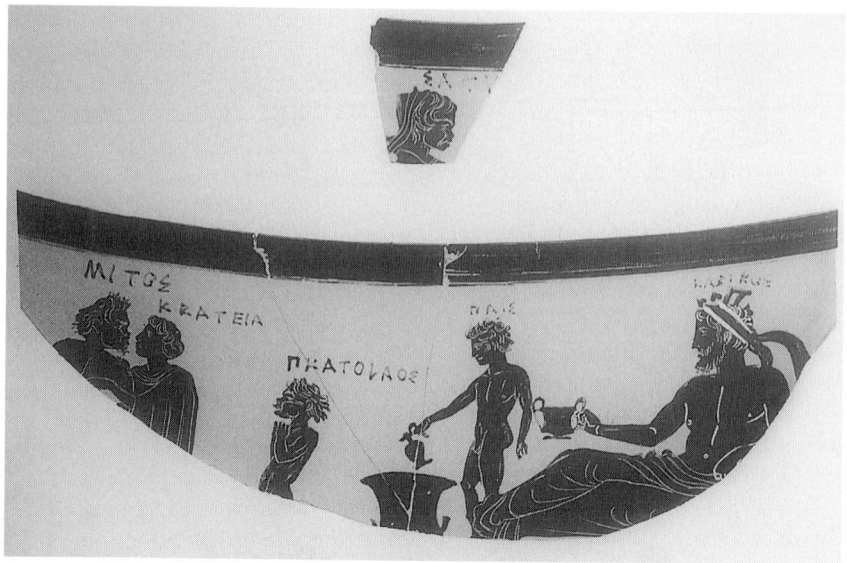

Figure 5.9 Wolters and Bruns 1940, 96.K1 = 4.62.302 (Wolters and Bruns 1940, pla. 44.1)

thus that he appears on the best known Kabirion-ware vase (Wolters and Bruns 1940, 96.K1 = 4.62.302), dated *c.* 410–400 BC (Figure 5.9). It is a symposium scene: Kabiros, propping himself up, holds a kantharos in his right hand, waiting for Pais, who stands before him facing away, to fill it from a pitcher which he is dipping into a krater. One of the remarkable things is that the artist has had to identify Kabiros and Pais by painting their names above their heads. Another vase (Wolters and Bruns 1940, 96, K2 = 4, 62, 297) dated 350–325 BC (Braun and Haevernick 1981, 26), shows, on one side, a reclining bearded figure leaning on his left elbow, holding a drinking horn in his right hand. He is approached by a family of mortals (that he is a god and they are human is clear from their respective sizes): a child, a man, two women. Between the humans and the god are traces of a bull. This is not a bull being brought to be sacrificed, for it, like the god, looks towards the worshippers. The combination of god and bull is enough to identify the former as Dionysiac, and in the context of the Kabirion, as Kabiros. On the other side of this vase is a symposium scene, with two pairs of men on couches, a flautist and a naked man dancing. All four symposiasts are bareheaded, and the left-hand pair have pygmy-like features, while the two on the right look more like portraits made to order. One man on each couch is young, the other old. A similar Dionysiac figure, with kantharos, appears on another sherd of the same ware (Wolters and Bruns 1940, 97, K3 = 4, 63, 305), while another (Wolters and Bruns 1940,

Figure 5.10 Wolters and Bruns 1940, 106.M4 = 4.64.358 (Wolters and Bruns 1940, 107, fig. 5)

97, K4) shows a Dionysiac god, holding a kantharos, wearing a headband on his head, while another hangs from the wall.[10]

A vase attributed to the Mystes Painter (floruit *c.* 400–375 BC), shows an outdoor scene with Hermes, Pan, and a female (Wolters and Bruns 1940, 106.M4 = 4.64.358 – the vase is lost) (Figure 5.10). She stands behind a rock, her head, but not her face, veiled, and her right arm raised. The gods stand on the other side of the rock, facing each other, right arms raised, left arms lowered and hands touching. Hermes hands Pan two branches with his left hand, and in his right he extends three branches and a mystic headband. To the right of this group are traces of two dancers and a flautist, on the opposite side of the vase a symposium scene, with two pairs of initiates on two klinai, being played to by a flute girl. All four symposiasts (a young man and an old one on each couch) are caricatured and wear the insignia of initiation (branches, headband tied into a bow). The three scenes seem to represent three of the activities conducted at the Kabirion: drinking, dancing, initiation. The scene with the two gods and the lady represents, I believe, the Kabiroi as Hermes and Pan, with the goddess, standing by the rock formation. Hermes and Pan are herdsmen's gods, and on this vase Pan is shown holding a shepherd's crook. A Dionysiac Kabiros is no cause for surprise at Thebes. As for Hermes and Pan, the Theban connection may be seen in the cult of the Mother of the Gods, with whom Pan was closely associated, especially by Pindar (Schachter 1986, 139).

Pan is being handed the insignia of initiation by his father Hermes. On the vase where the Dionysiac god is labelled Kabiros, he himself is depicted as an initiate, wearing the headgear reserved – as far as one can tell from other vases in the series – for initiates. If a god is himself an initiate, it follows that he is initiated into the mystery of some other god; it also follows that he is somehow subordinate to that other god. In the case of the Kabiroi, this would explain why they were more openly accessible than either the goddess or her partner. It would also explain why the Kabiroi are described as *hieros* – sacred – on four of the metal bulls. A god is not normally *hieros*, and to qualify a deity in this way is as much as to say that he is not a god of the first rank. They were attendant daimones, a role which suits the sense of the Semitic etymology from/kabir/, for the title need mean no more than "lord" or "mighty one".[11]

Cult activities: pre-Classical and Classical

It is impossible to date the beginnings of the cult. The earliest signs of any activity at the site are isolated sherds of Neolithic and Middle Geometric pottery, but there is no context for these, let alone a religious one. Schmaltz dated the earliest metal figurines to the tenth century BC. However, his dating depended entirely on style, there being no archaeological context (most of the figurines were dug up in the early excavations, and were found in dumps created when the western half of the sanctuary was razed to create a new level space for building during the second quarter of the third century BC). Nor was any allowance made for the fact that this was a provincial workshop. When Paul Roesch dated the votive inscriptions which were incised on thirty-seven of the bulls, he concluded that the inscriptions on five of them were between 50 and 100 years earlier than the dates given to the bulls. In the circumstances, it is preferable to leave the date of the beginning of the Kabirion open: the earliest datable object connected with the cult then becomes a bull dated 525–500 by Schmaltz, but following Roesch, at the end of the seventh or beginning of the sixth century BC. The letters incised on this bull are KA: this is enough to show that the Kabiroi were worshipped here at this time (Roesch 1985, E, 88, 29).

Permanent structures were not built at the Kabirion until the end of the Late Archaic period. Embedded in the floor of the Middle Tholos (18) was a short stretch of wall, M124, which seems to be the earliest datable surviving architectural element. Not enough survives to allow more than a guess at its function: perhaps part of an altar? There must, however, have been temporary buildings to house the activities of the clientele of the cult, traces of whose presence exist in the hundreds of miniature models of animals and glass beads, and in the numerous votive graffiti on sherds of drinking vessels.

The overwhelming majority of the votive statuettes of lead or bronze were bulls (Figure 5.11). This was not the only sanctuary where large numbers of metal statuettes of oxen were dedicated during the Archaic period and earlier. For example, most of more than the 570 bronze animals found at the sanctuary of Hermes and Aphrodite at Syme on Crete were bulls, as were close to 54 per cent of those found at Olympia. The bull as a votive offering was, therefore, not specific to any divinity, and says less about its divine recipient than it does about its human donor. Ownership of oxen was a sign of wealth. It required possession of enough land to pasture these relatively expensive

Figure 5.11 Bronze statuette from the Kabirion (Schmaltz 1980, pla. 13.246)

beasts. Offering a statuette of a bull to a god could serve a double purpose: overtly it entrusted the basis of a person's prosperity to the protection of the deity; on another level, it made a statement about the standing of the dedicator. Even more rarefied than the ownership of oxen and enough land to raise them was possession of horses, a luxury item if ever there was one, and it is no surprise that over 45 per cent of the early votive figurines at Olympia represented horses, a fitting dedication for an aristocratic worshipper.[12]

The custom of dedicating metal figurines of bulls seems to have tapered off towards the end of the sixth century, and continued at a lower rate until about the middle of the fourth. I deduce this from the fact that down to about 500 BC (that is, during the Archaic period), there were twenty-two dedications inscribed on metal bulls, whereas during the Classical period there were only twelve. Then, after a gap of about a century, there was one inscription dated about the middle of the third century, and two others at the end of it. I follow Paul Roesch in seeing these three as cases of the reuse of objects found in the course of one or other of the alterations made in the sanctuary. This is not to say that dedicating figurines of bulls was any less popular in the Classical period. The only difference was that most of the figurines were now made of terracotta. The terracotta animal figurines have not been published in detail and probably never will be, but at least as many of them were dedicated over the two centuries following the change in material as there had been metal bulls before it. The change in medium to terracotta has diminished the importance of these votive offerings in our eyes. Our attention has been diverted to the more obviously interesting spectacle offered by the Kabirion-ware vases. There is a kind of pecking order in what is noticed by modern scholarship: at the Kabirion, pride of place is taken by the figured vases and metal statuettes; next come the black glaze pottery and terracotta figurines; bringing up the rear are the thousands of glass beads found strewn about the site, and the Hellenistic inventories of votive offerings. These are our priorities, but not necessarily those of the ancient Greeks.[13]

Although no permanent dining building was built until the end of the Archaic period, eating and drinking in a ritual context must have taken place at the site long before then. Many of the sherds of black glaze ware which bear incised dedications must come from at least as early as the middle of the sixth century, to judge from the letter forms. Some of the names on the sherds are the same as those who dedicated metal bulls, and some are the names of women, so that dining at the Kabirion was, it appears, a family affair. Most of the early dining buildings at the Kabirion were round, their shape no doubt based on tents (nos. 12, 18, 28, M125). A possible apsidal building (29), which abuts on the Middle Tholos (18) would also have been based on a more fragile predecessor. Occupants of a round building would have been obliged to eat and drink sitting up, not reclining, which is entirely appropriate to a family occasion (Cooper and Morris 1990, 66–85).

The Lower Tholos (12), which was associated with the consort of the goddess, and the Middle Tholos (18), which was possibly connected with Kabiros and Pais, may have been the property of priestly families, one devoted to the Kabiroi, the other to the consort of the goddess. The existence of two hieratic families might explain why the early buildings at the Kabirion were grouped into two clusters (12 with 2, and 18 with 28, 29, and M125). Three graffiti – of which two seem to belong to the sixth century – record dedications by a priest, so the office did exist (*IG* 7, 3646, 3684, 3686).

It was not until late in the fifth century that a permanent structure designed especially for symposia was built. This is the "Rectangular Building" (2) near the Lower Tholos (12). But there is evidence for symposia earlier than this. Kabirion-ware vases, almost exclusively drinking vessels, custom-made for this sanctuary, are most easily understood in the context of the symposium, an upper-class, all-male phenomenon with undercurrents of pederasty. These vases begin to appear about the middle of the fifth century. Earlier still black glaze drinking vessels were used at symposia (as symposium scenes on Kabirion-ware vases show), and at least one sixth-century vase depicts a symposium scene. Even more telling is the sudden appearance early in the fifth century, and lasting to the end of the Classical period, of terracotta figurines of boys and youths – over 700 of them (Figure 5.12). To these can be added a small number of *kalos*-graffiti.[14]

The majority of Kabirion-ware vases were painted with floral or vegetative patterns. They were made until the second quarter of the third century. But Kabirion-ware is most famous for those vases which have scenes on them. These, besides being less numerous than the others, were also larger (as large as the largest of the black glaze kantharoi). Their manufacture ended in the third quarter of the fourth century. Scenes on Kabirion-ware

Figure 5.12 Terracotta statuette from the Kabirion (Schmaltz 1974, pla. 4.40)

vases say something about what went on at the sanctuary during the hundred and more years in which they were made. The change and eventual end of the genre can be attributed to the more or less sudden disappearance of patrons who would have commissioned figured scenes, and this — taken with the roughly contemporary cessation of both terracotta figurines and black glaze drinking vessels — must mean that there were no more symposia at the Kabirion. This should not be surprising: at about this time the flower of male Theban society was wiped out at Chaironeia, and the polis itself was obliterated, to be reconstituted twenty years or more later from survivors of the débâcle.

Anyone who tries to understand the scenes painted on these vases must remember that the picture may be the work of the craftsman, but the subject was chosen by the person who ordered it. Their great value lies in the fact that they were made specifically for use at a single sanctuary, to the specifications of one group of people (black glaze drinking vessels, on the other hand, like terracotta figurines, are not specific to a single place, and their significance varies with the contexts in which they were used). These pictures reflect the interests of a limited section of those who worshipped at the Kabirion, the upper-class males who took part in the symposia for which these large drinking mugs were made. If nothing else, they are an extremely valuable archive.[15]

Aside from scenes connected with the cult, a number of general themes can be identified: symposia, episodes from familiar stories (e.g. *The Odyssey*, the Battle of the Cranes and Pygmies, Kadmos), athletics, hunting. Many of the people in these pictures are depicted as grotesques or pygmies, and most are short and/or stocky, decidedly unheroic in appearance. Throughout there runs a strain of parody, even in the portrayal of gods and heroes. Some have seen in this the influence of Middle Comedy, and this is certainly not impossible. Whether plays were actually performed in the natural theatre at the base of the northern slope is, however, uncertain. There was, after all, a stream running across the valley at the bottom of the slope, and there were buildings on its opposite bank. The theatrical area of the Archaic and Classical periods may have been used only for the needs of initiation, as was the case in the Hellenistic and Roman periods, when a large podium filled the orchestra. It is prima facie unlikely that anything to do with the actual rite of initiation would have been represented openly. We have already seen how careful the faithful were to conceal the identity of the unnamed consort of the unnamed goddess.[16]

Certainly the vase painters who worked at the Kabirion were familiar with the artistic conventions of the day, and for their narrative, as opposed to genre, scenes they would have turned to well-known models, in this case illustrations of contemporary comedies. What singles out the Kabirion-ware is the use of pygmoid features which must reflect the influence of the Kabiric cult. Herodotos, writing about the sanctuaries of Hephaistos and the

Kabeiroi (father and sons) at Memphis, reports that their cult images resembled pygmies (3.37). There might have been cult images of the Kabiroi at the Theban Kabirion, and part of the ritual of initiation might have involved people dressed up as the Kabiroi.

In two cases human characters are not parodied, but instead look very like portrait studies, perhaps made to the order of the client. One is a symposium scene showing two pairs of men reclining (Wolters and Bruns 1940, 96, K2). One pair is caricatured, the other not. Is one pair masked, the other not? Did one of the latter commission the picture? It is impossible to be certain. The other is on the vase which shows and identifies the Dionysiac Kabiros and Pais (Figure 5.9).

Kabiros is looking at a group of three people, a man and woman – Mitos and Krateia – who are gazing intently into each other's eyes, and being watched by a naked boy, Pratolaos. The man and boy are caricatured, the woman not. A fragment with the head of an old woman – Satyra, not necessarily caricatured – may belong here. Kabiros and Pais are drawn on a slightly larger scale than the others, who must therefore be humans. This scene has been interpreted as Orphic, or comic. It could simply represent a family of worshippers (all the names are attested in Boiotia, save Krateia, and that is a common enough name). The fact that Krateia's features are normal suggests that this scene does show a family under the watchful or protective gaze of Kabiros (Schachter 1986, 93, n.2; cf. Daumas 1998, 39–40; Graf, this volume, p. 245).

The difficulties of interpreting scenes on Kabirion-ware vases are exemplified by this vase, and by another attributed to the Mystes Painter (Wolters and Bruns 1940, 108.M6 = 4.62.289) (Figure 5.13). It shows a procession, led by a dancer wearing what looks like a Phrygian cap and a long chiton, arms raised, hands clapping, a headband draped over each arm. She – or he – is followed by a naked old man, running, holding a staff in one hand, and carrying on his shoulders an aulos player (accompanying the

Figure 5.13 Wolters and Bruns 1940, 108.M6 = 4.62.289 (Wolters and Bruns 1940, pla. 33.1)

dancer no doubt), with headband and branches in his hair. Following them comes a cart drawn by a pair of mules (branches in their heads). On the cart are a man and woman. The man – caricatured – is dressed like an initiate, the woman holds a large round object – tympanon, mirror? – between them. They seem – the perspective is not clear – to be seated side by side looking at each other. Attempting to mount the cart at the rear is another man, holding a staff. This scene has been interpreted as an *hieros gamos* (a sacred marriage), or as part of the procession bringing celebrants to the sanctuary. Then again, it could be the "cast" of characters come to take part in some sort of *diathesis* or representation of the gods, as in the procession at Andania. Or it could be something else altogether.[17]

Vases which have scenes related to cult show events leading up to and following initiation. There are scenes of sacrifice, preparation for initiation, and symposia and general celebration afterwards. Events following initiation show participants wearing headbands with rectangular or triangular bows tied in them. Some of the vases show family groups. General festivities, as opposed to symposia and family dining, would probably have taken place in the open space south of the tholoi. In fact the entrance of the Lower Tholos (12) pointed in that direction, as would that of (29) if it was really an apsidal building.[18]

Cult activities: Hellenistic and Roman

Most of the surviving evidence for cult activity at the Kabirion comes from the late Archaic and Classical periods. This includes most of the votives and inscriptions, and all of the figured pottery of local manufacture. Inevitably there has been distortion in the way the cult has been interpreted, because scholarly interest has focused on them. Even Pausanias' discussion of the cult has been interpreted entirely in the context of the Classical and pre-Classical evidence.

And yet, the Kabirion flourished for at least another seven centuries after the end of the Classical period, and well beyond the lifetime of Pausanias. Worshippers did not stop going there, and indeed, during the Hellenistic and Roman periods the size of the sanctuary was progressively enlarged, and more, bigger, and better facilities were built – at state expense – to accommodate them. The cult was now definitely run by the state. One is reminded of what was to happen two centuries later in Messenia, when the priestly family which had run the Mysteries handed them over to the state, which proceeded to lay down strict regulations for the operation of the cult. Something like this might have happened at the Kabirion.

What probably did come to an end after the destruction of Thebes in 335 BC was lavish expenditure by individuals and families who seem to have operated the cult until then. But although there were no more symposia, dining continued at the sanctuary, and on a much greater scale than before:

the number of pieces of eating and cooking ware increases dramatically during the Hellenistic period. During the Roman period its place was taken by fine glassware, of which much was found on the site but only a small sample published.

The small number of votive offerings from the Hellenistic and Roman periods is deceptive. The inscription *IG* 7, 2420, of the middle and second half of the third century BC, lists supplementary offerings made in three archon years. These were items of gold, silver, and jasper. There must have been a much longer list of offerings, a cumulative inventory to which this list was attached, and a place to keep them. Objects of gold and silver are vulnerable to theft. Indeed, very few caches of Hellenistic and Roman votives have survived from antiquity, precisely because they were worth stealing. The surviving inscription may be said to be worth its weight in gold, because it shows that the Kabirion was a prosperous operation, and probably brought a great deal of profit to the polis of Thebes.

Although the architectural remains of the Hellenistic and Roman periods are hard to disentangle, it is possible to see that efforts were made to control access and direct internal traffic. Admission to the site, as we have seen, was controlled by the Entry Complex (11), and successive attempts were made to block access from the east at the site of the so-called "Niche" (16). Once inside, access to the theatral area was at first open, but later an attempt seems to have been made to channel people through a colonnade (4). Later still a passageway (21) led from the eastern end of the Southern Stoa (23) to the upper level of the Roman cavea (6), giving direct access to the "Upper Tholos" (17) and the Rock Formation. We can envisage a procession gathering in the southern part of the sanctuary, then going by way of (21) to (17) and the Rock Formation for preliminary sacrifices, before being seated in the theatre to watch new initiates being inducted on the Podium (5). It is possible that during the Roman period at least there were two stages of initiation (epopteia as well as myesis), with the second stage performed indoors in the *Anaktoron* (1) (Schachter 1986, 105).

The new physical configuration of the sanctuary also involved a theological change: the so-called "Upper Tholos" (17) took the place, at least partly, of the Rock Formation as the abode of the goddess, with the *Anaktoron* as the new home of the Kabiroi, replacing (18). The eventual disappearance of (12), the home of the goddess' consort, heralds a change in the makeup of the cult complex, with emphasis put on the goddess, on the one hand, and on the two Kabiroi on the other. Inscriptions now refer almost exclusively to Kab(e)iros and Pais together as equals, and once they are equated with the Theoi Megaloi, the Great Gods, of Samothrace (Schachter 1986, 89, and n.2).

The Thebans told Pausanias that the Mysteries lapsed after the expulsion of the Kabeiraioi by the Argives. The legendary successful siege of Thebes by the Argeioi may stand here for the historical capture of Thebes by Alexander in 335: can it be a coincidence that the Argead kings of

Macedonia traced their origins from Temenos? The initial revival of the Mysteries by Pelarge and Isthmiades, which is said to have happened at a place called Alexiarous ("stronghold"?) could have been connected with the initial expansion of the sanctuary late in the fourth century. The name "Pelarge" has echoes of both Samothrace and Dodona. It was the oracle of Dodona which advised the sacrifice of a farrowing beast to Pelarge. The early years of the third century would have provided the Thebans with a suitable occasion to consult this oracle, which was the recipient of large benefactions from Pyrrhos, with whom the Thebans were allied through the Aitolians, and who led an unsuccessful expedition to rescue Thebes from Demetrios Poliorketes in 292. The subsequent reorganization of the rites by Telondes might be a reflection of the final realignment of the sanctuary later in the third century. The sacrifice to Pelarge could have been performed at the so-called "Upper Tholos" (17).[19]

Pausanias refers to another organization of the Mysteries of the Kabirion by the Athenian Methapos, who was perhaps a member of the genos of Lykomidai. It is conventional to date this in the fourth century BC (another example of scholarship's focus on the Classical period). But there is nothing at the Kabirion during the first part of the fourth century – when Thebans and Messenians were very close – to attach to a doctrinal change. The only possible date within the fourth century would be towards the end, when, according to Pausanias (9.7.1), Messenians and Megalopolitans joined the Athenians in contributing to the reconstruction of the city. This is the period to which I have assigned the changes made by Pelarge and Isthmiades, and later by Telondes. It would suit Methapos as well, but there is a much more likely date for him. The key to this lies not in Thebes, but at Andania in Messenia. In 92 BC the Mysteries of Andania, which had been run by a priestly family, were handed over to the polis (*Syll*.3, 736 = *IG* 5, 1, 1390). At the time the gods receiving sacrifice were Demeter, Hagna, Hermes, Apollo Karnesios, and the Theoi Megaloi (line 34, 68–69). When Pausanias wrote of the cult, the gods were Demeter and Kore/Hagne, worshipped as Megalai Theai, Apollo Karnesios, Hermes (4, 1, 8; 4, 33, 4–5). In other words, between 92 BC and the third quarter of the second century AD there had been a change in the cult, with Great Gods ("Samothracian") being displaced by Great Goddesses ("Eleusinian"). The circumstances were ideal for calling in an outside authority to reorganize the ritual at Andania: there was no longer a priestly family who knew or could confidently produce a traditional procedure. The Lykomids, it is known, had connections with Eleusis, and the family itself was active during the early years of the Empire. I think it likely that Methapos or some other exegete worked at Andania at some time between 92 BC and the time of Pausanias, and that this was when he worked at Thebes as well. It may have been about the middle or second half of the first century BC, when the Roman cavea was built, or – probably – late in the first century AD when there seems to have been a further revival.[20]

Back to Pausanias

Despite Pausanias' commendable reticence, we can, with help from the archaeological remains, identify in his narrative several of the important features of this cult. First, it was a mystery cult, and must have been so from the very beginning. Second, the Mysteries were celebrated in honour of the Kabiroi and "The Mother". We can also confirm that the Kabiroi were father and son, for the Theban Kabiroi appear in the earliest documents as Kabiros and Pais, the latter occasionally being referred to as the Pais of Kabiros; that is, the son. In the cult *aition* as told to Pausanias, the recipients of the mystic rites were Prometheus and Aitnaios. Their role at the Theban Kabirion was to act as intermediaries between the goddess and her worshippers. In the story they are humans, Kabeiraioi (according to the manuscripts), but their own names are divine, and moreover are found in other Kabiric contexts. Although the aition is clearly influenced by the *Homeric Hymn to Demeter*, it may nevertheless mask the reality in which two Kabiroi, father and son, acted as the medium for initiates to approach the unnamed goddess. In cult, as opposed to myth, the Mysteries were celebrated in honour of the Kabiroi as well as the Mother. This apparent contradiction can be reconciled by regarding the Kabiroi as the goddess' servants, on a lower level, but still, by virtue of their connection with the rites, within the forbidden circle. Pausanias' history of the cult also refers to occasions on which the cult was interrupted and subsequently resumed under, as it were, new management; and elsewhere he mentions the Athenian Methapos as one who had organized the Mysteries at the Theban Kabirion. An examination of the archaeological evidence has allowed us to identify two of these breaks and reorganizations. And finally, the story Pausanias was told shows signs of how the cult was influenced by the mystery cults of Eleusis, Samothrace, and Lemnos. The sanctuary of Demeter Kabeiria and Kore, and indeed the very presence of Kore, were probably imported from Eleusis, while the story of how Demeter came to the city of the Kabeiraioi and gave the rites to two of them is straight out of the *Homeric Hymn to Demeter*; the names Pelarge and Telondes have a Samothracian ring about them, while Prometheus and Aitnaios seem to reflect the Lemnian cult (Schachter 1986, 88, n.7; 89, n.3; 94, n.5).

There is therefore nothing in Pausanias' account which, after considering the remains, does not ring true. But what he does not prepare us for is the wealth and variety of evidence from the site which, even in its imperfect state, has allowed us to try to reconstruct the history of the sanctuary and the nature of the cult.

Appendix: Chronological summary of architectural remains

The excavations

There were two series of excavations at the Kabirion, separated by almost seventy years, the first in the winter of 1887/1888 and the following spring, the second during the 1950s and 1960s. Preliminary summary reports were published of the first, and the first volume of what was intended to be the final publication appeared in 1940 (Wolters and Bruns 1940). Gerda Bruns, who had taken over the publication of the first volume and directed the later excavations, died before she could bring together the material for a complete and final publication, and it was left to others to bring out what she and her predecessors had excavated. A projected seventh volume was never published, leaving untouched the non-human terracotta figurines and the coins found on the site. The single most useful study of the site is the review of Heyder and Mallwitz 1978 by F. Cooper (1982), who clarifies the change in alignment. Details of his analysis require revision following the subsequent publication of the pottery in Heimberg (1982) and Braun and Haevernick (1981).

Architectural development

Detailed explanations of the dating and sequences are given in Schachter (1986, 74–88) and in the Addenda in Schachter (forthcoming). Heyder and Mallwitz (1978) divided the history of the site into six periods (actually seven, because they split Period IV into IVa and IVb). In 1986 I divided it into ten periods, which, following Cooper, I put into two phases (Schachter 1986). For the present publication I have tried to avoid a rigid framework. I have retained the numbering system of Heyder and Mallwitz (1978), with one or two exceptions, and with the addition of numbers symbolizing the different stages in a building's life; for example, the Lower Tholos, number 12, appears as 12.1, 12.2, and so on. Overall the numbers given by the archaeologists to buildings and pieces of wall seem to follow the sequence in which they were discovered.

Before the end of the sixth century BC
  M124 (Wall inside 18).
Late sixth/early fifth centuries BC
  Removed: M124.
  Added: P.1 (Sacrificial Pits, Phase 1); 12.1 (Lower Tholos, Phase 1); 18.1 (Middle Tholos, Phase 1: Perhaps the *naos kalos* of *Carmina Epigraphica Graeca* 1, 330).
Early Classical?
  Added: 28 (Tholos adjoining 18); 29 (Curved building, possibly apsidal, adjoining 18 [South Apsidal Building]); M125 (Tholos east of 28/18/29).

Circa last quarter, fifth century BC
    Changed: 12.2 (Lower Tholos, Phase 2).
    Added: 2 (Rectangular Building north-east of 12).
Classical?
    Changed: 18.2 (Middle Tholos, Phase 2).
Late fourth century BC
    Removed: 29 (South Apsidal Building).
    Changed: 12.3 (Lower Tholos, Phase 3).
    Added: 7.1 (Cavea, Phase 1); 17 (East Sacrificial Pits, "Upper Tholos"); WL16/17 (Water pipes); 19.1 (Conduit, Phase 1); 20.1 (Eastern Reservoir, Phase 1).
Late fourth century BC*?*
    Added: 8 (North Rectangular Building); M35/46 (South Rectangular Building); 10 (North Apsidal Building).
Late second quarter, third century BC
    Removed: 2 (Rectangular Building); 8 (North Rectangular Building); 10 (North Apsidal Building); 18.2 (Middle Tholos, Phase 2); M125 (Tholos east of 28/18/29); WL16/17 (Water pipes); possibly 28 (Tholos adjoining 18).
    Changed: 7.2 (Cavea, Phase 2); 19.2 (Conduit, Phase 2).
    Added: 3 (Retaining Wall); M57 (Buttress Wall); 16.1 ("Niche", Phase 1); WL6/7 (Water pipe).
Late second quarter, third century BC*?*
    Changed: P.2 (Sacrificial Pits, Phase 2); 12.4 (Lower Tholos, Phase 4).
    Added: 1.1 (Tholos: *Anaktoron*, Phase 1); 5.1 (Podium, Phase 1); 11.1 (Entry Complex, Phase 1: perhaps the *prothyron* of Wolters and Bruns 1940, 27, 4; the entry tokens published in *JIAN* 18 (1916/1917) 114 may be associated with this); D (Rectangular Building east of 11.1); 23 (Southern Stoa).
Late third century BC*?*
    Removed: M35/46 (South Rectangular Building); D (Rectangular Building east of 11.1).
    Changed: 1.2 (*Anaktoron*, Phase 2); 16.2 ("Niche", Phase 2); 11.2 (Entry Complex, Phase 2); M70/69/47/29/35a (Rectangular Building?).
First half of the second century BC*?*
    Removed: 12.4 (Lower Tholos, Phase 4).
    Changed: 16.3 ("Niche", Phase 3); 20.2 (Eastern Reservoir, Phase 2).
    Added: 13.1 (Western Stoa); 26 (Southwest Building); 24 (Western Reservoir: perhaps the *dute* referred to in *IG* 7, 2477).
Late second century BC*?*
    Removed: M70/69/47/29/35a (?Rectangular Building).
    Changed: 1.3 (*Anaktoron*, Phase 3); P.3 (Sacrificial Pits, Phase 3); 11.3 (Entry Complex, Phase 3).
    Added: 4 (Colonnade); M2a/M2, M3/M3a (Southern Buildings).

First century BC?
Removed: 7.2 (Cavea, Phase 2); M57 (Buttress Wall); M2a/M2, M3/M3a (Southern Buildings); WL6/7 (Water pipe); 19.2 (Conduit, Phase 2); 20.2 (Eastern Reservoir, Phase 2); 4 (Colonnade).
Changed: 16.4 (Niche, Phase 4); 5.2 (Podium, Phase 2).
Added: 6 (Roman Cavea); 15 (Cavea Wall); 9 ("Watch Room"); 21 (Corridor); 14 (Stairway).
Late first century AD?
Changed: 1.4 (*Anaktoron*, Phase 4: possibly the *anaktoron* of *SEG* 22, 418); P.4 (Sacrificial Pits, Phase 4).
Second half of the second century AD?
Removed: 26 (Southwest Building).
Changed: 13.2 (Western Stoa, Phase 2: probably the *oikoi* of *ArchDelt* 25 (1970[1971]) A, 134, 7).
Late
Added: 22 (Well); 25 (Tiled Floor).

Acknowledgements

The plans are based on Heyder and Mallwitz (1978), pls. 14 and 15, and Beilage 1. Permission to use these and to reproduce Figures 5.7–5.13 has been granted from the German Archaeological Institute.

Notes

1 I use the Boiotian dialect form "Kabir-" for the Theban cult. See Schachter (1986, 66, n.1). This cult has been studied in detail by Kern (1919, 1437–1442), Hemberg (1950, 184–205), Daumas (1998), and myself (1986, 66–110). The pieces by Kern and Hemberg were rendered largely obsolete when it was discovered in the 1950s that only a small part of the sanctuary had been excavated. Testimonia for the cult are listed in Schachter (1986, 66–73). What follows here takes account of work published since 1986. My own interpretation of the data has changed, in some cases substantially, and this chapter supersedes what I published in 1986.
2 The derivation of the name from Semitic/kabir/, "lord", "mighty one" was proposed by J.J. Scaliger in 1619: see Schachter (1986, 96, n.4). Samothrace: Hemberg (1950, 73–81), Cole (1984). The largest number of Kabeiroi sanctuaries was in Asia Minor, followed by the Aegean islands and Northern and Central Greece. Except for Lemnos and Thebes, whose beginnings were roughly contemporary, the evidence for these is mostly late: Hemberg (1950, 137–211). Lemnian Kabeiroi: Schachter (1986, 94, n.5). Boiotian male pairs: Schachter (1972, 20–21).
3 Theophoric names: of the fifteen names known from Boiotia, three are from Thebes, two each from Thespiai, Thisbe, Tanagra, and Oropos, one each from Halai, Akraiphia, and Chaironeia, and one unspecified. All except the polemarch are Hellenistic or later (Fraser and Matthews 2000, 478). Names from outside Boiotia (all Hellenistic): one each from Eretria (Fraser and Matthews 1987, 242), Athens? (Fraser and Matthews 1994, 244), Typaneai (Fraser and Matthews 1997, 227). Some of the Boiotians called *paillos* ("little Pais") could have been named after Pais: normally the title was given to dead infants, but at least one *paillos* grew up to be an

archon (Schachter 1986, 89, n.1; Fraser and Matthews 2000, 330). Coins: Heimberg (1982, 122–124). Kabirion-ware at Thespiai: Braun and Haevernick (1981, 413–415). Vases found at the Kabirion were in fragments, and it is suggested that the complete exemplars in various museums came from graves, mostly in the vicinity of Thebes (Braun and Haevernick 1981, 2). The Thespian woman in the sacred inventory: *IG* 7, 2420 lines 7–8. Dedication by an Aitolian: *IG* 7, 2467a.

4 My translation. Editors and translators rely on readings based mostly on emendations made by earlier editors. I have gone to the apparatus criticus of Hitzig's text (Hitzig and Bluemner 1907), which is still the only full one, and used forms attested in most cases by the majority of manuscripts. In one case I have accepted a correction to a manuscript ("Kabeiraioi" in paragraph two of the translation), in another an emendation ("men named Kabeiraians", paragraph one). The result is a reading which distinguishes consistently between men (Kabeiraioi, Kabeiritai) and gods (Kabeiroi), and calls the goddess of the cult Meter rather than Demeter.

5 In the interests of making the narrative as clear as possible, I have presented my reconstruction of the physical history of the sanctuary in an Appendix (see pp. 137–138).

6 Location of Kabirion: Wolters and Bruns (1940, pl. 1), Heyder and Mallwitz (1978, 7, fig. 2). The cemetery: Aravantinos ([1994] 1999) (500 m from the 88 km marker of the Thebes–Livadia road); cf. Blackman (2000, 59).

7 Rock formation: Schachter (1986, 74); cf. Clinton (1992, 14–27).

8 Prothyron: Wolters and Bruns (1940, 27, 4). Priests (hereditary): Wolters and Bruns (1940, 27, 4), *IG* 7, 2420, 2477. Kabiriarchs: *IG* 7, 2428, 2420. Paragogeies: *IG* 7, 2428. Dedications: *IG* 7, 2420. Entrance tokens: *Journal International d'archéologie numismatique* 18 (1916/1917) 114.

9 Theban prosperity middle to second half of the first century BC: Schachter (2000, 109). A statue erected at the Kabirion in honour of a hierarch may belong in this context (*IG* 7, 2518a). For a possible visit by Ovid (who had friends at Thespiai) see Schachter (1990). Recovery in the second half of the first century AD (building of *anaktoron*): Schachter (1986, 87, and n.5). Building of *oikoi* in the second century AD: Schachter (1986, 87–88); inventory list, second century AD: *IG* 7, 2425a.

10 On the bull and Dionysos, see Bérard (1976) and Dodds (1960, xviii, xx).

11 Ἱερός: Schachter (1986, 96, and n.2–3), Chadwick (1996, 150–161). Kabiroi as attendant daimones: Strabo (10, 3, 15 [470]), Schachter (1986, 96, and n.1).

12 Bulls at Syme: Lembesi ([1992] 1993, 13). At Olympia: Heilmeyer (1979, 196 [percentages], 275 [table]). Other sanctuaries with bull statuettes: Bevan (1986, i, 8992 and ii, 380–386) (she leaves out both Syme and the Kabirion). Different explanations have been proposed for why bulls were dedicated at the Kabirion. One is that they represented an idealized sacrifice, since evidence from animal bones found at the Kabirion shows that most of the beasts actually dedicated there were sheep or goats (Schmaltz 1980, 13). Another (Lembesi [1992] 1993) is that the dedication of bulls was connected with a ritual of maturation in the context of a homosexual partnership (part of the confusion which surrounds the interpretation of ancient practices is that we use the term "initiation" to describe both induction in a mystery cult and admission to a higher age-class group). Horses at Olympia: Heilmeyer (1979, 196).

13 In his review of Schmaltz (1980), Claude Rolley, while accepting an early date for the beginning of the series of bull figurines, argued (relying on Roesch's chronology) that their manufacture went on until late in the third century (Rolley 1986). I have doubts about the early dating. As far as the end is concerned, I am more influenced by the century-long gap which separated the latest three from their predecessors. Terracotta animals: Wolters (1890, 355–356). Glass beads: more glass beads were found at the Kabirion than at any other Greek sanctuary. Comparison with beads found elsewhere in Europe has shown that they range in date from the Early Archaic

to the Late Roman periods: Braun and Haevernick (1981, 97–110), Haevernick *et al.* (1987, 13–14, 23–24, 56, 63, 75, 77, 113–114, 117), Haevernick *et al.* (1995, 30, 118–120, 123–125, 128–130, 145, 147, 164, 166). Their significance is unclear, but it is fair to suggest that they were dedicated by women. Compare also the necklace of blue beads painted on a terracotta mask of Kore (?) from Boiotia: Mollard-Besques (1954, 96, C75).

14 Symposia: Boardman (1990, 124), Cooper and Morris (1990, 77–78), Murray (1990, 6, and n.14). Sixth-century symposium scene: *CVA* Deutschland 33 Berlin 4, 73 and pl. 200, 3–6. Terracottas: Schmaltz (1974). *Kalos*-graffiti: *IG* 7, 3596, 3597, 4122. Earlier symposia would have been held in temporary structures.

15 The dating of Kabirion-ware from the third quarter of the fifth century to the second quarter of the third is generally defensible, but dates assigned to individual pieces are no safer than those given to the metal bulls and black glaze kantharoi. For example, two of three sherds incised with the letter *H* are assigned to the latest period of manufacture: Braun and Haevernick (1981, 47 [129], 56 [22], the other being 50 [168]). But if *H* stands for H(ιαρός), a logical interpretation, they cannot be later than the second quarter of the fourth century, when the use of the epichoric alphabet was superseded by the Ionic (Vottéro 1996, 157–181, esp. 179–180). If Karen Braun's dating were correct, *H* would have to represent /αι/, which in the context is meaningless. In the general scheme of things, it makes no difference if individual pieces are misdated, but it is a useful reminder not to rely too heavily on subjective judgement.

16 Karen Braun (Braun and Haevernick 1981, 24–29) tries to match scenes on the vases with the known titles of lost plays. Michèle Daumas (Daumas 1998, 24–36, and elsewhere) interprets the scenes as depicting stages in initiation. (She turns it into something with Masonic overtones. We do not know if classical initiation rites included trials to determine worthiness. She also insists that only men were initiated, which flies in the face of the evidence, and requires her, for example, to interpret every woman shown on a Kabirion-ware vase as being really a man in drag.) The observations by Kilinski (1990, 37, 41–42) place Kabirion-ware in a natural line of succession from Archaic Boiotian pottery and provide a useful corrective to interpreting the scenes and motifs out of their true artistic context.

17 Schachter (1986, 100, n.2). Ἱερὸς γάμος (*hieros gamos*): Daumas (1998, 65–66). Procession: Loucas-Dourie (1992, 107–115). Διάθεσις (*diathesis*) at Andania: *Syll*.3, 736 = *IG* 5, 1, 1390 line 24.

18 The bow: Blech (1982, 213–214), discussing Wolters and Bruns 1940, 106, M3 = 4, 62, 291. The bow is also visible on Wolters and Bruns 1940, 96, K1 (4, 62, 302), 97, K4, 105, M1, 106, M4 (4, 64, 358), 4, 45, 103, 65, 369. Scenes analysed as preceding and following initiation: Schachter (1986, 100–101). Family groups: Wolters and Bruns 1940, 96, K1 (4, 62, 302), 96, K2 (4, 62, 297), 101, K25 (4, 62, 290), 101, K26 (4, 66, 389), 102, K29 (4, 65, 373).

19 Pelarge: Schachter (1986, 89, n.3). Dodona/Pyrrhos: Cloch (1952, 209), Will (1984, 105–107), Roesch (1982, 82). "Upper Tholos" (17): what survives are two concentric semi-circles north of, and three steps south of one of two bothroi sunk into the upper part of the cavea. This has been restored as a tholos, but it could have been an altar partly enclosed by a circular wall. Compare, for example, altars at Paros (Ohnesborg 1991, 122) and Pergamon (Sahin 1972, 25–28).

20 Methapos' date: *CB* 2, 105–106. Lykomids and Eleusis: Bourriot (1976, 1261, 1268–1269). Lykomids under the Empire: Bourriot (1976, 1268–1269), Davies (1971, no. 9238); see also Graf, this volume, p. 246.

References

Aravantinos, V., [1994] 1999: "Theta Eforeia Proistorikon kai Klassikon Archaioteton", *ArchDelt* 49B.1, 284–286.

Bérard, C., 1976: "ΑΞΙΕ ΤΑΥΡΕ", in P. Ducrey *et al.* (eds), *Melanges d'histoire ancienne et d'archeologie offerts a Paul Collart* (Lausanne, De Boccard), 61–73.

Bevan, E., 1986: *Representations of Animals in Sanctuaries of Artemis and Other Olympian Deities*. BAR International Series 315, Oxford.

Blackman, D., 2000: "Archaeology in Greece 1999-2000", *Archaeological Reports for 1999-2000* no. 46, 3–151.

Blech, M., 1982: *Studien zum Kranz bei den Griechen*. De Gruyter, Berlin and New York.

Boardman, J., 1990: "Symposium furniture", in O. Murray (ed.), *Sympotica* (Oxford University Press, Oxford), 122–131.

Bourriot, F., 1976: *Recherches sur la nature du Genos*. H. Champion, Lille and Paris.

Braun, K. and Th.E. Haevernick, 1981: *Bemalte Keramik und Glas aus dem Kabirenheiligtum bei Theben*. De Gruyter, Berlin.

Chadwick, J., 1996: *Lexicographica Graeca*. Oxford University Press, Oxford.

Clinton, K., 1992: *Myth and Cult. The Iconography of the Eleusinian Mysteries*. Svenska institutet i Athen. Stockholm.

Cloch, P., 1952: *Thèbes de Béotie*. Namur, Secrétariat des Publications, Facultés Universitaires.

Cole, S.G., 1984: *Theoi Megaloi*. Brill, Leiden.

Cooper, F., 1982: Review of Heyder and Mallwitz 1978, *Gnomon* 54, 56–63.

Cooper, F. and S. Morris, 1990: "Dining in round buildings", in O. Murray (ed.), *Sympotica* (Oxford University Press, Oxford), 66–85.

Daumas, M., 1998: *Cabiriaca: Recherches sur l'iconographie du culte des Cabires*. De Boccard, Paris.

Davies, J.K., 1971: *Athenian Propertied Families*. Oxford University Press, Oxford.

Dodds, E.R. (ed.), 1960: *Euripides, Bacchae*. Oxford University Press, Oxford.

Fraser, P.M. and E. Matthews (eds): *A Lexicon of Greek Personal Names* I (1987), II (1994) IIIA (1997) IIIB (2000). Oxford University Press, Oxford.

Haevernick, Th.E. *et al.* 1987: *Glasperlen der vorrömischen Eisenzeit*. Vol. 2. Hitzeroth, Marburg/Lanh.

Haevernick, Th.E. *et al.* 1995: *Glasperlen der vorrömischen Eisenzeit*. Vol. 4. Marie Leidorf GmbH, Espekamp.

Heilmeyer, W.-D., 1979: *Frühe Olympische Bronzefiguren. Die Tiervotive* = Olympische Forschungen XII. De Gruyter, Berlin.

Heimberg, U., 1982: *Die Keramik des Kabirions*. De Gruyter, Berlin.

Hemberg, B., 1950: *Die Kabiren*. Almqvist and Wiksell, Lund.

Heyder, W. and A. Mallwitz, 1978: *Die Bauten im Kabirenheiligtum bei Theben*. De Gruyter, Berlin.

Hitzig, H. and H. Bluemner (eds), 1907: *Pausaniae Graeciae Descriptio* III.1. O.R. Reisland, Leipzig.

Kern, O., 1919: "Kabeiros (*Kabeiros*) und Kabeiroi", in *RE* 10, 1399–1450.

Kilinski, K. II, 1990: *Boeotian Black Figure Vase Painting of the Archaic Period*. Von Zabern, Mainz am Rhein.

Lembesi, A., [1992] 1993: "Ta metallina zodhia tou Thevaikou Kaviriou", *Ephemeris* 131, 1–19.

Loucas-Dourie, E., 1992: "Some comments on the scene on the Cabiric vase, Athens N. M. 424", in R. Hägg (ed.), *The Iconography of Greek Cult in the Archaic and Classical Periods* = *Kernos Supplement* 1. Centre d'Étude de la Religion Grecque Antique, Athens–Liège.

Mollard-Besques, S., 1954: *Musée national du Louvre. Catalogue raisonné des figurines et reliefs en terre-cuite grecs, etrusques et romains* 1. Éditions des Musées nationaux, Paris.

Murray, O., 1990: "Sympotic history", in O. Murray (ed.), *Sympotica* (Oxford University Press, Oxford), 3–13.

Ohnesorg, A., 1991: "Altäre auf Paros", in R. Étienne and M.-T. Le Dinahet (eds), *L'espace sacrificiel* (De Boccard, Paris), 121–126.

Roesch, P., 1982: *Études Beotiennes*. De Boccard, Paris.

Roesch, P., 1985: Teiresias 15. *Appendix: Epigraphica* 15, 15–17.

Rolley, C., 1986: "Les bronzes grecs" (review article), *RA*, 385–389.

Sahin, M.Ç., 1972: *Die Entwicklung der Griechischen Monumentalaltäre*. Rudolf Habelt, Bonn.

Schachter, A. (forthcoming): *Cults of Boiotia 5: BICS Supplement* 38.5. Institute of Classical Studies, London.

Schachter, A., 1972: "Some underlying cult patterns in Boeotia", in *Teiresias Supplement* 1. Montreal.

Schachter, A., 1986: *Cults of Boiotia 2: BICS Supplement* 38.2. Institute of Classical Studies, London.

Schachter, A., 1990: "Ovid and Boiotia", in A. Schachter (ed.), *Studies in the Topography, History, and Culture of Boiotia* = *Teiresias Supplement* 3. Montreal.

Schachter, A., 2000: "The Daphnephoria of Thebes", in P.A. Bernardini (ed.), *Presenza e Funzione della Citta di Tebe nella Cultura Greca* (Istituti Editoriali e Poligrafici Internazionali, Pisa–Roma), 99–123.

Schmaltz, B., 1974: *Terrakotten aus dem Kabirenheiligtum bei Theben*. De Gruyter, Berlin.

Schmaltz, B., 1980: *Metallfiguren aus dem Kabirenheiligtum bei Theben*. De Gruyter, Berlin.

Vottéro, G., 1996: "L'alphabet Ionien-Attique en Béotie", in P. Carlier (ed.), *Le IVe Siècle av. J.-C. Approches historiographiques*. De Boccard, Nancy.

Will, É., 1984: "The formation of the Hellenistic kingdoms", in F.W. Walbank, A.E. Astin, M.W. Frederiksen, and R.M. Ogilvie (eds), *Cambridge Ancient History* VII.1. Cambridge University Press, Cambridge.

Wolters, P. and G. Bruns, 1940: *Das Kabirenheiligtum bei Theben* 1. De Gruyter, Berlin.

Wolters, P., 1890: "Das Kabirenheiligtum bei Theben. IV. Die Terrakotten", *AM* 15, 355–364.

6

MYSTERY CULTS IN ARCADIA

Madeleine Jost

No less than thirteen sanctuaries with mystery cults are known in Arcadia (Table 6.1).[1] Unfortunately, often only the existence of these cults is mentioned, without any information on their content. A more detailed knowledge of these cults can be obtained through the combination of archaeological evidence with the data from the literary and epigraphic texts. At Lykosoura, for example, the study of the buildings and chance finds from the *Megaron*, where the Mysteries were celebrated, allows the reconstruction of certain details of the ceremonial aspects of the Mysteries that are not mentioned in the literary sources, whereas the study of the drapery of the cult statue of Despoina provides further relevant information. This fortunate case is nevertheless unique, as for the remaining cults we are restricted to literary and epigraphic texts, which are silent in terms of the essential time of the "secret mysteries" (*IG* V 2, 265, line 22). Two honorary decrees from Mantineia, dated to 61/60 and 42/41 BC (*IG* V 2, 265, 266) mention, respectively,

Table 6.1 Mystery cults in Arcadia

Cult	Location	Source
Demeter Eleusinia	Pheneos	Paus. 8.15.1
Demeter Kidaria	Pheneos	Paus. 8.15.2–3
Demeter Thesmia	Pheneos	Paus. 8.15.3–4
Demeter Erinys/Lousia	Thelpousa	Paus. 8.25.4–7
Demeter (and Kore); Kore	Mantineia	*IG* V 2, 265, 266
Despoina, Demeter, Artemis and Anytos	Lykosoura	Paus. 8.37.8–9 (cf. *IG* V 2, 514, 515b, 516, 543)
Great Goddesses	Bathos	Paus. 8.29.1
Great Goddesses	Megalopolis	Paus. 8.31.7 (cf. *IG* V 2, 517)
Artemis	Kaphyai	Paus. 8.23.4
Dionysos	Heraia	Paus. 8.26.2
Dionysos	Phigalia	Schol. Lyc. *Alex.*, 211
Dionysos	Mantinike	Paus. 8.6.5
Antinoos	Mantineia	Paus. 8.9.8

the Mysteries of Kore and a *megaron* which probably housed the Mysteries of Demeter and Kore. In general, it is Pausanias who provides the most essential documentation: although he certainly was not present at each site on the day of initiation, he mentions the Mysteries which still existed in the second century of our era. Pausanias obeys a constant principle: the observation of the secrecy of the Mysteries. On the other hand, as we shall see, the obligation of silence does not seem to concern the entire *logos* on which the ceremony is founded, nor the whole of the rites of which it consists. As a result, despite our inability to shed light on the central rites of the Mysteries, we can restore their immediate context.

How were mystery cults defined (see Pakkanen 1996, 65–68)? In Arcadia, the word *mysteria*, which is applied to "secret things", appears in the decree *IG* V 2, 265 in connection with the Mysteries of Kore in Mantineia and in some inscriptions from Lykosoura in relation to the Mysteries of Despoina in the first and second centuries AD (*IG* V 2, 515b, line 10 and 516, line 15); we also find it in a scholion of Lycophron in connection with Dionysos at Phigalia (schol. Lycophr. *Alex*. 211). At Pheneos, Pausanias calls *mystai* ("mystes") the candidates for initiation (Paus. 8.15.1). From the same root we find in inscriptions the terms *myoumenoi* ("initiates", *IG* V 2, 543, lines 4–5), and *myesthai* ("to be initiated", *IG* V 2, 514, line 12). Lastly, in Pausanias' *Periegesis*, close to Tegea Dionysos carries the *epiklesis* Mystes, in reference to his initiation in the Mysteries of Eleusis (Paus. 8.54.5). Elsewhere, Pausanias uses the term *telete* ("festival, rite, initiation", from *telein*, "to achieve") for the Mysteries of Demeter (Paus. 8.15.1, 8.15.3, 8.15.4), Despoina (Paus. 8.37.2 and 8.37.8–9), the Great Goddesses (Paus. 8.29.1, 8.31.7) and Artemis (Paus. 8.23.1), as well as Antinoos (Paus. 8.9.8). *Atelestoi* twice indicates "the non-initiated" (Paus. 8.25.7 and 8.37.7). The term *orgia* ("cult objects, cult ceremony": Motte and Pirenne Delforge 1992) is reserved for Dionysos (Paus. 8.26.2, 8.5.5, 8.9.8; schol. Lycophr. *Alex*. 211). One can suppose that, in Pausanias' mind, these terms correspond to distinct realities, which unfortunately evade us, but in fact the three terms *mysteria*, *telete*, *orgia* indicate in more or less similar manners mystery ceremonies.

Divinities and places of Mysteries

The main divinities connected with mystery cults in Arcadia, as in other places, are Demeter and Kore (Figure 6.1). Under the *epiklesis* Eleusinia, Demeter was the subject of a *telete* at Pheneos where, according to Pausanias, the rites were the same as those of Eleusis (Paus. 8.15.1). Demeter has also Mysteries with typically Arcadian *epikleseis*, such as Demeter Kidaria and Demeter Thesmia at Pheneos (Paus. 8.15.3–4) and Demeter Erinys in Thelpousa (Paus. 8.25.7). Ceremonies associating Demeter and her daughter can be found at Bathos (Paus. 8.29.1) and Megalopolis (Paus. 8.31.7; *IG* V 2, 517, line 8), where they bear the name of the Great Goddesses, and also at

Figure 6.1 Demeter of Lykosoura (Athens, National Museum, neg. École Française d'Athènes)

Lykosoura, where Despoina, the girl-goddess, is the principal divinity of the sanctuary (Paus. 8.37.1 and 8.37.8–9). At Mantineia, the Koragia and the "sacred mysteries of the goddess" are celebrated in honor of only Kore (*IG* V 2, 265), which confirms the pre-eminence of the daughter versus the mother, which we observe at Lykosoura. Dionysos has orgiastic Mysteries in several places of Arcadia: close to Melangeia in Mantinike (Paus. 8.5.6), at Heraia (Paus. 8.26.2) and Phigalia (schol. Lycophr. *Alex.*, 211). At Heraia, Pausanias mentions a temple of Dionysos Polites ("Protector of the City") and another temple of Dionysos Auxites ("Who makes things grow"), as a building where the people of Heraia "celebrate orgiastic mysteries of Dionysos" (Paus. 8.26.1–2). The Mysteries are probably addressed to a universal Dionysos, rather than to Dionysos Auxites and Dionysos Polites; the second is a civic god for whom it is hard to imagine such ceremonies. It is also Dionysos in general, without any *epikleseis*, who is the object of *orgia* close to Melangeia (Paus. 8.6.5). The mention of Mysteries celebrated annually in honor of Artemis on Mt Knakalos, close to Kaphyai, is more unusual (Paus. 8.23.4), as the cult of Artemis is seldom a mystery cult: at Brauron, the *arkteia*, the rite central to the Brauronies, is called a *mysterion* ("mystery") by a scholiast of Aristophanes (schol. Aristoph., *Lysistr.* 645) and a *telete* by Hesychios (s.v. *arkteia*). Mysteries in honor of Artemis Pythia are known from Miletos (Rehm 1958, nos. 312, 326, 329, 333, 352, 360, 373, 381, 382), whereas some references to Mysteries of Artemis are known from Ephesos, Thasos, Mytilene, and Cyrene (Laumonier 1949, 61; Dobias-Lalou 2000, 210). In Arcadia proper, Artemis is associated with Despoina in the cult and probably the Mysteries of the *megaron* at Lykosoura (*infra*, p. 163). As for Antinoos, his cult at Mantineia was established by the Emperor Hadrian and comprised annual Mysteries (Paus. 8.9.7–8).

As far as the organization of the Mysteries is concerned, we are largely in the dark. In general, they were held annually, although at Bathos and Pheneos they were triannual (Paus. 8.29.1 and 8.15.2). Those ceremonies were generally celebrated within the civic framework, as indicated by Pausanias' references to the celebration of Mysteries by the inhabitants of the cities with the relevant sanctuaries: thus at Pheneos [*hoi Pheneatai*] ... *agousi* ... *teleten* (Paus. 8.15.1). The cult celebrated by the Meliasts close to Melangeia in Mantinike involved a male bacchic brotherhood, whereas nothing allows us to discern whether the worship was private or whether the Meliasts were, like the Koragoi at Mantineia (*IG* V 2, 265, line 27), ministers of the city (Paus. 8.6.5). At Lykosoura (Figure 6.2), the initiation fees provided significant sums to the city (*IG* V 2, 516, line 18) and the buildings (temple and *megaron*) and the cult group of Damophon indicate a certain opulence; in fact, the participants of the Mysteries probably came also from outside the city, for the cult was panarcadian. The text of *Periegesis* does not indicate a simple local sanctuary, like Pheneos, but a worship celebrated by all the Arcadians: "There is no divinity that the Arcadians venerate more than this Despoina", writes Pausanias (8.37.9) and it is to the Arcadians and not the inhabitants of Lykosoura that he attributes the celebration of the sacrifices and the Mysteries (Paus. 8.37.8). As far as the ministers of the cult are concerned, only one hierophant is attested, for the Great Goddesses of Megalopolis (*IG* V 2, 517, lines 8–9).

The locations of the sanctuaries with mystery cults are sometimes inside the cities (Mantineia, Megalopolis, Pheneos, Heraia and Phigalia), very close to them (Lykosoura, Figure 6.2), or a little further away (Pheneos, Kaphyai, Thelpousa, close to Melangeia, Bathos).[2] Urban sites and rural sites balance each other in number. Among the rural sites, two are close to springs (in Bathos and close to Melangeia). A location outside the city indicates a retreat of the worshippers, as is the case with initiation rituals. Thus at Kaphyai there are two sanctuaries of Artemis: one in the city devoted to Artemis Knakalesia, and another one devoted to Artemis (Pausanias does not mention an *epiklesis*), forming a "doublet", in the periphery of the *khora* on Mt Knakalos; it is in the latter that the Mysteries of the goddess were celebrated (Paus. 8.23.3–4).

Buildings reserved for the celebration of the Mysteries appear several times in the texts. Some could be located, even identified.[3] The people of Heraia had a building (*oikema*) where they celebrated orgiastic mysteries (Paus. 8.26.2). At Megalopolis, Pausanias mentions a large structure built for the celebration of the mysteries of the Great Goddesses. Was it a *megaron*? A lacuna in the manuscripts deprives us of the exact term, but the building was distinct from the *oikema* where the Periegete saw the statues of the founders of the Mysteries (Paus. 8.31.7). The word "megaron" appears on several occasions in the documents. A *megaron* is cited in Mantineia in inscription *IG* V 2, 266, line 27. Nikippa is honored in *IG* V 2, 265, line

Figure 6.2 Lykosoura: the temple and the steps (neg. M. Jost)

20 for having "given a roof to the mysteries" (Jost 1996, 196); she had probably had this building repaired, which was used at the same time for the Mysteries of Demeter and Kore (*IG* V 2, 266) and for those of Kore only (*IG* V 2, 265). Pausanias twice uses the word *megaron* for Arcadia. "At Lykosoura", he says, "close to the temple of Despoina, if one rises a little, there is to the right what is called (*to kaloumenon*) the *Megaron*. The Arcadians celebrate there the ceremonies with initiation and sacrifice to Despoina" (Paus. 8.37.8). By the expression *to kaloumenon*, the Periegete does not indicate a particular form of *megaron*, as Orlandini (1969–1970, 353) suggests; he quotes the local name of the monument. In Mantinike, close to Melangeia, "the Meliasts celebrate the orgiastic Mysteries of Dionysos and a *megaron* to Dionysos exists near the spring" (Paus. 8.6.5).

What does the word *megaron* signify? It seems that when it is used, like here, for a place where the Mysteries of Demeter or of Dionysos are celebrated, it indicates "an enclosed, sheltered place" (Hellmann 1992, 258–260; Bolanacchi-Condoléon 1992–1998, 473–490). It is a building, or at least an enclosure of walls, which protected the *mystai* from non-initiated eyes. To which we may add, according to the definition of Ammonios of Lamptrai, the idea of an altar (Tresp 1914, 91, no. 48). The *megaron* can contain pits (especially to bury the piglets of the Thesmophoria). The question whether the word indicates also underground structures, crypts, is more controversial and will not concern us here.

The site of Lykosoura offers, if we accept the traditional identification of Kourouniotes (1912, 142–161), a particularly illuminating example of a *megaron* (Figure 6.3). On the north slope of Terzi, to the southeast of the

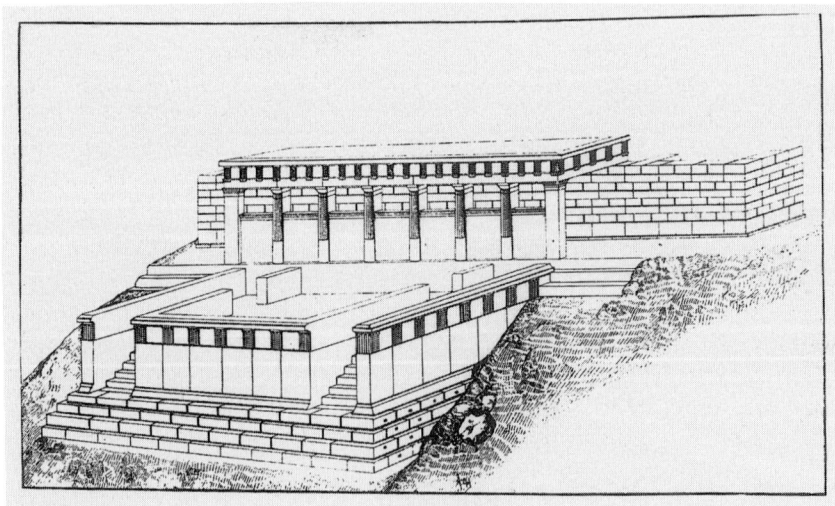

Figure 6.3 Lykosoura, reconstruction of the *Megaron* (after *ArchEph* 1912, 148)

temple, are found the remains of a building whose location corresponds to the references by Pausanias (8.37.8): "if one rises a little, there is to the right what is called the *Megaron*". On the *krepis*, it had a rectangular enclosure bordered by orthostats and framed by two staircases parallel to a wall. Above rose a portico, 9.50 m long, whose face consisted of half columns with stone slabs in between. Inside the enclosure must have been the altar: a large quantity of ashes and remains of carbonized bones were found there (Kourouniotes 1912, 148). Among the votive offerings found in the excavation, a series of terracotta figurines represent characters with heads of rams or bovids (Kavvadias [1897] 1898, 28; Kourouniotes 1912, 155–159). It may be, as we shall see on pp. 157–159, a representation of the actors of the Mysteries; these figurines thus constitute a major argument for the identification of this monument with the *Megaron* quoted by Pausanias.[4] This building is paralleled by the Great Altar of Pergamon (Kourouniotes 1912, 152) and possibly by the "Thesmophorion" on Thasos, built at the end of the fourth or the third century and perhaps contemporary (Muller 1996, 10–16).[5] Thus we have a building with such an arrangement that the ceremonies of the terrace were protected from public view, except for the portico, from where the old initiates (?) could see the rites (the height of the stone slabs did not exceed 1.36 m).

It remains to discuss the function of the ten steps laid out along the southern side of the temple on the slope of Terzi (Figure 6.2). The length of the higher steps is equal to that of the temple, whereas the length of the lower ones increases progressively. The width of the steps also increases gradually from the top (0.43 m) to the bottom (0.85 m) and so too their height (from 0.27 m at the top to 0.33 m at the bottom). *A priori*, this construction can be considered a supporting device; this is the idea proposed by Orlandos (1967–1968, 44 n.1, 45), who worked as an architect at Lykosoura. The slope is rather steep above the temple and the stone steps prevented the temple from being damaged by a landslide. Nevertheless, we can also think – and the two functions are not mutually exclusive – of a religious function. Loucas-Durie (1992, 87) suggests that spectators stood on the higher steps and sat on the lower steps. One cannot imagine, as do Ginouvès (1972, 68) and Orlandini (1969–1970, 354–357), that any event took place in the walkway to the east of the temple around the altar,[6] since from the steps to the east the view was indeed obstructed by the southern wall and the south-eastern corner of the temple. The distance of two meters between the steps and the temple is also insufficient to suggest *dromena*. On the other hand, the idea of *deiknumena* should not be excluded: it is possible that the priest appeared in the southern door frame to address the worshippers or to show them some object.

The reference to a *megaron* of Dionysos close to the source of the Meliasts in Mantinike is a rare occurrence of this term for Dionysos (Paus. 8.6.5). The word has been interpreted in different ways. Fougères (1898, 88–89, 266 n.8) considers it a great natural niche, a cave dug in the mass of Alogovrakhos, or a shadowy vault of ashes at the foot of Alesion. In the same spirit, Boyancé (1961, 117–118) identifies it with one of those bacchic caves, the importance of which in the Hellenistic period he has underlined, although these caves have their own designation (*antron*, *spelaion* or *mukhos*). An inscription of the Late Imperial period engraved on an altar in Thessalonike speaks in favor of a distinction between *megaron* and cave: a person would be at the same time, *archineokoros*, *archimagareus* (=*archimegareus*) and *pater spelaiou*, which seems to imply three different functions (Robert 1969, 990–1007). One will thus rather lean in favor of a monument, as in Heraia (Paus. 8.26.2). An enclosure wall found by Fougères and Bérard near the source Tripichi (source of Meliasts) has been identified by Fougères (1898, 86–89), thanks to the discovery of a statue of satyr with a flask, as the sanctuary of Dionysos. It is a rectangle measuring 37 × 22 m. Trenches opened in the interior did not allow the excavators to locate the building, either because it has disappeared as a result of the "low stability of the steep slope and the frequent erosion by rain" (Fougères 1890, 78), or because the trenches missed it.

An original monument is mentioned by Pausanias in relation to the Mysteries at Pheneos, the Petroma (Paus. 8.15.1–2). This consisted of "two large stones attached to each other". At the time of the *telete*, they were opened so that the writings relating to the Mysteries could be taken out and then placed back during the same night. Further up, there was a round top which contained the mask of Demeter Kidaria. The *mystai* were to meet in a room that Pausanias omits to mention. The Petroma was perhaps inside. At any rate, this cannot refer to a "rock cave" (Lévêque 1961, 107) nor even to an artificial cave dug in the rock, as some scholars have suggested (Stiglitz 1967, 136; Bérard 1974, 129). The description of Pausanias indicates man-made stones and suggests rather the idea of a stone receptacle with its lid; the whole construction would carry a hollow top. We can propose as a parallel a large stone cylinder discovered in 1959 in the sanctuary of Zeus at Lokroi Epizephyrioi, which contained bronze tablets bearing the administrative records of the sanctuary, dating to the fourth or third century (Maffre [2000] 2002, 310; Greco 1981, 76, 89–90).

On the other hand, the remains of the "telesterion" excavated by Kardara is not included here among the buildings sheltering the Mysteries, as the excavator relates this monument with an oracle in the "sanctuary of Aphrodite Erycine", which she excavated in northwest Arcadia (Kardara 1988, 129–143; *contra* Jost 1985, 59–60).

In Arcadia, as elsewhere, mystery ceremonies seem to have been celebrated at night. Pausanias (8.15.2) mentions this for the ceremonies at Pheneos and the scholiast of Lycophron for Phigalia (schol. Lycophr. *Alex.* 211), whereas lamps have been found at Bathos and Lykosoura (Bather and Yorke 1892–1893, 228; Loucas and Loucas-Durie 1985–1986, 563; cf. *IG*

V 2, 514, line 16). As far as the content of the Mysteries is concerned, information about those of Artemis and Dionysos is almost entirely non-existent. We only have one reference to dances and torches for Dionysos (schol. Lycophr. *Alex.* 211); in fact these are elements that often accompany the *orgia* of the god of the sap and the tree (Roux 1970, 61). For the other *orgia* of Dionysos, the existence at Heraia and probably also in Mantinike of buildings for the celebration of Mysteries suggests an organized and institutionalized cult. We will stress the Mysteries of Demeter and her daughter, for whom we have the richest information. Two cases arise: certain mystery ceremonies are supposed to derive from Eleusis, the ritual of which they reproduce; others, on the contrary, without being inevitably free from all "eleusinism", comprise original features and have a distinctly local character.

Demeter and Kore: the Eleusinian model

Demeter Eleusinia is not always accompanied by Mysteries. At Basilis, if we believe Nikias (according to Atheneus, *Deipn.*, 13.609 e–f), Demeter Eleusinia was honored in a *heorte* ("festival"), whose climax consisted of a beauty contest. The worship presented an undeniable character of antiquity and its contents had nothing to do with the eleusinian rites; the *epiklesis* Eleusinia was embedded in a substratum which remained dominant in the worship (see Jost 1985, 338–340, with the examination of the contestable thesis which attaches Eleusinia to an ancient Eleuthia). On the other hand, at Thelpousa, Demeter Eleusinia, her daughter, and Dionysos evoke the pantheon of Eleusis and we do not know if the absence of any reference to Mysteries by Pausanias conforms with reality or whether it was just an omission on his part (Paus. 8.25.3; Jost 1985, 311–312). Mysteries are certain at Pheneos: the Pheneatians, writes Pausanias, "celebrate a ceremony with initiation (*telete*) in honor of the goddess [Demeter Eleusinia], and affirm that the rites practised (*ta dromena*) at Eleusis and those instituted on their premises were the same (*ta auta*)"; the Periegete explains this similarity by a etiological legend: "Indeed, Naos arrived on their premises on the order of an oracle from Delphi, and Naos was a third generation descendant of Eumolpos" (Paus. 8.15.1). The whole matter is presented like a tradition of Pheneos. We can suppose that, in spite of her omission, Kore was associated with Demeter in the worship: we note the same gap concerning the sanctuary of Eleusis where it would be difficult to deny the role played by the daughter (Paus. 1.38.1–7). Moreover, Kore, according to a legend of Pheneos preserved by Konon, was carried away by Plouton to his underground kingdom through a crack of Mt Cyllene, in the territory of Pheneos (Konon, *Narr.* 15 = *FGrH* 26 F 1: cf. Imhoof-Blumer and Gardner 1964, 98).

In Megalopolis, the Great Goddesses, Demeter and Kore (called Soteira by the Arcadians) were also honored, according to Pausanias, in Mysteries which the local tradition attributed to founders who imitated the Eleusinian

Mysteries. At the time of Pausanias, in a building of the sanctuary, stood "human figures: those of Kallignotos and Mentas, and Sosigenes and Polos; it is them who instituted, they say, in Megalopolis, for the first time the mysteries of the Great Goddesses, whose rites are replicas of those of Eleusis" (Paus. 8.31.7).

It is difficult to define the character of the Great Goddesses of Megalopolis (on Kore's address as Soteira and the presence of Herakles Dactylos of Ida beside the Goddesses, see Jost 1994, 119–129). At any rate, they were sufficiently close to the goddesses of Eleusis so that their Mysteries replicated and copied those of Eleusis: this is what is probably indicated by the use of the word *mimemata*. Furthermore, even the name of the priestly functions was copied from Eleusis: a decree taken by the Achaeans at Lykosoura and roughly contemporary with Pausanias, quotes a certain Saon, "hierophant of the Great Goddesses", who is a "descendant of the founders of the Mysteries [of Megalopolis]" (*IG* V 2, 517, lines 8–9).

To what period can the "doublet" cults of Pheneos and Megalopolis be dated and what exactly is their connection to Eleusis? The answer is not simple.

At Pheneos, everything suggests a connection between Demeter Eleusinia and Eleusis, including the similarity of the rites and the etiologic myth of the local cult. There is thus no reason to see in the goddess a descendant of a "prehellenic" Eleuthia (Stiglitz 1967, 138–139; Jost 1985, 318). It remains to be understood how Mysteries, secret by definition, could have resulted in the "doublets" of Arcadia without demonstrating impiety on the part of those who spread them. A solution would be to consider the sanctuary of Demeter Eleusinia an offspring of Eleusis. *A priori*, this is suggested by the legend according to which the founder of the Mysteries of Pheneos was a descendant of Eumolpos, the priest of Eleusis. A parallel could be found in the legend narrated by the Phliasians: the ceremonies of the Mysteries celebrated at Keleai, close to Phlious, "replicated those of Eleusis" (Paus. 2.14.2). Despite the variations in some details, "the people of Phlious", writes Pausanias, "agree that they replicate the cult of Eleusis. They say that it was Dysaules, brother of Keleos, a refugee in their country, who instituted the initiation after having been driven out of Eleusis by Ion." Pausanias does not consider this local version accurate and doubts that Dysaules came from Eleusis. In fact, although Pausanias' arguments in this case are not valid,[7] we could still doubt that the priestly families of Eleusis would have sought to expand the cult. We would think rather that Eleusis, whose "uniqueness" is attested by some texts (Epiktetos, *Diatribai*, 3.21.11–14; *POxy* 1612; cf. Fraser 1972, 339–340), "wished to remain unique", as Burkert (1987, 38) has suggested; he concludes that "it largely succeeded in doing this"; indeed, the sanctuaries whose ritual can be related to Eleusis are exceptional.[8] Could we not think that at Pheneos, as at Keleai, the local legends that presented the founders of the Mysteries as coming from Eleusis had been invented by the Pheneatians and the Phliasians in order to authenticate their loan? The Arcadians, moreover, also gave to Arkas an Eleusinian master, Triptolemos, when he spread the cultivation of cereals in Arcadia (Paus. 8.4.1). While preserving the Mysteries of Demeter Kidaria, which were authentically Arcadian (Paus. 8.15.2–3), the people of Pheneos had assumed the right to introduce locally an Eleusinian "doublet". As the process could appear quite daring, they found support in the oracle of Delphi, which would have given the order to Naos to found the mysteries (Paus. 8.15.1).

How far back does this loan go? The tradition placed the action of Naos three generations after Eumolpos, which would mean the fourteenth century according to the mythical chronology given by the Parian Marble; thus, it lent a remarkable antiquity to him. Historically, the first indications that Eleusis was known in the Peloponnese do not date before the fifth century (Jost 1985, 354). Still, generalizations should be avoided: according to Herodotos, at the time of the Persian Wars the Spartan Demaratos "did not know the rites used in the mysteries of Eleusis" (Hdt. 8.65). We can suggest that the fifth century was the *terminus post quem* for this Eleusinian "doublet".

The Mysteries of the Great Goddesses at Megalopolis were established after the foundation of the city in 370/69, but we do not have definite evidence to date them either to the end of third or in the second century, as some authors do (Dickins 1905–1906, 128–130; Loucas-Durie, 1992, 89–92), or even earlier. A second-century date is based primarily on a reference to Sosigenes, the name of one of the founders, given as the father of a *damiorgos* in an inscription of Megalopolis of this time (*IG* V 2, 443, line 29). The existence of this Sosigenes suggests that the founders named by Pausanias were historical personalities (*contra* Stiglitz 1967, 22, n.22), but nothing proves that this was the founder himself and not one of his descendants, or even another person. Thus a dating to the third or second centuries is not certain, especially as there are arguments for an even earlier date. The sanctuary of the Great Goddesses, which was situated in the west part of the agora and corresponded to the sanctuary of Zeus Soter in the east, seems to belong to the original plan of this site. Furthermore, it contained statues brought from Trapezous at the time of the synoecism, when the inhabitants of this agglomeration were punished because they had refused to come to populate Megalopolis (Paus. 8.31.5). There does not exist a particular reason to think that the institution of the Mysteries was posterior to the establishment of the sanctuary. We would thus be inclined to propose that the Mysteries were founded shortly after the foundation of the *Megale Polis*.

The name of Sosigenes is, as Dickins (1905–1906, 129) pointed out, more frequent in Attica than in Arcadia. In the inscription of Megalopolis which quotes it, it must however designate a citizen of this city, since this person is the father of a *damiorgos* (i.e. a local magistrate). If Sosigenes had any relation to the founder, it would indicate an Arcadian origin of this personality; at any rate, it is doubtful that he would have been a "delegate" from Eleusis, as Dickins (1905–1906, 129) believed. We can thus consider the Mysteries of the Great Goddesses a loan by the city of Megalopolis, which intended to raise its religious prestige. That the worship needed to be authorized by Eleusis, insofar as it represented a disclosure of the Mysteries, is possible; but one can hardly imagine an initiative of Eleusis "to export" its Mysteries. As at Pheneos with Demeter Eleusinia and Demeter Kidaria, the mysteries of the Great Goddesses formed the Eleusinian equivalent of Mysteries with indigenous characters, definitely affirmed at Lykosoura.[9]

A somewhat particular case is presented by the Mysteries of Demeter Thesmia at Pheneos, where we suspect the existence of both Eleusinian and Orphic features. Before the introduction of Demeter Eleusinia and her Mysteries by Naos, Demeter, "in her wandering travels" would have been accommodated by the Pheneations; she would have given them, in thanks for their presents of hospitality, "all the vegetables, except broad bean". Trisaules and Damithales, who had received the goddess, instituted a festival with initiation (*telete*) in honor of Demeter Thesmia (Paus. 8.15.3–4). The subject of the reception of Demeter by the mortals is found in Attica, especially at Eleusis, where king Keleos receives the goddess in his palace (*Homeric Hymn to Demeter*, 179–230) and on the banks of Ilissos where Phytalos is given the fig tree by her as a sign of gratitude for his hospitality (Paus. 1.37.2). At Eleusis, after the return of Kore, Demeter returns to humankind the cultivated plants, of which she had deprived them, and establishes her Mysteries. The legend of Phytalos is closer to that of Pheneos (Demeter introduces a new cultivation), but it does not lead to the creation of Mysteries. The pheneatic tradition has its starting point, as in Attica (see Richardson 1974, 178), in the hospitality offered to Demeter by mortals, but an explicit bond between this reception, the gift of cultivation by the goddess and the Mysteries founded in her honor is found only in the Arcadian legend. The *epiklesis* Thesmia, "who taught the laws, the precepts [of agriculture]" to people, underlines this singularity (Jost 1985, 323–324).

"The reason for which broad bean is considered impure is the subject of a sacred *logos*", adds Pausanias (Paus. 8.15.4). The broad bean was a taboo, under the terms of a ritual prohibition which has a parallel in orphico-pythagorian doctrines. The broad bean of the Pythagorians relates at the same time to death and reproduction. A plant with a hollow stem, it is a passage point between the living and the dead. In addition, the broad bean "is indeed the marked source of generation in the plant world, to the extent that it appears as a mixture of blood and genitals in the fantasies of Pythagoreans" (Detienne 1979, 85). Under these conditions, to eat broad bean was like spilling blood: "It is a crime equal to eating broad beans and the head of one's parents", notes J. Lydus (*De mensibus* 4.43). The prohibition to consume broad bean derives from such views. It is difficult to determine how these doctrines could have been established at Pheneos. It is also attested at Eleusis, which was penetrated by orphism and pythagorianism as of the fifth century: "along the road [from Athens to Eleusis]", narrates Pausanias, "they have built a temple ... which they call temple of Kyamites (God of broad bean). I can say nothing certain about this: was he the first to sow broad beans? Did they take as a patron a hero because they could not bring back to Demeter the invention of broad beans? Those who have seen the ceremony of initiation at Eleusis or who have read the collections called Orphic know what I want to say" (Paus. 1.37.4). An Eleusinian intermediary is thus not excluded.

As for the rest of the Mysteries of Demeter Thesmia we know next to nothing. Even if the *epiklesis* Thesmia is related to Thesmophoros, it is not sufficient to suggest Thesmophoria there (Stiglitz 1967, 143), a celebration exclusively for women.

Demeter and Kore: the indigenous cults

Other Arcadian Mysteries have a clearly indigenous character, although an Eleusinian influence cannot be excluded. The mark of Eleusis is observed in the attributes which characterize cult representations, in particular the torch and the cist, a basket containing the sacred objects and on which Demeter often sits in the Eleusinian iconography. "In Thelpousa, the effigy of Demeter Erinys holds what is called the cist and, in her right hand, a torch" (Paus. 8.25.7). At Lykosoura, Demeter and Despoina are shown sitting in the center of the cult group; Demeter rests her left hand on the shoulder of Despoina in a gesture of tenderness reminiscent of the iconography of the Parthenon. "Demeter", writes Pausanias, "carries a torch in the right hand ... Despoina has a sceptre and what is called the cist on her knees; she holds the cist in her right hand" (Paus. 8.37.4). The distribution of cult attributes – the cist and the sceptre are in Despoina's hands – offers a material translation of the pre-eminence of this goddess, who gives her name to the sanctuary ("sanctuary of Despoina": *IG* V 2, 514). The Eleusinian influences remain superficial here and do not affect the essence of the cult, as we shall see later.

In more than one case we can get an idea of the originality of the Mysteries only through their cult environment, which suggests local divinities. Within the framework of the festival called Koragia, in Mantineia, Kore alone receives the Mysteries, as *IG* V 2, 265, lines 1–12 shows: "they were about to proceed to the secret Mysteries of *the* goddess", or the mention of the peplos of *the* goddess (ibid., line 20). Kore is here independent of Demeter and probably different from the attic Kore. The context of the Mysteries appears to indicate this: the essential moment of the festival of Koragia is indeed the transportation of the statue of the goddess from the temple to the house of a private individual. Whether it relates to the cycle of vegetation, celebrates the anniversary of the introduction of the cult, or commemorates a divine visit, the ritual that concerns Kore is specifically Mantineian (Jost 1996, 200).

At Bathos it is also the cult context which suggests that the Great Goddesses had a local character. The Mysteries were celebrated every two years, in relation to a spring called Olympias which flowed once every two years and close to which a fire burned. At the side they sacrificed to the Flashes, the Storms and the Thunderbolts (Paus. 8.29.1). The ceremony – not annual but triannual – was thus related to a natural phenomenon and it is reasonable to accept that it addressed old divinities of nature.

The Mysteries of Demeter Kidaria at Pheneos are illuminated by the *epiklesis* of the goddess and the rites which surround the *telete*. The *epiklesis* of the goddess derives from the name of a peaceful and solemn Arcadian dance (Jost 1985, 320–322). The dance is not frequently related to Demeter, and Pausanias does not provide any explanation for it: perhaps the Mysteries included some episode expressed by dances. The Periegete, without revealing any essential information, provides several interesting indications about the *telete*. After having described the Petroma (*supra*, p. 150) he indicates that "when they celebrate every two years the initiation known as 'major', they open these stones and, after having taken out the writings referring to initiation and read them so that the *mystai* hear them, they put them back the same night" (Paus. 8.15.2). During the "major" initiation, the priest also wears on his face the mask of Demeter Kidaria, which he has taken from the higher part of the Petroma, and he strikes with rods ("verges"), according to some tradition (*kata logon tina*) the inhabitants of the netherworld (Paus. 8.15.3).[10]

The "major" triannual *telete* concerned Demeter Kidaria. Perhaps the ordinary *telete*, which was to alternate with the preceding one, was that of Demeter Eleusinia whose sanctuary was close to that of Demeter Kidaria but distinct from it. Pausanias calls this ceremony simply *telete* (Paus. 8.15.1, and *supra*, p. 151). The initiation in the Mysteries of Demeter Kidaria was accompanied by two rites, which did not belong to the secret part of the Mysteries. As for the writings "referring to initiation", Pausanias does not of course reveal their content, which was reserved only for the *mystai*. One can think either of simple regulations of the Mysteries (Nilsson 1906, 344), or of written sacred texts which, like the orphic books (Sabatucci 1982, 43, 85), contained not only the indication of rituals but a myth relating to Demeter Kidaria; the reading of these texts would have constituted the essential moment of the night ceremony. The extreme veneration which the Petroma enjoyed (people swore by it: Paus. 8.15.2) would rather suggest the second possibility. One would thus have a second manifestation of the orphico-pythagorism at Pheneos (cf. *supra*, p. 154). As for the ritual of scourging, obviously Pausanias does not know its etiologic legend: it was to form part of the *logos* of the Mysteries to which he does not seem to have been initiated.[11] The priest – one would expect a priestess – face covered with the mask of Demeter Kidaria, struck the inhabitants of the netherworld: those were chthonic forces, which the priest called by exerting on them a kind of constraint. Behind the priest, it was the goddess herself who ordered the dormant forces to wake up to a new life.[12] The rite mentioned by Pausanias thus allows us to see in Demeter Kidaria an ancient divinity of vegetation, whose bonds with the dance *kidaris*, implied by the *epiklesis*, were perhaps clear for the *mystai* but remain obscure for us.

If we admit that the *logos* of Demeter Kidaria formed part of the Mysteries, this was not the case of the legend of Demeter Erinys in Thelpousa, which Pausanias describes in detail (Paus. 8.25.7): "When Demeter wandered in search of her daughter, Poseidon, according to the legend, started to follow her, taken with desire to mate with her; then, disguised as a mare, she went to pasture mixed with the mares of Onkos, but Poseidon realized that he has been tricked and mates with Demeter after having taken the shape of a male horse." From this union were born the horse Arion and a girl. The *logos* was thus known to all; only the name of Demeter's daughter was subjected to the secrecy of the Mysteries. An identical legend existed in Phigalia, where the absence of a mystery cult may have supported the diffusion of the legend (the girl there bore the name of Despoina: Paus. 8.42.1). Moreover, the horse Arion, born from the union of Demeter Erinys and Poseidon, was known in the *Iliad* and the *Thebais*, which lifted the secrecy (in the same manner, Pausanias 8.37.9 narrates how Persephone, the true name of Kore, was revealed by Pamphos and Homer).

The best-known Arcadian indigenous Mysteries are those of Despoina (the "Mistress") at Lykosoura, because the archaeological data come to alleviate Pausanias' silence. The excavations of the *Megaron* are of major interest because of the discovery by Kontopoulos of some 140 terracotta figurines with animal heads (Kavvadias [1897] 1898, 28; Kourouniotes 1912, 142, 155–159): they represent standing figures, about 15 cm tall, motionless, dressed with a himation, with the head of a ram or cattle; generally they carry a basket on the head; some are surely male, others could be female (Figures 6.4, 6.5). These statuettes are difficult to date: according to Kourouniotes the drapery of the older ones may suggest a fourth-century date, but the preserved specimens are not older than the second to first century BC. A more recent series would date to the first century AD. Perdrizet (1899, 635) suggested that these figurines were representations of divinities. This is not very likely; it seems, rather, that they represent masked people. They could have been priests and priestesses: both are attested in Lykosoura (Durie 1984, 137–147), whereas parallels can be seen in the cult of Demeter Kidaria at Pheneos, which was served by a masked priest (Paus. 8.15.3), or in the fragments of a small krater from Brauron on which a female priestess (?) and a man, carrying masks of bears, are represented (Kahil 1977; Reeder 1995, 322, 327–328 no. 100, with earlier bibliography).[13] These masked priests would have taken part in the *dromena* of the Mysteries. The basket that the figurines carry suggests, however, another possibility: couldn't these *kanephoroi* be initiates, who, after having taken

Figure 6.4 Figurine with criomorphic head (neg. M. Jost)

Figure 6.5 Criomorphic head (neg. M. Jost)

part in the procession while carrying the sacrificial material, would have dedicated these offerings, pointing out the task that they had fulfilled? Women could also be *mystai*, as attested by the sacred law which prohibits from initiation "pregnant or nursing women" (*IG* V 2, 514, line 12–13). At any rate, the number of the statuettes suggests that they were ex-votos offered by the worshippers: it is probable that besides the priests, the *mystai* also wore zoomorphic masks.[14] If the *kanephoria* were a common part in many festivals, wearing animal masks is unusual. We can cite the fragments of the above-mentioned small krater from Brauron, possibly two or three masks of the sanctuary of Artemis Orthia (Loucas and Loucas-Durie 1985–1986, 572, n.5) and the representations of the Cabiric vases from Thebes (Daumas 1998, 30–31). But only Cyprus offers real parallels: several figurines of the archaic period represent characters in the process of wearing or removing a mask of a bull, or holding it with both hands ("worshippers or priests": Laurens and Louka 1987, 23–32, with earlier bibliography). But the most obvious connection is provided by the sculpted decoration of the veil of Despoina.

One of the decorative bands on a skirt of the sculpted veil of Despoina[15] represents about fifteen characters disguised as animals (Figures 6.6, 6.7, 6.8;

Figure 6.6 The veil of Lykosoura (detail from the frieze 1)

some figures, very mutilated, are undecipherable). Besides other more conventional motifs (eagles and lightnings, marine *thiasos*, Nike carrying a *thymiaterion*), this procession of characters with animal appearance is original: by drawing parallels to the terracotta figurines from the *Megaron* one can attribute to it a religious significance related to the Mysteries of Despoina. The head and, in several cases, the ends of the limbs of these figures belong to the animal world, but they are dressed as humans and show human attitudes and gestures (some play music, others dance). Given these attributes, these must be humans disguised as animals, rather than animal demons (Dickins 1906–1907, 393–394): they wear masks and their arms and their legs are covered or prolonged by animal limb additions. According to the identifications suggested by Lévy (1968, 147–151), there are four musicians: a fox (?) playing the double flute and a horse playing a trigonon (?), then an equid playing the kithara and a horse blowing in a diaulos. The other figures (we can recognize two pigs, three rams and an ass) move while dancing. If the first is satisfied to beat time, several of them have a whirling movement which results in a torsion of the body, with the head turned to the back (Lévy 1968, 182). The second figure even recalls, by his attitude, the maenad of a black-figured

Figure 6.7 The veil of Lykosoura (detail from the frieze 2)

cup at Würzburg (Séchan 1930, 176, fig. 41). The animated dance performed by the masked figures situates us in an orgiastic environment.

Thus, the terracotta figurines found in the *Megaron* and the representations of the veil of Despoina make it possible to suggest that during the celebration of the Mysteries a procession of *kanephoroi* took place and dances were carried out by *mystai* and priests carrying masks and limbs of animals, perhaps on the terrace of the altar of the *Megaron*. This original rite suggests a divinity protecting animals, associated not with *one* particular animal, like Artemis at Brauron, but protecting various domestic species (the predator fox (?) is separate). The bulls, the rams and the pigs are animals related to the idea of fertility; the presence of equids recalls that at Phigalia Despoina was born from the union of Poseidon-horse with Demeter-mare (*supra*,

Figure 6.8 The veil of Lykosoura (detail from the frieze 3)

p. 157 and Paus. 8.42.1). As we shall see, the sacrifices at the *Megaron* and certain details of the cult group agree with the orgiastic character of the mystical ceremony.

Strictly speaking, the sacrifice conducted in the *Megaron* – of which ashes and fragments of burned bones have been found – is not part of the Mysteries as Pausanias describes them (Paus. 8.37.8). It constituted, however, an essential accompaniment and its atmosphere is reminiscent of the masked dances. The Arcadians, says Pausanias, "sacrifice numerous and abundant victims. Each one of them sacrifices whatever animal he has; instead of slicing the throat of the victims as in the other sacrifices, each one detaches a random member of the sacrificial animal by cutting it." The freedom of choosing the victims, as well as their abundance, is characteristic of these sacrifices. But most remarkable is the manner of killing the victims, which recalls the orgiastic cult of Dionysos: representations show indeed Maenads cutting up their prey not by tearing them, like the Bacchae of Euripides, but by cutting them randomly (Fuchs 1959, pls. 15–19). The sacrifices of the *Megaron* thus proceeded in the same unrestrained atmosphere as the masked dances. They contrast with the offerings of vegetables on the altar of Despoina, where fruits "of all the cultivated trees" were offered, except for the pomegranate (Paus. 8.37.7), which is reminiscent of the role played by this fruit in the *Homeric Hymn to Demeter* (370–374). Without repeating the Eleusinian character of the attributes of Demeter and Kore (*supra*, p. 155), we can observe in the cult group of Lykosoura several features which make it possible to confirm the connection of Despoina with the animals, as well as the orgiastic character of her Mysteries. This especially appears in the cult environment of the Goddesses.

Artemis was represented to the right of Demeter. She was shown as a huntress goddess, with a skin of stag, a quiver on the right shoulder, and a hunting dog at her side. In one hand she held a torch, in the other snakes, which indicate the chthonic component of her personality (Paus. 8.37.4; Jost 1985, 334–335). The association of Artemis with the central group, composed of Demeter and Despoina, astonished Pausanias, who tried to justify it with a legend probably borrowed from Herodotos (Paus. 8.37.6; Hdt. 2, 156): "[the tradition] which makes Artemis the daughter of Demeter, and not of Leto, comes from Egypt, and it is Aeschylos, son of Euphorion, who taught it to the Greeks". In fact, bringing together Artemis and Despoina is not due so much to their biological relationship, but rather to their natural affinities. The sphere common to both goddesses is the animal world. The Despoina evoked in the masked dances relates to the domestic animals, but, according to the Arcadians (Paus. 8.10.10), a legend also attributed to her a sacred hound, much like as in another legend a hound is attributed to Artemis: Arkesilaos, a ninth generation ancestor of Lydiades, had seen one day at Lykosoura a hound devoted to Despoina, overpowered by old age; its collar carried the inscription: "I was a fawn when I was captured, and Agapenor was then leaving for Troy". Affinities between Artemis and Despoina, which explain the presence of the former in the cult group, do not, however, appear to allow us to see in "Artemis" the "true name" of Despoina (Loucas-Durie 1987–1988, 401–419); it is better to accept that we cannot know the name, which was the object of a revelation to the *mystai*.

Another religious circle is evoked with Anytos, the Kouretes, and the Korybantes. Anytos was, according to the Arcadians, Despoina's fosterfather (Paus. 8.37.5; Loucas-Durie 1989, 105–114). He belonged to the race of the Titans and was represented armed, like the giant Hoplodamos next to Rhea (Paus. 8.36.2). As a Titan, he was responsible for Dionysos' sufferings (Paus. 8.37.3), which introduces an orgiastic note in the cult of Despoina – an element already noted. The Kouretes and the Korybantes, which were sculpted, the former on the footboard of the goddesses and the latter on the base of the cult group, belong to the same family of armed *propoloi* as Anytos. The Korybantes are associated with Rhea, under her various names (Mother of the Gods or Great Mother, Cybele in Phrygia); the Kouretes are related to the Great Kouros. Very often confused in the literature, they were considered in Lykosoura "two distinct races" and their legend was the object of a sacred *logos*, which formed part of the Mysteries of Despoina (Paus.

8.37.6; Jost 1985, 328). One can attach to the same religious sphere the altar of the Great Mother, in front of the temple (Paus. 8.38.7), the floor mosaic which covers the cella in front of the cult group (it represents two lions: Lehmann 1964, 191; *contra* Loucas-Durie 1987–1988, 401–419), as well as the motif of lions and tambourine, which decorates the footboard of the goddesses (Levy and Marcadé 1972, fig. 40).

Overall, the Mysteries of the *Megaron* probably had nothing to do with those of Eleusis. The maiden goddess, Despoina, was more significant there than Demeter; the sacrifices in which animals were randomly cut, the masked dances at the sound of the flutes or the kithara, the clash of arms and the cymbals of the Kouretes, the Korybantes, and the Great Mother indicate a much more "inspired" and "enthusiastic" climate, which makes the cult at Lykosoura original.[16]

In general, the secrecy of the Mysteries can be less absolute than it is sometimes believed. It always applies to the "true name" of the divinities, whose evocation is reserved only for the initiates. Certain divine legends remained secret, but whole passages were known to those who had not been initiated. Part of the ritual was also revealed, such as sacrifices at Lykosoura and rites at Pheneos, although their contents and significance remained secret. To these bits of knowledge are added the archaeological finds from Lykosoura. Ultimately, we can discern in the Mysteries of Arcadia both a strong Eleusinian influence and an original, distinct and indigenous core.

Notes

1 I would like to thank Michael Cosmopoulos for translating my text into English.
2 See Table 6.1. For the identifications of the sanctuaries of Megalopolis, Lykosoura, Melangeia, and Bathos, see Jost (1985, s.v.). For the sanctuary of Demeter Thesmia, in the Pheneatis, see Tausend (1999, 352–355). The locations of the other sanctuaries have not been identified.
3 See below for Lykosoura and close to Melangeia. The place called Bathos, where the Mysteries of the Great Goddesses were celebrated, could have been near the River Alpheios, at a location called "Vathy Rhevma". British excavations there have revealed material that points towards a female cult (see Bather and Yorke 1892–1893, 227–229). The existence of Mysteries would presuppose the presence of a building or a wall securing the secret of the rites, but no such structures were found at the site.
4 Orlandini (1969–1970, 349–353) has tried to identify this monument with the temple of Pan, mentioned above the *Megaron* by Pausanias (8.37.11). He draws his argument from a figurine of a satyr, found during the excavation of the *Megaron* by Kontopoulos (Kavvadias [1897] 1898, 28), which, however, could not have been the "small statue of Pan" mentioned by Pausanias. Furthermore, Orlandini cannot explain the presence of animal-headed figures in relation to Pan: he refers to a "climate of symbiosis" (1969–1970, 351) between the cult of Pan and that of Despoina, which remains to be proved. These figurines acquire their meaning only through their connection with the cult of Despoina, whose sculpted veil bears the same type of representations (*supra*, pp. 159–160). For affinities of the *Megaron* with prehistoric *telesteria* see Loucas and Loucas-Durie (1988, 25–34).

5 The *Megaron* of Lykosoura appears to have been contemporary with the temple. Kourouniotes dates it to the second century BC. The temple dates either to the second century (Dickins, 1905–1906, 112–120; Billot 1997, 278) or earlier (Jost 1985, 174–175).
6 Nielsen (2000, 120), as did Ginouvès before him, proposes that the steps extended towards the east (*contra* Léonardos [1896] 1897, 115 and pl. 1). Orlandini (1969–1970, 354–357) sees in the steps a "theatral area", whereas the main *Megaron* would have been an opening in the ground (*chasma*) or a sacred cavity (*bothros*) opened nearby, on the north slope of the Terzi hill. The possibility of the existence of this cavity should be taken with caution and a *megaron* open to the winds is not well conceived. Therefore, I agree with the identification proposed by Kourouniotes.
7 He draws his argument from the fact that Dysayles is not one of those to whom Demeter taught her Mysteries according to the *Homeric Hymn to Demeter* (vv. 474–476). The same thing could be said about Naos.
8 See Farnell (1907, 200–201). For Alexandria, Fraser (1972, 198–201) concludes that there were not any Mysteries in the proper sense of the term in the Alexandrine agglomeration of Eleusis, but only an important celebration in honor of Demeter. See also Sworonek and Traczkow (1981, 131–144).
9 Although it is not certain, it might be possible to assign to the cult of Demeter and Kore in Mantineia (*IG* V 2, 265) the same Eleusinian character of the goddesses as at Pheneos and Megalopolis, because of its apparent banality (Jost 1985, 345–346).
10 Paus. 8.15.3. *Hypochthonious* is a corrected form of *epichthonious*, which is traditioned by the manuscripts. *Epichthonious* offers an acceptable meaning (it reminds of human flagellations in Sparta), but the use of this poetic term to indicate people does not belong to Pausanias' prose.
11 When he knows a sacred myth but does not want to disclose it to those who have not been initiated, Pausanias always mentions it (cf. Paus. 8.37.6). For the reference to books, cf. also the Mysteries of Andania (Sokolowsky 1969, 120–129, no. 65, line 12), where we know of books placed by the hierophant Mnasistratos at the same time as a basket and the "rest of the objects that have been made for the Mysteries". The "books" of Andania are not easier to define than at Pheneos.
12 Cf. Bérard (1974, 80–82, 129), in connection with "the loud call" ("l'appel cogné"), which brings the *anodos* of Persephone.
13 It has been suggested that these two can be identified with Kallisto and Arkas (Reeder 1995, 327–328).
14 Loucas and Loucas-Durie (1985–1986, 561–578) suggest that these figurines correspond to the *agalma* mentioned in *IG* V 2, 514, line 15, among the objects that must "use those who present the offerings (*tous thyontas*) for the sacrificial ceremony". According to them, the figurines would have been "sacrificed" on the altar as substitutes for human sacrifices. This hypothesis does not appear well founded: *agalma* is not used for figurines and the verb *thyo* can apply to offerings that are not consumed, as the lamps of line 16 (cf. Casabona 1966, 72–75); see also Voutiras 1999, 235–249.
15 The date of the cult statue of Despoina is not known with certainty (see Lévy and Marcadé 1972, 967–1004). According to Marcadé, nothing in the style of the statue excludes a date to the third century. Themelis' suggestion, that the activities of Damophon took place in the end of the third or the beginning of the second century, is based on an inscription, the precise date of which is uncertain. See Themelis (1993a, 24–40; 1993b, 99–109; 1994, 31–32; 1996, 169–172, 184–185).
16 It remains unknown whether some ceremonies took place in the opening of the south gate to the temple (cf. *supra*, p. 199).

References

Bather, A.G. and V.W. Yorke, 1892–1893: "Excavations on the probable sites of Basilis and Bathos", *JHS* 13, 227–229.

Bérard, Cl., 1974: *Anodoi. Essai sur l'imagerie des passages chthoniens*. Institut suisse de Rome, Rome.

Billot M.-F., 1997: "Le décor des toits de Grèce du IIIe s. av. J.C. au IIIe ap. J. C", *BCH* 121, 235–290.

Bolanacchi-Condoléon, E., 1992–1998: "*Megarou Episkepsis, I*", *Horos* 10–12, 473–490.

Boyancé, P., 1961: "L'antre dans les mystères de Dionysos", *Rendiconti dell'Academia di Archeologia, Lettere e Belle Arti di Napoli* 33, 117–118.

Burkert, W., 1987: *Ancient Mystery Cults*. Harvard University Press, Cambridge, Mass.

Casabona, J., 1966: *Recherches sur le vocabulaire des sacrifices en grec des origines à la fin de l'époque classique*. Ophrys, Aix-en-Provence.

Daumas, M., 1998: *Cabiriaca. Recherches sur l'iconographie du culte des Cabires*. De Boccard, Paris.

Detienne, M., 1979: *Dionysos Slain* (trs. M. and L. Muellner). The Johns Hopkins University Press, Baltimore, Md.

Dickins, G., 1905–1906: "Damophon of Messene", *BSA* 12, 109–136.

Dickins G., 1906–1907: "Damophon of Messene II", *BSA* 13, 357–404.

Dobias-Lalou, C., 2000: *Le dialecte des inscriptions grecques de Cyrène*. Center d'Études Archéologiques de la Méditerranée, Paris.

Durie, E., 1984: "Les fonctions sacerdotales au sanctuaire de Despoina à Lykosoura-Arcadie", *Horos* 2, 137–147.

Farnell, L., 1907: *The Cults of the Greek States*, vol. 3. Clarendon Press, Oxford.

Fougères G., 1890: "Fouilles de Mantinée (1877–1888)(1)", *BCH* 14, 65–90.

Fougères, G., 1898: *Mantinée et l'Arcadie orientale*. Fontemoing, Paris.

Fraser, P.M., 1972: *Ptolemaic Alexandria*. Clarendon Press, Oxford.

Fuchs, W., 1959: *Die Vorbilder der neuattischen Reliefs*. De Gruyter, Berlin.

Ginouvès, R., 1972: *Le théâtre à gradins droits et l'Odéon d'Argos*. Vrin, Paris.

Greco, E., 1981: *Magna Grecia*. Laterza, Roma–Bari.

Hellmann, M.-C., 1992: *Recherches sur le vocabulaire de l'architecture grecque, d'après les inscriptions de Délos*. De Boccard, Athènes–Paris.

Imhoof-Blumer, F.W. and P. Gardner, 1964: *A Numismatic Commentary on Pausanias*. Argonaut, Chicago.

Jost, M., 1985: *Sanctuaires et cultes d'Arcadie*. Vrin, Paris.

Jost, M., 1994: "Nouveau regard sur les Grandes Déesses de Mégalopolis: influences, emprunts, syncrétismes religieux", *Kernos* 7, 119–129.

Jost, M., 1996: "Evergétisme et tradition religieuse à Mantinée au 1er siècle avant J.-C.", in A. Chastagnol, S. Demougin, and C. Lepelley (eds), *Splendidissima civitas. Hommage à Fr. Jacques* (Publications de la Sorbonne, Paris), 193–200.

Kahil, L., 1977: "L'Artémis de Brauron: rites et mystères", *Antike Kunst* 20, 86–98.

Kardara, K., 1988: *Aphrodite Erikyne, hieron kai manteion eis ten Boreiodutiken Arkadian*. Library of the Athens Archaeological Society 16, Athens.

Kavvadias, K., [1897] 1898: "Ekthesis ton pepragmenon tes Hetaireias kata to etos 1897", *Prakt*, 9–32.

Kourouniotes, K., 1912: "To en Lukosoura Megaron tes Despoines", *ArchEph*, 142–161.

Laumonier, A., 1949: "Le mysticisme artémisiaque", *Mélange V. Magnien*. Toulouse [s.n.] 59–64.

Laurens, A.F. and E. Louka, 1987: "Les masques chypriotes", *Cahiers du Gita*, no. 3, Oct., 23–32.

Lehmann, P.W., 1964: "The technique of the mosaic at Lykosoura", in L.F. Sanders (ed.), *Essays in Memory of K. Lehmann* (Augustin, New York), 190–197.

Léonardos, V., [1896] 1897: "Anaskafai tou en Lukosoura hierou tes Despoines", *Prakt*, 95–126.

Lévêque, P., 1961: "Sur quelques cultes d'Arcadie", *Information Historique*, 93–108.

Lévy, E., 1968: "Le groupe de Damophon à Lykosoura", thèse de 3e cycle inédite de l'Université de Strasbourg.

Lévy, E. and J. Marcadé, 1972: "Au musée de Lykosoura", *BCH* 96, 967–1004.

Loucas, I. and E. Loucas, 1988: "The *Megaron* of Lykosoura and some prehistoric telesteria", *Journal of Prehistoric Religion* 2, 25–34.

Loucas, I. and E. Loucas-Durie, 1985–1986: "La mention du mot *agalma* dans la loi sacrée de Lykosoura *IG* V 2, 514, l. 15", *Peloponnesiaka*, suppl. 13, vol. 2, 561–578.

Loucas-Durie, E., 1987–1988: "Le nom de la Théa Despoina (Tatien, *Ad Graec.*, 29 – Paus. VIII, 37, 6 et 9)", *Peloponnesiaka*, suppl. 16, vol. 2, 401–419.

Loucas-Durie, E., 1989: "Anytos, le parèdre armé de Despoina à Lykosoura", *Kernos* 2, 105–114.

Loucas-Durie, E., 1992: "L'élément orgiastique dans la religion arcadienne", *Kernos* 5, 87–96.

Maffre, J.-J., [2000] 2002: "Bulletin bibliographique: Pausanias, *Description de la Grèce, livre 8* (texte établi, traduit et commenté par M. Casevitz, M. Jost et J. Marcadé). Paris, Belles Lettres, 1998", *RevPhil* 74, 306–312.

Motte, A. and V. Pirenne Delforge, 1992: "Aperçu des significations de *orgia*", *Kernos* 5, 119–140.

Muller, A., 1996: *Les terres cuites votives du Thesmophorion de l'atelier au sanctuaire*. De Boccard, Paris.

Nielsen, I., 2000: "Cultic theatres and ritual drama in ancient Greece", in S. Isager and I. Nielsen (eds), *Proceedings of the Danish Institute at Athens*, 107–133.

Nilsson, M.P., 1906: *Griechische Feste von religiöser Bedeutung, mit Ausschluss der attischen*. Teubner, Leipzig.

Orlandini, G.A., 1969–1970: "Considerazioni sul *mégaron* di Despoina a Licosura", *Annuario* 31–32, 343–357.

Orlandos, A.K., 1967–1968: *He Arkadike Alifeira kai ta mnemeia tes*. Library of the Athens Archaeological Society 58, Athens.

Pakkanen, P., 1996: *Interpreting Early Hellenistic Religion. A Study Based on the Mystery Cult of Demeter and the Cult of Isis*. Helsinki, Foundation of the Finnish Institute at Athens.

Perdrizet, P., 1899: "Terres cuites de Lykosoura et mythologie arcadienne", *BCH* 13, 635–636.

Reeder, H., 1995: *Pandora's Box. Women in Classical Greece*. The Walters Art Gallery, Baltimore, Md.

Rehm, A., 1958: *Didyma, II. Die Inschriften*. Mann, Berlin.

Richardson, N.J., 1974: *The Homeric Hymn to Demeter*. Clarendon Press, Oxford.

Robert, L., 1969: *Opera Minora. Selecta: Epigraphie et antiquités grecques*, vol. 2. Hakkert, Amsterdam.

Roux, J., 1970: *Euripide. Les Bacchantes* I. Les Belles Lettres, Paris.
Sabatucci, D., 1982: *Essai sur le mysticisme grec*. Flammarion, Paris.
Séchan, L., 1930: *La danse antique*. De Boccard, Paris.
Sokolowsky, F., 1969: *Lois sacrées des cités grecques*. De Boccard, Paris.
Stiglitz, R., 1967: *Die Grossen Göttinnen Arkadiens. Der Kultname* ΜΕΓΑΛΑΙ ΘΕΑΙ *und seine Grundlage*. Österreichisches Archäologisches Institut in Wien, Vienna.
Sworonek S. and B. Traczkow, 1981: "Le culte de Déméter à Alexandrie", in L. Kahil, and C. Augé (eds), *Mythologie gréco-romaine, mythologies périphériques, études d'iconographie* (Center National de la Recherche Scientifique, Paris), 131–144.
Tausend, K., 1999: "Heiligtümer und Kulte Nordostarkadiens", in K. Taunsend (ed.), *Pheneos und Lousoi. Untersuschungen zu Geschichte und Topographie Nordostarkadiens* (Lang, Frankfurt am Main), 343–362.
Themelis, P.G., 1992: "The cult scene on the polos of the Siphnian Karyatid at Delphi", in R. Hägg (ed.), *The Iconography of Greek Cult* (Kernos Supplement 1, Athens), 49–72.
Themelis, P., 1993a: "Damophon von Messene – sein Werk im Licht der neuen Ausgrabungen", *Antike Kunst*, 36, 24–40.
Themelis, P., 1993b: "Ho Damophon kai he drasterioteta tou sten Arkadia", in O. Palagia and W. Coulson (eds), *Sculpture from Arcadia and Laconia* (Oxbow Books, Oxford), 99–109.
Themelis, P., 1994: "Damophon of Messene: New evidence, 1–37", in K. Sheedy (ed.), *Archaeology in the Peloponnese: New Excavations and Research* (Oxbow Books, Oxford), 1–37.
Themelis, P., 1996: "Damophon", in O. Palagia and J.J. Pollitt (eds), *Personal Style in Greek Sculpture* (Cambridge University Press, Cambridge), 154–185.
Tresp, A., 1914: *Die Fragmente der griechischen Kultschrifsteller*. Töpelmann, Giessen.
Voutiras, E., 1999: "Opfer für Despoina: Zu Kultsatzung des Heiligtums von Lykosoura *IG* V 2, 514", *Chiron* 29, 233–249 (avec la bibliographie antérieure).

7

TROPHONIUS OF LEBADEA

Mystery aspects of an oracular cult in Boeotia

Pierre Bonnechere

The *manteion* of Trophonius is among the best documented of ancient oracles, thanks to a striking chapter of Pausanias. There we hear how consultants underwent a long and unique preparation, after which they descended into the earth for the consultation itself, an experience so harrowing that for days after they found themselves unable to laugh. Students of Greek religion have tended to seize on the exotic details, sometimes ignoring issues of importance; more unfortunate yet, they have seen the consultation procedure as a late development, elaborated by the priests to add interest and draw clients to a threatened institution. In the present chapter I shall be giving a very different view.[1]

The *Trophonion* is not normally placed in relation to mystery cults. Several late sources, however, say right out that Mysteries were performed there. Two commentators of Gregory of Nazianzus, Cosmas of Jerusalem and the abbot Nonnus, refer to τελεταί (here to be understood as "mystery cult ceremonies") and associate them with consultation of the oracle. Among the scholiasts of Aristophanes, one speaks of μύησις ("initiation"); a second compares the mystery rites performed by those consulting the oracle of Trophonius to those of Eleusis.[2] This does not represent the misunderstanding of a much later period, nor a Hellenistic or Roman addition, but a legacy dating back at least to Classical times.[3]

Trophonius and mystery cults in the Hellenistic and Roman period

In Lebadean mythology and cult, the boundaries between the world beyond and the here-and-now are all-important. The Trophonius of myth lays the threshold of the Delphic oracle; he also builds the treasuries of Hyrieus and Augias, the nuptial chamber of Amphitryon, the temple of Poseidon at Mantinea, and indeed his own oracle. In all these tales he crosses the boundaries of worlds (Bonnechere 1999). This impression is confirmed by the complex mythological relationship that he holds with other heroes. Authors of the Roman era compare him to Amphilochus, Aristeas, Asclepius, Empedocles, Empedotimus, Heracles, the Dioscuri, the Magi and, very significantly, the Chaldaeans; some of these share distinct affinities with the Orpheotelestai. Strabo, inspired perhaps by Posidonius, mentions him in company with others who could communicate the will of the gods even after death: Amphiaraus and Zalmoxis, as well as Orpheus and Musaeus, co-founders of the Eleusinian Mysteries.[4] Nearly all these names, to various degrees, share a heroic form of immortality (macarism), an often chthonic quality involving a relationship with the beyond, oracular, medical and soteric power, the mastery of Truth and psychagogy.[5] As for the Lebadean cult, it is true to the myth of its founder: to consult Trophonius is to perform a *katabasis* – that is, to descend to the Underworld and come back through rituals which will be discussed below.[6] Such myth and cult are a fitting backdrop for Mysteries or at least elements of them.

In fact the elements of mystery cult are numerous. They are first mentioned explicitly in the *Embassy to Gaius* by Philo of Alexandria, dated approximately AD 40. Caligula, having identified himself with Dionysus, Heracles, and the Dioscuri, cast ridicule on "Trophonius, Amphiaraus, Amphilochus and their like, as well as their ὄργια καὶ χρηστήρια" ("mystery cults acts and oracles", *Embassy to Gaius*, 78 [and 93 for demi-gods]). The sense of "orgies" may be subject to controversy, but at the very least the term designates those objects manipulated during ceremonies of a secret nature – initiation rites and Mysteries – and by extension the ceremonies themselves (Motte and Pirenne 1992). The construction of the sentence seems to distinguish two groups: Dionysus, Heracles and the Dioscuri (i.e. those famed initiates present in the Classical iconography of Eleusis), and second, Trophonius, Amphiaraus and Amphilochus, three soothsayers conspicuous for their chthonic associations.[7] In ὄργια καὶ χρηστήρια Philo may have had in mind the three demi-gods, but he certainly did Trophonius and his consorts.[8]

The testimonies of the second century, moreover, leave no doubt that there were elements of mystery cult at the *Trophonion*, although it is difficult at first to grasp their exact purpose. Trophonius appears at times as an initiator who gives access to a higher level of personal accomplishment: Pausanias tells of Aristomenes, who having mysteriously lost his shield during a battle went on to a series of noble deeds after he had found it in Trophonius' precinct (theme of the beneficial *agalma* coming from the other world). According to Philostratus, Apollonius of Tyana made the descent at Lebadea, and after an unusual consultation of seven days, Trophonius confirmed him in his obedience to Pythagorean rules.[9] Tertullian speaking of mediators of the divine (Moses among Jews, Jesus among Christians), says that "Orpheus in Pieria, Musaeus at Athens, Melampus at Argos and Trophonius in Boeotia *initiationibus homines obligaverunt*" ("placed men in their service through initiations"). Origen, in reference to a list of heroes by Celsus which includes Trophonius, also mentions *teletai* in the context and associates them with the charlatanism of the Magi.[10]

Most interesting of all is Plutarch's *De genio Socratis*. In this work, the young Timarchus goes to the cave of Trophonius seeking an answer about the *daimôn* of Socrates. He receives a grand revelation of life's secrets – of reincarnation and the order of the cosmos. This dialogue, in which Trophonius is the possessor of *khresteria* and the revealer of *orgia*, proves the union of the two realities linked some decades earlier by Philo. It must be remembered that Plutarch, following Plato amongst others, placed among the principal concerns of elite lunar spirits, mediating between men and gods, not only the *performance of mysteries* (συνοργιάζουσι τῶν τελετῶν) and *soteric acts* (σωτῆρες ἔν τε πολέμοις καὶ κατὰ θάλατταν), but also *oracles* (χρηστηρίων ... ἐπιμελησόμενοι) – along with the *respect for justice* (φύλακες ἀδικημάτων).[11] Trophonius is to Plutarch one of these benign spirits.[12] In the philosophical myth in the dialogue *De facie*, this elite company of spirits, assistants to a lethargic and omniscient Cronus, is made by Plutarch the equal of the Idaean Dactyls, the Corybantes and moreover, the Trophoniads.[13] The last are enigmatic in many ways: although Boeotian, their ties to "Oudôra" remain unexplained, and their exact relations with Trophonius, evident from their name, cannot be determined.[14] Pausanias elsewhere identified the Idaean Dactyls with the Couretes who guarded the grotto of the infant Zeus, themselves assimilated to the Corybantes since Euripides.[15] A tradition of the fourth century BC has it that the Idaean Dactyls, in order to communicate the Mysteries to the human race, personally taught Orpheus, Trophonius' peer in Hellenistic and Roman sources. Since the Classical period, these same Dactyls had a role in the Mysteries of Samothrace, which they claimed to have founded; a founding role was also assigned to a certain Saon or Saos.[16] Now Pausanias indicates that the founder of the oracle of Trophonius was in fact one Saon of Acraephia, whom the hero had taught all the rituals to be followed, i.e. had initiated (Pausanias, 9.40.1–2). Even if a link between the two Saontes is not attested, the significance of the name (saviour, σῴζων), speaks eloquently for mystery cults. The gods who presided over Mysteries at Samothrace were well known for their soteric actions, notably sea rescues. At Lebadea, too, a fragment of Heraclides of Pontus already gives Trophonius the role of rescuer in a context of (Dionysiac?) Mysteries and war, but the quotation in the *Suda* is not clear.[17]

Strabo groups Trophonius with Orpheus and Musaeus and, furthermore, with Zalmoxis. This association with Zalmoxis, of whom modern scholars make a "Greek shaman" (e.g. Dodds 1965, 144), opens up other perspectives. Zalmoxis is already said by Herodotus to have had a κατάγαιον οἴκημα ("underground building"), which he inhabited for three years before returning "to earth", thereby convincing the Scythians that the soul is immortal. Hellanicus credited him with *teletai* and, like Herodotus, with the promise of immortality and the attaining of "everything good" (Hdt. 4.95; Hellanicus, *FGH*, 4F73).

In the course of this anecdote, Herodotus recalls the figure of Pythagoras, to whom Zalmoxis had been at one time a slave and then a student (Burkert 1972, 155–159; Graf 1988, 89–92; Hartog 1980, 102–126). Along the lines of Plato's myth of Er and the eschatological myths of Plutarch, Pythagoras was thought since the early third century BC to have visited the Underworld, where he saw Hesiod and Homer subjected to the worst torments because of their irreverence to the gods (Hieronymus of Rhodes cited by Diogenes Laertius, 8.21). It might be said that he acquired there a superior knowledge.[18] Hermippus somewhat later made fun of the story, saying that Pythagoras had simply – like Zalmoxis – disappeared beneath the earth in order to reappear wasted nearly to the bone. Since his mother had recorded events during his absence, he was able to demonstrate what passed for divine knowledge of them and persuaded his disciples of his divinity and immortality.[19] Burkert has proposed to see there a variation on μήτηρ; that is to say, Demeter to whom Pythagoreans are known to adhere.[20] Indeed, a tradition anterior to Timaeus held that Pythagoras only taught in subterranean chambers of limited access since only a mystery ritual would allow initiates to acquire supernatural knowledge.[21] Master of the doctrine of *metempsychosis*, he had even received from Hermes the power to remember everything.[22]

Is it a mere coincidence that Strabo (and perhaps Posidonius) link Trophonius and Zalmoxis? Quite the contrary: Trophonius operates in an underground chamber in the world beyond, where he reveals to Timarchus the secret of human incarnation. He harbours in his sanctuary the waters and the throne of Mnemosyne in person (Pausanias, 9.39). A different version, circulated among others by the early Christians, presents Trophonius in the image of Pythagoras and Zalmoxis: he had been but a man who, in his underground lair built to dupe the world, finally starved to death.[23]

Trophonius, Zalmoxis and Pythagoras then, according to independent traditions,[24] possessed a cave of similar nature, a privileged place where any individual could gain more than momentary access to the world beyond and to divine knowledge of all things, visible and invisible, past, present and future. The connection between revelation and chthonic sites was widespread: Epimenides, for example, possessed universal knowledge thanks to a fifty-seven year sleep in a cavern.[25] Pancrates of Lucian's *Philopseudes* acquired his magic after twenty-three years in the *adyta hypogaia* of Isis, well known for her Mysteries and subterranean chambers.[26] The "underground building" was certainly important in the mystery cults themselves. We have only to cite the *telesterion* at Eleusis and its *anaktoron* (Clinton 1992, 126–132), the *anaktora* of Isis or the mystery cult of the Dactyls if we accept the interpretation given of a magical papyrus by Betz (1980, 287–295). Plutarch (*De facie in orbe lunae*, 30, 944ce), we have noted, associated these same Dactyls with the Trophoniads, and their cult shared mystery aspects with them. As for underground chambers, we may also cite that of Orpheus, which Conon places at Libethra in Pieria, a building (οἴκημα) used for mystery cult ceremonies (τελεταί) forbidden to women.[27]

At the end of the Hellenistic and Roman periods numerous, though sometimes brief, references confirm the perception of Trophonius as the master of an oracle, in contact with the chthonic world and linked to initiation Mysteries. The two earliest witnesses for this period, Strabo (perhaps following Posidonius) and Philo, present him in the company either of Orpheus and Musaeus, founders of the Eleusinian Mysteries, to which Plutarch adds the Dactyls (also Tertullian, *Apologeticum*, 21.29), or else of mythological initiates of the Great Mysteries. Now, how was the oracle conceived before the Hellenistic and Roman period? Did it share more with the Mysteries than mere forms?

The perception of Trophonius and his oracle as Mysteries before the Roman era: the evidence of Aristophanes' *Clouds*

Thanks to Aristophanes' *Clouds* we have proof that the "underground building" of Trophonius, site of Timarchus' revelation, is not a late invention. I will not repeat here, except in brief, the detailed demonstration I have given in *REG*. The criticism of the nineteenth and twentieth centuries has been right to consider this play a parody of initiation to a mystery, but wrong to assume that Aristophanes had in mind a cult in particular: rather, he took features from this one and that to make a sort of generic product (Bonnechere 1998b, 436–480). In order to escape from his son's debts, the peasant Strepsiades decides to have himself initiated into the Mysteries of the Clouds. He goes to the φροντιστήριον (or Thinkery) where Socrates, the mystagogue, makes him go down into an underground room where he will be led to revelations: mastery of language and absolute knowledge of the *Nephelai* (489–490, 412, 841). The dull wits of the old peasant are a humorous stumbling block.

At the moment of descent into the earth and the beginning of the initiation proper, Strepsiades panics and implores Socrates (506–508): "First put into my hands a honey cake (μελιτοῦττα), for I am afraid to go down there, as if I were going down into Trophonius' cave".

Modern critics, while recognizing the parodic nature of the *Clouds*, have considered this merely a passing reference to the Lebadean cult, without wider significance for the play. Can it be that the Mysteries parodied by Aristophanes are largely Trophonian? This single reference, of course, is not enough to ensure, from the fact of the "underground building" of Trophonius in the imperial period, its existence in the fifth century. Other clues, however, give it force.

Described at length by Pausanias, the fateful descent in the *adyton* was preceded by a number of rituals, of which the last were these (9.39.7–8 and 11): the consultant, guided by the priests, drank from two nearby streams, Lethe and Mnemosyne.[28] He then reached the lair of Trophonius and went down the *adyton*, taking care to have in each hand a honey cake (μελιτοῦττα).[29] The *Clouds* closely mirrors this ceremony: Strepsiades is an old forgetful man (ἐπιλήσμων), and conscious of so being.[30] When Socrates asks him about his memory, he replies (483–485):

> [...] That depends, by Zeus:
> if someone owes me, I remember it very well (μνήμων πάνυ);
> if I have debts, alas, I forget everything (ἐπιλήσμων πάνυ)!

The place reserved by the poet for opposing the terms memory–forgetfulness, both at the end of the line, is significant. This is followed shortly by the invitation into the room of initiation, just as if Strepsiades had drunk from both springs (505–506).[31] Another comparison with Trophonius is invited by the precautionary measure of honey cakes in Strepsiades' moment of fear (506–508). The descent offers a very close parallel: καταβαίνων ("going down") designates Strepsiades' movement into the Clouds' initiation chamber as well as the consultant's into the cave of Trophonius. For Herodotus and Dicaearchus, the oldest witnesses, consultation at Lebadea was already a descent to the Underworld, designated by *katabainein* and *katabasis*.[32] Five key elements are thus combined in a few verses: memory, oblivion, fear, *katabasis* and honey cakes. These are united in a sequence that corresponds too perfectly with consultation of Trophonius to be a coincidence.

Beside these five elements, other references to the ritual of the *Trophonion* and its theoretical basis come also into play, especially the means and matter of revelation and the theme of acquired knowledge. More will be said of them below.

Another flagrant similarity between the Trophonian cult and the *Clouds* should first be mentioned: as the visionary returns groggy from Trophonius' cave, he is placed on the throne of Mnemosyne for reasons not entirely elucidated but surely related to the knowledge gained from the revelation (Pausanias 9.39.13):

The priests again, taking charge of the individual who comes back up from Trophonius, make him sit on the throne of Mnemosyne: he is not far from the *adyton*. Once seated there, they question him on the things he has seen and learned (ὁπόσα εἶδέ τε καὶ ἐπύθετο): once they have the information (μαθόντες) they send him back to his companions.

In other words, the priests search the consultant's memory after his encounter with Trophonius in order to understand what is contained in the revelation and to restore at the same time, no doubt, some order in his confused mind. This can be seen as an *anamnesia* of profound religious and philosophical truths. Mnemosyne is also closely related to the Aither, whence Timarchus for example returns, although in his case the enthronement is not explicitly mentioned, as though Plutarch wanted to indicate that the vision was completely understood by the young man in the cave itself.[33]

The Lebadean *thronosis* may have all the appearances of a late ritual, but comparison with the *Clouds* demonstrates that this is not so. The enlightenment Strepsiades receives is very much less than perfect, and that is because of his defective memory. Socrates reappears on the scene and orders him to leave the site of enlightenment with his σκίμπους ("small couch") so that he can lie down in view of everyone, in the Thinkery itself. The master, in a maieutic manner (627–693) and presenting all features of Trophonian ritual, tries to force his new disciple to meditate so as to profit from his enlightenment. Socrates in the role of priest (πρόπολος, 436; ἱερεύς, 359) then asks the appropriate questions, which he expects to be properly answered by one so freshly instructed (694–695, 696–697, 700–705, 731–793). But the litter of Strepsiades, which should serve as a place of revelation, is only the throne of Forgetfulness (630–631):

He forgets the paltriest things he learns,
before he's even learned them.

The joke gains point from an implicit comparison with Trophonius' throne of Memory, which in turn begins to look six centuries older than Pausanias.[34] The parallel between Strepsiades' "little bed" and Mnemosyne's throne is even more telling.[35] Considering the function of Lebadean θρόνωσις after revelation and the double enthronement of the *Clouds*, it would perhaps be useful to re-examine mystery initiations in terms of a possible twofold *thronismos* before and/or after initiation.

The oracle of Trophonius and Mysteries: the basic parallels

An oracle is the place of transition and communication *par excellence* between the world of gods and that of men. More precisely, it is a place where men can, by fixed procedures, raise themselves up into the realm of Truth and perceive whatever the gods choose to reveal. Mysteries are not essentially different. At most, they differ in the breadth and the intensity of the revelation, whose focus on a better earthly life and on the beyond places them on a higher emotional plane.

Among oracles, those foregoing an intermediary between divinity and consultant will tend to merge with the Mysteries, although there are exceptions.[36] Aelius Aristides, calling the written record of his contact with Asclepius "sacred speech" (ἱερὸς λόγος), clearly considered that the cult of this god could be seen as an elucidation of a Mystery, a term which he uses elsewhere. Similarly, an Orphic hymn says of Hygeia that she comes to help the *mystai*.[37] Nocturnal incubation brings about the co-penetration of two worlds, each one advancing by a step to encounter the other: the seeker who sleeps in the κοιμητήριον (room of incubation) and the god who appears in his dream. By this contact, the dreamer attains a vision that places him in the world of Truth and lets him see certain parts of it. Pausanias specifies moreover that Athenians claim to have shared with Asclepius the Mysteries at Eleusis, the second day of which was called *Epidauria*. This mystery aspect of Asclepius (called *soter* in an Orphic hymn) is well known already; it is useful to recall that Trophonius shares with him many traits of both character and cult.[38] Marcus Aurelius placed Mysteries between revelatory dreams, divination, and miraculous cures, precisely where Trophonius navigates.[39] One could with confidence extend the comparison to Isis (*pansoteira*) or Sarapis (Burkert 1992, 26; Versnel 1990, 45–47; for late antiquity see esp. Eitrem 1947).

The revelation of the *Trophonion* has always been surrounded by uncertainty. At the moment of revelation in the lowermost part of the *adyton*, the consultant is said by sources of Roman date to see sights and hear sounds. It has been theorized that the sights continue an ancient stratum of incubation, on which was grafted an Apollonian stratum (the sounds, since Apollonian oracles typically work through priests who deliver the response out loud); the cross would have come about in the remote archaic period with the arrival and success of Apollo in Boeotia. This idea is more clever than enlightening.[40] For one thing, the revelation is not one typical of incubation; for another, Apollo's presence at the *Trophonion* (we should note there is no Apollo Trophonius) is slight. Moreover, how could the two methods have been combined? If the consultant of Trophonius dreams, the priest cannot show or say anything to him, and the consultation then has nothing Apollonian about it; if on the other hand the consultant remains awake, then there is no oniromantic aspect. To hear sounds could conceivably be considered Apollonian, but how then are the sights to be explained unless we resort to a hypothesis typical of the seventeenth century and call it a hoax of the priests? That seems to me out of the question.

A reappraisal of the sources leads to a new and more appropriate solution. The consultation took place at night and only after a long and trying preparation of several days: confinement in an underground room, cold baths, prayers, abundant feasting, dances, sexual abstinence, music of the *aulos*, drinking of the waters of Oblivion and Memory, all in a state of increasing fear, and finally the discomforting enactment of a visit to Hades by a terrifying route through a dark pit.[41] This was not only a purification in the sense specific to Mysteries (Burkert 1992, 93–95; cf. the necessary purifications for initiates in the Thurioi tablets: IIA1–2, IIB1), but also a technique of rendering the consultant helpless, physically, emotionally and mentally, leaving him susceptible to auto-suggestion. Once in the black hole in the dead of the night and overcome with fear, the consultant must often have lost consciousness in a sort of hallucinatory syncope combined with auditory sensations. The oracle seems to have functioned by provoking in certain consultants "visionary trances",[42] which they perceived as the passage of their souls into another world.

That the flight of the soul out of body was implicit in consultation is clear as early as the fourth century BC in a lost text treating the descent into the cave of Trophonius. This text is by Dicaearchus, a member of the Aristotelian school, which was on other evidence fascinated by this subject (Detienne 1958–1960, 123–135; Wehrli 1944, 46–48; 1948, 47–49; 1969, 227–235): the fragments conserved speak of the possibility of the soul leaving the body, especially during sleep, and entering the world of Truth, something done much later, but still at Lebadea, by Timarchus. Even if the myth of the Plutarchan *De genio* is a fabrication, its framework is strictly in accord with tradition.

This idea of a "soul's voyage" is highly instructive. In the first place, it connects Trophonius to shamanistic milieux, though it must be said that the concept of shamanism in ancient Greece is a vague one. Zalmoxis, close to Trophonius in certain respects, may be taken as a sort of Greek shaman. Two others appear at Lebadea: Hermotimus of Clazomenae, associated with Trophonius in Timarchus' vision, and Phormion of Sparta/Croton, mentioned in Cratinus' lost play *Trophonius* (fifth century BC). These two Greek "shamans" – there are some ten of them in all – had at the very least a soul thought to depart their body leaving them lifeless in the meantime.[43]

In oracles of Trophonius' kind, the voyage of the soul and the vision served as a revelation with a "visible manifestation" and spoken explanation, all in an atmosphere very similar to those Mysteries whose essential character was to *experience* Truth through a montage of images combined with explanations.[44] Some Mysteries, those of Demeter or Meter, could also induce frenzied behaviour *in some participants*; this was experienced as an intense moment of privileged contact with the divinity.[45] This allows us to understand why from the time of Aristophanes, if not before, the oracle was considered (partially) as a mystery, and why the comic poet was able to establish an analogy between the (failed) enlightenment of Strepsiades and the consultant who descended into the cave of Trophonius. Along the same lines, it is not difficult to see why Plutarch in *De genio Socratis* chose the *Trophonion* as the scene for the apocalyptic and mysterious vision of Timarchus, whose myth is in fact called a "sacred speech" (24, 593a).[46]

A few remarks must be addressed to the contrast of sadness/joy central to certain chthonic passages (Alcestis) and fundamental to Mysteries like those at Eleusis or those of Meter, where the day of laughter followed a day of blood.[47] This opposition of terror and loss of laughter/rejoicing and recovery of laughter was indisputably present at the *Trophonion*: Pausanias (9.39.13) and all others emphasized the fear of the consultants and the loss of their ability to laugh, regained gradually after the face-to-face encounter with the divine; this aspect of the consultation can be traced back as far as Aristophanes.[48] The encounter with death is at the root of these rites, at the intersection once again of the Mysteries and the Pythagorean sect.[49] The sacred experience in Trophonius' cave, which left the consultant "unconscious of himself and others" but opened him to majestic visions, must have marked him for life, as did an initiation at Eleusis: "It was as though I were a stranger to myself."[50]

We should pause to compare the concept, central to much of Plato's work, that death is experienced as an initiation to Truth, to the pseudo-death during initiation to Mysteries, a partial introduction to Truth. This idea, developed in a often-quoted fragment of Plutarch, applies perfectly to an oracle that involves a transitory death, a sojourn in the world beyond and a partial revelation.[51] Lucius' initiation to Isis in Apuleius' *Metamorphoses* also makes clear the voluntary and temporary death in the formula "to approach the frontier of death and ... tread Proserpina's threshold". Since the *Homeric Hymn to Apollo*, is Trophonius not one who crosses the boundaries of worlds and lays down thresholds?[52]

Even a comparison of the speeches in the *Clouds* of Aristophanes and in Plutarch, both dealing with Trophonius, shows a real connection in thinking across five centuries. Just as Parmenides, after the flight of his soul and a voyage to the Underworld, learned *everything*, Strepsiades proclaims that initiation to the *Clouds* brings knowledge of "all things known to man" (412, 841); similarly Timarchus declares that he wants to know everything, for everything is worthy of wonder. To understand the world, the initiated Socrates lets his refined thought dissolve into the surrounding air, Strepsiades feels his soul fly away, and Timarchus surrenders it to the Aether, the place *par excellence* for uniting the soul with Truth in perfect *sympatheia*.[53]

Being without an intermediary, the Trophonian revelation has the same value as dreams sent (for example) by Asclepius. When this god appeared in the dreams of his patients he provided the cure immediately, as is attested in philosophical writings as well as in Galen and Rufus.[54] The methods of Trophonius are slightly different but the principle is the same: a revelation guaranteed by the divinity, whose effect is immediate. Furthermore, the trance involves a revelation that can be called *all-embracing*, in contrast to the usual forms of divination where an answer is given through an intermediary to questions of limited scope. The consultant of Trophonius certainly looks for an answer to a specific question, but he will discover it only in a greater state of transport, a vision far surpassing the exact object of his request. The most striking example is that of Timarchus, whose purpose is to ask after the spirit of Socrates but who sees passing before his closed eyes the very principles of life on earth.

Finally, investigation of the Lebadean background to Aristophanes' *Clouds* carries other consequences: the ritual of the springs of Oblivion and Memory and of Mnemosyne's throne,[55] said to be Hellenistic, find themselves projected several centuries into the past. The opposition of these waters now appears in a context with eschatological elements – do consultants not descend to the Underworld? – at the end of the fifth century BC, that is, before the first known "Orphic" tablet, and in mainland Greece. I shall not treat here the Orphic or Dionysiac Mysteries, however one may choose to name them: it will suffice to draw attention to this mystery element of the *Trophonion*.[56]

Lebadea, Eleusis and some additional traces of Mysteries

Now that continuity has been established between the Classical and the Imperial periods, let us return to some Hellenistic and Roman sources which associate the Mysteries of Trophonius with those at Eleusis, or at least encourage this association. The passage of Tzetzes comparing the wearing-out of the mantle of the *initiandi* in both cults is particularly interesting in light of a legend reported by Charax of Pergamon (probably under Hadrian). With Cercyon, who here appears as his half-brother, and with their father Agamedes, Trophonius robbed king Augias of his treasures. When Agamedes was caught in the king's trap, Trophonius killed and decapitated him so that the guilty family would not be identified; the two brothers then escaped. While Cercyon sought refuge at Eleusis, an "unwelcome guest", Trophonius fled with Agamedes' severed head; Augias followed his blood trail until the hero disappeared underground at Lebadea. The story has all the look of a patchwork created to explain the connection between the two cults. However, Cercyon is so little known that we can go no further.

Dietary restrictions are conspicuous in numerous incubatory cults, and their connection with Mysteries has long been known. At Eleusis their antiquity is without doubt, since in the fourth century BC a fragment of Melanthius mentions the cult rules regarding sacrifices with respect to mullet (*trigle*).[57] This fish appears alongside *melanouros* and *trygon* in a Lebadean list in a fragment of Cratinos' *Trophonius* (fr. 236, *PCG*). At the Mysteries of Demeter at Haloa, as a scholion of Lucian records, *trigle* and *melanouros* were also forbidden.[58]

Melanouros and *trigle* also figure among the foods forbidden to epileptics by some Greek doctors – specifically by those denounced in the Hippocratic treatise *On the Sacred Disease* (para. 1). It is apparent from that work that the two fish are considered unsuitable for sick persons because they disturb the stomach. Without venturing too far into the underlying thought, we may conclude that such foods were imagined to give rise to bad trances by troubling the digestion.[59]

In any case, abstinence occurred during the long preparation for Lebadean consultation and took place essentially in a small underground room, the οἴκημα consecrated to Agathos Daimon and Agathe Tyche. Though Good Fortune is habitually thought of as Hellenistic, in fact her cult enjoys a strong foothold from Classical times.[60] Before a journey to the Underworld she is by no means out of place. When apprised by Crito that his death is imminent, Socrates commends himself "to good Fortune!" because such is the will of the gods.[61] In the *Apology* (41c), Plato shows his master confident in the face of death as something good and not evil.[62] He knows that in the other world he will discourse with Orpheus and Musaeus among others. He is εὔελπις. This expression echoes the *fiducia* and *bona spes* of those initiated at Eleusis and in other mystery cults[63] and recalls Strepsiades of the *Clouds*, to whom the Chorypheus bids, just before his descent, happiness (512–513). Note also that according to Pausanias the pilgrim to the *Trophonion* leaves hopeful for the last part of his journey between life and death.[64]

Hadrian's demes at Antinoupolis

At the spot where his young favourite drowned in the Nile, Hadrian erected a city divided among ten tribes, each one comprising from three to five known demes.[65] The names used to designate these are reasonably assumed to reveal the emperor's interests. We find appropriately the Eleusinian Mysteries, which Hadrian held in high regard and in which he and Antinoüs were initiated to the *epopteia* in AD 128.[66] The tribe Athenaieus included a deme Eleusinios; the tribe Matid(e)ios, named after the empress Sabina's mother, counted Demetrieus, Thesmophor(e)ios and Kalliteknios among its five known demes, thus making an equivalence between Sabina's mother and Demeter;[67] the tribe Sab(e)inios comprised at least five demes: Harmonieus, Gamelieus, [Phy]talieus, Heraieus have long been associated with Hadrian's passion for things Eleusinian,[68] but the fifth deme, Trophonieus, and thus the place reserved for Trophonius, has remained problematic. Though arguments for Eleusinian reference (to the harvest and marriage in Gamelieus and Heraieus, to Kore in [Phy]talieus) appear now very weak, these demenames nonetheless have something Demetrian about them.[69] Harmonieus (and even Heraieus) would rather be associated with the Samothracian Mysteries and the wedding of Harmonia.[70]

Two explanations have been proposed. M. Guarducci's hypothesis that Hadrian consulted Trophonius is based on an inscription attesting that he travelled to Lebadea; the emperor would then have brought both chthonic cults to Antinoupolis. Beaujeu, following Weber, gives Trophonius (or another figure of the same name) a role in the Eleusinian Mysteries, one for which we have no trace of evidence.[71] We are now in a position to reverse Beaujeu's view: the excavations at Eleusis have not uncovered anything concerning Trophonius and it would be surprising that a cult figure important enough to be taken up by Hadrian should be completely lost in oblivion.

The existence of a deme Trophonieus, in the partial context of Mysteries and in close association with Demeter, should rather be taken to confirm Trophonius' role as a master of Mysteries. A brief re-examination of the demes at Antinoupolis provides an additional indication: the tribe Sebast(e)ios includes, besides that of Kaisar(e)ios, the demes Apollonios, Asklep(e)ios, Dioskour(e)ios and Herakl(e)ios. In these last names can be recognized the god and the three heroes unanimously connected to Trophonius by Imperial sources by virtue of their initiation in the Eleusinian Mysteries and subsequent immortality.[72]

Eubuleus–Eubulus

Another Eleusinian connection exists, more promising but at the same time less certain, for it partly relies on the contested identification of Eubuleus at Eleusis with the Eubuleus of the Orphic tablets. Though only lately recognized as such, Eubuleus was one of the great gods of the Eleusinian Mysteries, as much honoured as Triptolemus and the divine couple Theos–Thea (the Eleusinian names for Hades and Persephone). He had been the guide for (Persephone–)Thea on her return to the light and to the mourning Demeter (see esp. Clinton 1992, 56–63, and notably *IG* 1³.78 for sacrifices for each great divinity; less convincing is Sfameni Gasparro 1986, 102–110; 169–175). In cult, Zeus (Eu-)bouleus appears as the exact equivalent of Pluto, so that in the Attic Thesmophoria the presence of the one excludes the other (Clinton 1992, 60, based on Graf 1974, 172, n.72). However, Eubuleus at Eleusis has a separate role and is honoured independently from Zeus, Pluto and Theos.

In the part of the Eleusinian sanctuary traditionally called the "Plutonion", in which Clinton has convincingly identified the famous "Mirthless Rock" ('Ἀγέλαστος Πέτρα), a naturally formed seat, the excavation has brought to light the base of a statue of Eubuleus and what is perhaps his head, as well as a large stone relief of Lacratides, priest of Theos, Thea and Eubuleus.[73] In 1957, Paul Faure discovered there an angled tunnel a little over four metres long and nearly one metre in width, making the place an entry to the Underworld, the one used in the myth by Theseus himself. Modifications to the natural porch seem to confirm that the place was used for a *mise-en-scène*, notably in the *anodos* of Kore escorted by Eubuleus to her mother seated on the "Mirthless Rock".[74]

Now it happens that Eubuleus is not unknown at Lebadea. Small springs are visible today in the gorge below the tower of the medieval fort, on the left bank of the Hercyna. Together with the larger springs on the right bank, they are the most significant source of water for the river. One of the springs on the left bank issues from a narrow opening in the rock.[75] Above the opening can be seen the laconic inscription "Euboulou" in clear, regular letters of Hellenistic or Roman date ("that of Euboulos").[76] Eubulus is an equivalent to Eubuleus, as this appears from an Eleusinian inscription of the end of the fifth century and later in an Orphic Hymn.[77] Should we see here a reference to Eubuleus of Eleusis, or only a funerary inscription, given the proximity of another inscription commonly read as an epitaph: "[Nei]koboulou" ("that of Neikoboulos"; *IG* 7.3109)?

The question is not easily answered, for the second inscription is no clearer than its context. It is said to be composed of two parts at right angles: one, exposed to the elements, appears to have been worn away; the other is conserved on the inside of the grotto. It is not clear that the two pieces belong together, or even that they have been accurately reported. Even were such the case, a funerary inscription is unlikely in such a spot: so close to springs in an area obviously consecrated to a cult. The second inscription may well have a religious connotation that escapes us.

Our new understanding of the *Trophonion* allows some plausible suggestions to be made. That the sanctuary is a chthonic passage is borne out by the myth and cult of Trophonius himself, and also by the legend of the River Hercyna, supposed to have been discovered by Trophonius' daughter, a companion of Kore. Kore's mother, said to be the nurse of the infant Trophonius, had her temple in the grove (Pausanias, 9.39.2–5). That the name of Eubulus, a traveller between worlds in Eleusinian ritual, should be placed just above a narrow entry to the earth seems anything but coincidence. Elsewhere, Eubuleus is one of three gods invoked on the Orphic leaves of Thurioi and Rome,[78] in company with the Queen of the Underworld (Persephone) and Eucles.[79] Since the fifth century at the latest, the sanctuary at Lebadea harboured springs of Oblivion and Memory and a throne of Memory, and led the consultant to the world beyond. The presence of Eubulus there would have nothing extraordinary about it.

The sanctuary of Trophonius, then, was conceived since Classical times as an oracle very much like a mystery cult, both by its rites and by the nature of its revelation. The origin of this "hybrid" will no doubt remain hidden, given the lack of archaic sources, but it would be surprising if it arose entirely in the Classical period. However that may be, the Mysteries quite permeated the life of the *manteion*. Ancient testimony to that effect cannot be dismissed as coincidence, nor will the mystery elements be an imperial addition, meant to revive a sanctuary in decline.

Notes

1 This chapter is based on a monograph now in preparation. For the oracle of Trophonius see Pausanias, 9.39.1–40.2. For a recent overview: Schachter (1994, 66–89). Also: Betz (1983), Bonnechere (1998a, 1998b, 1999, 2002), Bonnechere and Bonnechere (1989), Brelich (1958, 46–59), Clark (1968), Dietrich (1965, 348–351), Gruppe (1916–1924), Levin (1989, 1637–1642), Nafissi (1995), Radke (1939), Schachter (1967, 1984), Simonetta (1994), Turner (1994).
2 Cosmas Hierosolymitanus on Gregory of Nazianzus, *Carmina*, 64.284 (*PG*, 68, 513).

Nonnus Abbas on Gregory of Nazianzus, *Oratio in sancta lumina*, 6 (*PG*, 36, 1069). Schol. to Aristophanes, *Clouds*, 508c, Holwerda; Tzetzes on Aristophanes, *Plutus*, 842, is rarely cited (the only exception is Walter 1939).

3 Burkert (1992, 14) has moreover insisted that it is false to consider Mysteries primarily late; on the link between oracles, Asclepius and Mysteries see ibid., 40.
4 Graf (1974, 22–39; 94–126) for the relationship between Eleusis and Orpheus from the end of the fifth century.
5 Bonnechere (2002). Strabo, 16.2.39 (=Posidonius, *FGH*, 87 F 70 (small characters); a fragment not reprinted in the editions of Theiler [1982] and Edelstein and Kidd [1989²]). Main sources: Aelius Aristides, *Asclepiades*, 38, 21, Keil; *To Sarapis*, 48, 25–32, Jebb; Celsus cited by Origenes, *Contra Celsum*, 3.34–35; Clemens of Alexandria, *Protrepticus*, 2.11.1; Cosmas Hierosolymitanus on Gregory of Nazianzus, *Carmina*, 64.284 (*PG*, 38, 512–513); Gregory of Nazianzus, *Carmina*, 1573, 10–12; *Contra Julianum (1)*, 4.59; *Epigrams* [in *Greek Anthology*], 8.29.1–3; *In sancta lumina* [*Orationes*, 39] (*PG*, 36, 340, 7–31); Lucian, *Assembly of the Gods*, 12; *Dialogues of the Dead*, 10 (and schol. *ad loc.*); Pausanias, 1.34.2; Philo of Alexandria, *Embassy to Gaius*, 78; Tertullian, *De anima*, 46.11.
6 Vocabulary in Schachter (1994, 80, n.2). *Katabainein* in Herodotus (8.134) and *katabasis* in Dicaearchus (fr. 13a–22, Wehrli), *c.* 350–300 BC. Later sources take up the same theme, particularly elaborate in Lucian, *Menippus*, esp. 22.
7 The three oracles have a somewhat similar mode of revelation: Amphiaraus proceeds by oniromancy (like Asclepius; Schachter 1981, 19–26), whereas his son, Amphilochus, and Trophonius, always associated in the Roman period, seem to use a half-conscious vision or trance (Amphilochus: esp. Cassius Dio, 72.7; Lucian, *Philopseudes*, 38; Tertullian, *De anima*, 46.11; Bethe 1894; Scheer 1993, 163–168; 222–253. Eleusis: Clinton 1992, esp. 78–84).
8 The comments of Philo (79–92) treat first Dionysus, Heracles and the Dioscuri, who are easiest to characterize.
9 Pausanias, 4.16.7; Philostratus, *Life of Apollonius*, 8.19 (also Eusebius of Cesarea, *Contra Hieroclem*, 44, 407).
10 Tertullian, *Apologeticum*, 21.29 (the reading *Trophonius* is assured despite small variants); from the Hellenistic period, *initiatio* corresponds to *myesis* (bilingual inscription of Samothrace: *SEG* 29.799). Celsus cited by Origenes, *Contra Celsum*, 3.34. On *telete*: Burkert (1992, 19–22).
11 Plutarch, *De genio Socratis*, 21–24, 589f–593a, esp. 21, 590b; *De facie in orbe Lunae*, 30, 944ce. Also Maximus of Tyre, *Dialexeis*, 12 (8).2 and 8; 12 (9).6–7.
12 Plutarch, *De defectu oraculorum*, 38–52, 431c–438d: conversations at Lebadea on the way in which spirits offer visions to receptive souls.
13 Plutarch, *De facie in orbe Lunae*, 30, 944ce (see Plato, *Laws*, 417b; also *De defectu oraculorum*, 13–14, 416a–417e. Cf. Motte and Pirenne (1992, 134–137, Vernière (1977, 260–261).
14 «τοὺς περὶ Βοιωτίαν ἐν †Οὐδωρα† Τροφωνιάδας». The emendation Λεβαδείᾳ is clearly unwarranted. Were the Trophoniads perhaps Trophonius' offspring (Pausanias, 9.39.5)?
15 Pausanias, 5.7.6. Ida: Aratus, *Phaenomena*, 35; Lactantius, *Divinae Institutiones*, 1.13; Euripides, *Bacchae*, 120–129. Also *Orphic Hymns*, prologue, 20–21; 38. Also Strabo, 10.3.19–22 (following Demetrius of Skepsis).
16 Dactyls: Ephorus, *FGH*, 70 F 104 (Diodorus, 5.64.4); Myrsilus of Lesbos, *FGH*, 477 F 2 (Pausanias, 9.30.4). The *Theoi megaloi* of Samothrace were close to the Dioscuri and occasionally identified with them: Cole (1984, 1593). Saon: Critolaus, *FGH*, 823 F 1; schol. to Apollonius of Rhodes, *Argonautica*, 1.916b. Samothrace formerly called Σαωκίς (Hesychius, s.v.); a mountain named Σαώκης (Nonnus, *Dionysiaca*, 13.397), or Σάον and Σάος (Lycophron, *Alexandra*, 78; Nicander, *Theriaca*, 472).

Another Saon, descendant of the founder of Mysteries at Megalopolis: *IG* 5^2 517, lines 8–9: see Jost in this volume.

17 Samothrace: Aristophanes, *Pax*, 276–279; Diagoras of Melus cited by Cicero, *De natura deorum*, 3.37.89 and cited by Diogenes Laertius, 6.59; Plutarch, *De facie in orbe Lunae*, 30, 944ce; schol. to Apollonius of Rhodes, *Argonautica*, 1, 916b. Lebadea: Heraclides, fr. 155, Wehrli (cited in *Suda*, s.v. Λύσιοι τελεταί αἱ Διονύσου). Indeed, the sceptic of Cicero's *De natura deorum* (3.22.56), discussing the several Hermes, mentions that of Samothrace, whose ithyphallic image was at the centre of local Mysteries (Hdt. 2.51) in association with the chthonic Hermes, Trophonius.

18 Burkert (1972, 158–159), followed by Graf (1994, 109). The association of Greek and Oriental wise men hails back to the Classical period at least; the lists are more numerous in the Roman period, but their principle is not new.

19 Hermippus cited by Diogenes Laertius, 8.41 (=fr. 20, Wehrli, =fr. 24, Bollansée). Pythagoras starving: Dicaearchus, fr. 35, Wehrli; Satyrus cited by Diogenes Laertius, 8.40.

20 The Master's house was in a sanctuary of Demeter, or became one after his death: Burkert (1972, 159). *Contra* Hartog (1980, 118), and Zhmud (1997, 114–115) who does not take into account all the available data.

21 Timaeus, *FGH*, 366 F 131 (Iamblichus, *Life of Pythagoras*, 143). Burkert (1972, 155, n.197, with bibliography). These chambers were sometimes even compared to those of Minos and of the Idaean cave. On teaching as an initiation to truth: Burkert (1972, 192–208, esp. 192–194).

22 Heraclides Ponticus, fr. 89, Wehrli. See Rudhardt (1988, 61) and Vernant (1982, 31–40).

23 Charax of Pergamon, *FGH*, 103 F 5; Cosmas Hierosolymitanus *on* Gregory of Nazianzus, *Carmina*, 64.284 (*PG*, 68, 512); Photius, s.v. Λεβάδεια; schol. to Aristophanes, *Clouds*, 508a and c, Holwerda, and 508b, Koster; Tzetzes on Aristophanes, *Clouds*, 506a.

24 Hartog (1980, 118). The age of the parallels is a prime importance. The first traces of a relation between Trophonius, divination and the world beyond go back to the *Homeric Hymn to Apollo*, the *Telegonia* and Pindar: Bonnechere (1999).

25 Diogenes Laertius, 1.109. Dodds (1965, 141–146); Leclerc (1992, 221–233). Initiates performed the initiation by three retreats into this grotto for nine days, clothed in black wool (a reversal of two "Pythagorean" rules). As an underworld passage, the cave was later said to have been the site of Pythagoras' initiation (Porphyry, *Life of Pythagoras*, 17): Faure (1964, 94–131). Apollonius of Tyana, an admirer of Trophonius, is said to have acquired his wisdom through dreams over three years (Graf 1984–85, 65–73).

26 Lucian, *Philopseudes*, 34–36 (Arnobius, *Adversus Nationes*, 43.1); Graf (1994, 107–110) notes the similarities between the Isis of Pancrates and the Pythagorean Demeter. In this dialogue Lucian also speaks of the oracle of Amphilochus at Mallus, which he considers a close double of Trophonius; the latter, moreover, is a magician-architect linked to Daedalus (Charax of Pergamon, *FGH*, 103 F 5; Pausanias, 9.39.8).

27 *FGH*, 26 F 1.45. According to Iamblichus (*Life of Pythagoras*, 146), Pythagoras had been initiated at Libethra by Aglaophamus, the successor to Orpheus. Space does not allow me to recount the legend of Rhampsinitus, quite close to Trophonius, Zalmoxis and Pythagoras. This "Pharaoh" was renowned for his οἴκημα and performed a *katabasis* during which he encountered Isis-Demeter, who gave him an *agalma* ("divine gift": Hdt. 2.121–122; Lloyd 1988, 52–59).

28 According to Pausanias, the two springs make the consultant forget his previous thoughts and let him remember the revelation.

29 Cakes: Schachter (1994, 81, n.2). Parallels: Herodotus (8.41), Pausanias (6.20.1), etc.

30 *Clouds*, 129, 414, 629–631 (ἐπιλήσμων and ἐπιλέλησται), 789–790 (ἐπιλησμότατον); also 887 and 1107.
31 The inversion of the order, Memory–Oblivion instead of Oblivion–Memory, adds an intentionally comic effect, to which we shall return.
32 *Supra*, n.6. *Contra* Betz (1983, 578).
33 The goddess was known in the Archaic period. Plato (*Critias*, 108d) mentions her as the most important of the divinities for remembering primal truths. She had therefore been the object of philosophical speculation, no doubt of speculation on the Mysteries. Like other details, the honey cakes are omitted by Plutarch, but his dialogue is not the record of a consultation. The speech itself, an *erotapocrisis*, is styled ἱερὸς λόγος ("sacred speech", 23, 593a). See also the Trophonian revelation received by Apollonius of Tyana (Philostratus, *Life of Apollonius*, 8.19); the account of it amounts to a Pythagorean treatise.
34 Pausanias cites the following directions: drink from oblivion in order to forget everything, then drink from memory to have total recall. On the threshold of his initiation, Strepsiades inverts the order of the Trophonian directions (and for that matter the "Dionysiac" tablets, which advise drinking only the cold water of Memory and avoiding the hot water of Forgetfulness), by invoking memory first and then forgetfulness. Seen from the Lebadean viewpoint of the second century AD, this would mean that he first cleared his mind, then drank waters of oblivion to be sure to remember nothing of what he had "learned" in the cave.
35 This second "*thronosis*" of the *Clouds* alludes to initiations only indirectly. It is known that a stool was used before or during these initiations, but not, it seems, after the revelation (e.g. Byl 1980, 11; 1994, 43; Dover 1968, 130–131; Guidorizzi 1996, 254). Marianetti (1993, 19–20, 23–27) considers two initiations in *Clouds* (lines 250–263, then 627–793) that would reflect the Eleusinian division into lesser and greater Mysteries. On the possibility of *thronismos* at Eleusis: Burkert (1983, 266–269; 1992, 81–82 and n.3; 130, n.21, n.36; 131, n.43 [iconography]). Also Dio Chrysostom, *Orationes*, 12.33; Plato, *Euthydemus*, 277c (in terms which suggest that it is at the beginning of the ceremony) with the commentary of Jeanmaire (1951, 131–138). Also Hesychius, s.v. Θρόνωσις; *Papyri Graecae Magicae*, 7.745–756, Preisendanz-Henrichs (τεθρονισμένος τοῖς θεοῖς, "enthroned by the gods"); *IG* 5.2.281: Mantinean dedication of a father to Antinoüs (master of Mysteries), for his dead son. Also Clinton (this volume), Cole (1984, 29), Dodds (1965, 84–86), Dover (1968, 130–131), Nock (1941), Rohde (1928, 302, n.1).
36 At Claros at the beginning of our era, the inscriptions suggest that the consultants underwent an initiation, *myesis*, before encountering the divine. Too little is known of this oracle to say more, though the *prophetes* seems the only one involved in divine contact (Macridy 1905, 164–165; 1912, 50–52; see also Iamblichus, *De mysteriis*, 3.11); the *adyton* of Claros, accessible only to initiates, is referred to as the οἶκος κατάγειος ("underground house"), equivalent to the "underground building" of the mystery cults mentioned above (Tacitus, *Annals*, 2.54: *specus*).
37 Ἱερὸς λόγος: *Orationes*, 42.4 and 11; 48.9 and 28. Mystery: *Orationes*, 23.16. Hygeia: *Orphic Hymns*, 68.12.
38 Pausanias, 2.26.8. The name *Epidauria* is obviously an addition of the late fifth or the fourth century, but the connection formed with Mysteries seems to me important (Clinton 1994). There is a tradition that the sanctuary of Sarapis at Alexandria had also been founded by, amongst others, Eumolpides Timotheus: Plutarch, *Isis*, 28, 362a; Tacitus, *Historiae*, 4.82–83. Egypt from the time of Hecataeus (*FGH*, 264 F 25; also Herodotus, 2.171) was considered the origin of Greek Mysteries, particularly those of Eleusis (see also an aretalogy of Isis at Maronea, third–second century BC: Grandjean 1975, lines 34–41). *Orphic Hymns*, 67.8.
39 *Letters to Fronto*, 3.10, p. 43, 15 Van den Hout. Also Aelius Aristides, *Orationes*,

48.32: the vision of Asclepius during a state between dream and wakening, which draws comparison with the experience of Mysteries.

40 Main sources: Maximus of Tyre, *Dissertationes*, 8 (14).2; Pausanias, 9.39.1–40.2; Philostratus, *Life of Apollonius*, 8.19; Plutarch, *De genio Socratis*, 21–22, 590b–593a; Clark (1968, 70–75).

41 Some details absent in Pausanias (9.39) are found in the fragments of comedy (*PCG*): Alexis, fr. 238–240; Cephisodorus, fr. 3–6; Cratinus, fr. 233–245; Menander, fr. 351–354. Other features of the initiation: being taken in charge by two Hermai, then by the priests, sight of an *agalma* reserved for the consultants in their final phase, change of clothing (linen tunic, fitted sandals) etc. About the final "aspiration" Plutarch and Pausanias are in total disagreement: I shall return to that elsewhere. Nor is this the place to elaborate on the linen (in Mysteries, see for example Apuleius, *Metamorphoses*, 11.10.2 and the commentary *ad loc.* of Griffiths 1975).

42 A term without any great scientific basis, but it serves the purpose.

43 Undertaking a journey to the Underworld to encounter a goddess named only as *Thea*, Parmenides is very close to the Mysteries (already seen by Burkert 1969). On Greek "shamanism": Bonnechere (2002), Zhmud (1997, 107–128).

44 Some sources imply that even the blind could see the Mysteries at Eleusis. Beyond the obvious "miracle" one must consider the possibility of an inner, culturally moulded vision (*Greek Anthology*, 9.298; Eucrates' ex-voto: Clinton 1992, fig. 78). The account of Mysteries in Dio Chrysostom (*Orationes*, 12.33), with a cosmic vision evoking that of Timarchus, speaks simply of sacred sights and sounds (also Cleanthus, *SVF*, 1, no. 538). On the feeling experienced at Eleusis, see also Proclus, *In Republicam*, 2, 108, 17–30 Kroll.

45 Dionysus: Cole (1980, 226–231), Dodds (1960), Corybantes: Dodds (1965, 71–89); in general Jeanmaire (1951, 105–219).

46 An interesting parallel: sailors who passed near Achilles' island in the Black Sea often *saw* Achilles (now a *daimon* like Trophonius) at exercise; others *heard* him singing; still others *saw* and *heard* him. Achilles would also appear to those who slept there: Maximus of Tyre, *Dissertationes*, 12 (9).7.

47 Meter: Sfameni Gasparro (1985, 56–63). Ref. in Burkert (1992, 68–69). Cf. Aelius Aristides, *Orationes*, 22.2: at Eleusis is found "what is most terrifying and most splendid of all that is divine for mankind". Note also a text of the Aristotelian corpus, *De Mirabilibus auscultationibus*, 101, 838b–839a Bekker, which brings together several Trophonian features: a certain tomb near a grotto of Lipara is said to be dangerous at night; loud laughter, accompanied by drums and cymbals, can be heard there; in this place a drunken man fell into a deathlike sleep and had an eschatological vision, waking just before his servants buried him. Drums and cymbals figure in the Mysteries of Meter/Cybele.

48 Bonnechere (1998b, 465–466); cf. Aristophanes (*Clouds*, 816–819). Other sources (especially proverbs) in Schachter (1994, 81, n.5). Diogenianus (1.8) enters the Trophonian proverb under a Demetrian saying: «'Αγέλαστος Πέτρα».

49 Bremmer (1992, 207–208). Laughter, Pythagoreanism and Trophonius: Semus of Delos, *FGH*, 396 F 10. We should add that Trophonius was considered μάκαρ in the Roman period, a term that resonates with Mysteries (Burkert 1992, 85).

50 Following the example of Sopater, Διαίρεσις ζητημάτων (C. Walz, *Rhetores Graeci*, 8, 114, 27 to 115, 1). Majestic visions: Plutarch, *De Genio Socratis*, 21–24, 589f–593a; *Sulla*, 17.1.

51 The consultation of the oracle, as shown in the myth of Timarchus, is unquestionably close to fr. 178, Sandbach, where are found: losing one's way, long and frightening wandering in total darkness, shivering, trembling, sweats and holy terror (the journey of Timarchus to the *adyton*, his loss of consciousness and temporary death), then marvellous light, pure sights, blossoming fields, voices, dancing, sacred

speeches and holy visions. The initiated man is free, crowned, celebrating the Mysteries and living with the pure and saintly (exactly Timarchus' vision). After his partial revelation, Timarchus received the total revelation in death two months later, as had been predicted. It matters little if the Mysteries of fr. 178 are Eleusinian or Orphic (Mylonas 1961, 265–266). Also Plutarch, *De recta ratione audiendi*, 47a; *De facie*, 943cd.

52 Apuleius, *Metamorphoses*, 11.23.6–8 (rather close to the myth of Timarchus: Griffiths 1975, 296–301). *Homeric Hymn*, 294–299 (Bonnechere 1999).

53 Plutarch places the myth of Timarchus in the *De genio Socratis*, and Maximus of Tyre, in his own dialogue of that name, cites Trophonius as well (*Dissertationes*, 8 [14].2).

54 Iamblichus, *De mysteriis*, 3.3 (also *IG* 4².1.127). Galen, *De libris propriis*, 19, 19 Kuhn; Rufus cited by Oribasius, *Collectiones medicae*, 45.30.11–15. This belief is not consistent: see the scepticism already present in some Hippocratic texts (*Epidemiae*, 1.10; *De humoribus*, 4; *De morbo sacro*, 2.72; *De affectionibus interioribus*, 48; *De diaera*, 4, *passim*).

55 Memory is associated with Pythagoras but also with the Orphics in the context of Mysteries (*Orphic Hymns*, 77.9–10: to make the *mystes* remember the holy *telete* and to avoid Forgetfulness).

56 A famous relief found at Lebadea represents the traditional initiation of a neophyte to Cybele or Meter in the presence of a chthonic god, Trophonius according to Walter (1939, 53–80). His interpretation was not accepted because the "sanctuary of Meter" seemed to be exterior to the *Trophonion*, and because Trophonius was not believed to have a part in Mysteries. Recently, however, it has been ascertained that the find-spot of the relief lies within the *Trophonion* (a summary by Daumas 1998, 78–79; her interpretation is disappointing). On Orphic tablets, see the chapters by Cole and Robertson in this volume, and the references cited there.

57 Melanthius, *FHG*, 326 F 2. The prohibited foods included: *trigle, galeos, mainis*, fish in general, wine, domestic fowl, beans, pomegranates, apples, flesh of animals improperly bled: Arbesmann (1929, 76–77), Deubner (1900, 14–28).

58 Schol. to Lucian, *Dialogues of the Courtesans*, 7.4 (280, 22–24, Rabe). Pythagoreans avoided these same foods: Diogenes Laertius, 8.1.33; Plutarch, *De liberis educandis*, 17, 12d: Parker (1983, 357–365). Trygon was Asclepius' nurse, buried at Telphousa in Arcadia (Pausanias, 8.25.11), and a connection can be "deduced" from the rule against eating the fish called *trygon* in incubatory cults.

59 The venom of the *melanouros* is discussed by Pliny, *Natural History*, 9.155. See also Apuleius, *Apology*, 40.5.

60 Hamdorf (1964, 37–39, 97–100) (T287, 290, 293, 297, 299, 301, 305, 308–309, 312, 314–316, 319–325, all anterior to 323 BC). Tyche is already a companion of Kore in the *Homeric Hymn to Demeter*, 420; also Empedocles, 31 B 103 (D–K).

61 Plato, *Crito*, 43d. Plato and the language of Mysteries: Riedweg (1987).

62 An Eleusinian thought, at least under the Empire: *IG* 2/3².3661, line 6.

63 Cumont (1949, 401–405), Joly (1955, 167–170). Also Burkert (1992, 24–25, 28, 37) (in the context of votive offerings and Mysteries), Merkelbach (1962, index, s.v. ἐλπίς), Sfameni Gasparro (1986, 123–124), Versnel (1985, 256–257). The sacrifice of a bull to Meter is "a sign of happiness" (*Corpus Cultus Cybelae Attidisque*, Leiden, 1977, 3.239); Plato, *Phaedo*, 67bc; 114cd (115e); *Republic*, 6, 496e. Main sources in the context of Mysteries: Aelius Aristides, *Orationes*, 22 ("Eleusinian"), 10, Behr; Cicero, *De legibus*, 2.14; Firmicus Maternus, *De errore profanarum religionum*, 22.1–2; Isocrates, *Panegyric*, 28; Iamblichus, *De mysteriis*, 2.6; Julian, *On the mother of the Gods*, 20; *Symposion*, 37, etc.; Plutarch, *De tranquillitate animi*, 20, 477ef; *De facie in orbe Lunae*, 28, 943cd; Xenophon, *Memorabilia*, 4.3.17.

64 Courage, to which the *initiandi* at Eleusis were exhorted by the verb θαρρεῖν, was as essential for visitors to Trophonius: Lucian (*Menippus*, 22) uses the verb when

65 Menippus *returns* to life by a shortcut leading through Lebadea. The last sacrifice determined whether the candidate was accepted: Trophonius therefore received only whom he wished, as did Isis in Apuleius (*Metamorphoses*, 11.21), informing the priests of her choice in a dream (cf. for Trophonius: Philostratus, *Life of Apollonius*, 8.19).
65 *P. Lond.* 1164: see Kühn (1913, 117–137), Montevecchi (1990, 183–195), Pistorius (1939, 44, 96–102), Zahrnt (1988, 669–706).
66 Summary in Beaujeu (1955, 165–172). Antinoüs also benefited from a mystery cult at Mantinea (near the temple of Poseidon built by Trophonius): Pausanias, 8.9.7–10.1 (games and statue representing the hero as Dionysus); Jost (1985, 128–129, 541–542).
67 In two Megarian inscriptions, Sabina is herself called Nea Demeter (*IG* 7.73 and 7.74). Thesmophor(e)ios seems correct despite the reading A[mallo]phorieus of Weber (1907, 177–178).
68 Weber (1907, 177–178), Beaujeu (1955, 171). *Trophonieus*: *P. Lond.* 1164, a6, a20, b6 (also k28: *Tryphoneus*). Harmonieus is to be preferred to Ar[otios] (Weber 1907, 106).
69 Antinoeia were also founded at Eleusis: *IG* 3^2.2042.
70 K. Clinton, personal communication.
71 Guarducci (1941, 155–156); *IG* 7.1675. Beaujeu (1955, 171) [based on Weber, 1907, 176–178, as Kühn 1913, 126 and Pistorius 1939, 99].
72 A triad present in the Eleusinian inscription concerning Hadrian's initiation (*IG* $2/3^2$.3575): Guarducci (1941, 150–151), Kühn (1913, 126).
73 Mirthless Rock: Clinton (1992, 14–27). Base of the statue: *IG* 2^2.4615; bust (Eubuleus or Iacchus [?]): Athens, MN, 181 (*c.* 330 BC), Clinton (1992, 57–58; 135, no. 4); relief of Lacratides (*c.* 100 BC; Clinton 1992, 51–53).
74 *BCH*, 82 (1958), 800–801 (map: Clinton 1992, 23). Schol. to Aristophanes, *Knights*, 785a, Koster. Ritual: Clinton (1992, 84–90), Sourvinou-Inwood in this volume.
75 When I was at Lebadea, in springtime 1998 and 1999, the grotto was almost flooded.
76 *IG* 7.3108. Of the two possible interpretations of Eubuleus, as the Eleusinian god or as a man, Schachter (1981, 221) seems to prefer the second.
77 *IG* 1^3.78.39; *Orphic Hymns*, 18.12–13; 41.5–8. In Pindar (*Pythian*, 3.93) *euboulos* is the epithet of Nereus, said (Hesiod, *Theogony*, 233–236) to possess absolute knowledge of truth and justice.
78 Thurioi: IIA1, IIA2, IIB1; Rome: IB1.
79 Εὐκλῆς seems to designate Hades (Hesychius, s.v.); we thus have a trilogy of Eleusinian type: Eubuleus and an infernal couple under other names. On the Lokrian *pinakes*, a man kidnaps Persephone, sometimes in the presence of Hades: could this be a version of the goddess' return effected by a hero who was a local Eubuleus without his Eleusinian torches? Clinton (1992, 73), following Kerenyi (1967, 173–174); also Sourvinou (1973, 12–21).

References

Arbesmann, P.R., 1929: Das Fasten bei den Griechen und Römern (Religionsgeschichtliche Versuche und Vorarbeiten, 21.1). Topelmann, Giessen.
Beaujeu, J., 1955: La religion romaine à l'apogée de l'empire. I. La politique religieuse des Antonins (96–192) (Collection d'études anciennes). Les Belles Lettres, Paris.
Bethe, E., 1894: "Amphilochos", *in RE*, 2, Stuttgart, 1938–1940.
Betz, H.D., 1980: "Fragments from a Catabasis ritual in a Greek magical papyrus", *History of Religions* 19, 287–295.

Betz, H.D., 1983: "The problem of apocalyptic genre in Greek and Hellenistic literature: The case of the Oracle of Trophonius", in D. Hellholm (ed.), *Apocalypticism in the Mediterranean World and the Near-East. Proceedings of the International Colloquium on Apocalypticism, Uppsala, August 12–17, 1979* (Mohr, Tübingen), 577–597.

Bollansée, J., 1999: *Hermippos of Smyrna and his Biographical Writings. A Reappraisal.* (Studia hellenistica, 35). Peeters, Leuven.

Bonnechere, P., 1998a: "Les dieux du Trophonion lébadéen: panthéon ou amalgame?", in V. Pirenne-Delforge (ed.), *Les Panthéons des cités des origines à la Périégèse de Pausanias*. Actes du Colloque organisé à l'Université de Liège du 15 au 17 mai 1997 (Kernos, suppl. 8, Liège). CIERGA, Liège, 91–108.

Bonnechere, P., 1998b: "La scène d'initiation des *Nuées* d'Aristophane et Trophonios: nouvelles lumières sur le culte lébadéen", *REG* 111, 436–480.

Bonnechere, P., 1999: "La personnalité légendaire de Trophonios", *RHR* 216, 259–297.

Bonnechere, P., 2002: "Trophonios: un héros 'chamanique'?", in J.M. Fossey and M.B. Cosmopoulos (eds), *Actes du IXe Congrès International sur la Béotie Antique*. Chicago (forthcoming).

Bonnechere, P. and M. Bonnechere, 1989: "Trophonios à Lébadée. Histoire d'un oracle", *LEC* 57, 289–302.

Brelich, A., 1958: *Gli eroi greci. Un problema storico-religioso*. Edizioni nell'Ateneo, Rome.

Bremmer, J., 1992: "Symbols of marginality from the early Pythagoreans to late antique monks", *G&R* 39, 205–214.

Burkert, W., 1969: "Das Proömium des Parmenides und die Katabasis des Pythagoras", *Phronesis* 14, 1–30.

Burkert, W., 1972: *Lore and Science in Ancient Pythagoreanism* (trs. E.L. Minar). Harvard University Press, Cambridge, Mass.

Burkert, W., 1983: *Homo Necans. The Anthropology of Ancient Greek Sacrificial Ritual and Myth* (trs. P. Bing). University of California Press, Berkeley–Los Angeles–London.

Burkert, W., 1992: *Les cultes à mystères dans l'antiquité* (trs. B. Deforge and L. Bardollet) (*Vérité des mythes*). Les Belles Lettres, Paris [Cambridge, Mass., 1987].

Burkert, W., 1993: "Concordia Discors: the literary and the archaeological evidence of the sanctuary of Samothrace", in N. Marinatos and R. Hägg (eds), *Greek Sanctuaries. New Approches*. Routledge, London and New York, 178–191.

Byl, S., 1980: "Parodie d'une initiation dans les *Nuées* d'Aristophane", *RBPh* 58, 5–21.

Byl, S., 1994: "Les Mystères d'Éleusis dans les *Nuées*", in S. Byl and L. Couloubaritsis (eds), *Mythe et philosophie dans les* Nuées *d'Aristophane (Ébauches)*. Ousia, Brussels, 11–68.

Clark, R.J., 1968: "Trophonios: The manner of his revelation", *Transactions and Proceedings of the American Philological Association* 99, 63–75.

Clinton, K., 1992: *Myth and Cult. The Iconography of the Eleusinian Mysteries*. The Martin P. Nilsson Lectures on Greek Religion, Delivered 19–21 November 1990 at the Swedish Institute at Athens. Acta Instituti Atheniensis regni sueciae, in 8°, 11, Stockholm.

Clinton, K., 1994: "The Epidauria and the arrival of Asclepius in Athens", in R.

Hägg (ed.), *Ancient Greek Cult Practice from the Epigraphical Evidence*. Paul Åström, Stockholm.

Cole, S.G., 1980: "New evidence for the Mysteries of Dionysos", *GRBS* 21, 223–238.

Cole, S.G., 1984: *Theoi Megaloi: The Cult of the Great Gods at Samothrace* (Études préliminaires aux religions orientales dans l'Empire romain, 96). E.J. Brill, Leiden.

Cumont, F., 1949: *Lux perpetua*. Paul Geuthner, Paris.

Daumas, M., 1998: *Cabiriaca. Recherches sur l'iconographie du culte des Cabires. De l'archéologie à l'histoire*. De Boccard, Paris.

Detienne, M., 1958–1960: "De la catalepsie à l'immortalité de l'âme. Quelques phénomènes psychiques dans la pensée d'Aristote, de Cléarque et d'Héraclide", *Nouvelle Clio* 10, 123–135.

Deubner, L., 1900: *De incubatione*. B.G. Teubner, Leipzig.

Dietrich, B.C., 1965: *Death, Fate and the Gods: The Development of a Religious Idea in Greek Popular Belief and in Homer*. University of London and Athlone Press, London.

Dodds, E.R., 1960: *Euripides* Bacchae. Clarendon Press, Oxford.

Dodds, E.R., 1965: *Les Grecs et l'irrationnel* (trs. M. Gibson). Flammarion, Paris.

Dover, K.J., 1968: *Aristophanes:* Clouds. Clarendon Press, Oxford.

Eitrem, S., 1947: *Orakel und Mysterien am Ausgang der Antike*. Albae Vigiliae, N.F., 5, Zurich.

Faure, P., 1964: *Fonctions des cavernes crétoises*. École française d'Athènes. Travaux et Mémoires des anciens membres étrangers de l'école et de divers savants, 14, Paris.

Graf, F., 1974: *Eleusis und die orphische Dichtung Athens in vorhellenistischer Zeit* (Religionsgeschichtliche Versuche und Vorarbeiten, 33). De Gruyter, Berlin and New York.

Graf, F., 1984–1985: "Maximos von Aigai. Ein Beitrag zu Überlieferung über Apollonios von Tyana", *Jahrbuch für Antike und Christentum* 27–28, 65–73.

Graf, F., 1988: "Orpheus. A poet among men", in J. Bremmer (ed.), *Interpretations of Greek Mythology* (Croom Helm, London), 80–106.

Graf, F., 1994: *La magie dans l'antiquité gréco-romaine. Idéologie et pratique*. Les Belles Lettres, Paris.

Grandjean, Y., 1975: *Une nouvelle arétalogie d'Isis à Maronée* (Études préliminaires aux religions orientales dans l'Empire romain, 49). E.J. Brill, Leiden.

Griffiths, J.G., 1975: *Apuleius of Madauros. The Isis-Book (Metamorphoses, Book XI)*. (Études préliminaires aux religions orientales dans l'Empire romain, 39). E.J. Brill, Leiden.

Gruppe, O., 1916–1924: "Trophonios", *in Roscher Lexikon der Mythologie*, 5 (Leipzig and Berlin), 1265–1278.

Guarducci, M., 1941: "Adriano e i culti misterici della Grecia", *Bullettino della Commissione Archeologica Comunale di Roma* 69 (Appendix: *Bull. Museo*, 12), 149–158.

Guidorizzi, G., 1996: *Aristofane*, Le Nuvole. Fondazione Lorenzo Valla Arnaldo Mondadori, Milan.

Hamdorf, F.W., 1964: *Griechische Kultpersonifikationen der vorhellenistischen Zeit*. Philip von Zabern, Mayence.

Hartog, F., 1980: *Le miroir d'Hérodote. Essai sur la représentation de l'autre*. Bibliothèque des Histoires. Gallimard, Paris.

Jeanmaire, H., 1951: *Dionysos. Histoire du culte de Bacchus*. Bibliothèque historique. Payot, Paris.
Joly, R., 1955: "L'exhortation au courage (ΘAPPEIN) dans les Mystères", *REG* 68, 164–170.
Jost, M., 1985: *Sanctuaires et cultes d'Arcadie*. Études péloponésiennes, 9. Vrin, Paris.
Kerenyi, K., 1967: *Eleusis, Archetypal Image of Mother and Daughter*. Bollingen Foundation, New York.
Kühn, E., 1913: *Antinoopolis. Ein Beitrag zur Geschichte des Hellenismus im römischen Ägypten. Gründund und Verfassung*. Universität Göttingen–W.F. Kästner, Göttingen.
Leclerc, M.-C., 1992: "Épiménide sans paradoxe", *Kernos* 5, 221–233.
Levin, S., 1989: "The old Greek oracles in decline", *Aufstieg und Niedergang der römischen Welt*, 2.18.2. De Gruyter, Berlin and New York, 1599–1649.
Lloyd, A.B., 1988: *Herodotus, Book II. Commentary 99–182* (Études préliminaires aux religions orientales dans l'Empire romain, 43, 3). E.J. Brill, Leiden–New York–Copenhagen–Köln.
Lloyd-Jones, H., 1985: "Pindar and the after-life", *Pindare*, Vandoeuvres–Geneva, 245–279.
Macridy, T., 1905: "Alterthümer von Notion", *JÖAI* 8, 155–173.
Macridy, T., 1912: "Antiquités de Notion II", *JÖAI* 15, 36–67.
Marianetti, M.C., 1993: "Socratic mystery-parody and the issue of ἀσέβεια in Aristophanes' *Clouds*", *Symbolae Osloenses* 68, 5–31.
Merkelbach, K., 1962: *Roman und Mysterium in der Antike*. Beck, Munich and Berlin.
Montevecchi, O., 1990: "Adriano e la fondazione di Antinoopolis", *Neronia* 4 (Coll. Latomus, 209). Latomus, Brussels, 183–195.
Motte, A. and V. Pirenne, 1992: "Les mots et les rites. Aperçu des significations de ΟΡΓΙΑ et de quelques dérivés", *Kernos* 5, 119–140.
Mylonas, G.E., 1961: *Eleusis and the Eleusinian Mysteries*. Princeton University Press, Princeton.
Nafissi, M., 1995: "Zeus Basileus di Lebadea. La politica religiosa del koinon beotico durante la guerra cleomenica", *Klio* 77, 149–169.
Nock, A.D., 1941: "A Cabiric rite", *AJA* 45, 377–381.
Parker, R., 1983: *Miasma. Pollution and Purification in Early Greek Religion*. Oxford University Press, Oxford.
Pistorius, P.V., 1939: *Indices Antinoopolitani*. Pistorius, Leiden.
Radke, G., 1939: "Trophonios", *RE*, 2nd series, 13, Stuttgart, 678–695.
Riedweg, C., 1987: *Mysterienterminologie bei Platon, Philon und Klemens von Alexandrien*. De Gruyter, Berlin and New York.
Rohde, E., 1928: *Psyché. Le culte de l'âme chez les Grecs et leur croyance à l'immortalité* (trs. A. Reymond). Payot, Paris.
Rudhardt, J., 1988: "Mnémosyne et les Muses", in P. Borgeaud (ed.), *La mémoire des religions* (*Religions en perspectives*, 2). Labor et fides, Geneva, 37–62.
Schachter, A., 1967: "A Boeotian cult-type", *BICS* 14, 1–16.
Schachter, A., 1981: *Cults of Boiotia*, 1 (*BICS*, Suppl. 38.1). London.
Schachter, A., 1984: "A consultation of Trophonios (*IG* 7.4136)", *AJPh* 105, 258–270.
Schachter, A., 1994: *Cults of Boiotia*, 3 (*BICS*, Suppl. 38.3). London.
Scheer, T.S., 1993: *Mythische Vorväter. Zur Bedeutung griechischer Heroenmythen im*

Selbstverständnis Kleinasiatischer Städte (Münchener Universitätsschriften. Münchener Arbeiten zur Alten Geschichte, 7). Munich.

Sfameni Gasparro, G., 1985: *Soteriology and Mystic Aspects in the Cults of Cybele and Attis* (Études préliminaires aux religions orientales dans l'Empire romain, 103). E.J. Brill, Leiden.

Sfameni Gasparro, G., 1986: *Misteri e culti mistici di Demetra*. L'Erma di Bretschneider, Rome.

Simonetta, R., 1994: "Nascita dell'oracolo di Trofonio", *Aevum* 68, 27–32.

Sourvinou, C., 1973: "The young abductor of the Locrian Pinakes", *BICS* 20, 12–21.

Turner, L.A., 1994: *The History, Monuments, and Topography of Ancient Lebadeia in Boeotia*. UMI, Ann Arbor.

Vernant, J.-P., 1982: "Aspects mythiques de la mémoire", in J.-P. Vernant, *Mythe et pensée chez les Grecs. Études de psychologie historique*, Paris, 1965 [1959], 80–107 (=J.-P. Vernant and P. Vidal-Naquet, *La Grèce ancienne. 2. L'espace et le temps*. Seuil, Paris 1991, 15–46).

Vernière, Y., 1977: *Symboles et mythes dans la pensée de Plutarque. Essai d'interprétation philosophique et religieuse des Moralia*. Les Belles Lettres, Paris.

Versnel, H.S., 1985: "'May he not be able to sacrifice'. Concerning a curious formula in Greek and Roman curses", *ZPE* 58, 247–269.

Versnel, H.S., 1990: *Inconsistencies in Greek and Roman Religion, 1. Ter Unus: Isis, Dionysos, Hermes. Three Studies in Henotheism* (Studies in Greek and Roman Religion, 6). E.J. Brill, Leiden.

Walter, O., 1939: "Κουριτικὴ τριάς", *JÖAI* 31, 53–80.

Weber, W., 1907: *Untersuchungen zur Geschichte des Kaisers Hadrianus*. B.G. Teubner, Leipzig.

Wehrli, F., 1944: *Die Schule des Aristoteles. Texte und Kommentar, 1. Dikaiarchos*. B. Schwabe, Basel.

Wehrli, F., 1948: *Die Schule des Aristoteles. Texte und Kommentar, 3. Klearchos*. B. Schwabe, Basel.

Wehrli, F., 1969: *Die Schule des Aristoteles. Texte und Kommentar, 7. Herakleides Pontikos* (2nd edition). B. Schwabe, Basel.

Zahrnt, M., 1988: "Antinoopolis in Ägypten: die hadrianische Gründung und ihre Privilegien in der neueren Forschung", *Aufstieg und Niedergang der römischen Welt* 2.10.1 (De Gruyter, Berlin and New York), 669–706.

Zhmud, L., 1997: *Wissenschaft, Philosophie und Religion in frühe Pythagoreismus*. Akademie Verlag, Berlin.

8

LANDSCAPES OF DIONYSOS AND ELYSIAN FIELDS

Susan G. Cole

Epic heroes die painfully and find no solace after death. The fame they crave demands a kind of bravery that would be useless if death had no sting. Their deeds survive them, but only in the memory of the living; the heroes themselves go to a place without rewards, where almost everyone receives the same treatment. In epic, death is a social experience and heroes are mourned by the entire community. In the world of the polis, the picture is quite different. The corpse is a polluted object, graves and cemeteries cluster along the roads leading out of the built city, and the funeral processions that join the two spaces emphasize a division between the living and the dead (Sourvinou-Inwood 1983, 45–48; 1995, *passim*). Funeral legislation enacted in the archaic period to curtail public demonstrations of grief during funerals actually accelerated the construction of elaborate private tomb monuments that recorded a family's loss. Death becomes a private affair. Mourning parents attempted to make heroes of dead adolescent children with epic hexameters (e.g., Friedlander 1948, no. 3),[1] but their sentimentality only called attention to the depth of their own grief. The dead who are named on their tombstones ask to be recalled as individuals, but when it became possible to make anyone a hero the issue of status had to take other forms.

As death itself became more ominous, the underworld was redistricted to accommodate a stratified afterlife. Amidst a background of endless loss and suffering, beliefs took root that envisioned part of the world of the dead as potentially a place of joy and happiness, with the promise in this life of some control. Divisions among the dead came to depend on prerequisites that could be satisfied only by personal experience. Rituals offered the necessary preparation, but the form and origin of such practices is obscured by the silence surrounding their performance. They were called *teletai* ("rites of fulfillment") because completion signified change in status and *mysteria* ("mysteries") because they could be revealed only to eligible candidates (the verb *muein* means "to close," usually taken to refer to the mouth).[2] Although we can now only speculate about the content of these rites, we are able to trace their influence by examining the evidence for segregation in the community of the dead.

Domata Persephoneia

The possibility of a divided landscape in the realm of the dead appears early in extant Greek literature, at the conclusion of the *Homeric Hymn to Demeter*. Crossing the boundary between darkness and light is contingent upon ritual experience. The poet says:

> Blessed is the mortal on earth who has seen these rites,
> But the uninitiate who has no share in them never
> Has the same lot once dead in the dreary darkness.[3]

Coming immediately after the account of Demeter's revelation of her Mysteries to the people of Eleusis, these lines break the flow of the narrative. Structured as a technical *makarismos*, the three lines have the shape of a ritual pronouncement of blessing. They do emphasize the power of Demeter's rites, but they also create the impression that the Mysteries at Eleusis were the only ones that offered the prerequisites for achieving special status after death. In practice, however, there were other mysteries that prepared participants for the opportunity of continual sunlight instead of eternal gloom.

For Homer, the world of the dead is dark and gloomy, clearly marked as separate from the world of the living. It is located beyond the edges of the earth, never reached by the sun. When Circe tells Odysseus that he must visit this place before he can reach his homeland, she is able to give him precise directions. She directs him to sail as far as the stream of Ocean and on the further shore, to seek the house of Hades at a place where Persephone's groves grow thick with high poplars and fruit-bearing willows. Here, at a rock where two rivers meet, he must spill the blood of sacrificial victims to rouse the dead and learn his way back home. Odysseus sails to the earth's edge, beyond the place where Dawn rises (*Odyssey* 12.3), where the sun never shines, and where there is always fog and darkness. Here he finds the grove of trees, the juncture of two rivers, and a meadow of asphodel (11.573).

The combination of water, trees, and refreshment should be pleasant, but the sights Odysseus describes are disturbing. The dead approach him in swarms, unable to speak unless animated by the blood of the animals he slays. Without blood, they are "witless," without activity, without pleasure and without future. When Odysseus sacrifices and prays, he addresses both Hades and Persephone, but it is Persephone alone who actually directs the dead and marshals them into groups for his interrogation (11.385). Odysseus catches sight of Minos, son of Zeus and former king of Crete, now a judge among the dead (11.573). A process of judgment is implied (although not explained) by the penalties meted out to the great criminals, mortals like Sisyphos, Tantalos, and Tityos, doomed to suffer forever for crimes against the gods. In this gloomy place the process of judgment separates out those who have offended the gods and doles out punishments, but nowhere in the underworld itself does Odysseus find any offer of eternal reward.

In the *Odyssey* the only hero singled out for special treatment is Menelaos, the least heroic hero of them all. Proteus predicts that Menelaos will not die but, still alive, be conveyed by the gods to the ends of the earth to dwell with Rhadamanthys in the Elysian Field (*Elysion Pedion*). Here he will find the "easiest life for mortals, in a place without snow, harsh winters, or rain," where "the stream of the Ocean constantly sends up breezes of the West wind, blowing briskly for the refreshment of mortals" (*Odyssey* 4.561–568, trs. R. Lattimore).

The striking images described by Circe, Odysseus, and Proteus – the streams of Ocean, the further shore, funereal trees, a particular white rock, or the fruitful plain – reflect the topography of the real world. Like the meadow of asphodel (11.573) or the water Tantalos tries to drink (11.583–584), such images are selected from a standard repertoire that does not require a complete inventory to conjure up feelings of dread. At the close of the *Odyssey* itself, when Penelope's suitors withdraw to the house of Hades, they come to a place along the shore of Ocean where we can recognize the meadow of asphodel from Odysseus' earlier visit (cf. 11.573 with 24.13). A scholiast, commenting on this passage, tells us what the epic audience may have actually believed: that asphodel grows here because this plant takes away the desire to eat and drink. These are activities the Homeric dead do not need. Further recitation of detail is unnecessary. For an audience experienced with conventional formulae, only a sketch is required to establish the location and to indicate that we are at the entrance to the house of the dead.

Odysseus' descriptions of the afterlife are not presented as part of the main narrative of the epic, but indirectly, in flashback, protected from scrutiny by the conventions of prophecy and reported speech. Odysseus presents himself as the first mortal to sail alive to the domain of Hades (*Odyssey* 10.501–502), but the poet's description of the journey and the recital of Odysseus' experiences is shaped by the requirements of epic genre and relies on a background of formulaic descriptions. The narrative assumes a topography familiar to the audience, and the techniques that create distance between the main plot of the epic and the inserted story call attention to the special status of Odysseus' journey.

In epic, heroes die often. Every death is regretted, every victim noticed, but ultimate destinations are rarely mentioned and the experiences of the dead rarely described. Like death itself, the realm of the dead also demanded respectful speech and special gestures. Hades was the Zeus of the other world, but it was Persephone whose word carried terror. Her name conjured up such fear, in fact, that in ordinary speech it was rarely used (Plato, *Cratylus* 404c–d).[4] As bride of Hades, this *arrhetos kore*[5] grew up to be queen of the dead, but her job had associations that made her name too dreadful to pronounce. Even when she was worshipped together with Demeter, mother and daughter were addressed simply as "The Two," an expression nevertheless so powerful that only women were actually supposed to utter it. In Aristophanes' *Frogs* Persephone is simply *he theos*, "the goddess,"[6] and Death, although a god, receives no offerings. As Aeschylus says toward the end of the drama, quoting a line from one of his own plays: "Alone of the gods, Death does not crave gifts" (Ar. *Frogs* 1392; cf. Aesch. *Niobe* Fr. 161.1 Radt). Prayers to Persephone were either prayers to the dead or curses on the living.[7] No parent ever considered naming a daughter after her (Parker 2000, 54–55), and it should be no surprise to discover that even the place where she dwelt had no name of its own. We are in the habit of calling this place the "underworld," but the Greeks themselves, seeking security in euphemism, preferred simply *domata Persephoneia* or, more often, *domata Haidou* ("Persephonian domains" or "halls of Hades"). To avoid precision they used circumlocution or synecdoche, with expressions like Ploutonia ("Pluto's Spaces"), Charoneia ("Charon's Corners"), Acheronteia ("Realms of Acheron"), or "House of Lethe."

Hesiod knows a dark, gloomy place at the ends of the earth, where the Titans were hidden and grieving monsters tied and bound (*Theogony* 617–620; 729–731). He also knows the Islands of the Blest, where a generation of heroes untouched by war remain eternally at ease enjoying the earth's natural bounty.[8] In Hesiod's poetry, however, there are no distinctions among the ordinary dead. The first poet to draw sharp boundaries between underworld realms is Pindar. He distinguishes two populations of the dead, divided in death on the basis of behavior in life (*Olympian* 2.57–60). For Pindar, all owe the same debt to death, but there are some who can meet Persephone's price (Pindar Fr. 133, quoted by Plato, *Meno* 81b). These are the people who kept their oaths and never troubled the earth or disturbed the sea (Pindar, *Olympian* 2.64, 66). They live a life of "perpetual equinox" (the phrase is from Dover 1993, 60), without pain, separated from those who suffer for their offenses against the gods. The especially privileged after three cycles of life and death would keep company with Rhadamanthys and dwell in eternal sunlight at the "Isle of the Blest." This is a place very much like Hesiod's Islands of the Blest, where flowers and trees are always in bloom, and fresh water always flows (Pindar *Olympian* 2.70–74).[9] Those whose wits are too weak to discern the requirements for a life rightly lived will suffer an eternity of pain. Not for them, the "meadows of purple roses," the frankincense trees," or the "trees with golden fruits" (Pindar F 129 Maehler).

When we read Pindar, we know that the water Tantalos once tried in vain to drink will be available to those who arrive thirsty, but qualified and prepared to partake. The fruits that once hung from the trees over Tantalos' head – pears, pomegranates, apple, sweet figs, and ripe olives – are the same as the gleaming fruits of the earth, grown here without human labor and now available, but only to the just. In the *Odyssey* offenses in this world are requited in the next, but rewards are given freely by the gods. For Pindar, rewards are simple, but they must be earned. Heaven is a place with good weather, plenty of fresh water, and free fruit (Pindar *Olympian* 2.61–75).

Mad women and *Frogs*

Pindar divides the population of the dead on the basis of behavior. In the *Homeric Hymn to Demeter* it is visual experience of special rituals that defines *mystai* as fulfilled (*teleioi*), prosperous (*olbioi*), and blessed (*eudaimones*). Those who achieve a special ritual status are distinguished from those who have not had the same experience. The latter, those who are not initiated, are "incomplete" (*ateleis,* line 481). Only those who had seen the rites could avoid the damp darkness of the halls of Hades and reach the sunlight of the blessed. A painting at Delphi by the fifth-century painter Polygnotos of Thasos depicted the famous dead who dwelt with Hades. Pausanias, who describes this painting in meticulous detail, singles out those labeled as "uninitiated," for this reason doomed to perform the useless labor of carrying water in broken vases. Pausanias notices no relation between rank in death and behavior in life (10.25.1–31.12), but already by Polygnotos' day the connection between the two had become a factor in assigning status to the dead. Pindar's concerns about respect for oaths and the requirements of community life were broadened. The Eleusinian initiates who play a major role in Aristophanes' *Frogs* make it clear that the rites at Eleusis were not available to those who violated the trust of other citizens.

Aristophanes' *Frogs*, a play that opened at Athens in 405 BCE, was written shortly after Euripides' *Bacchae*, performed originally in Macedonia and produced at Athens only after Euripides' death in 406 BCE. Both plays feature Dionysos as a principal character and the members of the chorus as ritual participants. Both incorporate rituals and ritual language, and in both the god appears in disguise. In the *Bacchae* the female attendants of Dionysos who accompany him from Asia function as chorus and set an example of reverence and correct worship. In contrast, the women of Thebes refuse to recognize the god and are driven to a frenzy of inappropriate behavior as a result. In Aristophanes' *Frogs* the chorus of Eleusinian initiates sets an example of ritual propriety. As "blessed *thiasoi*" (*eudaimonas thiasous*, 156), these initiates partake of a most beautiful radiance (*phos kalliston*, 155) and dance amid beds of myrtle (*murrinonas*, 156). Other dramatists had represented a *nekuiya* on stage,[10] and Kritias, contemporary of Sophocles and

Euripides, even used a chorus of initiates to complement the *katabasis* of Theseus. Aristophanes' chorus of initiates, however, is a major character with a special role to play, carefully integrated into the action of the play. This chorus functions as informant and collective guide to the underworld, because its members are experienced initiates. Like the *mystagogoi* appointed to supervise candidates for initiation, they guide Dionysos and describe the route, show him the sights along the way and introduce the local residents. Aristophanes was careful to structure his lyric passages within the framework of the plot so that he did not disturb the integrity of his chorus. The action of the play begins in real time in the real world. Aristophanes takes 315 lines to introduce us to Dionysos and his mission to Hades. He had to postpone the parodos,[11] because, since the initiates are already dead, Dionysos cannot meet them until he enters their realm. Their status, nevertheless, will be an important check on their reliability.

In the *Bacchae* Dionysos instructs by dividing those he punishes from those he protects. His landscape is a remote mountain glen teeming with animal and plant life, where milk flows almost unbidden from the ground and ivy can drip with sweet honey. The Dionysian meadow is attractive, but it can also be ominous (Euripides, *Bacchae* 103–770; 1043–1152). One moment a place for ritual and source of spontaneous nourishment, the next moment the Dionysian haunt can become a place of murder and bloody dismemberment. The chorus sings of a meadow, where the fawn, an animal dear to Dionysos, plays among lush moisture and green plants (862–876). Like the clearing where Pentheus dies, the meadow where the fawn sports connotes lavish abundance and freedom from care; but even such gifts have a price. Although the fawn may be free to cavort, the meadow conceals the intrusion of death in the form of the hunter's snare.[12]

Euripides' Dionysos is in complete control of the dramatic situation and needs no guide. In Aristophanes' *Frogs*, however, it is Dionysos himself who is in need of instruction (Lada-Richards 1999, 51–60). The god's journey to an alternative universe is staged as a guided tour for his audience, one that "initiates" them to the possibilities they will someday face. Aristophanes, who draws on the traditional topography of the underworld, recognizes a divided landscape and marks out the special places reserved for his chorus of initiates. The members of the chorus are well informed about requirements for entry. The major qualification is still ritual, and the chorus knows that the Mysteries are not open to all.[13] Herakles, himself a famous initiate, explains the distinction between qualified and unqualified. Penalties are exacted for violating community responsibility. The three offenses are swearing false oaths, ignoring the obligations of hospitality, and striking a parent (147–150).[14] These are dangerous acts that threaten family unity and social cohesion. The chorus of initiates returns to the same theme in the lyric passage that follows, concluding with a song that explains the importance of acting with justice toward outsiders and fellow citizens.[15] The text of their choral song is quoted in a short inscription on a little Hellenistic altar at Rhodes:

> By Aristophanes:
> For on us alone
> do the sun and the divine
> daylight shine, all of us who
> 5 have been initiated
> and who maintained a reverent
> manner toward strangers
> and private citizens.[16]

The anonymous initiate who displayed this text at Rhodes, by isolating this particular passage, called attention to the poet's claim that standards for social behavior were part of the preview of the Mysteries. These lines are quoted from a passage that creates a significant moment in the play. Timed to mark an important transition, this song accompanies the moment when Dionysos walks up to the door of Hades as he prepares to cross the last boundary between the living and the dead.

The singers are in a good position to testify to the benefits of initiation. Because they are dead, they have already achieved the rewards of sunlight, mobility, and pleasant surroundings. Immune to the unpleasantness of those scorned by Persephone, they now dwell in a protected space at the boundary between life and death – as Herakles says, "along the road itself, right at the door of Pluto's place" (161–163). Protected by ritual, they inhabit a pure space. Their meadow and their grove are not shrouded in darkness, but streaming with light. Those inexperienced in *bakcheia* are excluded from their Mysteries.[17] Separated by gender into two groups, the chorus divides for ritual. Males withdraw to a grove to dance for the goddess, while females celebrate an all-night ceremony (*pannychis*) in their own flowered meadow. Protected in death by ritual, the chorus does not have to deal with the "sewers of mud" or the rivers of "ever-flowing diarrhoea" that torment those who committed crimes against their fellow citizens (144–146).[18] For the chorus, meaningful experience in the other world consists of eternal performances of the rituals that got them there in the first place.

The meadow of judgment

The year of Aristophanes' *Frogs* was a year of war and political uncertainty at Athens. Aristophanes exploits Euripides' recent death by sending Dionysos on a mission to bring a famous dead playwright back from the underworld to solve Athens' problems. In a play where the chorus is so obviously associated with the Eleusinian Mysteries, however, we might well ask: "Why Dionysos?"

A possible answer may lie in the contents of a grave in Hipponion, a little Greek town in South Italy not far from Lokroi. Here, some time during the last years of the fifth century or the early years of the fourth, a woman took with her to the grave a tiny gold tablet to guide her soul on its last journey. The inscribed tablet describes what her soul could expect to find "on the other side." On the slip of gold, beaten thin and carefully folded, sixteen lines of poetry in more or less dactylic hexameters give directions for a scripted performance at the door of Hades' domain. Providing the itinerary for the journey and a script for recital, the little gold tablet gives precise instructions about where to go, what to do, and what to say in order to reach a place like the sunlit meadow, where Aristophanes' chorus of initiates dances for Persephone. The text from Hipponion can be translated as follows:

> This is the task of Memory; when you are about to die...
> – – – – [line missing?] – – – –
> into the broad halls of Hades, there is to the right a spring;
> and standing next to it a white cypress tree;
> arriving down there, the souls of the dead grow cold.
> Do not go near this spring at all.
> But in front of it you will find the cold water flowing forth from
> the lake of Memory; and guardians pass above.
> But they will surely ask you, with their crowded thoughts,
> for what reason you seek out the darkness of dank Hades.
> Say: "I am the child of Earth and of starry Sky,
> and I am parched with thirst and I am perishing. But give me quickly
> cold water to drink from the lake of Memory."
> And above all, they will announce you to the king under the earth.
> And above all, they will give you to drink from the lake of Memory.
> And what is more, when you have drunk, you will travel a road, a sacred
> road, which other famous *mystai* and *bakchoi* also tread.[19]

Greek texts on gold designed to protect the soul after death have been turning up in graves throughout the Mediterranean since 1835, and new items continue to appear almost every year. Thus far, more than forty inscribed gold tablets have been identified in sepulchral contexts.[20] All seem to have been designed for the same journey, a journey over which, it turns out, Dionysos presides.

Questions of unity and origin are difficult to answer. First of all, the tablets cluster in three far-flung geographic areas: Thessaly–Macedonia, western Crete, and Sicily–S. Italy (see Table 8.1). Outliers have also cropped up at Manissa and Mytilene and in Elis and Achaia. Moreover, themes and content do not correlate neatly with geographic distribution. Texts from Thourioi were anomalous in their coded reference to regeneration, rebirth, and apotheosis until two tablets from Pelinna were published in 1987.[21] Name tags, badges, and greetings with *chairein* are heavily concentrated in Macedonia, but greetings with *chairein* also appear elsewhere, at widely separated sites in South Italy (Thourioi) and on Crete.[22]

Tablets show variation in size, form, and content. They have been found in contexts of both cremation and inhumation and in the graves of both males and females (although in more female contexts than male). Tablets were placed on the chest, near a hand, at the base of the skull, in the mouth, over the mouth, or under the head. Some are long, others are short; some are rolled, others folded; some give only the dead person's first name, a few give only ritual status. Longer texts are written on small, rectangular pages; name tags are more likely to take the form of little leaves of sacred plants (myrtle, grape, or olive). Two longer texts from Pelinna are written on golden pages shaped like ivy leaves. Some name tags are in the form of an *epistomion* (a band placed across the mouth). Two "tablets" are simply gold coins over-scribed with the name of a single individual. At least seven uninscribed gold sheets, together with an eighth, ruled for writing but without text, seem to be imitations of the inscribed gold leaves. Two of the forty-four tablets are inscribed on silver.

Once considered to divide neatly into two distinct categories (see Zuntz 1971, 277–286, for preliminary outline), the collection has now grown so large and the categories so overlapping that similarities have become as significant as differences. Certain repeated themes and images nevertheless stand out, especially the anticipation of a journey to the underworld, a confrontation with a divine gatekeeper, a landscape with trees and water, and formulae for ritual responses. The conclusion to be drawn from the total collection is that those who took such texts to the grave (or their relatives) had confidence in entitlement to special treatment after death. In one way or another, the texts assume that eligibility was established by ritual and confirmed after death by recalling or reciting esoteric information that could have been learned only through that ritual experience.

The tablet from Hipponion is the oldest and also the longest example in the series. Written in Ionic with an overlay of the local Doric dialect of Hipponion, the text preserves traces of what must have been an earlier Ionic model.[23] It is therefore very likely that the model for this text originated elsewhere, perhaps in Ionia itself. The expectations expressed in the text and the obvious connection to initiates (*mystai*) and bacchic followers (*bakchoi*) of Dionysos could even predate Pindar (Cole 1980, 227–238, for connections with Dionysos).

Texts on the gold tablets serve a variety of purposes. They greet the gods, appease Memory, refer to drinking special water, point out a special route, answer questions about identity, give passwords, remind a divinity of a participant's status, give the names of individual initiates, recall required ritual, or repeat ritual formulas. They assume that the gods will be able to recognize those eligible for special treatment. The Hipponion text alludes to

Table 8.1 Gold tablets: dispersal, date, and content

Group	Location	Date	Burial	Gender	Shape
P1	Pelinna (Thessaly)	Late 4 cent. BCE	Inhumation	Female?	Ivy leaf
P2	Pelinna (Thessaly)	Late 4 cent. BCE	Inhumation	Female?	Ivy leaf
B1	Petelia (Italy)	Before 350 BCE	Inhumation/published 1836	Male?	Rectangular
B2	Pharsalos (Thessaly)	350–320 BCE	Found with ashes in bronze hydria	Female?	
B3	Eleutherna (Crete)	3/2 cent. BCE		Male?	Rectangular
B4	Eleutherna (Crete)	3/2 cent. BCE		Son	Rectangular
B5	Eleutherna (Crete)	3/2 cent. BCE		Son	
B6	Mylopetra (Crete)	3/2 cent. BCE		Daughter (thygater)	Rectangular
B7	Stathos (Crete)	3/2 cent. BCE		Son	
B8	Stathos (Crete)	3/2 cent. BCE		Son	
Graf B9	Thessaly? (Malibu)	4 cent. BCE		Son	Rectangular
B10	Hipponion (Italy)	c. 400 BCE	Inhumation	Female	Trapezoidal
B11	Entella (Sicily)	3 cent. BCE?			
B12	Pherai (Thessaly)	Late 4 cent. BCE			
A1	Lesbos Thourioi	Unpublished Before 350 BCE?	Inhumation (mound)	Male?	Rectangular
A2	Thourioi	Mid-4 cent. BCE?	Inhumation (mound)	Male?	Rectangular
A3	Thourioi	Mid-4 cent. BCE?	Inhumation (mound)	Male	Rectangular
A4	Thourioi	Mid-4 cent. BCE?	Partial cremation	Male?	Rectangular
A5	Rome	2 cent. CE		Female	Rect/rolled
C	Thourioi	Mid-4 cent. BCE?	Cremation: same as A4		
D1	Eleutherna (Crete)	3 cent. BCE?			

LANDSCAPES OF DIONYSOS AND ELYSIAN FIELDS

Placement	Type	Imagery	Password	Mysteries	Divinity	Name
On chest		Animal/milk/wine			Bacchic one; Persephonea	
On chest	Combined	Animal/milk/wine	Ho bakchios me eluse		Persephona	
?	Memory					
In bronze hydria		Hydria/rape of Oreithyia				"Asterios"
	Memory	Dying of thirst				
	Memory	Dying of thirst				
	Memory	Dying of thirst				
	Memory	Dying of thirst				
	Memory	Dying of thirst				
	Memory	Dying of thirst				
	Memory	Dying of thirst				
	Memory	Dying of thirst/sacred road		Mystai and bakchoi	Queen under the earth	
	Memory	Dying of thirst	Symbola		Queen under the earth	
		Sacred meadow	Symbola: Andrike-paidothurson	Mystes	Brimo	
Near hand	Purity	Lightning/penalty	Blessed + god instead of mortal		Phersephoneia	
Near hand	Purity	Lightning/penalty			Phersephoneia	
Near hand	Purity	Lightning/penalty			Phersephoneia	
	Kid in milk	Sacred meadows/groves	Chaire		Phersephoneia	
In gold cylinder	Memory/purity		Benediction		Eukles/Eubouleus	Caecillia Secundina
	Epistulary salutation		Chairein		Plouton/Phersoponeia	

Table 8.1 Continued

Group	Location	Date	Burial	Gender	Shape
D2	Sfakaki (Crete)	25 BCE–50 CE	Cist grave/ bronze coin on chest	Male?	Epistomion
D3	Aigion (Achaia)	3 cent. BCE			Myrtle leaf
D4	Pella (Macedonia)		With 12 uninscribed leaves	Male	Myrtle Leaf
D5	Pella (Macedonia)			Male	Myrtle leaf
D6	Pella (Macedonia)	Late 4 cent. BCE		Female	Myrtle leaf
D7	Pella (Macedonia)	Late 4 cent. BCE		Female	Myrtle leaf
D8	Pella (Macedonia)	Late 4 cent. BCE		Female	Leaf
	Pella (Macedonia)	Early 2 cent. BCE	Names orig. in ink?		Uninscribed tablets
D9	Aigai	Hellenistic		Female	Leaf
D10	Methone (Macedonia)	4 cent. BCE	Female	Leaf?	Mouth
D11	Paionia (Macedonia)	Late 4 cent. BCE		Male	Leaf?
D12	Elis	3 cent. BCE		Female	Myrtle leaf
D13	Elis	3 cent. BCE		Female	Myrtle leaf
D14	Alkeyes Kitros (Th)	Philip II?		Female	Gold coin
D15	Alkeyes Kitros (Th)	Philip II?		Male	Gold coin
E1	Thurioi				Silver uninscr.
E2	Poseidonia				Silver tablet
E3	Cosenza	ca. 400 BCE		Female?	Uninscribed tablets
E4	Manissa	Early Roman Imp	tomb 483		Inscribed fragment
	Sfakaki (Crete)	2 cent. BCE			3 uninsc. tablets
	Montesarchi				29 stamped lines

a traditional infernal landscape divided into at least two regions, with access to a preferred place restricted to those who can prove that they are qualified. The Pelinna tablets and A1 and A4 from Thourioi imply that rebirth will follow death. Other tablets give actual passwords and programmed ritual responses. In fact, three of the new texts (one from Pherai and the two from Pelinna) have considerably enlarged our corpus of Greek ritual language.[24] The text from Pherai (Thessaly) even calls the secret password it records by its technical name, *symbola*. The same term also appears at Entella in Sicily, at the southern extremity of the spill zone. Other tablets emphasize personal identification, assuming that although many might apply, only those prepared will be admitted.

Many divinities are mentioned. Gods include Persephone, Plouto, Brimo, the Bacchic one (Dionysos), as well as traditional figures like Eukles (pos-

LANDSCAPES OF DIONYSOS AND ELYSIAN FIELDS

Placement	Type	Imagery	Password	Mysteries	Divinity	Name
Base of skull	Epistulary salutation				Plouton/ Phersopone	
Mouth	Badge			Mustes		
	Badge/ name tag			Mustas		Dexilaos
	Badge/ name tag			Mustas		Philon
	Name tag				Phersepone	Philoxena
	Badge/ name tag			Mustes eusebes	Persephone	Poseidippos
	Name tag					Hegesiska
	Badge/ name/sal.		Chairein		Phersepone	Philiste
Name tag						Phulomaga
	Name tag					Bottakos
Under head	Name tag					Euxega
Under head	Name tag					Philemena
Mouth	Name tag/ charonian					Xenariste
Mouth	Name tag/ charonian					Andron
2 now lost						
	Badge		I belong to x of the goddess			
2 earrings		Earrings: KOR, LUS				

sibly equivalent to Plouto) and Eubouleus. These divine names are also associated with Mysteries elsewhere. The terms used to describe groups of worshippers should be a clue, but the dead themselves are identified by generic titles (*mystai, bakchoi,* or *mystes eusebes*) that do not obviously refer to a readily definable ceremony. In fact, we have several choices. *Mystai* is a generic term, used of initiates of the Eleusinian, Dionysian, and Samothracian Mysteries, as well as any number of independent groups associated with various divinities, indigenous and foreign, early and late. *Bakchoi* is a technical term for followers of Dionysos, used to rank initiates in Dionysian groups in the Hellenistic and Roman periods. It could also refer to worshippers with no obvious connection to mystery ceremonies. *Mystes eusebes*, "reverent initiate," is the technical expression for an initiate of the Samothracian Mysteries and the official title used in initiate lists inscribed in stone at the home sanctuary. So far it has turned up on a gold tablet only once, but it may be significant that this tablet comes from Macedonia. The fact that the same tablet is also inscribed with the name of Persephone, however, suggests that we are not dealing with a Samothracian initiate.

The tablets that record these terms make no reference to evidence for sanctuary-based mystery ceremonies. In fact, they contain no references to temples, sanctuaries, or sacred places. We are therefore probably justified in assuming that required rituals were not associated with a specific place or a specific sanctuary. Any rituals certifying completion of the ceremonies that generated these texts must have been privately organized, performed in obscurity, and under no official control. We are familiar with ceremonies that fit this description because such rites are mentioned (with scorn) by Plato and Demosthenes. These writers hold in contempt the freelance priests who conducted ceremonies of purification and initiation in private homes (Plato, *Republic* 364b–365a; Dem. 18.259). Demosthenes' description of Aeschines reading from book rolls to prompt his mother as she conducted purification rituals for paying customers in her own home is intended to cast doubt on the status of the family as well as the ceremonies. Plato, with a certain distaste, associates similar rituals with Musaios and Orpheus and attributes to them a *logos* about eschatology complete with suggestions for avoiding punishments like wallowing in mud or drawing water in a sieve (*Republic* 363d–e). Both writers connect unregulated initiation and purification ceremonies with texts. The possession of privileged texts and the ability to reproduce them meant prestige for the purveyors of these ceremonies. The circulation of texts coupled with the high regard for the written word and the emphasis on memory accounts for any consistencies in ritual and ideology.

Plato's disapproval is shared by the anonymous fourth-century author of the commentary preserved on the Derveni papyri.[25] This writer has little confidence in initiations for private consumption peddled by self-trained practitioners; nor is he impressed with the public initiations performed in the cities (Obbink 1997, 43, for a translation). A pedant with philosophical aspirations, the author of the texts recorded on the Derveni papyri was not interested in rituals that offered security after death because he believed that initiates did not really understand what they saw and heard. The man who took a copy of this commentary to his own funeral pyre must also have been unimpressed by rituals that promised good times for the dead. He preferred exegesis of cosmology and theogony. His philosophical ambitions, however, were not shared by the practical initiates who chose to be buried with gold tablets. They may have had little confidence in their own memories, but they did expect to be rewarded.

The Derveni commentator distinguishes between ritual solutions for the problem of knowing and remembering (as practiced in the Mysteries) and philosophical access to knowledge tested by textual analysis (Obbink 1997). He had no confidence that meaning could be found in ritual or that through ritual experience candidates could truly understand what the Mysteries claimed to teach. He does not mention texts like those on the gold tablets, but he is acquainted with hymns that may be related. The distinction made by the Derveni commentator between two ways of knowing is a sign of a split between ritual tradition and a new, self-conscious intellectual discourse on the nature of divinity. Sixth- and fifth-century evidence from Olbia, however, including a bronze mirror inscribed with a Dionysaic ritual cry and bone tablets inscribed with the phrases like "Life–Death–Life" provide material evidence for the bacchic initiation ceremonies at Olbia described by Herodotus (4.79) (see Zhmud 1992). The ritual context therefore stretches back to the late archaic period, providing a pedigree for the contrasts between death, rebirth, and even apotheosis (i.e., on the tablets from Thourioi and Pelinna). Until we have more information, it seems safe to assume that the texts on the tablets – short, contradictory, heterogeneous, and unpredictable – are more likely the product of independent groups supervised by inspired leaders than the result of a particular philosophical movement.[26]

The content of the tablets is certainly eclectic. Because enjambment is not a characteristic of the longer texts, lines from one can easily do service in another. Texts combine direct address with description, dialogue with monologue, and recitation of ritual phrases with assertions of identity. The soul engages in dialogue.[27] Divine stewards of the other world question new arrivals and expect answers. They ask: "Why are you here?" "Who are you?" "How are you?" The tablets themselves also make pronouncements and give instructions:

> "Blessed and most happy you will be god instead of mortal."
> "And then you will be a lord among the other heroes."
> "Go to the right . . . observe very carefully."
> "Hail, you who have experienced what you have never experienced before."
> "Once human you have become a god."
> "A kid, you fell into the milk."
> "*Chairen*! *Chairein*! Take the right-hand road to the sacred meadows and grove of Phersephoneia."
> "Now you died and now you were born, thrice blessed one, on this day."
> "Tell Phersephona that the Bacchic one himself has released you."
> "Enter the sacred meadow!"
> "For the *mystes* is without punishment."
> "A bull, you leapt into the milk."
> "Suddenly you leapt into the milk."
> "A ram, you fell into the milk."
> "You shall have wine as your blessed honor."
> "Caecilia Secundina, go in peace, you have become divine."

The soul is expected to make a scripted response:

> "I am the child (son, daughter) of Earth and the starry Heaven."
> "I am parched with thirst and I perish."
> "Give me quickly cold water to drink from the lake of Memory."
> "I belong to the heavenly lineage; and you yourselves know this."
> "But I am thirsty and I am perishing; but give me quickly cold water flowing from the lake of Memory."
> "My name is Asterios, and I am parched with thirst, but give me to drink from the spring"
> "A kid, I fell into the milk!"
> "I belong to the child of the goddess!"

The soul also responds with acclamation and ritual response:

> "Pure, I come from the pure ones, o queen of those under the earth!"
> "Man–child–thyrsos! Man–child–thyrsos!"
> "Brimo! Brimo!"
> "Greetings, Plouton and Phersepone!"

The "other world" of the tablets is familiar, recognizable by the now traditional signs: springs, a lake, a cypress tree, sacred meadows and groves. The *mystes* approaches sacred Persephone as a suppliant, longing to sink into the lap of the mistress-queen.[28] Some initiates thirst for the water of Memory; others have become divine (the process is described as being struck by lightning), still others expect rebirth.

The purity of the soul is matched by the purity of the tablet itself, for gold is pure by nature, whole, and unchanging. Impervious to the effects of rust, verdigris, and time, the metal stakes a claim to timelessness.[29] The soul in passage has need of the stability of gold because the consequences of the impending choice are long-lasting. At the critical moment, choice requires a clear mind, access to memory, a ready response, and, above all, the right answer. The text on the tablet provides a "cheat" sheet for the soul, but it is also a substitute for the soul's own voice. The tablet is the vehicle for its own message, for if all else fails, the tablet itself can speak. The written text implies a belief in the power of the written word, but if the gods of the dead must witness performance of ritual speech, what exactly is the purpose of the written text itself? Is it only a trigger for memory? A ticket to the meadow of the blessed?[30] A reminder to retain the memory of past life? (see Zuntz 1971, 380.)

Status after death is determined by ritual experience, but it also depends on access to memory. Those buried with a text like the one from Hipponion, were not willing to share the shadowy existence of the Homeric dead, deprived of memory unless animated by the blood of victims slain in ritual. Memory certifies personal identity, ritual status, and the content of rituals learned earlier. The written word is a stimulus, but it also provides a token by which the gods recognize those deserving special treatment. Passage at death is complicated because, as the tablets make clear, it is the responsibility of the soul to remind the gods of its own eligibility. The dead themselves, in other words, must deal with the possibility of the gods' indifference. The texts do not console, but rather provide a plan for action because the soul must make a choice whose effects will be permanent. The soul must therefore know three things: (1) the right route; (2) the correct passwords and ritual responses; and (3) its own identity. Above all, the soul must remember which water to drink. There will be no second chance.

We see from Aristophanes' *Frogs* that there are distractions. Charon's ferry stops at the Plain of Forgetfulness (186), a place like Plato's Field of Lethe and River of Oblivion, where souls lose memory. Later tomb inscriptions will describe the water of Lethe as bitter (Merkelbach and Staube 1998, 07/08/02). We read from his epitaph that one Eunonomos, by choosing to drink from a spring that "does not speak," drank the drink of silence and had to take the road to Hades. Euonomos implies that he had a choice between two springs, but that the water of memory was available in only one. The choice was up to him. The springs at Lebadeia, where, according to Pausanias, there was a spring of Lethe and a spring of Memory, may be relevant.[31] The tablets imply that even initiates might need help. The text is therefore an aid to memory. The dead cannot be trusted to find their own way.

But how accurate are the instructions on the tablets? The tablet from Petelia advises the soul to avoid the spring on the left and to choose the other, the one flowing from the lake of Memory. The tablets from Pharselos and Hipponion, on the other hand, advise against the spring on the right. The tablet from Entella warns against a lake on the right. Tablet A4 from Thurioi advises the soul to take the right-hand road. None of the tablets actually prescribes water from a spring on the right, but what is the poor soul from Petelia to do if, relying on her tablet, she finds that she has drunk the wrong water?

Why should the dead need Memory anyway? Tomb inscriptions are ambivalent. Epitaphs describe the post-mortem experience as a journey with several possible destinations: a place under the earth, among the stars, the Elysian plain, or an imaginary landscape in the underworld. For some, the experience is described as sleep or loss of consciousness; for others, as an eternal banquet with free food in the land of the blessed (*choros ton eusebon*; see Chaniotis 2000). Memory itself was a handicap because memory of a past life could emphasize the grief of separation. An epitaph at Knidos describes a dead wife able to appear to her husband for a brief visit because, as she says, "I have not yet drunk the very last water of Lethe, daughter of

Aidoneus" (Merkelbach and Staube 1998, 01/01/07). Another woman is unable to forget her beloved brothers even though she has drunk the "drink of Lethe of those under the earth" (Merkelbach and Staube 1998, 04/07/07).

In the *Phaedrus* Plato casts the journey of the soul to the forms in terms of metaphors from the Mysteries. His comparison of the soul's vision of the forms to the vision of the Mysteries assumes that initiates were expected to remember the content of the initiation ceremony. For Plato, the soul trying to be freed from the cycle of rebirth and earthly existence had to free itself from all earthly attractions (Plato, *Phaedrus* 248c–256d). Memory of a past life for such souls was not an advantage. Plato also describes a system of roads and judgments for the soul after death. He recommends the road to the right (*Republic* 614b), by which the souls of those who have lived a life of justice travel upward to return to the meadow where they began, in order to choose lots for the next life. Before returning to earth to take up a new life, each soul had to pass through the torrid Plain of Forgetfulness to drink the water of oblivion, water that no ceramic vessel could hold (621a). There could be no memory of a past life when beginning the next. In other dialogues Plato uses different metaphors, but the message is similar. The *Gorgias* concludes with the topography of a plain where a decision must be made. Here, at a *triodos* (crossroads) the road splits in two directions. Three judges divide the earth between them. Aiakos takes Europe, Rhadamanthys Asia, and their brother Minos sits as a judge of appeals. Souls are anonymous because judges cannot know a soul's earthly identity (524e). Stripped naked, the judge's soul scans the naked, petitioning soul, and according to a law in force since the time of Kronos, those judged righteous go to the Isle of the Blest (523a–b).

There is no judgment scene like this in any of the golden tablets, but there is the pressure of anxiety about passing a test. In the *Frogs*, Aristophanes' Dionysos sets up a test to conclude the contest between Aeschylus and Euripides. To determine the winner, he weighs their poetic metaphors on a balance scale (*stathmos*; Aristophanes, *Frogs* 1365). The procedure is a parody of the scene in Aeschylus' *Psychostasia*, the play where Zeus weighs souls of heroes to decide who deserves death (Sommerstein 1996, 280). In the *Frogs* we have the opposite situation. Here Aristophanes' Dionysos weighs words to determine which dead poet will make the return journey back to the living. Aeschylus almost wins with the heavy line quoted at the beginning of our discussion: "For Death alone of the gods does not desire gifts." Death cannot be bribed. The line suggests that the role of Dionysos, referee in this mini-contest between Aeschylus and Euripides, may be no accident. Those familiar with his role in the Mysteries for the *mystai* and *bakchoi* of the gold tablets would not have been surprised.

The new tablet from Pherai invites the soul to enter the sacred meadow, "for the *mystes* is without penalty" (*SEG* 45.646). If there were a scene of judgment in the procedure for which this tablet served, it would have been over quickly. Pindar says that the helpless dead who die in this world pay the penalty immediately (*Olympian* 2.57–2.58). Tablets A2 and A3, from Thourioi, contain the line "And I have repaid the price in exchange for deeds not at all right." But, as the tablet from Pelinna has it, "Tell Persephona that the Bacchic One himself has released you." Here, finally, we find the clue that might explain the role of Dionysos. The god himself is not a judge, but he presides over the transition where the process of judgment must take place.[32] We have arrived at the meadow near the gates of Hades, the place where Aristophanes' chorus of Eleusinian initiates sing their ritual song, the song that connects respect for strangers and fellow citizens with the Mysteries (Ar. *Frogs* 454–459). The image of the meadow also recurs in other accounts of post-mortem experience. Plato's descriptions of the meadow of decision are ominous, whether it is the meadow with two exits that ends the *Republic* (Plato *Republic* 619c–d) or the meadow of the *Gorgias* where three judges preside over the place where the path splits (Plato, *Gorgias* 524a). The meadow where the *bakchoi* assemble may be a place of anxiety, but it is not a place of gloom.

The bacchic meadow in the texts of the gold tablets is a place of promise because the souls of the tablets are protected by their bacchic *teletai*. Dionysos will mediate. As the only god who shares his own epithets with his worshippers (Cole 1980, 234), he is also the only god who can share with them the benefits of his divine status. He is the god for those critical transitional moments right up to and including the interchange at Pluto's door. A fourth-century vase now in Toledo, in fact, depicts Dionysos at precisely this moment, stepping up to the entrance to the House of Hades and shaking hands with Hades himself (Johnston and McNiven 1996, 27–34 and pl. 1). The central scene is framed by familiar Dionysiac figures and companions: Aktaion with Pentheus and Agave on the right, a satyr and two maenads on the left, and a childish Paniskos and Kerberos below. Dionysos seems to be negotiating here on behalf of his Theban cousins whose challenges and sufferings are recounted in Euripides' *Bacchae*. Whatever the result, the important image is the gesture at the center, the handclasp, a gestural *symbola* that joins Dionysos and Hades. The two have come to an agreement.

Dionysos is the one who negotiates; Persephone is the one who decides. Tablet A4 at Thourioi advises the soul: "Take the right hand road to the sacred meadows and grove of Phersophoneia!" A2 and A3 explain: "And now I have come as a suppliant to sacred Phersephoneia." The meadow is the place where the decision will be made.[33] The new tablet from Pherai in Thessaly invites the soul: "Enter the sacred meadow; for the *mystes* is without punishment." Initiates protected by Dionysos expect easy transit. Those from Macedonia and Eleutherna, who wear their badges courageously to the grave, greet the goddess without fear: "Greetings to Pluton and Persephone!" "Greetings to Persephone!" They give their own names with no expectation of retribution: Dexilaos, Philoxena, Poseidippos,[34] Philiste, Phulomagna, Bottakos, Hegesiska.

When a gold tablet was placed in a grave there was no need of an outward sign.[35] Tablets were not for the living. They were written to prepare the soul for the encounter with the gods of the dead. No one else needed to know they existed. Tomb inscriptions, in fact, rarely allude to expectations for special treatment after death, and even when they do, much is left unexplained.[36] Epitaphs rarely make appeals to memory. We do hear that souls have gone to the Isle of the Blest, reached the land (*choros*) of the blessed gods, or that they now dwell among the stars. In the context of rewards, however, forgetfulness is still something to be avoided. A man named Hekatodoros is described by the inscription at his grave as conveyed to the banquets of the gods on Olympos because he "did not drink the water of Lethe" (Merkelbach and Staube 1998, 01/20/27). An eight-year-old boy escaped the house of gloomy Persephone only because he did not drink the water of Lethe (Merkelbach and Staube 1998, 01/20/29).

We have come a long way from the undifferentiated and powerless dead in the epic underworld. The initiates from Macedonia proudly wear their name tags when they set out on their journey, ready to greet the gods at the border crossing. Name tags break the rule of anonymity established for the naked souls facing the judges stripped naked in Plato's version. The gold tablet initiates in general have expectations very different from those of the Homeric dead, whose appetites are choked off and stifled by asphodel. The dead who satisfy Dionysos do not need to fast. Scenes of Dionysiac feasts and symposia in the other world figure prominently among the work of fourth-century Italiote vase painters (Jaquet Rimassa 1998, 19–41), suggesting that the pleasures of the other world are the pleasures of a perpetual Dionysiac banquet where no one had to wash the dishes (Graf 1974, 98–102). Plato may not have approved (Plato, *Republic* 364e–365a; Riedweg 1998, 373), but modest rewards were enough when faced with the permanent tedium of the underworld. Security was the issue that really mattered.

The meadow of the tablets is a mythic space. Greek lands were not often blessed with verdant meadows, and real crops were produced only by means of hard work. The Dionysian meadow, in contrast, requires no labor because it is a land lush without cultivation. The landscape of the tablets is like the meadow where Aristophanes' chorus dances, a place moist with dew and full of flowers (Aristophanes, *Frogs* 326, 344, 373, 448). Whether located high in the mountains (as in Euripides' *Bacchae*), or at an entrance to the underworld (as at Eleusis, Hermione, Lerna or the mythical Nysa of the *Homeric Hymn to Demeter*), meadows, clearings, and glades were not funereal spaces (Motte 1973, 239–247). The mythic meadow of the tablets, located in an area between life and death, was not the end of a journey. The terms "Elysian Field" and "Isle of the Blest," denoted a place of spontaneous cultivation, far removed from ordinary life and completely unconnected with any known city or land, where special souls could dwell undisturbed with the gods. Achilles, according to some, was translated to the Isle of the Blest, beyond the place where ordinary mortals could hope to rest, but only because his mother interceded with Zeus (Pindar, *Olympian* 2.79–80). Another version has Achilles buried in a golden amphora, a gift from Dionysos (*Odyssey* 24.73–75). Does the golden amphora from Dionysos represent a vestige of an alternative terminus for Achilles? In a short dialogue falsely attributed to Plato, the "land of the pious" (the *choros ton eusebon* mentioned in tomb inscriptions) is a place of flowered meadows and a final destination for philosophers and poets, where those who have been initiated have front row seats ([Plato] *Axiochos* 371d–e); but there is no mention of an Isle of the Blest or an Elysian Field for the initiates of the gold tablets (Lloyd-Jones 1985, 277). The "mystic path" (*mustikon oimon*) to Rhadamanthys mentioned in a fragment of a poem by Poseidippos may complicate the route,[37] but Plutarch indicates that, for some initiates, the meadow may be only a detour or temporary haven. In a passage thick with imagery of the Mysteries he describes a "meadow of Hades" as a resting place for the souls that have passed the test of judgment. Here, selected for reward, they rest until purified of their earthly existence (Plut. *Moralia* 943c). For the *bakchoi* and *mystai* of the tablets, there is an expectation of more to come. Even the meadow is only a transitional space, not a final destination.

The souls of initiates may still need to crib, but the path to the meadow is open, the right ritual response can be recalled, and memory can still be sustained by drinking the right water. Not everyone was eligible. Polygnotos depicted Orpheus sitting on a hill in the underworld, leaning on a willow, in a place Pausanias recognized as the Homeric grove of Persephone (Pausanias 10.30.6). Sokrates, on the point of death, happily anticipated the possibility of meeting Orpheus and Musaios in that other world (Plato, *Apology* 41a). Orpheus, however, did not tarry long in the grove. If Sokrates really wanted to converse with Orpheus, he would have had to be very quick. As Plato tells the story elsewhere (*Republic* 620a), Orpheus himself had already passed right through the meadow and back. This time he chose for his next existence not the life of a man, but the life of a swan. Memory served him well. He had retained just enough recollection of his former life to know that he did not want to be born again from woman.

Notes

1 Almost half of archaic epitaphs are for young people; Sourvinou-Inwood (1995, 297).
2 See, however, Clinton's chapter in this volume.
3 *Homeric Hymn to Demeter* 480–482; translated by Helene Foley (1993, 26). The sentiments are repeated with formulae so similar that the ideas expressed must have been widely honored. Compare Pindar F 137 Maehler. The same division is implied elsewhere; see Sophocles F 837 Radt; Isoc. 4.28; *AP* 11.42; *IG* ii^{2}3661.5–6.
4 Gods whose names were avoided were called *anonumoi* (see Henrichs 1991, especially 181 n.41 [Persephone] and nn.73–75 [Hades, "the barren"]).

5 "The girl whose name could not be spoken," Euripides, *Helen*. 1307; cf. Aristophanes, *Frogs* 337, 378. Pausanias calls "Kore" a "nickname" (3.2.9): *epiklesis*. In part, her association with rites about which there could be no conversation protected her from casual speech.
6 Even her servant in the underworld avoids using her name; Aristophanes *Frogs* 504.
7 Circe prays to Hades and Persephone (*Odyssey* 10.534). See Aeschylus, *Psychagogoi* F 273 Radt, for appeals to the dead. Plato has reservations about such appeals; *Laws* 909b. Underworld gods are treated with care because they are associated with retribution, not because they are "dark or uncanny" (as suggested by Pulleyn 1997, 90). Representations of sacrifice to Demeter and Kore are not common (see van Straten 1995, 77).
8 *Works and Days* 167–173, with line numbering problems (see West 1978).
9 Compare Pindar, *Threnos* 3 (F 129 Maehler, from Plutarch's *Letter of Consolation to Apollonios*, where the lines are called a "description by Pindar of the *eusebeis* in the house of Hades."
10 Aeschylus, *Psychagogoi*; Sophocles, *Niptra*, *Aithous*; Kritias, *Perithoos*. Kritias' *Perithoos* also had a chorus of initiates, but confusion about the date obscures for us whether this play was produced shortly before or shortly after *Frogs*.
11 Of the extant, complete plays of Aristophanes, the *Frogs* has the latest parados, at line 316; only *Peace*, with the entrance of the chorus at line 301, comes close.
12 Motte (1973, 233–237, 309 n.91).
13 The issue of normative behavior is not as uncomplicated as Guthrie implied when he said, "The emphasis on ritual action and lack of positive teaching meant that on the doctrinal side . . . the mysteries lay open to any influences which the passage of time, and the changing character of the worshippers, might bring to bear." (Guthrie 1954, 290).
14 On which, compare Guthrie (1954, 292), Richardson (1974, 311), Sommerstein (1996, 169, on lines 145–153).
15 Sommerstein (1996, 169), on respect toward insiders and outsiders. Aeschylus was from the deme of Eleusis.
16 Pugliese Carratelli (1940, 119); the inscription reproduces Aristophanes, *Frogs* 454–459, diverging from most mss. in line 4 in supplying *hieron* for their mistaken *hilaron*.
17 Aristophanes, *Frogs* 357; the term refers to comic language and derives its comic punch from reverence to bacchic rituals of initiation (emphasized by *etelesthe* and *teletais* in the same speech).
18 Aristophanes F 156.3, for a river of cloacal muck; Sommerstein (1996, 169), for summary of the bibliography.
19 Translation of the text established by Sacco (2001, 32–33).
20 This count includes the published gold myrtle leaves inscribed with initiates' names. Riedweg (1998, 389–398) edits the longer texts known in 1996 and includes brief descriptions for those at that time still unpublished. Since then, in addition, many more name tags have been located in Macedonia, and important longer tablets from Pherai, Entella, and Sfakaki (near Rethymno) have been published.
21 On Pelinna, see Segal (1990), Graf (1993).
22 For the new tablets from Crete, see Gavrilaki and Tzifopoulos (1998).
23 Iacobacci (1993, 263) argued for a Doric nucleus with Ionic accretions, but, as Sacco (2001, 27–33) has shown, the new tablet from Entella confirms, as Janko (1984, 98) argued, that the original dialect was Ionic.
24 Hordern (2000, 131) makes a distinction between "verbal exchanges which no doubt reflect things said during the mysteries" and ritual texts. The corpus of Greek ritual utterance assembled by Porta (1999), provides a typology for classifying

phrases identifiable as ritual speech. Dionysiac contexts account for a relatively high proportion of the collection.
25 Janko (2001), argues that he is Diagoras of Melos; Kahn (1997), suggests Euthyphro.
26 Burkert (1982), for the distinction, and Burkert (1987, 31–33), for itinerant practitioners. Kingsley (1995), exaggerates the significance of the evidence for Pythagorean communities and the influence of Empedokles. Graf (2000), minimizes the distinction between theoretician and practitioner.
27 For the form of this kind of speech, see Riedweg (1998, 375); he distinguishes three kinds of language (responses or liturgy from initiation ritual, a *hieros logos*, and ritual language performed at the grave of an initiate). See, too, Baumgarten (1998).
28 Early fourth-century terracotta statuettes of a small winged figure on the lap of a seated female from Medma, colony of Lokroi are interpreted by Hadzisteliou-Price (1969; 53–54) as the soul of the initiate embraced by Persephone.
29 "Neither moth nor weevil can devour gold" (Pindar *Olympian* 1.1, 3.42; cf. Pausanias 1.15.4, 8.47.2 for time and rust).
30 Betz (1998, 400), for the tablet as a sign by which the initiate will be recognized; Albinus (2000, 130–140), for the lake and the meadow.
31 The oracle of Trophonios at Lebadeia had two springs. Enquirers drank first from the water of Lethe, to forget anything that might distract them from hearing the god's response, and later, after receiving an oracle, from the water of Memory to remember the god's message (Pausanias 9.39.8). See Bonnechere's chapter in this volume.
32 The Argives threw a lamb into a pit as an offering to Dionysos Pulaochos (guardian of the gateway); Plutarch, *Isis and Osiris* 364–365.
33 For the meadow in this role, see also Diodorus Siculus, 1.96.5; Plutarch F 178 Sandbach. For the suggestion that in the Gurob papyrus a meadow was mentioned in conjunction with the line that mentions a river, see Horden (2000, 137).
34 For the suggestion that this Poseidippos is the Hellenistic poet from Pella who lived for some time in Alexandria, see Dickie (1998), drawing on an earlier article (1995).
35 For the distinction between internal, private testimony and external, public epitaph, see Tortorelli Ghidini (1995, 468).
36 Cole (1993) for tomb inscriptions that mention Dionysiac themes and discuss Dionysiac initiates.
37 Lloyd-Jones (1963); *Supplementum Hellenisticum* 705.

References

Albinus, L., 2000: *The House of Hades: Studies in Ancient Greek Eschatology*. Aarhus University Press, Aarhus.
Baumgarten, R., 1998: *Heiliges Wort und Heilige Schrift bei den Griechen: Hieroi Logoi und verwandte Erscheinungen*. Gunter Narr, Tübingen.
Betz, H.-D., 1998: "Zur Lehre vom Menschen in den orphischen Goldplättchen," in F. Graf (ed.), *Ansichten griechischer Rituale* (B.G. Teubner, Stuttgart and Leipzig), 399–419.
Burkert, W., 1982: "Craft versus sect: The problem of Orphics and Pythagoreans," in B.F. Meyer, and E.P. Sanders (eds), *Jewish and Christian Self-Definition in the Greco-Roman World* (Fortress Press, Philadelphia), 1–22.
Burkert, W., 1987: *Ancient Mystery Cults*. Harvard University Press, Cambridge, Mass.
Chaniotis, A., 2000: "Das Jenseits: Eine Gegenwelt?," in T. Hölscher (ed.), *Gegenwelten: zu den Kulturen Griechenlands und Roms in der Antike*. (Munich and Leipzig), 159–182.

Cole, S.G., 1980: "New evidence for the Mysteries of Dionysos." *GRBS* 21, 223–238.
Cole, S.G., 1993: "Voices from beyond the grave: Dionysos and the dead," in T.H. Carpenter, and C. Faraone (eds), *Masks of Dionysos* (Cornell University Press, Ithaca, N.Y.), 276–295.
Dickie, M., 1995: "The Dionysiac Mysteries at Pella," *ZPE* 109, 81–86.
Dickie, M., 1998: "Poets as initiates in the Mysteries," *Antike und Abendland* 44, 49–77.
Dover, K., 1993: *Aristophanes*, Frogs. Clarendon Press, Oxford.
Foley, H., 1993: *The Homeric Hymn to Demeter*. Princeton University Press, Princeton.
Friedlander, P., 1948: *Epigrammata: Greek Epigrams in Verse from the Beginnings to the Persian Wars*. University of California Press, Berkeley.
Gavrilaki, I. and Y.Z. Tzifopoulos, 1998: "An 'Orphic–Dionysiac' gold *Epistomion* from Sfakaki near Rethymno," *BCH* 122, 343–355.
Graf, F., 1974: *Eleusis und die orphische Dichtung Athens in vorhellenistischer Zeit*. Walter de Gruyter, Berlin.
Graf, F., 1993: "Dionysian and Orphic eschatology: New texts and old questions," in T.H. Carpenter and C. Faraone (eds), *Masks of Dionysos* (Cornell University Press, Ithaca, N.Y.), 239–258.
Graf, F., 2000: "Text and ritual. The Corpus Eschatologicum of the Orphics," in G. Cerri (ed.), *La Letteratura pseudepigrafa nella cultura greca e romana* (Istituto Universitario Orientale, Naples), 59–77.
Guthrie, W.K.R., 1954: *The Greeks and their Gods*. Beacon Press, Boston.
Hadzisteliou-Price, T., 1969: "'To the Groves of Persephoneia...' A group of 'Medma' figurines," *Antike Kunst* 12, 51–55.
Henrichs, A., 1991: "Namenlosigkeit uhnd Euphemismus: Zur Ambivalenz der chthonischen Mächte im attischen Drama," in H. Hofmann (ed.), *Fragmenta Dramatica: Beiträge zur Interpretation der griechische Tragikerfragmente und ihrer Wirkungsgeschichte* (Vandenhoeck and Ruprecht, Göttingen), 161–201.
Hordern, J., 2000: "Notes on the Orphic papyrus from Gurob," *ZPE* 129, 131–140.
Iacobacci, G., 1993: "La laminetta aurea di Hipponion: Osservazioni dialoettologiche," in A. Maracchia (ed.), *Orfeo e l'orfismo* (ruppo Editoriale Internazionale, Rome), 249–264.
Janko, R., 1984: "Forgetfulness in the golden tablets of Memory," *CQ* 34: 89–107.
Janko, R., 2001: "The Derveni papyrus (Diagoras of Melos, *Apopyrgizontes Logoi?*): A new translation," *CP* 96, 1–32.
Jaquet Rimassa, P., 1998: "Dionysos d'ici et Dionysos d'ailleurs," *Pallas* 48, 19–41.
Johnston, S.I. and T.J. McNiven, 1996: "Dionysos and the Underworld in Toledo," *MusHelv* 53, 25–36.
Jordan, D., 2001: "'Written' instructions for the dead. An example from Mordovia," *ZPE* 134, 80.
Kahn, C.H., 1997: "Was Euthyphro the author of the Derveni papyrus?," in A. Laks and G.W. Most (eds), *Studies on the Derveni Papyrus* (Clarendon Press, Oxford), 55–63.
Kingsley, P., 1995: *Ancient Philosophy, Mystery, and Magic*. Oxford University Press, Oxford.

Lada-Richards, I., 1999: *Initiating Dionysos*. Clarendon Press, Oxford.

Lloyd-Jones, H., 1985: "Pindar and the after-life," *Pindare*, Entretiens Sur L'Antiquité Classique 31 (Vandoeuvres, Geneva), 245–283.

Lloyd-Jones, H., 1963: "The seal of Posidippus", *JHS* 83, 75–99.

Merkelbach, R., 1999: "Die goldenen Totenpässe: Ägyptisch, orphisch, bakchisch." *ZPE* 128, 1–13.

Merkelbach, R. and J. Staube, 1998: *Steinepigramme aus dem griechischen Osten I*. B.G. Teubner, Stuttgart and Leipzig.

Motte, A., 1973: *Prairies et jardins de la Grece antique*. J. Duculot, Brussels.

Obbink, D., 1997: "Cosmology as initiation vs. the critique of Orphic Mysteries," in A. Laks and G.W. Most (eds), *Studies on the Derveni Papyrus* (Clarendon Press, Oxford), 39–54.

Parker, R., 2000: "Theophoric names and the history of Greek religion," in S. Hornblower and E. Matthews (eds), *Greek Personal Names, Their Value As Evidence* (Oxford University Press, Oxford), 53–80.

Porta, F.R., 1999: "Greek Ritual Utterances and the Liturgical Style." Ph.D. Diss. Harvard University.

Pugliese Carratelli, G., 1940: "Versi di un coro delle 'Rane' in un'epigrafe rodia," *Dioniso* 8: 119–123.

Pulleyn, S., 1997: *Prayer in Greek Religion*. Clarendon Press, Oxford.

Richardson, N.J., 1974: *The Homeric Hymn to Demeter*. Clarendon Press, Oxford.

Riedweg, C. 1998: "Initiation–Tod–Unterwelt," in F. Graf (ed.), *Ansichten griechischer Rituale. Geburtstags-Symposium für Walter Burkert* (B.G. Teubner, Stuttgart and Leipzig), 359–398.

Sacco, G., 2001: "Ges pais eimi, Sul. v. 10 della laminetta di Hipponion," *ZPE* 137, 27–33.

Segal, C., 1990: "Dionysus and the gold tablets from Pelinna," *GRBS* 31: 411–419.

Sommerstein, A.H., 1996: *Aristophanes*, Frogs. Aris and Phillips, Warminster.

Sourvinou-Inwood, C., 1983: "A trauma in flux: Death in the 8th century and after," in R. Hägg (ed.), *The Greek Renaissance of the Eighth Century B.C.: Tradition and Innovation* (Acta Instituti Atheniensis Regni Sueciae, 4.30 Stockholm), 33–48.

Sourvinou-Inwood, C., 1995: *Reading Greek Death*. Clarendon Press, Oxford.

Tortorelli Ghidini, M., 1995: "Lettere d'oro per l'Ade," *La Parola del Passato* 50, 468–482.

van Straten, F.T., 1995: *Hiera Kala*. E.J. Brill, Leiden.

West, M.L., 1978: *Hesiod, Works and Days*. Clarendon Press, Oxford.

Zhmud, L., 1992: "Orphism and graffiti from Olbia," *Hermes* 120, 159–168.

Zuntz, G., 1971: *Persephone*. Clarendon Press, Oxford.

9

ORPHIC MYSTERIES AND DIONYSIAC RITUAL

Noel Robertson

The role of Dionysus in Orphic belief

Orphic belief, as it was finally expressed in the multi-volume creation story or *Rhapsodies* of late antiquity, held that this world would have been a better place but for a thwarting of the original design. The Orphic creation story, like others, proceeded from phantasmagorical beginnings to the triumph of Zeus, but represented Zeus as intending a further and final development. For he begot a successor god and even enthroned him while still a boy: this was Dionysus son of Persephone, herself both Zeus' own daughter and his queen. The ruination of this plan by the Titans leaves us with the same imperfect world under Zeus, and with Persephone and Dionysus as we know them, respectively queen of the underworld and lord of wine and its all-too-fleeting happiness. Yet knowledge of the plan is redemptive for one who passes from this life to the next, to the realm of Persephone. Orphic believers also acted out their faith in ritual, as prescribed in other books. Such then is the picture as we see it later – after the *Rhapsodies* were compiled from a mass of pre-existing material, no earlier than the second century BC, possibly much later.

Orphic belief and ritual existed in some form in the fifth century BC, being referred to by Herodotus and Euripides and others. It is a question therefore of how much of the belief and ritual concerning Dionysus goes back to that time – a time when Dionysus was one of the chief gods of every Greek city, worshipped at seasonal festivals with elaborate public rites and with another kind of belief, the local myths pertaining to each festival. Perhaps unexpectedly, it is archaeology which in recent decades has contributed striking new details of Orphic belief and ritual: they draw us especially to this matter of Dionysus. The Derveni papyrus, recovered from a funeral pyre in Thessaly, contains a truncated commentary by a ritual adept upon an Orphic creation story that is itself, apart from the commentary and the burial, conjecturally dated to ca. 500 BC or even the sixth century.[1] Gold leaves inscribed with Orphic mementoes have emerged from far-flung graves, the earliest dated to ca. 400.² In fifth-century Olbia bone plaques more cryptically inscribed were cherished by the living and left behind both in a public square and in private houses (Dubois 1996, no. 94). The evidence for Dionysus can be summarized as follows.

Though the Derveni papyrus breaks off while Zeus is still a new ruler in the creation story, it dwells on the identity of the goddesses Rhea and Demeter (col. xxii) – not mother and daughter as in ordinary belief, but the unitary figure who is first mother of Zeus and then, by Zeus, of Persephone as mother-to-be of Dionysus.³ So this creation story was indeed headed for the outcome we know from the *Rhapsodies*. The commentator on the story professes to have studied rites as well as books, not only sombre rites addressed to underworld deities and to the dead (cols. ii–iii, vi), and private rites performed by *magoi* and other specialists and by initiates on their own account (cols. vi, xx), but also public rites conducted "in cities" and observed by the multitude (col. xx, lines 1–2). These would certainly include the festivals of Dionysus.

Turning to the gold leaves, we see that the persons buried with them expected to meet Persephone in the underworld and were prepared to introduce themselves with a few apt phrases recalling the great events of the Orphic creation story.⁴ They had also been fortified by ritual, and were advised to say so: "Tell Persephone that *Bakchios* himself has set you free!"⁵ Either the story or the ritual had taught them mystic names for Persephone and her son, which were now produced as "symbols."⁶ The rites were no doubt private and secret, but the initiate was likened to the sacrificial victim of Dionysus' public worship; namely, a vigorous male animal, kid or ram or even bull.⁷ And he had the title *bakchos*, a higher one than *mystes*, like a reveler at Dionysus' festivals.⁸

At Olbia the bone plaques were employed in rites which had to do both with "Dionysus" and with "Orphic" belief. Yet the plaques are widely scattered in the city; some have emerged from the area north of the agora, called the *Temenos*, a square larger than the agora itself; they were carved and polished and inscribed with a careful hand (the same hand appearing on more than one plaque), so as to be distributed among the faithful and then retained.⁹ The rites in question were doubtless private rather than civic, and yet they were conspicuous. Now it is just such rites, and at Olbia, that we hear of in a famous passage of Herodotus (4.79) – private rites of Dionysus *Bakcheios* that were conspicuous to all and indeed offensive to strait-laced Scythians. From the epigraphic record we happen to know as well that Dionysus *Bakcheios* was honored with civic cult and age-old ceremony in the mother city of Miletus and in her numerous colonies, including Olbia.¹⁰ During the fifth century, then, something of the civic cult was put to private use by Orphic believers.

In sum, the new evidence shows that Dionysus was important to the Orphics from the outset, and that he came to them from the general background of public worship. To understand Orphic ritual and belief we must go back to the rites and myths of Dionysus in Greek cities. This has not been the usual approach. Scholars have relied upon a supposed category of "initiation rites" which is thought to entail beliefs and imagery about death and rebirth.[11] But the category confuses different kinds of so-called initiation. The original Greek initiates or *mystai* did not join a separate social group, a tribe or band or sect or livelihood. They lent themselves instead to the civic cults of, chiefly, Dionysus or Demeter and sought to promote the fertility of the corresponding part of nature, vine or grain. It was fertility magic that set them apart. Only when the community effort began to lose its hold did *mystai* form private associations, like the Orphics. Initiation rites as a topic of comparative religion are irrelevant.

Ritual elements shared by Orphic and other creation stories

In the Orphic creation story Dionysus, as Zeus' successor, was attacked and killed by the Titans. This is the episode which we may hope to explain from public worship, not from any private initiation rites. But let us be aware that other episodes before this, episodes common to both Orphic and other creation stories — the various *Theogonies* of Greek literature — are likewise to be traced to public worship. It is a general feature of Greek myths (and the creation story incorporates a series of lesser myths) that they are closely tied to ritual. A myth was told to explain a rite, and at the end of the telling the rite was held up as proof that the myth had happened so. In Greek literature the myths have of course moved away from their original setting, and the ritual counterpart goes unmentioned but for special cases, as at the conclusion of a few tragedies, or in later, learned prose and poetry. But the ritual always continued as before (that is the nature of ritual) and was familiar to everyone (similar festivals were celebrated in every city). It gave rise to new stories, or to variations of the old.

Until the Orphics introduced Dionysus, the creation story culminated with Zeus. As an infant, Zeus was hidden by his mother Rhea in a mountain cave on Crete, and marvelously suckled (by a nymph, or a goat, or bees), and attended by dancing Curetes. Thus preserved, he overthrew Cronus and ended the tyrant's reign, which however was also known as a gentle pastoral regime, a Golden Age. So much, though not with uniform detail, is common to every *Theogony* of which we are sufficiently apprised: Hesiod, Musaeus, Epimenides, the Cyclic *Theogony* summarized by [Apollodorus], the Orphic *Rhapsodies*.[12]

Behind it is the ritual of the ancient pastoral goddess called Rhea in the story, but in cult the Mother, more fully the Mother of the Gods (Robertson 1996a). Behind the nursing in the cave is her spring festival *Galaxia*; behind father Cronus is her summer festival *Kronia*; behind the succession of divine generations is her cult title (antedating any story) "the Mother of the Gods," the gods being all the lesser powers of nature. The Mother's worship was celebrated in many cities, and some of them had their local versions of the nursing of Zeus. A cult at Lyctus in Crete happened to be famous in early days, and on Hesiod's authority this remote locale continued to be part of the usual creation story; it was said of Epimenides that he had visited the cave himself. Among the other instances, Athens contributed to Musaeus' *Theogony* in virtue of the Mother's cult on the like-named Museum Hill (Robertson 1996a, 246–253 [Hesiod and Epimenides], 255–263 [Musaeus]).

In the Orphic creation story the number of divine generations was increased, reaching seven in the *Rhapsodies*. From Zeus onward the Cretan cave, alias the cave of Night, was retained as the setting for successive matings and nursings (*Orph*. fr. 58, from the *Theogony* of Hieronymus and Hellanicus; frs. 105, 107, 150–152, 156, 162, from the *Rhapsodies*). Here Zeus mated with his mother, Rhea/Demeter, and begot Persephone; here he mated with Persephone and begot Dionysus; the Curetes danced attendance on both Persephone and Dionysus. But a new element was added: Zeus took the form of a snake to mate with Rhea/Demeter and again to mate with Persephone.[13] The snaky guise comes from Zeus' own worship, from his cult as *meilichios*.

Zeus *meilichios* is a god of earth's bounty and of household stores, and in votive reliefs is quite typically represented as a large bearded snake, coiled and rearing up (Jameson *et al.* 1993, 82–85, 94). His festival *Diasia* fell in early spring, at the beginning of the lenten period when stores are declining; it could be regarded as the very greatest festival of Zeus (Thuc. 1.126.4–6).[14] At just the same season, probably within a few days, a festival came round to honor Persephone – the festival *Antheia* (or a similar name) in Demeter's cycle, which marks the earing of the grain and its mythical analogue, the return of the grain maiden from the realm below.[15] Zeus *meilichios* and Persephone might well seem a nuptial pair.

No doubt they were so regarded before the Orphics adopted them for the creation story. Zeus *meilichios* was especially prominent at Selinus, where coins dating to the later fifth century BC unmistakably depict the nuptials: a great snake rears up before a woman seated on a rock, and she takes him tenderly to her naked bosom.[16] And since Persephone's spring festival was widely celebrated in the west, in Sicily and in southern Italy, it may be that the story reached the Orphics from this quarter. But at Athens, too, both festivals – of Zeus and Persephone – were famous, and were close together on the ground in Agrae as they were in the calendar, and Persephone's was said to commemorate the matter of Dionysus, which must be the Orphic creation story.[17] This ritual complex was as widespread as the festivals of the Mother that inspired the original story.

In portraying Dionysus as successor, the Orphics borrowed a colorful item from the Mother's worship. Zeus set the little boy upon a throne, from which he was afterwards lured away by the Titans.[18] At the festival *Galaxia* actual thrones were "spread" to receive the goddess and her partners as imagined by the worshippers: they are a constant feature of the Mother's cult and iconography (Robertson 1996a, 252, 259–263, 297). Thrones were also taken over for private rites, called "Corybantic," in which an initiate, or a mental patient, was thus seated while others executed a frenzied dance around him, this too deriving from the Mother's festival (the Corybantes, alias Curetes, are her partners) (Linforth 1946). The Orphics adopted the throne as a sign of Dionysus' kingship. But Dionysus and the Mother had been associated in just this way even prior to the Orphic creation story.

Both deities are notorious for the frenzied activity, a virtual madness, with which their worshippers seek to revive the neighboring upland tracts of vineyard or of pasture. It was therefore said of Dionysus that as a boy, i.e. between the mythical stages of infancy and manhood, he went mad but was cured by the Mother, whom he chanced to meet in the mountains. The boy's madness is shown in early red-figure painting, which may reproduce a lost tragedy (Carpenter 1993; 1997, 35–41; Robertson 1995b, 291–292); the manner of his cure is shown in Hellenistic reliefs – he is perched on a throne, and Corybantes dance round him (Stambolidis 1987, 69–73, 150–152, pls. 7b, 32d from Cos, altar of Dionysus; *LIMC* Kouretes, Korybantes 31a–b from Perge, theatre). It was further said, as a narrative motif, that the madness was caused by vengeful Hera, and again the Orphics followed suit, saying that Hera incited the Titans against Dionysus.

We see that the creation story, in any version from Hesiod to the Orphics, was much indebted to public ritual, especially the Mother's. For believers, the story was authenticated by the ritual, abiding proof of those events of long ago.

Dionysus in Delphic myth and ritual

Dionysus' fate was recounted at length, with curious detail, in the *Rhapsodies* (*Orph*. frs. 208–214, 240). Let us start here and then move back in time.

The Titans drew the little boy away from the throne which made him king. They whitened their faces with gypsum, and displayed a mirror and some tricksy toys – jointed doll, knucklebone, ball, top, bull-roarer, etc. Thus beguiled, Dionysus followed the Titans to meet a horrible end. They cut him into pieces, which they boiled and roasted and ate. The heart alone, still beating, was saved by Athena and carried to Zeus, who made use of it in begetting the second Dionysus, son of Semele.[19]

Much of this was enacted in the private rites of Orphic believers. Several sources for the story refer to such rites, and there is independent confirmation. A papyrus from Gurôb in the Fayyûm gives directions for mystic rites of Dionysus while invoking Persephone and Rhea/Demeter and the Curetes and listing as "symbols," and as the contents of a basket, a mirror and several toys.[20] Orphic ritual also worked its fascination upon a wider audience. In the papyrus fragments of Lollianus' novel *A Phoenician Story* a gang of outlaws bind themselves together as professed "initiates" by killing a boy and removing his heart to consume in sacramental fashion.[21] A verse inscription from Smyrna bids regular worshippers of Dionysus to abstain from the heart of any sacrificial victim.[22]

The origins of this strange story have long been disputed. It is acknowledged that a few details, similar but discrepant, are heard of long before, being located at Delphi. But it has not been recognized that they derive from Dionysus' festivals as celebrated at the great sanctuary.

Both Callimachus and Euphorion said that Dionysus, son of Persephone, was laid to rest at Delphi by Apollo, beside his own tripod (Callim. fr. 643, cf. *Aet.* ii fr. 43 [50 Massimilla] 117; Euphorion fr. 13 Powell, cf. fr. 36). It was a burial of his limbs, which had been torn and scattered by the Titans but also retrieved by them and placed in the tripod basin. Plutarch, versed in Delphic antiquities, knows the story and the burial place (Plut. *Is. Os.* 35, 365A; "beside the oracle place" = beside the tripod). In a different story, ascribed to the poet Dinarchus, the burial is of Dionysus, son of Semele, who died at Delphi after fleeing from his assailant Lycurgus.[23] Since Lycurgus is notorious from Homer onward for savagely wielding an axe or the like, we may suppose that the remains of this Dionysus were likewise mangled limbs.

As to the son of Persephone, the Titans scatter the limbs, then throw them into the tripod basin; Apollo buries them beside the tripod. We can only guess at the intervals involved. Since any story needs to motivate the action, there must have been an interval between the scattering of Dionysus' limbs and their retrieval, during which the Titans changed their minds, perhaps being warned by Zeus.[24] It was convenient to say that the Titans placed the limbs in the basin, but that Apollo buried them.

Delphi was famous for dividing the honors of cult between Apollo and Dionysus. Apollo held sway in spring and summer, but Dionysus in winter while Apollo was away. In feigning that Dionysus is buried by Apollo, the story looks to a ritual event of spring. Apollo on his first arrival, says a celebrated story, killed the serpent Python, and of Python too it was said that the remains were buried beside the tripod, obviously the same ritual event.[25] Python, as an earlier denizen of Delphi, is also linked with Dionysus: at that earlier stage, before Apollo arrived, it was Dionysus who gave oracles from the tripod.[26]

If the burial of Dionysus is a ritual event of spring, the tearing and scattering will be a ritual event of winter. It is true that in the story as we have it Delphi is not specified as the setting of the first stage. And it is also true that just at Delphi Dionysus son of Semele is associated with another ritual event of winter, the revel of the Thyiads who fling about on Parnassus, even in the cold and snow, so as to "wake," and no doubt to nurse and dandle, the baby god in his cradle.[27] In this case a ritual event, the revel of women, is expressly tied to a mythical episode: the nursing of the infant Dionysus. Now other myths of Dionysus, which we will come to, have much to say of the nursing of infants by devoted mothers, though the infants are usually royal scions rather than the god himself. The myths are located at cities where the worship of the wine god especially flourished, and at each of them we may infer the corresponding rite, a revel of women in the hills. These myths are revealing in another way. The nursing, for all its tenderness, is followed by a frightful tearing and scattering of one of the infants.

We shall find in examining the other myths that a sacrificial animal was torn and scattered at a winter celebration. So it was at Delphi. In the sculpture of the Siphnian Treasury Thyiads are shown reveling in one scene and in another brandishing a sacrificial victim.[28] At Delphi, then, we have two successive events, the tearing and scattering in winter and the burial in spring. The first event fell within the three winter months when Dionysus held sway, the second within the spring and summer months when Apollo did. It is not that the two events inaugurate the two periods, which are defined rather by the long series of Apolline festivals extending throughout the fair weather season (Plut. *De E ap. Delph.* 9, 389C).

These successive rites of winter and of spring recur wherever Dionysus is worshipped, in the three main dialect areas. The festival names at Delphi are not recorded.[29] *Thyia* ("revel-rites") was probably a name for the winter festival here as at Elis.[30] But Delphi chose to set itself apart from other cities by assigning highly individual names to standard festivals – witness the Delphic calendar of months, in which nearly half of the eponymous festivals are otherwise unheard of.[31] Two months of winter and spring are coordinate: *Poitropios* = December and *Endyspoitropios* = April, apparently named for "suppliant-rites" and "grimly suppliant-rites."[32] It could be our pair of festivals.

Thus the story known to Callimachus and Euphorion, of how Dionysus was killed and afterwards buried beside the Delphic tripod, derives from two standard festivals of Dionysus, in winter and in spring, as celebrated at Delphi. Callimachus and Euphorion speak of the son of Persephone: it is the Orphic creation story, as then current. Dinarchus speaks of the son of Semele, and it is impossible to say whether that story arose independently from Delphic ritual or merely rang the changes on the other.

The elaboration of the story in the *Rhapsodies*

The version of the *Rhapsodies* with which we began differs from the earlier one only by reason of elaboration. This will be apparent as soon as we examine the differences.

Much was said in the *Rhapsodies* of how the Titans practiced on the little boy. Since it was essential to lure him from the throne, they first assumed some merry ways. The whitened faces as much as the mirror and the toys were meant to amuse and entice, not to intimidate.[33] To daub the face with some handy pigment, gypsum or soot or even mud, is typical of the sportive conduct of fertility rites, including those of Dionysus.[34] Accordingly, the whitened faces may have entered the story early. If so, they led on to the mirror and the toys, which only then became the symbolic tokens of private rites.[35] In any case, the emphasis is due to the sentimental regard for children that prevailed in later times.[36]

This tender scene was succeeded in the *Rhapsodies* by one of horror, in which the Titans slash or tear the child into pieces to boil and roast and eat; only the heart remains. The cooking and eating are incompatible with the earlier version known to Callimachus and Euphorion, in which the torn remains are buried beside Apollo's tripod at a spot that was always pointed out.[37] In a rival story the son of Semele was buried here after being hacked up by Lycurgus: he was certainly not cooked and eaten. In yet another story Python was buried here after being dispatched by Apollo: he was certainly not cooked and eaten.

There was however, for Callimachus and Euphorion, a preliminary to the burial. The limbs of Dionysus, as also the bones of Python, are placed in the tripod basin before they are buried beside it. It was the Titans who did this for Dionysus. Euphorion is quoted as saying so, and seems to say as well that they put him in the fire:

†ἀν πυρὶ Βάκχαν δῖαν ὑπὲρ φιάλην† ἐβάλοντο.[38]

Cooking over a fire is of course the fundamental use of a tripod basin, but is not otherwise heard of at Delphi, where Apollo's tripod is the emblematic seat of his prophetess. The line quoted is corrupt throughout. It is likely that in the course of misunderstanding words have been transposed, so as to produce the halting rhythm of the first two feet and the strangest of corruptions, ἀν for ἐν. Perhaps the line should be mended as follows:

Βάκχον ἅτ' ἐν πυρὶ δῖον ὑπὲρ φιάλης ἐβάλοντο
("Holy Bacchus they threw upon the basin *as if* into the fire")

It was *as if* they were about to cook him on the tripod, says Euphorion wryly. The cooking is a momentary fancy.

Clement of Alexandria preserves a composite version of the story, with some details from Hellenistic poetry and others from the *Rhapsodies* (*Protr.* 17.2–18 = *Orph.* frs. 34–35). He found it in the learned source, which he follows closely if selectively in reviewing pagan mysteries.[39] For Clement, as for his source, the Mysteries are rites commemorating the adventures of the gods, though Clement decries the rites as unseemly and the adventures as disgraceful.

Clement tells how the Titans beguiled and then tore and finally cooked Dionysus, how Athena carried off the heart, how Zeus blasted the Titan – all this surely from the *Rhapsodies*. He also quotes two lines of Orpheus describing the toys, likewise surely from the *Rhapsodies*. The toys are scornfully identified by Clement as the "symbols" of commemorative ritual. That is all we hear of ritual, which Clement tends to omit. In recounting the adventure, however, Clement also tells how the Titans, before cooking Dionysus, placed a basin on the tripod which thus served for boiling the limbs, and how Zeus afterwards gave the limbs to Apollo to bury, and how Apollo carried them to Parnassus for the purpose. This much comes from Euphorion or other Hellenistic poetry, except that Zeus transmits the limbs. Clement's source must have pointed to the Delphic tripod and the burial site as commemoration. It was his interest in ritual that led him to produce a composite version of the story.

In the *Rhapsodies* the Titans did indeed both cook and eat the little boy. Since the story was now divorced from Delphi and the burial place, there was no point in saying that the pieces were retrieved and buried. Instead it followed the usual line of stories about a little boy butchered for a cannibal feast: stories of Pelops, of Tereus' and Thyestes' sons, of the pathetic victims of Lycaon. Those stories too were often embellished with grisly details of the cooking. Yet we should note the generic difference between myths which had always dwelt on a cannibal feast and this myth of Dionysus which had not. In the first kind the little boy stands for a sacrificial animal which is cooked and consumed by the worshippers. In Delphic myth the boy Dionysus, like other little boys in other Dionysiac myths, stands for an animal victim which is torn and scattered in a drastic fertility rite. The Delphic myth was assimilated to the first kind by the Orphics.

In the *Rhapsodies* again the heart is the only part of Dionysus that is saved from the cannibal feast; it contributes to the begetting of the second Dionysus. It was an obvious choice. At any sacrifice the internal organs were removed at once from the slaughtered animal, first among them the palpitating heart, which made a gory spectacle.[40] Thereafter it might be singled out for burning up on the altar.[41] More often, however, the organs were either burnt up together or consumed together by the worshippers, or divided impartially between these uses. When worshippers of Dionysus abstained from the heart in second-century Smyrna, this was a consequence of Orphic belief, as we saw above. The Orphic story does not draw on any particular rite, but gave rise to imaginary ones, such as the oath-taking in Lollianus' novel, as we also saw.[42]

Similar stories in other cults of Dionysus

As earlier Orphics told the story, Dionysus was torn and the pieces were scattered; then they were retrieved and buried at Delphi. The story came from Delphic cult. Similar stories, though the victim is not as a rule the god himself, were told about other local cults of Dionysus: in Boeotia and the northeast Peloponnese and at a couple of other Dorian and Aeolian places, otherwise on mythical terrain. The restricted range shows that the story pattern arises in the first instance not from any literary vogue but from Dionysus' ritual as practiced in certain areas.

The stories are similar to the Orphic one both in outline and in detail. The Orphics said that the rule of Dionysus was opposed by the Titans, with horrible violence. Since this is a creation story, Dionysus is the short-lived sovereign of the world. In local stories it is Dionysus the wine-god who is opposed by local persons; yet the horrible violence is the same. The victim is a royal scion, whether child or youth; he is torn and scattered; the pieces are retrieved and buried.

These other stories are obviously relevant. Yet they include something more than the killing and the burial; they begin with earlier events which are essential to the pattern. We first see nursing mothers devoted to their offspring, and then we see the nursing interrupted and the mothers put to flight. The interruption is typically due to a fit of madness, and the killing is a further consequence. We must consider each story as a whole.

Let us follow geographic order. When Dionysus arrived at Orchomenus, the three daughters of king Minyas were nursing new-born sons; they persisted in doing so, though commanded to revel for the god, and he drove them mad and they tore one of the infants (Gantz 1993, 736–737; *LIMC* Pentheus [?]65, [?]68). Plutarch describes a rite associated with the story (*Quaest. Gr.* 38, 299E–300A). The priest of Dionysus takes a sword and pursues a group of women reputedly descended from the royal family. Plutarch regards this as perpetuating a desire for vengeance on the killers. If, however, the ritual action is to be matched with one in the story, it is like Dionysus falling on the women and driving them mad.

Aeschylus and Euripides both told how Dionysus arrived at Thebes and drove the women mad so that they tore young king Pentheus (Gantz 1993, 481–483; *LIMC* Pentheus 1–70). Both drew on the actual worship of Dionysus, for which Thebes was renowned above all other cities; we may be sure that Euripides, in describing the women's conduct of long ago, means it to be plausible in comparison with Aeschylus and in the light of the reality. The women's actions at Thebes are the same as at Orchomenus, though motivated differently.[43] They all obey the god's command to revel, and are led by three royal mothers, daughters of Cadmus. According to a close observer in Euripides' play (whose report serves to counter ignorant suspicion), they initially behave as tender nursing mothers. Again they are driven mad; twice in fact: first by intruding rustics and then by Pentheus. Again they attack and tear victims: first cattle – and almost the rustics too – and then Pentheus, his own mother taking the lead. They both tear and scatter: the pieces of Pentheus are volleyed with such fury that they catch and hang in trees and slither into crevices on the ground. Afterwards they are painstakingly sought for and gathered up and buried.

Elsewhere in Boeotia we have only story fragments. At Haliartus, as at Delphi, Dionysus himself, a baby god, is the subject; he was nursed here and also bathed in a local stream (Callim. *Aet.* ii fr. 43 [50 Massimilla] 86–92; Plut. *Lys.* 28.7–8). At Tanagra women reveling for Dionysus are attacked by Triton, who comes out of the sea as they take a purifying bath; but the god appears and saves them (Paus. 9.20.4). Just beyond the border of Boeotia, at the Attic village Icarium, we find a piquant variation, probably first contrived by the learned Eratosthenes (Merkelbach 1963, 486–519; *LIMC* Ikarios i, 1–4). Icarius, the local eponym, welcomes Dionysus on his arrival but is torn and buried because of a misunderstanding; and he is not a youth but a gaffer, and the bereaved woman is not his mother but his daughter.

At Argos too, Dionysus visits women with madness, either the three daughters of King Proetus or else all the nursing mothers, who then tear their children. But there is no supporting detail, and of the royal daughters it is more often said, and much more fully, that they offended not Dionysus but Hera, being flighty girls rather than mature women.[44] We may suspect that the Argive episodes as relating to Dionysus are merely copied from Boeotia, all the more since Argos has quite a different story about Dionysus and his women. They arrive together from overseas, and are attacked as they revel; it is even said that Dionysus himself was killed by Perseus (Piérart 1996; *LIMC* Dionysos 800–801). Though this story is attested much later than the others, it gives the appearance of being an authentic local *aition*.

The story of the Titans assaulting Dionysus was situated both at Patrae in Achaea and on Crete. Of course it was borrowed from the Orphics at both places. But it answered to local belief as well. At Patrae the story also told of Dionysus' nursing beforehand, and on Crete it was commemorated by a festival: the picture of biennial rites gives authentic detail.[45]

Besides Boeotia, we should consider Aeolian Lesbos. Mytilene has a prosaic moralizing tale of how a mother, and wife of Dionysus' priest, slew her son in a rage on the very day of the festival; it was divine retribution, since the priest had murdered a man and secretly buried the body (Ael. *Var. Hist.* 13.2: again, biennial rites with authentic detail). For the sake of the story, the burial of a victim is antecedent to the slaying of a child.

Two old and famous stories, about Lycurgus and Orpheus, transport us to the distant land of Thrace. They do not originate in any memory or observation of Thracian custom. In Greek myth Thrace is the land of winter: persons live there, things happen there, because they belong to that season. In the one story, baby Dionysus is nursed by the nymphs on a Thracian mountain, until wicked King Lycurgus assails them and they flee (Gantz 1993, 113–114; *LIMC* Lykourgos i, 1–81). In the other, women reveling for Dionysus on a Thracian mountain encounter Orpheus and tear and scatter him; his head was later buried on Lesbos or elsewhere (West 1990, 26–50; *LIMC* Orpheus 7–70; buried head: Robert 1920, 406–408).

It will be seen that every story fits the same pattern: (1) women nurse; (2) they are suddenly checked and routed; (3) they tear and scatter a nursling; (4) the remains are retrieved and buried. Only Euripides' *Bacchae*, incomparably richer than any other source, gives us all the stages and full details of each; the others overlap at different points. The Orphic creation story confines itself to the last two stages: the first two are superfluous, since Dionysus is born and reared in the Cretan cave just like Zeus, as a fully accredited successor. Thereafter the creation story joins up very neatly with the pattern.

Dionysiac ritual

Behind the Orphic creation story we were able to discern the Delphic festivals of Dionysus. But even at Delphi there was more to the winter festival than appears in the story; there was the Thyiads' rite of waking the baby in his cradle. We now see that myths of Dionysus often begin with a nursing, the first of our four stages; so the corresponding rite was widespread. Let us investigate the ritual of Dionysus that stands behind all four stages of the narrative.

The ritual has not hitherto been well understood. It can even be maintained that the details in Euripides' *Bacchae* owe little to contemporary practice, and that later practice was modeled on the *Bacchae*. This is to invert the normal relationship between life and literature; it is implausible when the *Bacchae* is considered in isolation, and impossible when so many stories show a converging pattern. There will be a common background of ritual over the area covered by the stories.

For local varieties of Dionysiac as of other ritual there is a form of evidence which has been slowly growing without being much noticed: the month names in the local calendars of Greek cities.[46] At each city the months are named for festivals, those of Dionysus prominent among them. The names are almost solely known from documentary inscriptions; to assemble them and put them in order has been a long and drawn-out task. But now we have the usual names for Dionysus' festivals throughout the Greek world. They differ as between the main dialect areas, between the Ionic domain on the one hand and on the other both the Aeolic and the Doric and northwest-Greek domains. In the Ionic domain Dionysus' two festivals, of winter and of spring, are the *Lenaia* and the *Anthesteria*. In the Aeolic, etc., domain they are the *Theodaisia* and the *Agriania* (*vel sim*.). It is these two that we are concerned with as the background of the stories.

The month *Theodaisios* is attested at seven cities, *Agrianios* (*vel sim*.) at eleven; at two of these cities both months are attested. The numbers are impressive, given the very sporadic attestation (far more so for this domain than for the Ionic, where *Lenaion* and *Anthesterion* are attested at eighteen and at twenty cities). Dionysus' festivals were important occasions each year.[47] And yet the showing of the calendars seems to conflict with a leading feature of Dionysus' festivals as remarked by literary sources. The celebrations were "trieteric" or biennial; they came round at two-year intervals.[48] The purported rule extends to both winter and spring festivals and to both of our domains. For this conflict no likely explanation has ever been suggested.

I can think of only one. Dionysus' festivals did indeed come round every year at the same two seasons, winter and spring, under the same two names. But the festival business, the ritual, was not the same each year. The ritual of one winter was not repeated until the second year after; in successive winters the festival business was markedly different. Likewise in spring. The complete ritual sequence took two years. Any one form of celebration, in winter or in spring, was biennial.

Nature supplies a reason why it should be so. The growth and maturation cycle of vine and wine is longer than that of other crops. Grain as the other staple crop is sown and harvested each year in a cycle which once formed the very rhythm of human life. But vine and wine take a year and a half: from the pruning and other operations of the first winter, through the growth and ripening of spring and summer, through vintage and pressing, through the fermentation of the second winter, up to the opening and tasting of the new wine in the spring. Along the way the community performs the magic rites that strengthen nature and its precious gift. Demeter, after the great festival of the sowing, has a series of lesser ones at the sprouting, the earing, the harvest, the threshing, the ingathering, all within eight months or so, from October to June.[49] Dionysus, we now see, has a series of four considerable festivals in the winter and spring of successive years.

In the ritual of both Demeter and Dionysus it is especially women who exert their own proven fertility on behalf of the more uncertain fertility of nature (Robertson 1991, 4, 17–18, 23–26, 28–31; 1995a, 193–197, 200–203). Whereas Demeter's women were sequestered in great sanctuaries, Dionysus' women somehow reveled. The four stages of each story, as distinguished above, correspond to the four successive celebrations of winter and of spring which themselves accompany the critical stages of nature's growth and maturation cycle.

Some of the actions are linked with festivals in sources already indicated. The first stage, the nursing, is so linked at both Delphi and Haliartus. At Delphi, the Thyiads' rite of waking the baby goes with their winter revel on Parnassus. At Haliartus, the winter festival *Theodaisia* is celebrated beside Cissusae, the "Ivy" spring where Dionysus' nurses cleansed the baby at his birth. At Cyrene too the *Theodaisia* commemorate the story of Dionysus and his nurses (Suda s.v. Ἀμφιδρόμια).

The second stage, the routing of the women, is so linked at Orchomenus, Tanagra, and Argos. At Orchomenus the priest pursues the women at the biennial *Agriania*, a celebration of the spring festival. At Tanagra the women are attacked by Triton as they take a purifying sea-bath, which they could only do in clement weather, in the spring. At Argos, where the women are attacked by Perseus, the sea-bath is indicated by their local name, ἅλιαι ("sea-women"), and by their supposed arrival from overseas; the attack is commemorated by cult-places near the agora (Paus. 2.20.4, 22.1).[50] We can add the neighboring Arcadian city of Alea.[51] Here the women are scourged at a biennial celebration which has the local name Σκιέρεια [ἱερά] ["Rites] of the shady places"; that is σκιερά as a substantive (Paus. 8.23.1). It is the vineyards with their spring foliage which are thus endearingly evoked.[52]

We see that the first two stages are linked with the festivals of winter and spring. The third stage, the tearing of the victim, is likewise linked with the winter festival, which then must be the celebration of the second year. Orpheus is torn by women reveling for the god in Thrace, the land of winter (and he is said to have been mourning throughout the previous winter months). On Crete the tearing of Dionysus is commemorated by an actual festival, in which the tearing of an animal victim is mentioned as part of the ritual.[53]

The story and the ritual unfold together. At each stage the actions are meant to produce the like effect in nature. The women first, in winter, go up to the hills where the vines are exhausted and ravaged and nearly lifeless; they make a show of waking and nursing a new-born child. But in spring, as the vines burgeon with the male potency which will become the grape clusters, the women's care is no longer wanted and the men make a show of chasing them away. In the next winter, after the male potency has been harvested – after the crushing of grapes into pools of juice – the women go to the hills again and make a show of tearing and scattering a young male animal. But in spring, just before the fermented juice is opened and its mature strength revealed, the community makes a show of gathering the remains and restoring the victim.

It is the actions of the two winter festivals, the nursing and the tearing, on which our stories largely dwell. So do artistic renderings, especially vase painting; they too provide a view of ritual, an independent one. The nursing, though it was only mimicked by the women, must be depicted in art with an actual baby, and this is always the god Dionysus (*LIMC* Dionysos 682–686, 691, 696–703, Mainades 103; Carpenter 1997, 52–59). The ritual tearing was of young animals, goats or deer, and is so depicted; the women moreover wield knives, and the victims are sliced apart, not torn.[54] In this respect the scenes in art are much closer to the reality. And they remind us, as the stories mostly do not, how important animal victims were in the ritual of Dionysus.

Animal vigor as well as human fertility was brought to bear on nature. This was the original purpose of animal sacrifice in all its varied modes; but no other mode was so drastic or demonstrative as the slicing and scattering in the hills.[55] The god himself, the power of vine and wine in nature, was equated with the animal victim. Dionysus is often described or depicted as bull-horned; he is summoned to appear as a bull (Plut. *Quaest. Gr.* 36, 299A–B), and cult images showed him as a bull (*Is. Os.* 35, 364F; cf. *LIMC* Dionysos 154–159). The worshippers acted out their belief. On Tenedos they pampered a gravid cow and treated the delivery as a childbirth; they fastened boots, *kothornoi*, on the new-born calf to show it was the very god; then they slaughtered it (Ael. *Nat. An.* 12.34).

The belief is central, for it produces the festival names *Theodaisia* and *Agriania*. The second element of *Theodaisia* is *daio* ("divide"); "feast" is a secondary meaning, inasmuch as feasting follows a division of the meat.[56] These are "[rites] of dividing the god."[57] The name of the spring festival occurs in widely varied forms: *Agriania, Agrionia, Agerrania*. There was probably an effort to disguise or alter the meaning, as will happen with holy names (for efforts of this kind, see Robertson 1996a, 282–286). The first two forms have an obvious resemblance to *agrios* ("wild"), though they cannot properly be so derived.[58] The third form *Agerrania*, which is Aeolic, points rather to *ageiro* ("gather"): these are "[rites] of gathering [the remains]."[59] The two names denote the culminating actions of the second winter and spring.

Like other fertility rites, those of Dionysus expressed the ancient magical belief that man and animal and nature are one. And like the others, they issued later in professed Mysteries, in secret rites and stories which surprisingly revealed to man his rightful place in the world. When the Orphics told how the child Dionysus through being torn and scattered gave promise of another life hereafter, they only appropriated for themselves the earlier religion of Greek cities.

Notes

1 *ZPE* 47 (1982) *sub fin.* 1–12 (the only complete text, but provisional and unauthorized); Laks and Most (1997) (authorized English translation of the complete text); Tsantsanoglou (1997, 93–95) (authorized text of cols. i–vii, as renumbered); also Obbink (1997, 42–43, 48) (semi-authorized texts of cols. xx and xxii).

2 Riedweg (1998, 389–398) (re-edition of nearly all published items, old and new, and list of those unpublished); add Gavrilaki and Tzifopoulos (1998) (Rethymno area, Crete).

3 The equation between Rhea and Demeter is extended by the syncretizing commentator to other matronly goddesses, and for this he finds warrant in a different Orphic book, of *Hymns*, whence the line *Demeter Rhea Ge Meter Hestia Deio* (col. xxii lines 11–12) – which goes to show that the equation of the first two had long been common coin among the Orphics. Obbink (1994) restores a passage of Philodemus

4 Either "Persephone" or "queen of those below" or "queen below" is prominent on most of the leaves (P 1–2, A 1, 2–3, 4, 5 – I follow Riedweg's enumeration, incorporating earlier ones). "Queen below" is plausibly read on the Hipponium leaf (B 10), and plausibly restored on another from Entella (B 11). The dead person mostly describes himself as being of kindred race with the gods, a race going back to Earth and Sky (A 1, 2–3, B 1, 2, 3–9, 10, 11). In leaves from Thurii he speaks as well of a fatal lightning strike (A1, 2–3). All this is to situate himself within the Orphic creation story. The gods, Titans first and then the rest, descend from Earth and Sky, as in other creation stories; in the Orphic story man too shares this descent, as the result of a lightning strike. After the Titans slew Dionysus, Zeus blasted them with his lightning and created man from the residue of soot.

5 Leaves from Pelinna (P 1–2). On the Hipponium leaf (B 10), "initiates and *bakchoi*" follow a separate path in the underworld, doubtless to the door of Persephone's palace. An Apulian crater (Munich 3297, the name-piece of the Underworld Painter) shows a family of initiates, husband and wife and little son, standing before Persephone and the palace with the lyre-playing Orpheus as their spokesman: (*LIMC* Hades 132; Schmidt 1991, 32–33). Schmidt (1991, 42–44), adduces another scene by the Underworld Painter in which Orpheus presides at a seeming initiation ceremony in this world. On an earlier vase (Toledo museum no. 1994: 19), Dionysus himself stands beside the palace and the royal pair, and clasps the hand of Hades. Johnston and McNiven (1996) argue for the Orphic Dionysus, son of Persephone, but since he is surrounded by the wine god's retinue, and by the stricken family from Thebes, it is undoubtedly the son of Semele in search of his mother, as others have assumed.

6 A gold band from Pherae, 350–300 BC, gives the heading "symbols" and the names *Andrikepaiothyrsos, Brimo*, and directs the initiate to enter the meadow of the blessed without any post-mortem punishment (*SEG* 45: 646; Tsantsanoglou 1997, 114, 116–117; Riedweg 1998, 362, 388, 390).

7 Leaves from Pelinna and Thurii: "I/you, kid/bull/goat/ram, leapt/fell into milk" (P 1–2, A 1, 4). The "goat" instance is to be restored on one of the Pelinna leaves (Robertson 1995b, 289–290).

8 *Mystai kai bakchoi* (B 10). The two titles are likewise used successively in Eur. *Cretes* (fr. 472 Nauck = 635 Mette = 79 Austin), but at an interval, and with an accumulation of detail, which show that the second is grander than the first. The sequence [*mystes*], *neobakchos* was restored by Sokolowski (1962, 90, lines 8–9) (Callatis, *s.* ii *a.*, giving rules for initiates in a local cult), and is adopted by Avram (1995), but {. . . *oute bakchos ou}/te neobakchos* seems much likelier.

9 Vinogradov (1991, 81–82), rightly infers widespread public participation, but with social and political consequences which are too hypothetical. Parker (1996, 485), entertains "the skeptical view" that the plaques did not belong to members of a sect but saw only transitory use by an officiating priest; their provenance however is against this. Other suggestions must be left open. Perhaps the bone material derives from shared sacrifices (West 1983, 18). Perhaps the schematic drawing of a ship evokes the processional conveyance of Dionysus' spring festival (Dettori 1996, 308–310).

10 Ehrhardt (1988, 169–170, 467–468). A temple block at Miletus is inscribed with a rule for the awful rite of *omophagion embalein*, "throwing in the raw-eating," our only documentary reference (Sokolowski 1955, 48).

11 So West (1983, 140–175), the latest full-scale study. Against the category is Robertson (1990, 426–429).

12 Hes. *Theog.* 477–484, 492–496; Musaeus *Vorsokr* 2 B 8; Epimenides *Vorsokr* 3 A 1 § 111, B 21–24; [Apld.] *Bibl.* 1.5–6; *Orph.* frs. 150–156.
13 So too Ov. *Met.* 6.114; Nonn. *Dion.* 5.568–569, 6.156–164. There was "a Cretan tale" to similar effect: Zeus became a snake so as to elude Cronus, and also changed his nurses into bears, whence this group of constellations in the sky (schol. Arat. 46). Whether the source is Epimenides is disputed: *Vorsokr* 3 F 23 vs. *FGrH* 468 F 5.
14 Robertson (1992, 21–22, 135). Hesiod draws on the *Diasia* in rendering the transition from the Golden Age to the reign of Zeus. When gods and men gather for the first time under Zeus, the left-over Titan Prometheus contrives that men shall enjoy a hearty meal of black pudding made from an ox (*Theog.* 535–561). At the *Diasia* people gather from far and wide in a sombre mood, but enjoy a hearty meal of black pudding made from an ox.
15 Robertson (1992, 25–26; 1996b, 346–347, 359); cf. Nilsson (1906, 356–359) on the festivals *Anthesphoria* and *Herosantheia*. The *Anthesphoria* as a festival of Hipponium – the festival name is implicit in Strabo's description (6.1.5, p. 256) – can be recognized as the occasion of the "Locrian plaques," Locri being the mother city of Hipponium. At Athens the *Diasia* fell on 23rd *Anthesterion*, and "the Lesser Mysteries" in the same month on an unknown day, but probably at mid-month, the usual time for the festivals of Demeter's cycle.
16 Zeus *meilichios* at Selinus: Jameson *et al.* (1993, 28, 89–103). The coins: Zuntz (1971, pl. 15c). According to Jameson *et al.* (1993, 95), Selinus has no example of Zeus *meilichios* in snake form; but the coins go unmentioned.
17 "The Lesser Mysteries are performed as a representation of the matter of Dionysus" (Steph. Byz. s.v. *Agra*). Deubner (1932, 70) thinks of Iacchus, but that figure of Demeter's autumn festival had no story of his own to represent (see Robertson 1998, 559–561).
18 *Orph.* fr. 208, cf. Nonn. *Dion.* 6.165–166, 169; *LIMC* Dionysos 267, an ivory pyxis showing the enthronement among several Orphic scenes.
19 Citations from the *Rhapsodies* do not show what the use was. But in Hyg. *Fab.* 167.1 Zeus very suitably grinds the heart and gives it to Semele in a potion. Furthermore, Lollianus and the Orphic *Argonautica* must have had authority for describing the culinary preparation of a heart in oath-taking (*infra*, n.21). On the other hand, Firm. Mat. *De Err.* 6.4 (=*Orph.* fr. 214) tells how Zeus placed the heart inside a gypsum image of Dionysus. This is regarded by Henrichs (1972, 70) and by West (1983, 163) as a plausible ceremony. Yet it could hardly lead to the begetting of the second Dionysus in the *Rhapsodies*, and a commemorative image agrees better with the Euhemerist outlook of Firmicus' source, for whom Zeus and Dionysus are a Cretan tyrant and his son.
20 *Orph.* fr. 31, second century BC. The names *Brimo* and *Irikepaige* (voc.) are anticipated on the gold band from Pherae, where they, rather than toys or any objects, are the "symbols" (*supra*, n.6).
21 Henrichs (1972, 92–93, fr. B 1 *recto*; 96–97, fr. B 1 *verso*). The outlaws slice the heart, add barley meal and oil, cook the organ and collect the blood, and swallow either slices or bites. In the Orphic *Argonautica* (316–318) Orpheus pounds the heart of a bull (*thrausas* mss: *erusas* Schneider), lays it on cakes, and sprinkles oil and sheep's milk, all in what is meant to be an oath-taking.
22 Sokolowski (1955, 84 line 13), second century. It is a typical attempt of that period, matched by the flowering of oracles at Clarus and elsewhere, to impart a higher tone, in this case Orphic and Pythagorean, to conventional worship, in this case Dionysus'.
23 *FGrH* 399 F 1 = *SH* 379B. Philochorus *FGrH* 328 F 7 and Cephalion *FGrH* 94 F 3 are cited too, but Jacoby has doubts about both, as also about the date of Dinarchus. West (1983, 151) is more accommodating. Tatian, *Adv. Gr.* 8, confuses the burial place with the *omphalos*.

24 In a version (*Orph.* fr. 35) intermediate between this one and the *Rhapsodies*, the Titans boil the limbs in a tripod basin, but not at Delphi, and also roast them on spits, but do not eat them before Zeus hurls his lightning; Apollo is then given the limbs and "brings them to Parnassus" for burial. We come to it below (see p. 226).

25 Python's bones like Dionysus' limbs go into the tripod basin and then are buried (Hyg. *Fab.* 140.5; Serv. Verg. *Aen.* 3.360). Roman poets played as well on the resemblance of *cortina* ("basin") and *corium* ("hide") (Serv. Verg. *Aen.* 3.92, etc.), whence also Eust. on Dion. Per. 441 (his author more conventionally thinks of Python coiling round the tripod).

26 Hyp. Pind. *Pyth.*, p. 2 Drachmann. In Eur. *Iph. Taur.* 1243–1244 Parnassus is already reveling for Dionysus when Apollo arrives.

27 Wintertime: Plut. *De Prim. Frig.* 18, 953D, etc. Waking the baby: Plut. *Is. Os.* 35, 365A. Plutarch to be sure has embarked on a comparison of Dionysus with Osiris, who was not awakened as a baby; but his phrase *hotan hai Thuiades egeirosi ton likniten* draws on Delphic cult and falls outside the argument. Nilsson (1957, 38–45) does not succeed in showing that the Thyiads meant to summon the dead god from the underworld.

28 Themelis (1992). The *polos* of the surviving Caryatid shows, at the back, women reveling; at the front, a woman dangling a slaughtered animal. Themelis rightly equates them with the Thyiads. For other, disputed, renderings of the Thyiads, see Villanueva Puig (1986, 38–40, 47).

29 It is often affirmed, as by Nilsson (1906, 284), that the month *Dadaphorios* is named for the torchlight of our revels on Parnassus. But the many *-phoros*, *-phoria* compounds of ritual all refer to the carrying of objects in a procession: the revels are not a processional torch-bearing.

30 Besides the Thyiads, Delphi has a cult-site Thyia with an eponymous nymph (Hdt. 7.178, *passim*). On the festival at Elis, producing the month-name *Thyios*, see Nilsson (1906, 291–293). Note, however, that in the federal calendars of Thessaly and Boeotia the month *Thyios* falls in spring, and at Lamia, Melitaea, and Phthiotic Thebes it is unplaced: Trümpy (1997, index 1 s.v.). It seems that either celebration, in winter or in spring, could be called *Thyia* ("revel-rites"): we know that either could be called simply *Dionysia*.

31 Delphic month names which are both exceptional and peculiar – in that they do not match festival nomenclature as otherwise known – are *Boathoos* (cf. *Boadromios vel sim.*), *Dadaphorios*, *Bysios*, *Endyspoitropios*, *Ilaios*. Most Greek cities have hardly any exceptional and peculiar month names (apart from the foreign names on Crete and Cyprus). The festival names of Delphi's eight-year cycle are also unparalleled: *S(t)epteria*, *Charila*, *Herois*.

32 The festival *Poitropia* is mentioned but not illuminated by the rules of the Labyadae (*Corpus des inscriptions de Delphes* 1.9 D 5) and a decree of Chaleium (*FdD* 3.3.145). Now at Chaleium and elsewhere in West Locris it gives its name to a month of spring, *Poitropios* = March or April. For the rest, the calendars in question have only one Dionysiac month, *Dionysios* = December at Physcus, named for the winter celebration. Again, see Trümpy (1997). On this showing, *Poitropia* may be a regular name for the spring festival, and the Delphic nomenclature may be re-duplication.

33 Modern comment always assumes that the Titans whiten their faces to be scary, and we are told how tribal and other initiates undergo a virtual death while their tormentors impersonate spirits (e.g. West 1983, 154–155). It is true that white faces may look like the dead (as in another, but surely unrelated, line of Euphorion, fr. 88 Powell), and true again that Harpocration s.v. *apomatton* likens Aeschines' practice of smearing initiates with mud to the Titans coating themselves with gypsum: a fateful

precedent for modern research; but any harum-scarum conflicts with the Titans' purpose of deceiving Dionysus. Nonnus calls the whitened faces a deception (*Dion.* 6.169–170), as Clement does the toys (*Protr.* 17.2 = *Orph.* fr. 34).

34 Revellers at the Attic vintage festival smear their faces with gypsum (Plut. *Prov. Alex.* 30 Crusius = *Corp. Paroemiogr. Gr. Suppl.* 16); ithyphallic performers with soot (Semus *FGrH* 396 F 24); girls dancing for Artemis with mud (Paus. 6.22.2). Nonnus in his varied references to faces smeared with gypsum attributes them to female Bacchants as well (*Dion.* 29.274, 34.144, cf. 47.733).

35 West (1983, 156–157), points to a mirror from Olbia of the late sixth century, on which the owners inscribed their names with the cry *euai* (Dubois 1996, no. 92). But a mirror is an uncanny object that may lend itself to religious faith without being used in ritual. Nilsson (1955, 671–672), thought that the Orphic story was behind the toys, notably tops, dedicated from an early date at the Cabirium of Thebes; but this cult was much concerned with children anyway.

36 Children are generally prominent in later mysteries: see Lambrechts (1957), who unconvincingly explains that thoughts of the afterlife dwelt on those who died young. Nilsson (1957, 106–115) holds that Dionysus' Mysteries were influenced in this respect by the myths about the infant god (he might have said, about other infants too), which seems circular.

37 To judge from (?)Philochorus *FGrH* 328 F 7, it was perhaps only a certain area in the temple, which happened to include an actual base, that could be said to bear an imaginary epitaph.

38 Quoted by schol. Lycophr. *Alex.* 207. I have obelized, as Pfeiffer does, on Callim. fr. 643: ἐν πυρὶ Βάκχον δῖον edd., φιάλης Lobeck, ὑπερφίαλοι O. Müller (this can be ruled out, since the tripod basin is in question).

39 On this source see Robertson (1996b, 367–372). The extent of his interest in ritual is better seen in the case of Demeter's Mysteries, about which he contributes unique detail to the scholia on Lucian.

40 Luc. *Sacr.* 13; Gal. *Plac. Hipp. et Plat.* 2.4; Hsch. s.v. καρδιουλκίαι. A curse tablet adjures Hecate to "cut out the heart" of the detested person (*SEG* 30.326).

41 Suda, Etym. Magn., *Lex. Rhet.* ed. Bekker s.v. καρδιωσάμενος, -οι; Hsch. s.v. καρδιοῦσθαι. In third-century Ephesus the rules of official procedure refer to a general category of sacrifice, probably all but holocausts, as καρδιουργούμενα and ἐκμηριζόμενα (*Ephesos* 9.1.1, D 1, F 14), i.e. victims whose heart and thigh(s) are burnt up.

42 Eubulus *Semele or Dionysus* fr. 94 Kassel-Austin should perhaps be mentioned in order to be dismissed. Dionysus complains, in lines which are hopelessly corrupt, of certain sacrificial portions, including the heart. This passage, along with several others, is quoted only to show the stinginess of worshippers.

43 Eur. *Bacch.* 229–230, 680–682 (royal mothers), 699–702 (nursing), 722–723, 729–730 (intruding rustics), 734–747 (cattle torn and scattered), 760–764 (men bloodied), 1125–1139 (Pentheus torn and scattered), 1216–1221, *Chr. Pat.* 1466–1472 (pieces gathered for burial). Carpenter (1997, 114–117), argues too ingeniously that Euripides is indebted to generic scenes in vase painting.

44 Robertson (1983, 153–162), *LIMC* Proitides 1–7. The Hesiodic version which spoke of Dionysus doubtless appeared in the *Melampodia*, not in the *Catalogue* as West has it (F 131 = [Apld.] *Bibl.* 2.26). West (1985, 79) objects that in a context full of *Catalogue* material [Apld.] cannot mean the *Melampodia* by citing "Hesiod"; but this is [Apld.]'s only style for any Hesiodic work, used of the *Melampodia* at F 275 = *Bibl.* 3.71; his purpose here is to distinguish a Hesiodic work from Acusilaus (*FGrH* 2 F 28). Aeschylus' *Xantriai* very likely showed Hera afflicting the daughters of Proetus. S. Radt on *TGrF* F 168, a controversial papyrus fragment, flatters me by claiming my conjecture λάἰχος εὐκλείας (line 11) for his own.

45 Patrae: Paus. 7.18.4. Pausanias emphasizes the looming threat which the Titans

posed, and says that Μεσάτις ("Midmost") as a district of Patrae was named from the episode, presumably because the child was surrounded by his enemies. Crete: Firm. Mat. *De Err.* 6.5 = *Orph.* fr. 214.

46 The calendar details which follow are easily verified through the indexes in Trümpy (1997).
47 Less common Dionysiac month names that probably refer to the winter festival are *Eiraphios* (1) and *Euonios* (1); those that probably refer to the spring festival are *Bakchion* (2), *Iobakchios* (1), *Dithyrambios* (1), and *Pithoigion* (1). The commoner *Dionysios* (15) and *Thyios* (6) can refer to either (*supra*, n.30). *Daisios* is the Macedonian variant of *Theodaisios* (*infra*, n.57).
48 For some references and discussion, Jost (1985, 433–434). Inscriptions, too, mention trieteric celebrations. *Hom. H. Bacch.* 11–12, the earliest reference, was emended, or rather rearticulated, by T.W. Allen so that the *aition* becomes the slicing of Dionysus into three pieces; Casadio (1999, 86, n.13) cites subsequent opinion.
49 In Attica, where the evidence is fullest, we have the series *Thesmophoria*, *Proerosia*, *Chloaia*, *Antheia*, *Kalamaia*, *Skira* (see Robertson 1992, 26, n.81; 1996b, 232, n.38, 247–252).
50 Marchetti (1994, 147) offers a conjectural location for one of the cult-places. As to the purported rite and monument for a daughter of Proetus, see Robertson (1983, 159, n.39).
51 When the Dorian eponym Pelops treacherously murders the Arcadian eponym Stymphalus, this archetypal crime is oddly compounded by a tearing and scattering of the limbs ([Apld.] *Bibl.* 3.159). It is as if the Dorians were typified for their neighbors by the winter festival.
52 Ibycus extols the blossoms and "shady branches" of a vineyard in spring (*Poetae Melici Graeci* 286), and Leonidas' blossoms "of shady fruitage" are perhaps the same, and belong to an Arcadian countryman (*Anthologia Palatina* 6.154 = *Hellenistic Epigrams* 97).
53 "They tear a live bull with their teeth" (Firm. Mat. *De Err.* 6.5). Rather, they dismember it with knives, and the dreadfulness is heightened by the language of "raw-eating" (Robertson 1995a, 199).
54 *LIMC* Mainades 9, 13, 16, 30, 33, 38, 40, 42, 45. Literature gives occasional glimpses, as when the Titans use knives on Dionysus (for these sources, West 1983, 160, n.72) or Icarius is hewed and bludgeoned with various rustic implements (Nonn. *Dion.* 47.116–124, 163–176).
55 Robertson (1990, 432–436; 1991, 15–16, 18–21, 25–26; 1995a, 197–199).
56 It is nearly always assumed that *Theodaisia* is a synonym of *theoxenia*, so that both are "[rites] of feasting/hosting a god," as with couch and table (e.g. Jameson 1994, 36, n.5). But there is no suggestion of this in ancient sources who mention or gloss the festival name *Theodaisia*. Unlike *theoxenia* it never occurs as a descriptive term, only as a festival name, which *Theoxenia* seldom is. Nor does it demonstrably refer to any god but Dionysus. Nor is Dionysus known as a recipient of couch-and-table hospitality: the magic embodiments of the wine god are not to be so regarded. For *Theodaisia* we require a meaning altogether different from *theoxenia*.
57 The sense "divide" is supported by the analogy of *geo-* and *kreo-daisia, -daites*. Plutarch holds up *isodaites* as one of the epithets of Dionysus that refer to his tearing and scattering (*De E apud Delphos* 9, 389A). Note too that whereas Macedon was notorious for the savagery of its Bacchic revels (Plut. *Alex.* 2.7–9, *passim*), the rites are there attested by the variant month name *Daisios*.
58 Wildness keeps its appeal for modern theorists who treat of mental structures; for linguistic argument they offer the hypothesis of "a vanished god" whose name varied (Trümpy 1997, 126–127, after W. Burkert). Festivals, however, are generally named for definite ritual actions; wild gods are not wanted here.

59 Nilsson (1906, 271–273, and more doubtfully 1955, 598) favored *ageiro*, but thought of the Agriania, like the Anthesteria, as a "gathering" of the dead, who came up with Dionysus from the underworld. For the Agriania this view has been generally given up, but still persists for the Anthesteria (against it, Robertson 1993, 197–208).

References

Avram, A., 1995: "Un règlement sacré de Callatis," *BCH* 119, 235–252.

Carpenter, T.H., 1993: "On the beardless Dionysos," in T.H. Carpenter and C.A. Faraone (eds), *Masks of Dionysus* (Cornell University Press, Ithaca, N.Y.), 185–206.

Carpenter, T.H., 1997: *Dionysian Imagery in Fifth-century Athens*. Clarendon Press, Oxford.

Casadio, G., 1999: *Il vino dell'anima. Storia del culto di Dioniso a Corinto, Sicione, Trezene*. Il Calamo, Rome.

Dettori, E., 1996: "Testi 'orfici' dalla Magna Grecia al Mar Nero," *Parola del Passato* 51, 292–310.

Deubner, L., 1932: *Attische Feste*. Keller, Berlin.

Dubois, L., 1996: *Inscriptions grecques dialectales d'Olbia du Pont*. Droz, Geneva.

Ehrhardt, N., 1988: *Milet und seine Kolonien* (2nd edition). Lang, Frankfurt.

Gantz, T., 1993: *Early Greek Myth. A Guide to Literary and Artistic Sources*. Johns Hopkins University Press, Baltimore, Md.

Gavrilaki, I. and Y.Z. Tzifopoulos, 1998: "An 'Orphic–Dionysiac' gold *epistomion* from Sfakaki near Rethymno," *BCH* 122, 343–355.

Henrichs, A., 1972: *Die Phoinikika des Lollianos*. Habelt, Bonn.

Jameson, M.H., 1994: "*Theoxenia*," in R. Hägg (ed.), *Ancient Greek Cult Practice from the Epigraphical Evidence* (Åstrom, Stockholm), 35–57.

Jameson, M.H., D.R. Jordan, and R.D. Kotansky, 1993: *A Lex Sacra from Selinous*. Greek, Roman and Byzantine Monographs 11. Duke University, Durham, N.C.

Johnston, S.I. and T.J. McNiven, 1996: "Dionysos and the underworld in Toledo," *MusHelv* 53, 25–36.

Jost, M., 1985: *Sanctuaires et cultes d'Arcadie*. Vrin, Paris.

Laks, A. and G.W. Most, 1997: "A provisional translation of the Derveni papyrus," in A. Laks and G.W. Most (eds), *Studies on the Derveni Papyrus* (Oxford University Press, Oxford), 9–22.

Lambrechts, P., 1957: "L'importance de l'enfant dans les religions de mystères," in *Hommages à W. Deonna* (Collection Latomus 28, Brussels), 322–333.

Linforth, I.M., 1946: "The Corybantic rites in Plato," *U. of Cal. Publ. in Classical Philology* 13.5, 121–162.

Marchetti, P., 1994: "Recherches sur les mythes et la topographie d'Argos," *BCH* 118, 131–160.

Merkelbach, R., 1963: "Die Erigone des Eratosthenes," in *Miscellanea di studi alessandrini in memoria di A. Rostagni* (Erasmo, Turin), 469–526.

Nilsson, M.P., 1906: *Griechische Feste von religiöser Bedeutung, mit Ausschluss der attischen*. Teubner, Leipzig.

Nilsson, M.P., 1955: *Geschichte der griechischen Religion* 1 (2nd edition). Beck, Munich.

Nilsson, M.P., 1957: *The Dionysiac Mysteries of the Hellenistic and Roman Age.* Gleerup, Lund.

Obbink, D., 1994: "A quotation of the Derveni papyrus in Philodemus' 'On Piety'," *CronErcol* 24, 111–135.

Obbink, D., 1997: "Cosmology as initiation vs. the critique of Orphic mysteries," in A. Laks and G.W. Most (eds), *Studies on the Derveni Papyrus* (Clarendon Press, Oxford), 39–54.

Parker, R., 1996: "Early Orphism," in A. Powell (ed.), *The Greek World.* Routledge, London.

Piérart, M., 1996: "La mort de Dionysos à Argos," in R. Hägg (ed.), *The Role of Religion in the Early Greek Polis* (Åstrom, Stockholm), 141–151.

Riedweg, C., 1998: "Initiation–Tod–Unterwelt: Beobachtungen zur Kommunikationssituation und narrativen Technik der orphisch-bakchischen Goldblättchen," in F. Graf (ed.), *Ansichten griechischer Rituale. Geburtstags-Symposium für W. Burkert* (Teubner, Stuttgart), 359–398.

Robert, C., 1920: *Die griechische Heldensage 1. Landschaftliche Sagen.* Weidmann, Berlin.

Robertson, N., 1983: "Greek ritual begging in aid of women's fertility and childbirth," *TAPA* 113, 143–169.

Robertson, N., 1990: "Some recent work in Greek religion and mythology," Pt. 1, *EMC* n.s. 9, 419–442.

Robertson, N., 1991: "Myth, ritual, and livelihood in early Greece," in M. Silver (ed.), *Ancient Economy in Mythology: East and West* (Rowman and Littlefield, Baltimore, Md.), 3–34.

Robertson, N., 1992: *Festivals and Legends. The Formation of Greek Cities in the Light of Public Ritual.* University of Toronto Press, Toronto.

Robertson, N., 1993: "Athens' festival of the new wine," *HSCP* 95, 197–250.

Robertson, N., 1995a: "The magic properties of female age-groups in Greek ritual," *AncW* 26, 193–203.

Robertson, N., 1995b: Review of T.H. Carpenter and C.A. Faraone (eds), *Masks of Dionysus,* in *EMC* n.s. 14, 286–292.

Robertson, N., 1996a: "The ancient Mother of the Gods. A missing chapter in the history of Greek religion," in E. Lane (ed.), *Cybele, Attis and Related Cults* (Brill, Leiden), 239–304.

Robertson, N., 1996b: "New light on Demeter's mysteries: the festival Proerosia," *GRBS* 37, 319–379.

Robertson, N., 1998: "The two processions to Eleusis and the program of the Mysteries," *AJP* 119, 547–575.

Schmidt, M., 1991: "Bemerkungen zu Orpheus in Unterwelts- und Thrakerdarstellungen," in P. Borgeaud (ed.), *Orphisme et Orphée en l'honneur de J. Rudhardt* (Droz, Geneva), 31–50.

Sokolowski, F., 1955: *Lois sacrees de l'Asie Mineure.* De Boccard, Paris.

Sokolowski, F., 1962: *Lois sacrées des Cités grecques, Supplément.* De Boccard, Paris.

Sokolowski, F., 1969: *Lois sacrées des Cités grecques.* De Boccard, Paris.

Stambolidis, N.C., 1987: *O bomos tou Dionusou sten Ko.* Publications of the Archaeologikon *ArchDelt* 34, Athens.

Themelis, P.G., 1992: "The cult scene on the polos of the Siphnian Karyatid at Delphi," in R. Hägg (ed.), *The Iconography of Greek Cult* (Kernos Supplement 1, Athens), 49–72.

Trümpy, C., 1997: *Untersuchungen zu den altgriechischen Monatsnamen und Monatsfolgen.* Winter, Heidelberg.
Tsantsanoglou, K., 1997: "The first columns of the Derveni papyrus and their religious significance," in A. Laks and G.W. Most (eds), *Studies on the Derveni Papyrus* (Clarendon Press, Oxford), 93–128.
Villanueva Puig, M.-C., 1986: "À propos des Thyiades de Delphes," in *L'association dionysiaque dans les societés anciennes* (Collection de l'École française de Rome 89, Rome), 31–51.
Vinogradov, J.G., 1991: "Zur sachlichen und geschichtlichen Deutung der Orphiker-Plättchen von Olbia," in P. Borgeaud (ed.), *Orphisme et Orphée en l'honneur de J. Rudhardt* (Droz, Geneva), 77–86.
West, M.L., 1983: *The Orphic Poems.* Clarendon Press, Oxford.
West, M.L., 1985: *The Hesiodic Catalogue of Women.* Clarendon Press, Oxford.
West, M.L., 1990: *Studies in Aeschylus.* Teubner, Stuttgart.
Zuntz, G., 1971: *Persephone.* Clarendon Press, Oxford.

10

LESSER MYSTERIES – NOT LESS MYSTERIOUS

Fritz Graf

In most scholarly accounts since Franz Cumont, ancient mystery cults are narrowly confined to a small number of cults that, furthermore, are surprisingly symmetrically arranged – the three old Greek mystery cults of Demeter in Eleusis, of the Great Gods of Samothrace, and of Dionysos, and the three younger "Oriental" cults of Isis (and the other Egyptian gods of her circle), the Great Mother, and Mithras.[1] But there were more mystery cults than that in the Greek and Graeco-Roman world, as any reader of Pausanias knows: in his "Description of Greece", he listed a not inconsiderable number of what he called "a Rite", *telete* – the Rite of the Great Goddesses in the ancient capital of Messenia, Andania, and in Megalopolis and Trapezous in Arcadia, of Demeter Eleusinia in Arcadian Pheneos and of Hagna in Lykosoura, of Demeter in Phlious on the Corinthian Gulf and of Dionysos and Demeter in nearby Lerna, of Hecate on the island of Aegina, of the Kabeiroi in Thebes and of Hera in Argive Temenion,[2] not to mention the Mysteries of Eleusis. In some cases, the local tradition Pausanias is reporting connects those rites with the Eleusinian Mysteries;[3] in others, Pausanias does not dare to talk about the rites in detail, since they are secret;[4] and in yet other cases, testimonies besides Pausanias (mostly inscriptions) call them outright Mysteries, *mysteria*.[5] There can thus be no doubt that these local cults are phenomenologically comparable to the six major cults. Inscriptions, less easy accessible than Pausanias' books, give considerably more: they attest to a wide variety of Mysteries, both as part of major cults and as isolated rituals, and often performed by the members of one of the cultic associations that were becoming an important feature of social life from later Hellenistic times onwards (see esp. Poland 1909).

Scholars of an earlier generation used to scoff at these later Mysteries, since they seemed to lack the religious seriousness associated with mystery cults; Martin Nilsson, for one, asked whether the term "mysteries" in these contexts was more than a figure of speech, and few scholars disagreed.[6] From a position that has taught us to distrust such statements as potentially ethnocentric, it would be easy to refute Nilsson; after all, his favourite late antique mystery cult is an association "that felt united by its mysteries, its rituals, and its faith... The future would belong to mystery cults that formed communities".[7] The problem, however, raises an intriguing question of method. How are we to understand the term "Mysteries" (or rather *mysteria*), when the term covers a much wider ground than the six major mystery cults that, to most of us, determine what mystery cults are? A closer look at some of these "lesser mysteries" imposes itself. It will become clear that we deal with cults that, on the one hand, preserve some rather archaic features and that, on the other, have been transformed into something very different in the complex society of the Roman Empire.

Traces of hoary antiquity? Peloponnesian mystery rites

Among the Peloponnesian mystery cults mentioned by Pausanias, the one outstanding cult, as to documentation and importance, is the cult of the Great Gods (or, as Pausanias has it, Great Goddesses) in Andania in Messene.[8]

"I may not talk about the Great Goddesses (for it is to them as well that they perform the rite in the Karnasian grove), since I regard them as second only to the Eleusinian festival in awesomeness" – thus writes Pausanias when he is about to describe the grove close to the ruins of Andania, the former royal city of Messenia (Paus. 4.33.5). The religious awe that the rite inspired in Pausanias must have had to do both with the character of the ritual and its hoary antiquity. In his long account of Messenian history, Pausanias had given ample room to the early history of the cult of Andania. Andania's first queen, the eponymous heroine Messene, received the rite from Eleusis at the very dawn of human history, from Kaukon, a somewhat enigmatic hero – the Peloponnesians regarded him as the grandson of the hero Phlyos, the Athenians as the great-grandson of none less than Gaia herself, according to "the Demeter hymn of Musaios for the Lykomidai" (Paus. 4.1.5; for the Lykomidai, see below). The Mysteries of Andania thus derive from those of Eleusis, but are at the same time assumed to be as old as human society in Messene. Twice in the years to come, Athenians reformed the cult, thus renewing and strengthening the link with the rites of Demeter and Kore in Eleusis. First, in the time of the Athenian kings, Lykos, the banished son of King Pandion, introduced, among other things, a purification rite still in use in Pausanias' time (Paus. 4.1.6). Later, a certain Methapos made some changes; he was an Athenian ritual expert who had also founded the Mysteries of the Kabeiroi near Thebes and had his statue dedicated in the sacred enclosure of the Attic Lykomidai where the clan was performing their own brand of Mysteries (Paus. 4.1.5–9. 2.6), whose (mythical or historical) member he must have been. The main change in the Mysteries, though, happened in much clearer historical times, when, after the Spartan defeat at Leuktra in 371, the Theban and Argive victors restored the

Messenian state, with Messene as its newly founded capital. The Mysteries were central, according to Pausanias: Kaukon, the founder of the Mysteries, appeared in a dream both to the Theban victor Epameinondas and to Epiteles, the Messenian whom the Argives had made commander of the Messenian forces. While to Epameinodas Kaukon promised eternal fame if he would give back their state to the Messenians, Epiteles got a more complex message: he should dig on Mount Ithome, the sacred mountain of the Messenians, at a place where yew and myrtle were growing together. Epiteles obeyed and found an ancient bronze urn that he brought to Epameinondas; after a prayer and a sacrifice, Epameinondas opened it and found a text written on a tin foil: it turned out to be "the rites of the Great Gods, as deposited by Aristomenes", the hero of the Messenian resistance to Sparta whose defeat had made possible the Spartan conquest of Messenia (Paus. 4.26.6–8). The members of the Messenian priestly families copied this text into books: they thus obtained ritual books that guaranteed the authenticity of the mystery rites performed after 379 (Paus. 4.37.5).

The cult of the Great Goddesses of Andania, then, is intimately connected with the existence of the Messenian state: its beginning went together with the reconstruction of the cult, and this reconstruction was sanctioned and legitimized by the ritual text left by Aristomenes that had miraculously been found, through the intervention of the original founder of the cult, Kaukon. There can be no doubt that both stories – the story of how Queen Messene received the Mysteries, and of how the Messenian commander Epiteles found the text that shaped the refounded cult – must have been invented shortly after the foundation of Messene;[9] the Great Goddesses, Kaukon, Messene, and Aristomenes loomed large in the sacrifices and prayers that marked the foundation of the new capital and state (see the list in Paus. 4.37.6). When, in 92/1 BC, a member of the priestly families, Mnasistratus, reformed the Mysteries, he again referred to these books which he handed over to the Messenian state (see note 10). The cult of Andania and the Messenian state determine each other.

The relationship between the Mysteries and the state, though, is complex, as the inscription of 92/1 shows; in this inscription the outward organization of the Mysteries is meticulously detailed:[10] the Mysteries are the responsibility of the council and the assembly of Messene, but the actual business is delegated to several bodies, among them the large group of "Holy Men" (*hosioi*). Mnasistratus had pushed for these new regulations; he also donated the sacred books, but he kept for himself the leading position in the procession and the custody of the sacred fountain named Hagna, which entailed participation in all sacrifices connected with the fountain. Presumably the same Mnasistratus – called here "hierophant" – had asked the oracle of Apollo Pythaeus in Argos about the Mysteries; the god, however, addressed his answer to all Messenians: the Mysteries are their affair, whatever interest Mnasistratus had in their reform (Deshours 1999).

The regulations of 92 BC keep carefully away from anything that was secret; they distribute obligations and prerogatives and regulate the rituals that were visible to all participants in the festival: the great procession of the priests and other functionaries, with the initiates and the sacrificial animals that must have been led from the city of Messene to the sanctuary of the Great Goddesses in the Karnasian grove, and the sacred meal of the "Holy Men" that took place after the sacrifices and to which the priests and priestesses, the musicians and Mnasistratus and his family were invited. They also list all the animals and their recipients that have to be sacrificed, with their divine recipients: "A pregnant pig for Demeter, a two-year old pig for the Great Gods, a ram for Hermes, a boar for Apollo Karneios, a sheep for Hagnan; furthermore, a ram and three piglets for the purification and one hundred sheep for the 'first initiates' the neophyts"; this could argue for a restriction of their number to exactly one hundred. Purification rites belong to the preliminary phase of all mystery cults, before coming into close contact with the divine; in Andania, purification could take place either in the grove of Lykos or, more spectacularly, in the theatre. The sacrifices to the divinities must have taken place in the grove, as part of the secret ritual, as did dances for which the regulations list the musicians. Hermes and Apollo Karneios had their statues in the grove (Paus. 4.33.4). Hagna – whom the initiates identify with Demeter's daughter Kore – had her spring with altar and statue (Paus. 4.33.4; Sokolowski 1969, 65, 84–86). Demeter and Kore form the link with Eleusis, whatever the original nature of Hagna, "The Pure One" had been; Apollo Karneios, among the Peloponnesians, is a predominantly political god; Hermes, whose statue carries a ram, is a god of herdsman and their world outside the city. The Great Gods are more enigmatic: the inscription depicts them as the main divinities who had a temple in the sanctuary; Pausanias, however, chose to write about the Great Goddesses as the main divinities (Piolot 1999). Ordinarily, the Great Gods belong together with male ecstatic groups like the Kabeiroi, Kouretes and Korybantes and are connected, among other places, with the Samothracian Mysteries (Hemberg 1950; Cole 1983); Hermes and Demeter – in her Arcadian form that is closer to the great mother goddesses than the ordinary Greek form – have links with them, while Persephone does not. Thus, it might be that we glance at least at an earlier constellation of a group of male gods around a mother goddess – a constellation that then had been "normalized", perhaps through the influence of Eleusis, by understanding Hagna as Kore which gave Pausanias the possibility to focus on the couple of the Great Goddesses, Demeter and her daughter.

Pausanias' long story of the origins and early history of the Messenian Mysteries connects them with three other mystery cults. Foremost are the Mysteries of Eleusis: to link the Messenian cult with the Eleusinian Mysteries gave them nobility and antiquity;[11] they were the most important and, at least in the eyes of Greeks from the classical epoch onwards, the most ancient mystery cult, which was thought responsible for nothing less than civilizing humanity through Demeter's gift of grain. The presence of Demeter and Kore among the mystery gods easily justified this interpretation, and other Peloponnesian mystery cults equally derived from Eleusis, among them the Mysteries of Demeter Eleusinia in Pheneos and of the Great Goddesses of Megalopolis in Arcadia. Pausanias regarded the rites of the Goddesses in Megalopolis as a copy of those in Eleusis, without giving details that could confirm his view.[12] In Pheneos, again according to Pausanias, the ritual books of the Mysteries were kept in a sacred rock and taken out only for the trieteric Greater Mysteries when the priest, wearing the mask of Demeter Kidaria, was beating the earth with a rod; the rites had been instituted to Pheneos by Naos, the grandson of Eumolpos, the first Eleusinian hierophant.[13] In all these cases, it is rather a propagandistic move by the local priesthood than accurate information.

The connections with the Theban Kabeirion and the Athenian Lykomidai are more tenuous and hinge on the enigmatic personality of Methapus; they might reflect not much more than Pausanias' scholarly mind or the wish of the Andanian priesthood to connect their Mysteries with another famous sanctuary – Thebes would be an obvious choice, given the key role the Thebans played in the refoundation of the Messenian state. This is not to say that the Theban Mysteries would not share some traits with Andania. Their mythology brings in Demeter and the theme of humanity's early age: the Mysteries were said to have been instituted by Demeter Kabeiraia when she entrusted sacred objects to the Kabeiros Prometheus and his son Aitnaios; the goddess and her daughter had a sacred grove next to the Kabeirion where only the initiates could enter (Paus. 9.25.5–9), and a vase from the sanctuary portrays, among others, a Pratoloas, "First Human".[14] Furthermore, Pausanias – who is very reticent about who the Kabeiroi are – asserts that their rites were performed for them and the Mother (Paus. 9.25.6): this recalls the Andanian constellation. Inscriptions and images from the sanctuary show a bearded Kabeiros and his *Pais* ("boy"); this couple appears as the local form of the Panhellenized Kabeiros Prometheus and his son Aitnaios. Theban youngsters dedicate their toys, presumably at the end of their boyhood, and among the votive statuettes, boys wearing a conical cap (a "pilos") are numerous (see Burkert 1977, 421); such a cap is worn both by the Holy Men in Andania (Sokolowski 1969, 13, 65) and by the Dioskouroi who, like the Kabeiroi, sometimes are called "Great Gods" (Hemberg 1950); the same type of cap is worn by the divine blacksmith Hephaistos, patron of another mystery cult of Kabeiroi on the island of Lemnos and, in genealogy, father or grandfather of the Kabeiroi (Akusilaos, *FGrHist* 2 F 20; Pherekydes, *FGrHist* 3 F 48). Aitnaios ("he who belongs to Aitna") recalls the Sicilian volcano where Hephaistos' workshop was located. The connections are hazy, but again a vaguely common background can be made out, where male initiation groups, blacksmiths' associations and a Great Goddess play a role.

The same holds true to an even larger degree for the Mysteries of the Athenian clan of the Lykomidai, the clan of Themistokles. Their sanctuary was outside Athens, in Phlya, a village whose eponymous hero was Phlyos, the grandfather of Kaukon. Information is late and scant (Plut. fr. 24, see also Themist. 1 [after Simonides, fr. 627]; Paus. 1.31.4). The Mysteries are thought older than the Eleusinian ones and their main divinity is again a Great Goddess (whom Pausanias identifies with Gaia); we also hear about an altar to her and about other altars, among them the one of Persephone Protogonos, "First-Born". The clan was said to use very old hymns in its cult, such as a hymn of Mousaios that told how Demeter visited Phlyos and, presumably, brought the cult. The influence of Eleusinian mythology is obvious, and some of the divinities have epithets that look rather late; but the fact that a single family regarded their ancestral cult, in whatever transformation, as a mystery cult seems significant: mystery cults play an important role in determining group identity, and it seems possible to argue that the Eleusinian Mysteries as well started out as a clan cult.[15]

Fancy transformations? Anatolian mystery cults of the imperial epoch

The Greeks regarded the central Peloponnese not unjustly as a repository of hoary traditions that went back to the epoch before the Dorian invasion, whenever that was. Another region of old traditions is Anatolia – although the documentation for its cults is most often contained in inscriptions from the imperial epoch and, at least when away from the Aegean west coast, has certainly been transformed through the process of a more recent Hellenization. In the epigraphical evidence for Mysteries, Anatolia looms large indeed: many of its major cults – not only those of the Great Goddess Cybele and her relatives – were said to have contained such a rite, and private mystery associations abound.

The major oracular shrines of Western Anatolia were the ones in Klaros and in Didyma; from both, inscriptions attest to Mysteries. In Klaros, during the first and second centuries AD many of the theopropoi, the official delegates by their city to the oracular god, left epigraphical records; some of these officials claim that, besides consulting the oracle, they "also performed the mysteries", or that the theopropos "went down after his initiation" or that "after initiation and going in, he received the oracle".[16] "Going in", *embateuein*, means having access to the complex and labyrinthine combination of passageways and chambers in the foundations of the Clarian temple, ordinarily was reserved to the priest.[17] The initiation, then, must have been the ritual one had to undergo if one wanted to have access to this space that even the priest could not enter without "many preliminary rites" (Iamb. *Myst* 3.11): such an initiation was optional, not all the visitors of the shrine needed to come that close.[18] In the oracle of Apollo at Didyma, Mysteries were regularly connected with the hydrophoros of Artemis Pythie, "the highest office open to a woman in Didyma" (Fontenrose 1988, 128): at the term of her office, many hydrophoroi receive praise also for having performed the Mysteries.[19] We lack the means to determine whether this too was a specific initiation of a hydrophoros, or whether she had also to preside over mystery rites that were open to some visitors of the oracle.

But the best-known sanctuary of Western Anatolia was the Artemision of Ephesus, and Ephesus itself had become the leading city in the region, not the least because it harboured also the imperial cult of the province Asia. Ephesus had several mystery cults and was proud of them – already King Lysimachus, who established the city in its later place, had provided for "mystery rites and sacrifices" as a decree from the time of Commodus has it (Wankel *et al.* 1979–1984, 26, line 3). One could honour a city official for his "piety as to the mysteries" (Wankel *et al.* 1979–1984, 702), and a letter to the proconsul of AD 88/9 reminded him that "kings, emperors and governors" had always favoured the mystery cults of Demeter Thesmophoros and Karpophoros (Wankel *et al.* 1979–1984, 213). Besides these cults and the Mysteries of Dionysos (Wankel *et al.* 1979–1984, 275, 293, 1250; no. 1595 combines the Mysteries of Demeter with those of Dionysos Phleus) and Aphrodite Daitis (Wankel *et al.* 1979–1984, 1202), about which information is scarce, two complexes of epigraphical texts attest, in the imperial epoch, to mystery cults in connection with the most important institutions of Ephesus, the prytaneion and the Artemision, the political and the religious centres of the town. Several inscriptions from the sanctuary of Artemis honour the priestess of Artemis for her conduct during her office – "she performed the sacrifices and the mysteries in a dignified way" (Wankel *et al.* 1979–1984, 987, 988, 989, 3059) – and thank a priestess (the name is lost) for "having renewed all the mysteries of the goddess and instituted them in the traditional manner". In another text, the same honour is accorded to a hierokeryx, a sacred herald,[20] and the grave inscription of a high functionary of the temple mentions that he "fulfilled all mysteries" (Wankel *et al.* 1979–1984, 4330, third century AD) – Mysteries clearly were an important part of Artemis' cult. As is to be expected, in none of these texts are details of the mystery rituals mentioned.

The other body of evidence for Mysteries comes from the prytaneion, the political and religious centre of the city of Ephesos; here, the Ephesians had cults of Hestia Boulaia, but also of other divinities whose cults were established during the imperial age: Artemis, *Pyr Aphtharton* ("Indestructible Fire"), the divine personification of the eternal fire that burns on every public hearth and from which the Ephesian prytanis takes the fire "to kindle the fire on all the altars"[21] – Sopolis ("City-Saver"), Demeter Karphophoros[22] and her daughter, an oracular Apollo,[23] and, of course, the reigning emperors. A small group of inscriptions, all from the later second or third century AD, concern the prytanis, the supreme magistrate of the city, and his performance of mystery cults and sacrifices. Three times, a prytanis (or one of his relatives) is thanking the main divinities of the prytaneion, especially Hestia Boulaia, at the end of office for having "absolved" the Mysteries,[24] while once mystery rites are at least mentioned as part of his obligations.[25] Again, any detail beyond the simple performance of *mysteria* is absent. The main texts from the same building, written on its columns, are membership lists of a "college" whose (ordinarily) six members were calling themselves "Pious Kouretes" (*Kouretes eusebeis*) adding, after the late first century AD, the title *philosebastoi* ("loyal to the emperor").[26] The lists begin in the time of Augustus and last into the early third century, with some changes in the number and roles of ritual functionaries listed which alone informs us about the rituals they perform. Ordinarily, there are a *hieroskopos* ("inspector of entrails"), a specialist for fumigations, and a flute player; later texts add others – a trumpet player, a dancer (*akrobates*), a basket bearer, a perfume bearer. We easily infer sacrifices, libations, ritual music and dance from these lists, but we lack the means to decide whether, over time, the rites became more sumptuous, or the Kouretes delegated more and more rites to specialists, or the lists become more detailed (so Knibbe 1981, 79–80). Other functionaries of the group are the *hierokeryx* and the hierophant – functions that are best known for the Mysteries of Eleusis but are, in the imperial age, by no means confined to them; but at least the presence of the hierophant must imply mystery rites in which this official "revealed the sacred things". Some of the members appear in high civic offices, about half of them are Roman citizens, and their title "loyal to the emperor", which they share with all high officials of Ephesos, points to their closeness to the imperial house and to their participation in the ruler cult that is so prominent in Ephesos. In short, the Kouretes belong to the ruling class of imperial Ephesos.

The ritual duties of the Kouretes are closely related to the manifold ritual activities of the prytanis, with whom they must have shared the building. When a prytanis, under the emperor Commodus, collected money in order to restore "The Sacred College of the Kouretes" the contributors were all former prytaneis (Knibbe 1981, 53 no. B54 [=Wankel *et al.* 1979–1984, 47; AD 180/192]); an inscription connects the Mysteries that the prytanis performed "for the safety of our community" with the Kouretes (Knibbe 1981, 59 no. D3 [=Wankel *et al.* 1979–1984, 1077; ante AD 211/12]), and at least in one case a prytanis could act as their leader.[27] According to a law inscribed in the second or third century about the duties of the prytanis – an excerpt from a "traditional law", *patrios nomos* – the prytanis is advised in these duties by the "official hierophant" assisted by all the ritual functionaries of the Kouretes, and controlled by the Kouretes and the hierophant, who can fine him for infractions in the rites. It is obvious that his ritual duties were much too complex to be performed without instruction, help, and the possibility of mistake by a layman and politician: this again points to the complexities of mystery rites.

The two bodies of evidence – one for Mysteries of Artemis, the other for Mysteries of the Kouretes in the prytaneion – are bridged and united by a report given by the geographer Strabo (14.1.20 pp. 639–640). There is, outside the city of Ephesos, and close to a stream, a sacred grove named Ortygia. Here, Leto is said to have given birth to her daughter Artemis, despite the hostility of Hera; the Kouretes – armed dancers – were dancing around the newborn baby in order to keep away the jealous rival. This story, reflecting the distinction between two birth places of the twins that were already present in the *Homeric Hymn to Apollo* and that contradicts the better-known story of the birth on Delos,[28] is modelled after the myth of Zeus' birth in Crete (Kallim. hymn 1.52–53; Apollod. 1.1.7 *passim*) and is the etiological myth for a group of human Kouretes who, in Strabo's record, meet annually in Ortygia on Artemis' birthday and perform banquets "and some mystic sacrifices" (Strab. 14.1.20 pp. 639–640).

Strabo was writing before what must have been the Augustan establishment of the Kouretes in the prytaneion. The College of the Kouretes, though, antedates him; the first epigraphical attestations date to the late fourth or early third centuries BC, and although their function is not quite clear from these texts, they seem to be positioned at some point between the sanctuary of Artemis and the city of Ephesos (*Ephesos* 4:1 S. 82 No. 2 [Knibbe 1981, A1]; Knibbe 1981, A2 [wall block, originally from the sanctuary of Artemis]). But since Strabo reflects the situation in the Hellenistic epoch, they must already have performed their Mysteries at a festival of Artemis.

Behind this group – in myth, armed young dancers; in ritual, men belonging to the elite of Ephesos and its temple of Artemis – one discerns an older ritualistic background. The name "Kouretes" points to a well-known phenomenon especially, but not exclusively, from Crete – to a body of young warriors who formed the future citizen body and who performed their rites in the service of Zeus and his mother Rhea, another Great Goddess; the best-known ancient text is the famous hymn to Zeus, Greatest Kouros, from Cretan Paleocastro.[29] The remote culture of Crete, as already Ephoros was aware of, retained ritual traditions that in other places were abolished or transformed long ago.[30]

This, however, is prehistory. Already the Hellenistic Kouretes, whom we discern only very dimly, seem to look different, and even more so those reformed in early Augustan time whose organization and rituals are attested in the inscriptions. The same inscriptions suggest that during the imperial age the Mysteries must have changed again; but we do not know what the attested reform under Commodus changed. What is visible, however, is that a multitude of gods were introduced into the prytaneiaon during the imperial age: the inscriptions mention not only the traditional and old Hestia Boulaia, but also the "Indestructible Fire" (*Pur Apharton*), Sopolis ("Saviour of the City") and, most intriguing, Demeter Karpophoros and her

Daughter.[31] Apollo arrived in the early second century,[32] Demeter Karpophoros not much later (Wankel *et al.* 1979–1984, 1210 *c.* AD 120); she had not only her statue, but her sanctuary inside the prytaneion. But she was connected with the cult of the emperors already in the time of the emperor Tiberius, when Livia is identified with her,[33] and in AD 83/4 a letter to the Roman proconsul Mestrius Florus attests to the Mysteries that combine the cult of Demeter Karpophoros and Thesmophoros and of the emperors, with large groups of initiates (Wankel *et al.* 1979–1984, 213): at this time, these Mysteries seem independent from the cults on the prytaneion.

At least in the third century things look different: there must have been mystery rites by prytaneis and Kouretes, not only in Ortygia for Artemis but also in the prytaneion. Demeter seems to have played a role here: among the ritual functionaries that thank Hestia and the gods in the prytaneion appears the "basket-bearer" the woman who carried the basket of Demeter in her processions.[34] Demeter was thus part of the cults in the prytaneion – the only uncertain thing is whether her rites were independent from other rites or whether her Mysteries were fused with earlier mystery rites in the prytaneion that were mainly concerned with Hestia. It is noteworthy that already, more than a century earlier, two female prytaneis – Claudia Trophime in AD 92/93, and Tullia in about AD 170 – in several poems addressed to Hestia gave expression to a "fire-theology" that finds parallels in the Orphic hymn to Hestia, written perhaps for a second century Bacchic mystery community in Western Asia Minor.[35] Whatever the developments are, we discern a complex situation where mystery cults are connected not only with the traditional Eleusinian goddesses, but with Artemis on the one hand and with the exponents of the Ephesian state on the other. The rites which our texts call mystery rites were complex and, presumably, secret; they defined the character and founded cohesion of the performing group, the Kouretes and their prytanis, and they were seen as being vital for the identity and existence of the city of Ephesos. In a wider diachronic perspective, moreover, these *mysteria* derive from rituals that can be connected with rituals that performed the introduction of young men into the group of male adult citizens. In an anthropological reading, rites like these go together with tribal initiation rites in which secrecy as a form and change of status as a function were predominant features (Harrison 1927, 1–29). There is at least one other case where rites that functioned in archaic Greece as rituals of introduction into adulthood are labelled, in Imperial times, mystery rites: an inscription from the island of Amorgos calls the dedication of a youth's hair to Asklepios' traditional Mysteries.[36] The rite is better known from neighbouring Paros, where the hair usually is labelled "ephebic" or "young man's hair".[37]

Another western Anatolian centre was Stratonikeia in Caria, a town connected with two major sanctuaries of divinities that might well predate its Seleucid foundation: Hekate in Lagina and Zeus Panameros. High above the city plain, at its southern end, was the large and impressive sanctuary of

Zeus Panameros and Hera, mentioned by no ancient literary text: here too, the rich epigraphical finds attest to a mystery cult (Oppermann 1924; Laumonier 1958, 221–343, esp. 292–322; Sahin 1979/1981, nos. 100–354).

Again, the texts, all from the second or third centuries, are rather uniform. They honour a priestly couple at the term of their office which ordinarily lasted one year, rarely an entire penteteris. The husband was priest of Zeus, the wife priestess of Hera, and they were selected either during the Heraia, or the festival of Zeus, the Komyria. All have Roman citizenship, all belong to a small group of families who obviously shared the priesthoods among themselves, but had other offices as well: we deal again with the local elite. The priestly couples officiated in two festivals – in the Panamereia to Zeus Panameros, the major festival of the sanctuary that lasted ten days, and in the Komyria and Heraia. These two festivals lasted two days and took place at the same time in two places – a place called Komyrion somewhere outside the sanctuary, and in the sanctuary; while the men performed the Komyria, the women performed the Heraia in the main sanctuary.

Mysteries are connected with the Komyria only. In its course, the priests feasted the male citizens, foreigners, and slaves at a banquet in the Komyrion, while their wives offered another banquet to the wives of the citizens and foreigners and to the female slaves in the sanctuary. Participation in the Komyria thus seemed restricted to the males (although there is a rare exception to this gender division I. Strat 248, but the syntax is hazy), and drinking was as important as eating. Details are hazy and focus on the lavish banquets: the priests provided meals and ample provision of wine – in one case also tents during the two days, in another also wood for the sacrifices.[38] Banquets that fed everybody – the citizens, Romans, foreigners, resident aliens, and slaves (Sahin 1979/1981, no. 174) – and animal sacrifices could not have been secret; the Mysteries then were something else, whatever they were. Scholars had different ideas – that the banquets realized "a mystical communion" among the participants (Oppermann 1924, 66–69), or that the gender separation and the polarity between Zeus and Hera pointed to sacred marriage as the key to the rites (Laumonier 1958, 310). But sacred marriage (Avagianou 1991) is as unwarranted by our sources as is mystical communion, and both concepts have lost their popularity anyway. Still, the all-male group, given over not only to eating but also to heavy drinking, is suggestive; heavy drinking also dominated the Mysteries of the Kabeiroi in Thebes and on Lemnos: we might deal with a transformation of an earlier rite under the pressures of Imperial beneficence and lavishness.

Drinking and feasting is present not only in those rites but also in another mystery rite from western Asia Minor, known already in early Hellenistic time: the rites of the Kyrbantes or Korybantes in Ionian Erythrai. They are attested in a list of civic priests and a sacred law that regulates the sale of their priesthood.[39] These inscriptions, again the only documents for this specific cult, do not use the term, nor do they, naturally, inform us about secret rites – but they use the verb "to initiate" (*telein*); a yet unpublished text from the same rite also refers to the initiates as *kekorubantismenoi* ("those who have become Korybants"), an expression closely related to the *bebakcheumenoi* ("those who have become bakchoi") in the famous graveyard regulation from fifth-century Cumae in Italy[40] and, no less important, to the Ephesian designation of former Kouretes as *kekoureutekotes*, "those who have been Kouretes" (Wankel *et al.* 1979–1984, 47.7 [=Knibbe 1981, 53 no. B54.7]): in all three cases, the perfect participle designates someone who not only has performed the rite but who has been transformed into a new and lasting state of being through his initiation. The Erythraen cult, as usual, does not give away how this was achieved; as usual, the inscriptions only give the well-known facts. The cult has a priest and a priestess, and their tasks are gender-defined: the priest initiated the men, the priestess the women. Part of this initiation ritual, certainly a preliminary rite, is a bath. Another rite is what the key text calls *kraterismos* ("rite around a krater"); this points to the preparation and consumption of wine. It fits that the two groups of Korybantes are called *Euphronisioi* and *Thaleioi*: this associates them with the Greek words for ample meals, and the joy of festivals. The cult is attested in other places in southwestern Asia Minor, the adjacent Dorian Islands including Crete, and Athens; literary sources focus on ecstatic dancing and, contrary to all epigraphical evidence, make the Korybantes into servants of the Great Mother. Aristophanes and his contemporaries thought that the rite would cure madness, as could the Mysteries of Hekate on Aegina and the cult of Asklepios – Athenians of the fifth century thus sought above all its healing and purificatory powers.[41] The same could be true for the Erythraeans, although they must have vastly enjoyed the drinking bouts and banquets as well: it is another instance of what Burkert termed "the extraordinary experience", triggered here, as in the Dionysiac Mysteries, through the collective consumption of alcohol – warning us against the too easy assumption that wine alone was responsible for the closeness of Bacchic and Corybantic ecstasy (Philo, *Vit. Cont.* 12, a passage that seems more indebted to Plato, *Symp.* 228B, 234D than to actual ritual).[42] That they accepted its priesthoods as part of their civic institutions, at any rate, should warn us from seeing these Mysteries only as the rites of a marginal private association.

In the imperial epoch, the Korybantic rites have disappeared from direct, epigraphical attestation, as opposed to literary references that, however, do not necessarily reflect contemporary attitudes. The Mysteries of Hekate on Aegina, which Aristophanes and his contemporaries had viewed as having as high healing powers for madness as the Korybantic rites, survive and even thrive.[43] Pausanias visited and described the sanctuary with its cult image by Myron (Paus. 2.30.2); the Mysteries were held annually and were thought to have been founded by Orpheus. The orator Dio insists on the purification rites before which the priests "invoke and point to many and various sorts of *phasmata*, ghosts" sent by Hekate: he might speak from direct experience (Dio, *Or.* 4.90). Libanius knows of a contemporary who, as a "leader of the thiasos", sailed to Aegina to participate in the cult (Liban. *Aristoph.* p. 426B); as the vocabulary intimates, at this time the rites were comparable to those of Bakchos. But pagans of the later fourth century AD did not only, or not even in the first place, look for ecstatic experience: Fabia Aconia Paulina, wife of Vettius Agorius Praetextatus, praises her deceased husband as "a pious initiate who kept in his innermost mind everything that has been found in the sacred rites and who, with manifold learning, adores the divine power". He shared this endeavour with his wife, introduced her "to all mysteries", and even "exempted her from death's destiny".[44] Of these cults, besides the Mysteries of Eleusis, Cybele and Mithras, were those on Aegina where she served as a hierophant: her husband taught to her, the servant of Hecate, her "triple secrets"[45] – whatever these secrets were, the Mysteries provided less "extraordinary experience" than soteriological hope and theological and philosophical knowledge.

This voice, at the very end of paganism, is uncommonly explicit about the gains of initiation, and in its stress on the cognitive aspects of religious experience it reflects its own time. It must be stressed, however, that these theosophic insights are as much coming from a learned initiate – Praetextatus, who also in Macrobius' *Saturnalia* is the spokesman for theosophy – as through whatever instruction happened in the rites themselves. In this, they continue earlier philosophical explications of mystery rites, as Porphyry's allegorization of the Mithraic rites or the emperor Julian's *Oration on the Great Mother*:[46] it would be wrong to assume that the popularity of mystery cults in general resulted from such a need. If anything, a result of such a cognitive view of Mysteries is theurgy, whose adept is called an initiated in the *Chaldaean Oracles*.[47]

The popularity of mystery cults during the imperial epoch is visible not only in the mysteria connected with civic cults that have been discussed so far but even more so in the many mystery associations that are attested, not the least again in Asia Minor. In a fascinating paper, Peter Herrmann collected all the evidence just for one small city, Sardis in Lydia, and came up with "a quite diverse spectrum of such cultic organisations".[48] Often enough we lack any information going beyond the existence of such an association, whose members dedicate an honorary inscription to an outstanding fellow member or official, or put up a grave inscription for a fellow initiate. Rarely enough, we gain more insight into the history, the rituals or the beliefs of these groups.

On a stele from a Pisidian town dated to the first half of the first century AD, the children and grandchildren honour a certain Trokondas, son of Osaeis and grandson of Hermaios, and his daughter Artemis, hereditary priest and priestess of Artemis Ephesia, for having watched "with integrity and in befitting manner over the solemn mysteries of the goddess which were discovered and transmitted" (Horsley 1992). The somewhat unusual mention of Trokondas' grandfather might be read as indication that Hermaios was the founder of the Mysteries, who also had built the temple and erected the cult image – an image that appears on the accompanying relief where a male in a toga and with a garland in his left hand (obviously Trokondas) is pouring a libation over an altar, on whose other side a small ox is standing under the statue of an enthroned and matronal goddess[49] – definitely not the Ephesian Artemis in any of her iconographical guises,[50] but an indigenous Mother equated with the famous goddess. Nothing in the sacrificial scene on the relief points to Mysteries; it is a common iconographical expression of traditional piety. The text, however, refers to "discovered and transmitted mysteries with their sacred rites".[51] The key term is "discovered" (*heurethenta*, literally "found"); the foundation of the Mysteries was stimulated by a discovery. This recalls the story from Andania how the revival of the Mysteries relied on the text left by Aristomenes and discovered at the time of the foundation of Messene, or the other story from Magnesia on the Maeander of how the institution of Bacchic Mysteries was provoked by the appearance of a statue of Dionysos inside a broken tree.[52] In this latter case, a Delphic oracle explained the consequences of this miracle; in the former, a dream vision ordered the discovery. It is to be assumed that it was not only the Andanian books that were transmitted in the family of the priests until they arrived with Mnasistratos but that also that the Bacchic image was handed down through generations of priestesses: the Magnesian maenads were organized in three thiasoi that derived from the three sisters of Kadmos. Whatever caused the foundation of these Mysteries, it was no simple adoption of the Ephesian cult but a more complex process that made the priestly family the sole possessors of ritual knowledge.[53] This fits into a pattern that goes as far back as the Eleusinian Mysteries where Demeter had revealed the rites to the ancestors of the leading priestly families (*Hom. H. Cer.* 473–476), and the same is true not only for the Mysteries of Andania but also, for example, for an association of initiates of Sarapis in Hellenistic Delos, for the private Mysteries of Sabazios in Athens where the priestess officiated together with her son, the rhetor Aeschines, as his adversary Demosthenes is only too glad to point out, or for the rites of Dionysos Kathegemon in Pergamon where the son took over after his father fell ill.[54]

In this rare case, we still glimpse the institution of a new mystery cult; in another case, we see at least the ritual mechanism that gave it its status. Among the inscriptions from Sardis is a dedication by "the initiates and worshippers (*mystai kai therapeutai*) of Zeus"; its editor connected it with another honorary inscription by the "worshippers of Zeus who are among those who have access to the adyton" – which would show that the "initiates and worshippers" are one and the same group. If this is so, then this group defines itself by at least one specific ritual privilege: the access to the sacred space inside the temple of Zeus – a space to which otherwise only the priests would have access; the Mysteries, one assumes, prepared the individual for this privileged access to the divinity. This reminds us of the Mysteries in Apollo's sanctuary in Klaros that permitted the initiate to enter the space otherwise reserved to the priest, where he met with his divinity. But to prepare for and be allowed direct contact with a divinity is a function of most mystery cults: the images on an urn and a sarcophagus in Rome show, in forceful symbolism, how an Eleusinian initiate of the Lesser Mysteries could approach Demeter and her sacred snake without fear;[55] the Eleusinian initiation brought close contact with Persephone, as the Euripidean Herakles claims (Eur. Her. 610–613), the Isis Mysteries with the gods of above and below (Apul. Met. 11.23).

If the initiates could have close contact with the divine sphere, all the more so their priests. In a story typical for late antiquity, Eunapius tells how under Julian the last-but-one Eleusinian hierophant could foresee the future of his institution, and how Julian called him to Gaul, "performed together with him some things known only to them" and found the strength to depose Constantius.[56] On a much smaller scale, and some 150 years earlier in Lydian Thyateira, the children and the "initiates of the gods" dedicated an altar to their deceased priestess, on which she herself promises: "If you want to know the truth from me, pray at this altar, and you will obtain what you want in a vision, by night and day":[57] the deceased priestess, closer to the gods than her initiates, mediates between the gods and the initiates. At the end of the following century, with Vettius Agorius Praetextatus and his wife Paulina, this cognitive gain from initiation becomes a source of theosophy.

But these are only the refined ends of the spectrum of expectations. At the other end stand things which every pious pagan would expect from his or her gods. As the prytanis Tullia in Ephesos in AD 170 phrased it: her careful service in all the sacrifices and mysteries of her offices made her confident that the gods would grant her health, a long life and children that resembled their mother.[58] And a long inscription from Aeolian Kyme that regulates the construction of new buildings for the Mysteries of the otherwise unknown god Mandros ends with a promise and a threat: "whosoever participates in the mysteries, if he keeps them and guards them undisturbed, may he obtain accessible and fruitful land, the birth of legitimate children and participation in all goods, but he who thinks otherwise should obtain the opposite of this".[59] This is not very different from promises and threats in many official prayers or treaties in Greece.

Summary

Mysteries, then, were on the one hand a firm part of pagan religion; they appear less exceptional than when looking only at the six major cults – an insight that is also relevant for the much-debated question of whether and how early Christianity was influenced by them.[60] Nevertheless, there is a bundle of characteristics that do not apply equally to all mystery cults but, when taken together, sketch how pagans might have understood the term.

Mystery cults defined and confirmed identity – from political groups such as in the Mysteries of Andania that are intimately connected with Messenia, to clan cults such as the Mysteries of the Lykomidai or to cultic associations in the towns and cities of the Empire. Unlike other rites that achieve the same aim, mystery rites do so by keeping the ritual means secret; the shared knowledge among group members is a powerful means of defining group identity against those who lack this knowledge. Secrecy, and its corollary knowledge among the initiated, also is the basis for the cognitive aspects of late antique mystery cults that we observed and where knowledge of the ritual was subordinated to the theosophical knowledge.

These rituals very often transformed the person who underwent them. The linguistic for this transformation is, as we saw, the participle perfect. These participles not only express the lasting effect of the rites of Bakchos, the Korybantes or Kouretes – the initiates actually have become Bakchoi and Korybantes, they have exchanged a former identity against one which is as close to their gods as a human being can get; and even having served as an Ephesian Kouretes left its imprint for the rest of one's life. This movement is the extreme form of what we have observed already: that mystery rites open up access to the divinity; but while in Eleusis, Klaros or in the cult of Zeus in Sardes the distance between the divinity and the human worshipper is only reduced, in the cults of Dionysos, the Korybants or the Kouretes, it is virtually eliminated. One is tempted to ascribe this to ecstatic experiences, were it not for the Ephesian Kouretes, where no hint of ecstatic rituals beyond the magnitude of a symposium is visible. Another way of changing is the permanent change of status achieved in life-crisis rituals; we saw that at least in one case ordinary puberty rites could be classified as mysteria (whereas it was only the Christians that transformed the wedding rites into a mysterium).

Outward expression of group identity was, often enough, a sumptuous common meal, often with more than ordinary consumption of wine. It is these meals that the inscriptions and texts often talk about: they needed to be visible, either by excluding non-members or, in the euergetic culture of imperial cities, by inviting everybody. In these cases I would assume that nevertheless a distinction between those who underwent the Mysteries and those who were invited was maintained, the invitees forming the necessary outsiders whose perception of the initiated as different was vital in the dialectic process of secrecy and knowledge.

Notes

1 There are few exceptions to this – Meyer (1993) includes also the Mysteries of Andania, and the important chapter on mystery cults in Burkert (1977) presents several of the lesser known cults; Burkert (1987) very much returns to the canonical six major cults, as does e.g. Metzger (1984, 1259–1423).
2 Paus. 4.1.5–9 (Andania), 8.15.1–4 (Pheneos), 8.19.1 (Trapezous), 8.31.1–9 (Megalopolis), 8.37.1–10 (Lykosoura), 2.14.1 (Phlious), 2.30.2 (Aegina), 2.37.1–6 (Lerna), 2.38.2 (Temenion).
3 Connection with Eleusis: Phlious (Paus. 1.14.1), Megalopolis (8.31.7), Lykosoura (8.15.1–2), Andania (4.33.4–5).
4 Secrecy: Andania (4.33.4), Lerna (2.37.5), Temenion (2.38.2).
5 Epigraphical evidence: Andania (Sokolowski 1969, 65 and the oracle SIG^3 735), Lykosoura (*IG* V.2, 515–516, see also Paus. 8.37.9 "uninitiated"), Hekate in Aegina (*Corpus Inscriptionum Latinarum* VI 1779, with a *hierophantria*).
6 Nilsson (1974, 369). The critical voices: Nock (1952, 177, 213, here 185 = Nock 1972, 797 ["we must not underestimate their emotional depth or overestimate their antiquity and dissemination"]); more direct is Robert (1960, 2838, n.3).
7 Nilsson (1974, 371–372). Nilsson talks about the association of the god Mandros in Kyme (cf. p. 255).
8 The most detailed account is still Margherita Guarducci (1934). Nadine Deshours is preparing a monograph on the cult; see also Deshours (1993, 1999).
9 For the myth of Queen Messene, see Deshours (1993, 39–60).
10 Sokolowski (1969, 65); translation in Meyer (1997, 55–59).
11 For the Athenian image of the Mysteries as "the double gift of Demeter, the greatest one: grain that caused us to live differently from animals, and the mysteries that give to all participants a better for the end of their life and the entire time afterwards", see Isocr. *Or.* 4.28.
12 Paus. 8.31.6. Jost (1985, 342–343) argues for taking this information seriously; the founders of Megalopolis in 368/7 borrowed the Eleusinian Mysteries. This seems difficult to accept, given the uniqueness of Eleusis, and the presence of a hierophant in *IG* V.2, 517 is no proof.
13 Paus. 8.15.1–4; see Jost (1985, 317–324).
14 The picture in Nilsson (1974, fig. 48.1).
15 See Graf (1985, 274–277, 490), Bremmer (1994, 85). An earlier version of this theory is in Speiser (1928, 362–372).
16 The inscriptions known at this time are collected by Picard (1922a, 303–304; 1922b, 190–197, esp. 191–192); they were published by Th. Macridy (1905, 165 no. V.4, line 15; 1912, 50 no. 14, 51 no. 16, 52 no. 20, 46 no. 2).
17 Tac. *Ann.* 2.54.2 says that the priest, in order to prophesize, descended into a cave; Iamb. *Myst.* 3.11, closer to the architectural realities, locates his prophesy "in a subterranean room".
18 For a discussion of *embateuein* see esp. Nock (1952, 177–213; 1972, 798), Nilsson (1974, 476), Robert (1954, 28–29 [=Robert 1969–1990, VI 548]).
19 Rehm and Harder (1958, nos. 312, 326, 327, 329, 333, 352, 373, 381, 382).
20 Edited in *OeJh* 59 (1989) 717 no. 6.
21 This obligation is the first in the list of his sacred duties from the second or third century (Sokolowski 1962, 121; Wankel *et al.* 1979–1984, 10, 121 [=Knibbe 1981, 57 no. D1]).
22 She had a sanctuary in the pryncion, Knibbe (1981, 57 D1 [=Wankel *et al.* 1979–1984, 10, line 28]).
23 See Keil (1939, 119–128), Knibbe (1981, 101–105).
24 Knibbe (1981, 55 no. C1 [=Wankel *et al.* 1979–1984, 1060; after AD 214/15]).

Knibbe (1981, 169 no. N4 (=Wankel *et al.* 1979–1984, 1058, second or third century AD]); see also Wankel *et al.* (1979–1984, 1069, second or third century AD).

25 Knibbe (1981, 59 no. D3 [=Wankel *et al.* 1979–1984, 1077, emperors Marcus Aurelius and Geta]). The list of his duties does not mention mystery rites.
26 Knibbe (1981), Rogers (1999), Graf (1999). Guy Rogers prepares a monograph on the Mysteries.
27 See Knibbe (1981, 61 no. D7 [=Wankel *et al.* 1979–1984, 613a, before AD 193), where two groups of Kouretes are distinguished by the names of their leaders, one of whom is prytanis. Also the prytanis M. Aurelius Menemachus renovates "the sacred college of the Kouretes" and gives a list of former prytaneis who contributed to this renovation, and of (former and acting) Kouretes.
28 Hom. *H. Ap.* 14. Leto gave birth "to the girl in Ortygia, to the boy on rocky Delos", the birth of both on Delos, for example, in Ovid *Met.* 6.331–336; Apollod. 1.25.
29 See for the hymn West (1965, 149–159); for the background Graf (1999).
30 The priest and hierophant of the Mysteries of the Kouretes in Termessos who still was a boy (*Tituli Asiae Minoris* III:1, 194, *c.* AD 210) does not reflect archaic traditions but is a not unusual case of a boy purchasing a priesthood which he then will hold through his entire life; the incumbant belongs to a family with several priests of local Mysteries.
31 See Keil (1939, 119–128) also Merkelbach (1980).
32 He is introduced as "oracular", shortly after AD 104 (Knibbe 1981, 27 no. B24 [=Wankel *et al.* 1979–1984, 1024]). The two texts from the third century cited in note 34, though, mention Apollo Klarios in his stead.
33 Wankel *et al.* (1979–1984, 4337 [*c.* AD 19/23]): The Demetriasts honour Servilia Secunda, the priestess "of the Imperial Demeter Karpophoros", i.e. of Livia Augusta.
34 Knibbe (1981, 55 no. C1 [=Wankel *et al.* 1979–1984, 1060; after AD 214/15]; 62 no. E3 [=Wankel *et al.* 1979–1984, 1064, second/third cent.]; 66–67 nos. F10–12 [=Wankel *et al.* 1979–1984, 1070–1072; after AD 212]).
35 For the poem of Claudia, see Knibbe (1981, 62 no. F1 [=Wankel *et al.* 1979–1984, 1062]); of Tullia, Knibbe (1981, 65 no. F5 [=Wankel *et al.* 1979–1984, 1068]); also see Merkelbach (1980). The Orphic hymn to Hestia is no. 84; for its origin, see, *inter alia*, West (1983, 28–29).
36 *IG* XII:5.173, 175; see Rubensohn (1902, esp. 225–229).
37 Delos: Engelmann (1975). Aeschines: Demosth. *De cor.* 259–260. Pergamon: Fränkel (1890, no. 248).
38 Tents: I. Strat. Sahin (1979/81, 203 [under M. Aurelius, between AD 164 and 166]); wood: Sahin (1979/81, 205, line 27).
39 Engelmann and Merkelbach (1974, nos. 201, 206), Graf (1985, 319–334); a new fragment of no. 206 published by Himmelmann (1997).
40 The new text, a *pierre errante* in Samos, has been brought to my attention by Dr Klaus Hallow in Berlin, whom I thank. For the Cumae text, Jeffery (1961, 240 no. 21); see esp. Turcan (1986, 227–246).
41 Ar. *Vesp.* 119–123; Eur. *Hipp.* 141–144; [Hippocr.] *Morb. sacr.* 1; Plat. *Symp.* 215E. *Ion* 553E. *Leges* 790E; see Linforth (1946, 121–162), Dodds (1951, 77–79).
42 Burkert (1987, 89–114); see esp. 112–113 where he cites Philo.
43 For these Mysteries, see Lobeck (1829, 242), Nilsson (1906, 398–399), Johnston (1999, 144–145).
44 *Corpus Inscriptionum Latinarum* VI:1.1779 (=Dessau 1892–1916, 1259); the verses also in Buecheler and Lommatzsch (1895–1897, 111 [=Courtney 1995, no. 32, with English translation]). D13–15 *tu pius mustes sacris teletis reperta mentis arcano premis divumque numen multiplex doctus colis sociam benigne coniugem nectens sacris;* 21–24 *tu me, marite, disciplinarum bono puram ac pudicam sorte mortis eximens in templa ducis ac famulam divis dicas. te teste cunctis imbuar mysteriis.*

45 Courtney (1995, no. 30): *Hecates ministram trina secreta edoces.*
46 See the commented editions by Fontaine *et al.* (1987) and Ugenti (1992).
47 Or. Chald. Fr. 132 des Places; see also the passages from the Neoplatonists, collected by Lewy (1978, 444–445 nos. 1e and 11).
48 Herrmann (1996, 315–368); the citation is on p. 339.
49 Horsley (1992, pl. 31). The first editor, after careful deliberation, took her to be the enthroned daughter; but this seems much less likely: the ordinary arrangement of votive reliefs puts the humans on one side of the altar, the divine recipients of the sacrifice on the other side.
50 For the two forms – standing with two torches, and as with many "breasts" (multimamma) – see Fleischer (1973) and Rogers (1991).
51 The term *hieroteles* ("with their sacred rites") is unique in extant Greek.
52 Kern (1900, no. 215a).
53 Less clear are the Mysteries of Artemis in Thyateira (*Tituli Asiae Minoris* V.1, 995) where the priestess is honoured "who performed the mysteries of the goddess and her sacrifices splendidly and at great expense" – the formula is standard.
54 Delos: Engelmann (1975). Aeschines: Demosth. *De cor.* 259–260. Pergamon: Fränkel (1890, no. 248).
55 Urna Lovatelli and Torre Nuova sacrophagus, see Mylonas (1961, 205–207 with figs. 83, 84).
56 Eunap. *Sophist.* 476 (I thank Sarah Iles Johnston for this).
57 *Tituli Asiae Minoris* V: 1055 (see Robert 1937, 129 no. 6).
58 Knibbe (1981, 64 no. F4 [=Wankel *et al.* 1979–1984, 1063], 5–6). Her wish reproduces a formula often used in oaths, e.g. Aeschin. c. Ctes. 110–111 or *SIG*3 1219, 25–27.
59 Engelmann (1976, 86 no. 37; first or second century AD). This was the association that found, more than anyone else, the favour of Nilsson (*supra*, n.7).
60 The scholarly literature is immense. Good guides are Nock (1952, 1972), Wiens (1980, 1248–1284), and Colpe (1992, 203–228).

References

Avagianou, A., 1991: *Sacred Marriage in the Rituals of Greek Religion.* European University Studies, Series 15, Bd. 54. Berne.

Bremmer, J.N., 1994: *Greek Religion.* Greece and Rome. New Surveys in the Classics 24. Oxford.

Buecheler, F. and E. Lommatzsch (eds), 1895–1897: *Carmina Latina Epigraphica.* Leipzig and Berlin.

Burkert, W., 1977: *Griechische Religion der archaischen und klassischen Epoche.* Kohlhammer, Stuttgart.

Burkert, W., 1987: *Ancient Mystery Cults.* Harvard University Press, Cambridge, Mass.

Cole, S.G., 1983: *Theoi Megaloi. The Cult of the Great Gods at Samothrace.* Études Préliminaires aux Religions dans l'Empire Romain 96, E.J. Brill, Leiden.

Colpe, C., 1992: "Mysterienkult und Liturgie. Zum Vergleich heidnischer Rituale und christlicher Sakramente", in Carsten Colpe, Ludger Honnefelder, and Matthias Lutz-Bachmann (eds), *Spätantike und Christentum. Beiträge zur Religions- und Geistesgeschichte der griechisch-römischen Kultur und Zivilisation der Kaiserzeit* (Akademie Verlag, Berlin), 203–228.

Courtney, E., 1995: *Musa Lapidaria. A Selection of Latin Verse Inscriptions.* Scholars Press, Atlanta.

Deshours, N., 1993: "La légende et le culte de Messénie ou comment forger l'identité d'une cité", *RÉG* 106, 39–60.
Deshours, N., 1999: "Les Messéniens, le règlement des mystères et la consultation de l'oracle d'Apollon Pythién à Argos", *RÉG* 112, 463–484.
Dessau, W. (ed.), 1892–1916: *Inscriptiones Latinae Selectae*. Berlin.
Dodds, E.R., 1951: *The Greeks and the Irrational*. University of California Press, Berkeley.
Engelmann, H., 1975: *The Delian Aretalogy of Sarapis*. Études Préliminaires aux Religions dans l'Empire Romain 44. E.J. Brill, Leiden.
Engelmann, H., 1976: *Die Inschriften von Kyme*. Inschriften griechischer Städte aus Kleinasien 5. R. Habelt, Bonn.
Engelmann, H. and R. Merkelbach, 1974: *Die Inschriften von Erythrai* 2. Inschriften griechischer Städte aus Kleinasien 3. R. Habelt, Bonn.
Fleischer, R., 1973: *Artemis von Ephesos und verwandte Kultstatuen aus Anatolien und Syrien*. Etudes Préliminaires aux Religions dans l'Empire Romain 35. E.J. Brill, Leiden.
Fontaine, J., A. Marcone, and C. Prato, 1987: *Guiliano Imperatore. Alla Madre degli Dei*. Fondazione L. Valla, Milan.
Fontenrose, J.E., 1988: *Didyma. Apollo's Oracle, Cult, and Companions*. University of California Press, Berkeley.
Fränkel, M., 1890: *Die Inschriften von Pergamon*, vol. 1. W. Spemann, Berlin.
Graf, F., 1985: *Nordionische Kulte. Religionsgeschichtliche und epigraphische Untersuchungen zu den Kulten von Chios, Erythrai, Klazomenai und Phokaia*. Bibliotheca Helvetica Romana 21. Schweizerisches Institut in Rom, Rome.
Graf, F., 1999: "Ephesische und andere Kureten", in H. Friesinger and F. Krinziger (eds), *100 Jahre Österreichische Forschungen in Ephesos. Akten des Symposions Wien 1995* (Verlag der Österreichischen Akademie der Wissenschaften, Vienna), 255–262.
Guarducci, M., 1934: "I culti di Andania", *Studi e Materiali di Storia delle Religioni* 10, 174–204.
Harrison, J.E., 1927: *Themis. A Study of the Social Origins of Greek Religion* (2nd edition). Cambridge University Press, Cambridge.
Hemberg, B., 1950: *Die Kabiren*. Almquist and Wiksell, Uppsala.
Herrmann, P., 1996: "Mysterienvereine in Sardeis", *Chiron* 26, 315–368.
Himmelmann, N., 1997: "Die Priesterschaft der Kyrbantes in Erythrai", *EpigAnat* 29, 117–121.
Horsley, G.H.R., 1992: "The Mysteries of Artemis Ephesia in Pisidia. A new inscribed relief", *AnatSt* 42, 119–150.
Jeffery, L.H., 1961: *The Local Scripts of Archaic Greece*. Clarendon Press, Oxford.
Johnston, S.I., 1999: *Restless Dead. Encounters Between the Living and the Dead in Ancient Greece*. University of California Press, Berkeley and Los Angeles.
Jost, M., 1985: *Sanctuaires et cultes d'Arcadie*. Études Péloponésiennes 9, Paris.
Keil, J., 1939: "Kulte im Prytaneion von Ephesos", in W.M. Calder and J. Keil (eds), *Anatolian Studies Presented to W.H. Buckler* (Manchester University Press, Manchester), 119–128.
Kern, O., 1900: *Die Inschriften von Magnesia am Maeander*. W. Spemann (1900) and De Gruyter, Berlin, 1967.
Knibbe, D., 1981: "Der Staatsmarkt. Die Inschriften des Prytaneions", *Forschungen*

in Ephesos IX/1/1. Verlag der Österreichischen Akademie der Wissenschaften, Vienna.

Laumonier, A., 1958: *Les cultes indigènes en Carie*. Paris.

Lewy, H., 1978: *Chaldaean Oracles and Theurgy. Mysticism, Magic, and Platonism in the Later Roman Empire* (2nd edition). Études Augustiniennes, Paris.

Linforth, I., 1946: "The Corybantic rites in Plato", *University of California Publications in Classical Philology* 13, 121–162.

Lobeck, C.A., 1829: *Aglaophamus Sive de Theologiae Mysticae Graecorum Causis Libri Tres*. Königsberg [1829] (repr. Darmstadt 1968).

Macridy, Th., 1905: "Altertümer von Notion", *ÖJh* 8, 155–173.

Macridy, Th., 1912: "Antiquités de Notion II", *ÖJh* 15, 36–67.

Merkelbach, R., 1980: "Der Kult der Hestia im Prytaneion griechischer Städte", *ZPE* 37, 77–92 [repr. in W. Blümel, B. Kramer, J. Kramer, and C.E. Römer (eds), *Hestia und Erigone. Vorträge und Aufsätze* (B.G. Teubner, Stuttgart and Leipzig), 52–66].

Metzger, B., 1984: "Classified bibliography of the Graeco-Roman mystery-religions 1924–1973", with a Supplement 1974–1977, in *Aufstieg und Niedergang der Römischen Welt,* II 17:3 (De Gruyter, Berlin and New York 1984), 1259–1423.

Meyer, M. (ed.), 1993: *The Ancient Mysteries. A Sourcebook. Sacred Texts of the Mystery Religions of the Ancient Mediterranean World*. Harper and Row, New York.

Mylonas, G.M., 1961: *Eleusis and the Eleusinian Mysteries*. Princeton University Press, Princeton.

Nilsson, M.P., 1906: *Griechische Feste von religiöser Bedeutung mit Ausschluss der attischen*. Teubner, Leipzig.

Nilsson, M.P., 1974: *Geschichte der griechischen Religion* (3rd edition). C.H. Beck, Munich.

Nock, A.D., 1952: "Hellenistic Mysteries and the Christian Sacraments", *Mnemosyne* 5, 177–213.

Nock, A.D., 1972: *Essays on Religion and the Ancient World*, edited by Zeph Stewart. Harvard University Press, Cambridge, Mass.

Oppermann, H., 1924: *Zeus Panamaros*. Religionsgeschichtliche Versuche und Vorarbeiten 19:3. Giessen.

Picard, Ch., 1922a: *Ephèse et Claros. Recherches sur les sanctuaires et les cultes de l'Ionie du Nord*. Paris.

Picard, Ch., 1922b: "An oracle d'Apollon Clarios à Pergame", *BCH* 26, 190–197.

Piolot, L., 1999: "Pausanias et les mystères d'Andanie. Histoire d'une aporie", in J. Renard (ed.), *Le Péloponnèse. Archéologie et histoire* (Actes de la rencontre internationale de Lorient, 12–15 mai 1998, Rennes 1999), 195–228.

Poland, F., 1909: *Geschichte des griechischen Vereinswesens*. Leipzig.

Rehm, A. and R. Harder, 1958: *Die Inschriften von Didyma*. Didyma II. Berlin.

Robert, L., 1937: *Études Anatoliennes*. Paris.

Robert, L., 1954: "Les fouilles de Claros". Conférence donné à l'université d'Ankara le 26 octobre 1953 (Ankara 1954), 28–29 (=Robert 1969–1990, VI 548).

Robert, L., 1960: "Recherches épigraphiques. VI. Inscriptions d'Athènes", *Revue des Études Anciennes* 1960, 316–324 (=Robert 1969–1990, 2832–2840).

Robert, L., 1969–1990: *Opera minora selecta: epigraphie et antiquites grecques*, 7 vols. Amsterdam.

Rogers, G.M., 1991: *The Sacred Identity of Ephesos. Foundation Myths of a Roman City*. London.
Rogers, G.M., 1999: "The Mysteries of Artemis at Ephesos", in H. Friesinger and F. Krinziger (eds), *100 Jahre Österreichische Forschungen in Ephesos. Akten des Symposions Wien 1995* (Vienna), 241–250.
Rubensohn, O., 1902: "Paros III. Das Asklepieion", *AM* 27, 199–238.
Sahin, S., 1979/1981: *Die Inschriften von Stratonikeia*. Inschriften griechischer Städte aus Kleinasien 21–22, Bonn.
Sokolowski, F., 1962: *Lois sacrées des Cités grecques, Supplément*. De Boccard, Paris.
Sokolowski, F., 1969: *Lois sacrées des Cités grecques*. De Boccard, Paris.
Speiser, F., 1928: "Die eleusinischen Mysterien als primitive Initiation", *Zeitschrift für Ethnologie* 60, 362–372.
Turcan, R., 1986: "Bacchoi ou bacchants? De la dissidence des vivants à la ségrégation des morts", in Olivier de Cazanove (ed.), *L'association dionysiaque dans les sociétés anciennes. Actes de la table ronde organisée par l'École Française de Rome (25–25 mai 1984)* (Rome), 227–246.
Ugenti, V., 1992: *Giuliano Imperatore. Alla Madre degli Dei*. Galatina.
Wankel, H. *et al.* (eds), 1979–1984: *Die Inschriften von Ephesos*. Inschriften griechischer Städte aus Kleinasien 11–17, Bonn.
West, M.L., 1965: "The Hymn of the Curetes", *JHS* 85, 149–159.
West, M.L., 1983: *The Orphic Poems*. Oxford.
Wiens, D.H., 1980: "Mystery concepts in primitive Christianity and Its environment", *Aufstieg und Niedergang der Römischen Welt* II 23:2 (Berlin and New York), 1248–1284.

11

CONCLUDING REMARKS

Michael B. Cosmopoulos

At the end of this project it will be useful to draw a brief picture of the main points contributed by the book. The most striking characteristic of Greek mysteria is the large number of mysteric cults and the wide range of deities worshipped. Until now, scholarship and popularized books on Greek religion have focused on the major divinities, mostly Demeter/Kore and the Kabeiroi, and have created a somewhat biased view of Greek Mysteries. The chapters in this book make it very clear that such a view does not correspond to reality. Not only are the gods worshipped in several mystery cults unrelated to Demeter, but many cults developed independently of Eleusis and for different reasons. At Thebes, the Kab(e)iric cult seems to have been introduced as early as the eighth or the seventh century as a private cult and taken over by the polis after the fourth century. Other mystery cults can be traced back to Archaic *rites de passage*, transformed into mysteria during the Roman period. The origins of the Andanian Mysteries can be traced back to the political motivations of the Messenian state of the early fourth century. In general, most mysteria (Thebes, Andania, Phlya, several cults in Arcadia and probably Eleusis itself) started as private, clan or family cults, before they were turned into secret cults. At Eleusis it is possible that an "advent festival" predated the mystery cult; this festival could have taken on a metaphysical character in the sixth century, when it became a mysterion by the addition of an initiation ritual involving a *katabasis*, a simulation of descent to Hades and the search for Persephone. A ritual search is also attested at Samothrace, where the initiates wandered in the dark in search of Harmonia. In this case, however, the conclusion of the ritual was not the reunion of Mother and Kore, but the sacred marriage and a sexual union between Harmonia and Cadmus.

The chthonic connection is always strong, as it is in overcoming the fear of death that Mysteries find their most useful justification. In Levadeia the sanctuary of Trophonios could have been a chthonic passage and could have related to Eleusinian and Orphic rituals through Eubulos. A divided Netherworld, as it appears in the *Homeric Hymn to Demeter*, needs to be overcome if the individual wants to preserve any hope of a happy afterlife. The function of Mysteries as rituals providing a "special knowledge," which offers the possibility of a better place in the underworld, is revealed by the journey of the soul, as this is described by the tablets found in graves in different parts of the Greek world, revealing the belief that status after death was determined by ritual experience.

Initiation is, of course, common in all mystery cults. Two of the major cults, at Eleusis and Samothrace, and several minor ones (such as Pheneos, for example) seem to have used similar initiation rituals, at least as far as we can deduce from the terminology employed (*mystes–myoumenos–telete*). At Samothrace, it is possible that part of the preliminary initiation was also the Korybantic rite of *thronosis*.

The picture that emerges from the study of individual mysteria suggests a long tradition with many common elements. Although, as mentioned above, our view of Greek mystery cults should not be centered at Eleusis, it is undeniable that the radiance of the Eleusinian Mysteries in the Hellenistic and Roman world did lead to the formalization and, if such a word can be allowed, the "mysterization" of several cults. Besides the similarities in initiation rituals between Eleusis and Samothrace, the borrowing of Eleusinian purification rites at Andania and Phlya confirms the close interaction of major and minor Mysteries, especially in the Hellenistic and Roman periods, and the impact that Eleusis had on other mysteria. Outside the world of secret mysteric rituals, a loose connection can be observed between mysteria and oracular cults, such as the sanctuary of Trophonios at Levadeia, which seems to have been considered, at least since Classical times, both an oracle and a mystery cult. Orphic Mysteries seem closely connected to dionysiac beliefs and rituals and form a special case: although they may have originated in the worship of Dionysos in archaic Greek cities, they were not attached to any public sanctuary.

A final point that needs to be raised is the connection between the realm of soterological rituals and the pragmatic world of politics and finances. Some mysteria were established as the result of political actions in order to foster civic union, such as those of Andania. In the Hellenistic and Roman periods several cults, from Eleusis to Ilion, were used by the *poleis* to generate and secure benefits from the powerful Hellenistic kingdoms and Rome. In most cases, mystery cult sanctuaries and/or the cities that sponsored them profited financially from the initiation fees of the *mystai*.

In general, one cannot help but feel awe for the tremendous impact that mysteria exercised, not only on the Greek psyche but also on so many aspects of the Graeco-Roman world. Only when we consider how mystery cults were born, matured, and developed alongside with Greek culture, and how they survived until the end of antiquity, can we begin to appreciate the effect they have had on western civilization. The continuity and diversity of Greek mystery cults reflect a system of spiritual beliefs that lasted for 2,000 years; perhaps this should help us to place our modernized, globalized, and mechanized world into perspective...

INDEX

Academy 32
Accius 72
Achaea 204, 228
Acheronteia 196
Achilles 92, 186, 212–13
Acraephia 171; see also Akraiphia
Acragas 54
Acusilaos 236
Advent festivals 32
adyton 173, 174, 176, 185, 186, 254
Aegina 241, 252, 257
Aelian 46, 73
Aeneas 102
Aeschines 71, 206, 235, 250, 254
Aeschylos 227, 236; *Psychagogoi* 196, 214; *Psychostasia* 210
Aetna 31
Agamedes 179
Agave 211
Agerrania 232; see also Agriania; Agrionia
Aghios Kosmas 15
Agrae 221
Agriania 230, 231, 232; see also Agerrania; Agrionia
Agrianios 230
Agrionia 32, 35, 46, 232; see also Agerrania; Agriania
Aidoneus 209
Aither 175
Aitnaios 113, 135, 245
Aitolians 134
Ajax 92
akousmata 33
Akraiphia 138; see also Acraephia
Aktaion 211
Alesion 150
Alexander the Great 74, 92, 114, 134
Alexander IV 74
Alexandria 29, 31, 47, 58, 165, 170, 185, 215
Alexiarous 114, 134
Alogovrakhos 150

Alpheios 164
Altars 1, 8, 15, 16, 19, 59, 65, 81–6, 88, 91, 92, 93, 115, 126, 140, 148, 149, 150, 161, 163, 199, 222, 226, 244, 246, 254, 255
Ambrosiaster 74
Amphiaraos 122, 170
Amphilochos 170, 184
Amphion 122
Amphitryon 169
amyetos 55, 56, 59, 60, 65, 72
anamnesia 174–5
Andania 51, 65, 72, 74, 114, 132, 134, 165, 241, 242, 243, 244, 245, 254, 256, 257, 263, 264
Andocides 57
Andrikepaiothyrsos 233
anodos 75, 165, 181
Antheia 47, 221, 237
Anthesphoria 234
Anthesteria 229, 238
Anthesterion 47, 51–2, 230, 234
Antilochos 92
Antinoos 143, 144, 146
Antinoupolis 76, 180–1
Antiochos Hierax 100, 101
Antiochos I 93, 100
Antiochos II 100
Anytos 143, 163
Aphrodisiasts 54
Aphrodite 126, 150, 246
Aphrodite Daitis 246
Apollo 16, 32, 43, 68, 92, 100, 106, 176, 223, 224, 225, 243, 246–7, 250, 255
Apollo Karneios 106, 134, 244
Apollo Pythaeus 243
Apollodoros of Athens 32–3
Apollonios of Rhodes 65, 181, 183, 214
Apollonios of Tyana 170, 184, 185
apomatton 235
Arcadia 143–68, 187, 241, 245, 263
archimagareus 150
archineokoros 150

INDEX

archon basileus 44
arcteia 146
Argos 170, 228, 231, 243
Arion 157
Aristarche 101, 106
Aristeas 170
Aristides 30, 39, 74–5, 175–6, 183, 185, 186, 187
Aristomenes 170, 243, 254
Aristonicos 102
Aristophanes 146, 170, 177, 198, 200, 252; *Clouds* 33, 43–4, 173–5, 178–9, 180, 183, 184, 186; *Frogs* 45, 66–7, 196, 197–9, 209, 210, 211, 212; *Peace* 52, 198
Arkesilaos 163
arrhetos kore 196
Arsinoe 61, 101
Artemis 42, 143, 144, 147, 151, 159, 161, 163, 236, 247, 249, 250, 253
Artemis Ephesia 253, 254
Artemis Orthia 159
Artemis Propylaia temple 42–3
Artemis Pythia 146
Artemis Pythie 247
Artemision of Ephesos 247
Asklepeios 73, 122–3, 170, 175, 178, 181, 185, 187, 250
Askra 112
Assos 101, 106
Asterios 208
ateleis 197
atelestos 55, 56
Athena Ilias 92, 102
Athenaieus 180
Athenians 25, 36, 54, 134, 185, 242, 252
Athens Archaeological Society 20
Attalos I 101, 102
Attalos II 101, 102
Attalos III 102
Attis 96
Augias 169, 179
Augustin 35
Augustus 90, 248
aulos 131, 176
Axieros 68
Axiokersa 68
Axiokersos 68

Bacchae 55, 56, 162, 183, 198, 211, 212, 229; *see also* Bacchai
Bacchai 55
Bacchants 236
Bacchic 55, 56, 64, 203, 204, 207, 210, 237, 250, 252, 254
Bacchic initiation 55, 56
bacchoi 55, 200, 202–3, 205, 210–11, 213, 233
bacchos 219

Bakchion 237
Bakchios 219
Basedow, M. 86–7, 90, 104, 106
Basilis 151
Bathos 143, 144, 147, 150, 156, 164
bebakcheumenoi 252
Blegen, C.W. 80–1, 84–5, 87–91, 95, 97, 104, 106
Boadromios 235
Boathoos 235
Boedromion 33, 39, 40, 51–2, 65
Boiotia 112, 113, 114, 122, 131
Bottakos 205, 211
Braun, K. 140
Brauron 146, 157, 161
Brauronies 146
Brimo 36, 203, 204, 207, 233, 234
Bysios 235

C. Flavius Fimbria 89
Cadmos 67–8, 69, 75, 76, 228; *see also* Kadmos
Caligula 170
Callimachos 75, 223, 225
Campana 59
Capua Vetere, Mithraeum 74
Caria 250
Caryatid 235
Celsus 171, 183
Cercyon 179
Ceres 29, 30, 35
Chaironeia 32, 35, 130, 138
Chaldeans 170
Chaleium 235
Charax of Pergamon 179, 184
Charon 196, 209
Charoneia 196
Chloaia 47, 237
Choes 54
Christianity 29, 256
Christians 170, 172, 256
Circe 194, 195, 214
Cissusae 231
Claudia Trophime 250
Clement of Alexandria 29, 31, 58, 59, 226, 235–6
Clouds 33, 43–4, 173–5, 178–9, 180, 183, 184, 186
Commodus 247, 248, 249
Conon 151, 173
Corinth 94, 99
corn 35–8
Cornutus 35
Corybantes *see* Korybantes
Cos 222
Cosmas of Jerusalem 169
Cratinus, *Trophonius* 169
Crete 126, 194, 200, 202–3, 204, 220, 221, 228, 229, 231, 232, 235, 249, 252

INDEX

Cronos 64, 171, 220, 234
Cumont, F. 187, 241
Curetes 220, 221, 222; *see also* Kouretes
Cybele 80, 93, 95–7, 99, 101–2, 104, 105, 163, 187, 246, 253
Cyllene, Mt. 151
Cyprus 159, 235
Cyrene 146, 231

Dadaphorios 235
Daedalos 184
Daisios 232, 237
damiourgos 153
Darcque, P. 1–2
Dardanos 69, 75, 80, 93, 97–9, 102, 105
Daumas, M. 140
Delos 73–4, 94–5, 186, 249, 250, 254
Delphi 42, 102, 151, 153, 169, 197, 222–30, 235, 251
Demaratos 153
Demeter Eleusinia 39, 143, 151, 152, 154, 241, 245
Demeter Erinys 143, 144, 155, 157
Demeter Erinys/Louisa 143
Demeter Karpophoros 247, 249–50
Demeter Kidaria 143, 144, 150, 153, 154, 156, 157, 245
Demeter of Lykosoura 145
Demeter Thesmia 143, 144, 154, 155, 164
Demeter Thesmophoros 155, 247, 250
Demetrieus 180
Demetrios Poliorketes 51, 58, 134
Demetrios of Skepsis 183
Demosthenes 71, 206, 254
Derveni papyrus 218
Despoina 94, 106, 143–6, 148, 155, 157, 159–64
Dexilaos 205, 211
Diasia 234
diathesis 132
Dicaearchos 174, 177, 183
Didyma 100, 246–7
Dinarchos 223, 224
Dio Chrysostom 63, 185, 186, 253
Diodoros 35, 38, 64, 67, 68, 75, 96, 99, 113, 183
Dionysia 32, 35, 235
Dionysian 198, 205, 213
Dionysios (month) 224, 237
Dionysos Auxites 145–6
Dionysos Bakcheios 219
Dionysos Kathegemon 254
Dionysos Phleus 247
Dioskour(e)ios 181
Dioskouroi 69, 124, 170, 183, 245
Diotima 53, 59
Dipolieia 54
Dithyrambios 237

divination 53, 88, 172, 176, 178
Dodona 114, 134, 140
Domata Persehoneia 194–7
Dowden, K. 51, 52, 82
drama mystikon 29
dromena 149, 151, 157
Dysaules 152

Eétion 69
Egyptian 241
Eiraphios 237
Eleusinian Mysteries 1, 25, 27, 30–1, 33, 35, 36, 39, 45–8, 50, 56, 151–2, 245, 264
Elcusinion, Agora 26, 40–1, 51, 57, 60
Eleusinios 30, 74–5, 181
Elis 200, 204, 224
Elysian Field 193, 195, 212
Elysian Plain 209
Empedocles 170, 187
Empedotimos 170
Endyspoitropios 224
Entella 201, 202–3, 204, 209, 214, 233
Epameinondas 243
Ephesos 54, 100, 235, 247, 249, 250, 255
Ephoros 67, 68, 69, 75, 183, 249
Epidauria 73, 185
Epidauros 16, 17, 19
Epimenides 27, 172, 221
Epiphanios 47
Epiteles 243
epopteia 36, 37, 51, 52, 56–7, 58, 59, 60, 65, 133, 180
Er 172, 252
Eratosthenes 228
Eretria 138
Eros 59
erotapocrisis 185
erotika 72
Erythrai 251
Eubouleus 59, 75, 181, 182, 203–4, 205
Euboulos 181, 236
eudaimones 197
Eumolpidai 51, 60
Eumolpos 45, 151, 152, 153, 245
Eunapios 255
Eunonomos 209
Euonios 237
Euphorion 162, 223, 225, 226
Euripides 54, 69, 71, 171, 199, 210, 214, 218, 227, 228; *Bacchae* 55, 56, 162, 183, 198, 211, 212, 229
Euthydemos 185
Eutresis 15

Fabia Aconia Paulina 255, 258
Fayyûm 222
Fimbria 89, 103

267

INDEX

Gaia 242, 246
Galaxia 221, 222
Gamelieus 76, 180
Gregory Nazianzenos 29, 169, 182–3, 184
Gurôb, Fayyûm 222

Hades 30, 31, 33, 34, 38–9, 55, 74–5, 176, 181, 188, 194–200, 209, 211, 213, 233, 263
Hagna 140, 241, 243, 244
Halai 138
Haliartos 228, 230–1
Hall of the Choral Dancers, Samothrace 61, 67
Haloa 179
Hannibal 102
Harmonia 67–8, 69, 180, 263
Harmonieus 76, 180
Harpocration 235
Hecate 235, 241, 253
Hector 92
Hegesiska 205, 211
Hekate 33, 250, 252, 257
Hellanicos 171, 221
Hellas 114, 120
Helos, Laconia 39
Hephaistos 112, 130–1, 245
Hera 31–2, 222, 228, 241, 249, 251
Heraclides of Pontos 171
Heraia 143, 146, 147, 148, 149, 151, 251
Heraieus 76, 180
Herakl(e)ios 181
Herakles 59, 170, 183
Herakles Dactylos 152
Hercyna 182
Hermaios 253–4
Hermes 31, 38, 67, 68, 75, 112, 125–6, 134, 184, 244
Hermione 212
Hermippos 172
Hermotimos of Clazomenae 177
Herodotos 52, 54, 55, 92, 112, 130–1, 153, 163, 171, 172, 174, 183, 184, 185, 207, 218, 219
Herois 235
Herosantheia 234
Herulians 91
Hesiod 112, 172, 188, 196, 221, 222, 234, 236
Hestia Boulaia 247, 249
hiera 33, 38, 40, 44
hierokeryx 247, 248
hierophant 32–3, 35, 38, 46, 71, 146, 152, 165, 243, 245, 248, 253, 255
hierophantes 29, 46, 249
hierophantis 29
hieros gamos 132
hieros logos 215
hieroteles 259
Hippolytos 36–7, 75

Hipponion 71, 200, 201, 202–3, 208–9; city of 223, 234
Hipponion Tablet 71
Homer 157, 172, 194, 223
Homeric Hymn to Apollo 178, 184, 249
Homeric Hymn to Demeter 2, 30, 45, 74–5, 135, 154, 163, 165, 187, 194, 197, 212, 264
Hopladamos 163
Hygeia 176
Hyrieus 169

Iakchos 47, 59
Iasion 67, 69, 75, 99
Ibycos 237
Icarion 228
Idean Dactyls 171
Ilaios 235
Ilion 79–81, 84, 91, 92, 93, 94, 95, 98, 99, 100, 101–3, 105, 106, 130, 264
Ilissos 154
Imbros 68, 95
Iobakchios 237
Irikepaige 234
Isis 30, 172, 176, 178, 184, 187, 241, 255
Ithome 243
ithyphallicism 68

Jesus 170
Jews 170
Julian, *Oration on the Great Mother* 187, 253, 255

Kabeiraia 114, 245
Kabeirion 57, 94, 245
Kabeiritai 113, 114
Kabeiroi 68, 69, 95, 112, 113, 114, 130–1, 241, 242, 244, 245, 251, 263
Kabiriarchai 118
Kabirichos 122
Kabiroi 112, 122, 125, 126, 127, 130–1, 133, 134, 139
Kabiros 122, 124, 125, 127, 131, 135, 139
Kadmilos *see* Kasmilos
Kadmos 68–9, 130, 254; *see also* Cadmos
Kaisar(e)ios 181
Kallignotos 152
Kalliteknios 180
Kalydon 106
kanephoria 159
Kaphyai 143, 146, 147
Kasmilos (or Kadmilos) 68
katabainein 174
katabasis 170, 174, 198, 263
katharmos 56, 70
Kaukon 242, 243, 246
kekatharmenos 55, 58, 59
kekorubantismenoi 252
kekoureutekotes 252

268

INDEX

Kennell, N. 41–5
Kerykes 51, 60
Klaros 246, 255, 256
Kleanthes 35
Knakalos 146, 147
Knidos 209
Komyria 251
Komyrion 251
Konon 151
Kontopoulos, K. 157, 164
Koragia 39, 145, 155
Korakou 15
Korybantes 63–4, 163, 164, 171, 186, 222, 244, 251, 256
kothornoi 232
Kouretes 163, 164, 171, 222, 244, 248, 249, 250, 252, 256; *see also* Curetes
Kourouniotes, K. 1, 2, 6, 11, 13, 148, 149, 157, 165
Krateia 131
kraterismos 258
Krisa 15
Kritias, *Perithoos* 197–8
Kronos 210
Kyamites 155
Kyane 39
kykeon 31
Kyloneion *agos* 27
Kyme 99, 112, 255, 257
Kynortion, Mt. 16, 18

Labyadae 235
Laconia 39
Lacratides 181
Lactantius 30–1, 32, 34, 37, 66, 183
Lambrinoudakis, V. 16
Lamia 235
Larysion, Mt. 32, 35
Lebadean 173, 175, 178–80
Lebadeia 169, 170, 171, 174, 177, 179–83, 187, 209
Lemnos 57, 64, 75, 95, 112, 135, 138, 245, 251
Lenaia 230
Lerna 212, 241, 257
Lesbos 183, 202–3, 228, 229; *see also* Mytilene
Lesser 36, 47, 51–2, 53, 58, 59, 72, 234, 241, 255
Lesser Mysteria 52, 58, 59, 60, 72
Lesser Propylaea 36
Lethe 174, 196, 209–10, 212, 215
Leto 163, 249
Leuktra 242
Libanius 253
Libethra 173
Livy 74, 102
Locris 235
Lokroi 150, 200, 215
Lollianus 223, 226, 234

Lovatelli Urn 59
Lower Tholos, Kabeirion, Thebes 116, 118, 119, 122, 127, 128, 132, 136
Lucian 34, 71, 179, 187, 236; *Philopseudes* 172, 183
Lycaon 226
Lycourgos 223, 225, 228–9
Lyctos 221
Lydia 253
Lydiades 163
Lykomidai 134, 242, 245, 246, 256
Lykophron 98
Lykos 242, 244
Lykosoura 94, 106, 143–9, 152, 154, 157, 160–5, 241, 257
Lynch, K. 84, 106
Lysimachos 247

Macrobius, *Saturnalia* 253
Maeander 254
Magi 170, 171
Magna Mater 97
Magnesia 254
magoi 219
Maleatas 16
Mallus 184
Mamurt Kale 97, 100
Mandros 255, 257
Manissa 200
manteion 169, 182
Mantinike 143, 146, 148, 149, 151
Marcus Aurelius 114, 176
Mardonios 114
Maronea 185
Matid(e)ios 180
Medma 215
Megalesion 100
Megalopolis 134, 143, 144, 147, 152, 153, 154, 164, 183, 241, 245, 257
Megara 26
Melampos 170
Melangeia 144, 146, 147, 164
melanouros 179, 187
Meliasts 146, 148, 149
Melitaea 235
Melite 45, 95
Memory 174, 175, 176, 179, 182, 187, 200, 201, 202–4, 208, 209, 210, 213; *see also* Mnemosyne
Memphis 131
memyemenos 58, 71
Menadier, B. 83, 97, 104, 106
Menelaos 195
Mentas 152
Messene 99, 134, 242, 243–4, 254
Mestrius Florus 250
metempsychosis 172
Meter 100, 122, 139, 177, 187

269

INDEX

Methana 16, 17
Methapos 114, 134, 140, 242
Migonion 32
Miletos 146, 219
Miletus 219
mimemata 152
mimesis 29, 34
Minos 184, 194–5, 210
Mirthless Rock 115, 181
Mithraeum, Capua Vetere 74
Mithraic mysteries 65
Mithras 241, 253
Mithridatic wars 89
Mitos 131
Mnaseas 68, 112
Mnasistratos 243
Mnemosyne 172, 174, 175, 179, 203; *see also* Memory
Moses 170
Mount Cyllene 151
Mount Kynortion 16, 18
Mount Larysion 32, 35
Mounychion 52
Mousaios 170, 171, 173, 180, 220, 246
Musaeus 220
Museo Nazionale Romano 72
Muses 32, 68
Mycenae 16, 17, 21
myesis 51, 52, 56, 57, 58, 59, 60, 61, 62, 63, 65, 70, 176, 183
Mylonas, G.E. 2, 4–8, 11–16, 20, 29, 31, 36–7, 45–7, 94, 187, 259
myoumenoi 33, 57, 144
Myron 252
Myrsilos 183
mystagogoi 51, 65, 118, 198
mystagogue 50–1, 66, 173
mystai 26, 44, 47, 50–2, 55–8, 62, 65, 66–7, 70, 144, 148, 150, 156, 159, 161, 163, 185, 197, 200, 201, 203, 205, 210, 213, 220, 233, 264
mysterion 29–30, 36, 146
mystes 50–1, 54, 55, 57, 60, 65, 66, 144, 187, 203, 205, 207, 208, 210, 211, 219, 264
Mystes Painter 125, 131
Mytilene 146, 200, 228; *see also* Lesbos
Mytileneans 92

Naos 151, 153, 154, 245
Naupaktos 114
nekuiya 197
neobakchos 233
Nike 160
Nikippa 147
Nilsson, M. 39, 46, 71, 156, 234, 235, 236, 238, 241, 257, 258, 259
Nonnus 75, 169, 183, 236
Nysa 212

Odysseus 94, 194, 195
Odyssey 130, 194, 195, 197, 213
Olbia 207, 218, 219, 236
olbioi 197
Olympia 106, 126–7
Olympos 30, 212
omphalos 235
Orchomenos 227, 231
Orcos 35
Origen 171
Oropos 138
Orpheotelestai 170
Orpheus 45, 170–1, 173, 180, 206, 213, 229, 231, 233, 234, 252–3
Orphic poetry 45
Orphics 179, 219, 220, 221, 222, 226
Ortygia 249, 250
Osiris 30, 235
Ovid 39, 96, 139

Pais 122, 124, 128, 131, 134, 135, 138, 245
Palladion 98–9
Pan 75, 112, 125–6, 164
Panathenaia 54
Pancrates 172
Pandion 242
Parmenides 177, 178
Parnassos 223, 226, 231, 235
Paros 134, 250
pater spelaiou 150
Patrae 228, 236
Patroclos 92
Peace 52, 198
Pelarge 113–14, 134, 135
Pelinna 200, 201, 202–3, 204, 207, 211, 233
Peloponnese 153, 227, 246
Pelops 226, 237
Pentheus 198, 211, 227, 228
peplos 39, 155
Pergamon 93, 94, 95, 98, 100, 101–3, 134, 149, 179, 184, 187, 258
Perge 222
Persephone Protogonos 246
Perseus 228, 231
Petelia 202–3, 209
Petroma 150, 156
Phaedo 55, 58, 59, 180
Phaedrus 56–7, 58, 65–6, 210
phallos 36–7
Pharaoh 184
phasmata 33, 253
Pheneatis 164
Pheneos 143, 144, 146, 150, 151, 152, 154, 156, 157, 164, 241, 245, 264
Pherai 201, 202–3, 210, 211, 214
Pherekydes 95, 245
Phigaleia 143, 144, 147, 150, 157, 161

INDEX

Philetairos 97, 101
Philios, D. 2, 13
Philip II Arrhidaios 74
Philiste 205, 211
Philo of Alexandria 170
Philocteta 72
Philostratos 170, 185, 186
Philoxena 205
Phliasians 152–3
Phlious 152–3, 241, 257
Phlyos 242, 246
Phrygians 36
Phulomagna 211
Phylakopi 16
Physcos 235
Phytalos 154
Pieria 170, 173
Pindar 53, 125, 184, 188, 196, 197, 210–11, 213, 215
Pithoigion 237
Plato 171, 172, 178, 185, 206, 209, 212, 213, 252; *Cratylus* 196; *Euthydem.* 63, 65; *Euthydemos* 185; *Gorgias* 210, 211; *Meno* 196; *Phaedo* 55, 58, 59, 180; *Phaedrus* 56–7, 58, 65, 210; *Symposium* 53, 59, 71; *Theatatus* 71
Ploutonia 196
Plutarch 33, 34, 38, 43–4, 46, 51, 53, 72, 173, 175, 186, 213, 214, 223, 227, 235, 237; *De facie* 171, 172, 178, 184, 187; *De genio Socratis* 171, 177, 185, 187; *Isis and Osiris* 215; *On the Soul* 66
Pluto 181, 196, 199, 211
Poitropia 235
Poitropios 224
Polos 152
Polygnotos 197, 213
Porphyry 253; *Life of Pythagoras* 184
Poseidippos 205, 211, 213
Poseidon 157, 161, 169, 187
Posidonios 172, 173, 183
Pottery 15, 16, 17, 18, 19, 84, 96–7, 122, 126, 127–8, 130, 136, 149, 157, 159, 161, 165
Pratolaos 131
Priam 92
Pringsheim 52, 72
Proetus 228, 237
Proklos 30
prophetes 185
propoloi 163
Proserpina 30, 66, 68, 178
Proteus 195
protomystai 51
Pseudo-Augustine (Ambrosiaster) 74
psyche 33
Ptolemy II 65
Purifications 53
Pylos 16, 17

Pyr Aphtharton 247
Pyrrhos 134
Pythagoras 172, 179, 184, 187
Pythagorean 170, 177, 184, 185, 215, 234
Python 223, 225

Rhapsodies 218–22, 224–6, 235
Rhea 163, 218, 220, 221, 222–3, 249
Richardson, N.J. 45, 47, 154, 214
Roesch, P. 126, 127, 140
Rolley, C. 127
Rome 97, 98, 100, 101–3, 105, 182, 202–3, 264
Rose, Brian C. 79–81, 83–4, 86–8, 89, 90, 91, 93, 95, 97, 101, 102, 106

Sab(e)inios 76, 180
Sabina 180
Sacrifices 16, 17, 18, 19, 39, 53, 92, 96, 133, 147, 159, 161–2, 164, 179, 181, 194, 219–20, 243, 244, 247, 248, 249, 251, 255
Samos 31–2, 258
Samothrace; Hall of the Choral Dancers 61, 67; Hieron 61, 94, 106; Propylon 61, 64; Rotunda of Arsinoe 61
Samothracian 50, 62, 65, 67, 68, 76, 79, 93–9, 101, 102, 104, 105, 180, 206, 244
Samothracian Gods 68, 79, 93–9, 101, 102, 104, 105, 133
Saon (Saos) 152, 171
Sarapis 176, 185, 254
Sardis 100, 253, 254, 256
Satyra 131
Scamandreia 79
Schliemann, H. 79
Schmaltz, B. 126, 127, 129
Scyles 53, 55
Sebast(e)ois 181
sekos 47
Seleucid dynasty 92, 100
Seleucos II 100
Selinus 221
Semele 222, 223, 225, 233, 236
Sfakaki 204, 214
Sibyl 102
Sicily 30, 200, 202–3, 204
Siphnian Treasury, Delphi 224
Sisyphos 195
Smyrna 59, 223, 226
Socrates 59, 171, 173–5, 178, 180
Solon 27, 43–4
Sopater 72, 186
Sophocles; *Aithous* 214; *Niptra* 214
Sopolis 247, 249–50
Sosigenes 152–4
spells 53
S(t)epteria 235
Stesimbrotos 112

INDEX

Strabo 64, 71, 89, 92, 95, 99, 106, 139, 170, 172, 173, 183, 234, 249
Stratonikeia 250
Strepsiades 173, 174, 175, 177, 178, 180, 185
Suda 171, 231, 236
symbola 203, 204, 211
Syme 126
sympatheia 178
Syracuse 38, 39

Tablets 16, 71, 75, 150, 176, 179, 181, 185, 200–4, 206–9, 211–13, 236, 264
Tanagra 138, 228, 231
Tantalos 195, 197
Telegonia 184
teleioi 197
Telesterion 1, 2, 3, 5, 7, 8, 11, 13, 14, 15, 26, 33–4, 38, 39, 44, 46, 66–7, 73, 94
teletai 30, 46, 53, 54, 55, 56, 58, 171, 193, 211
telete 29–30, 51, 52, 53, 54, 55–6, 57, 58, 59, 60, 63, 65, 69, 70, 71, 72, 108, 144, 150, 151, 154, 156, 183, 187, 241, 264
Telondes 114, 134, 135
Temenion 241, 257
Tenedos 232
Teneric Plain 114
Tereus 226
Tertullian 29, 36–7, 170, 173, 183
tetelesmenos 55, 56, 58
Teumessos 113
thamakos 122
Thasos 69, 146, 149, 197
Thebais 114, 157
Theban Kabiroi 112–42
Thebes (Boiotian) 68, 94, 112, 113–15, 118, 119, 125, 132–4, 139, 159, 197, 227, 233, 236, 241, 242, 245, 251, 263; Thebes (Phthiotic) 235
Thelpousa 143, 144, 147, 151, 155, 157
Themistokles 246
Theodaisia 230, 231, 232
Theodaisios 230
Theoi Megaloi 68, 69, 133, 134
Theon of Smyrna 59
theoxenia 237
Thera 106
Therai, Laconia 39
Theseus 69, 181, 198
Thesmophoria 45, 47, 55, 71, 148, 155, 181, 237
Thesmorphor(e)ios 180
Thespiai 113, 139
Thessalonike 150
Thessaly 200, 202–3, 204, 211, 218, 235
thiasoi 71, 197
Thisbe 138
Thompson, H. 90, 96, 97, 99
Thourioi 200–1, 202–4, 207, 211

Thrace 45, 228–9, 231
Threpsiades, I. 2
thronismos 63, 175
thronosis 62–3, 64, 72, 73, 175, 264
Thyateira 255, 259
Thyestes 226
Thyia 32, 35, 224
Thyiads 223, 224, 229, 230–1, 235
Thyios 235, 237
thymiaterion 81, 160
thyrsos 55, 56, 208
Timarchos 171, 172, 173, 175, 177, 178
Timeotheos 185
Titan 163, 234
Tityos 195
Tonaia 31–2
Torches 29, 30, 31, 34, 59–60, 67, 94, 151, 259
Torre Nova Sarcophagus 59
Trapezous 153, 241
Travlos, I. 1, 2, 3, 15, 19, 43, 45, 60
Triton 228, 231
Trokondas 253–4
Trophoniads 171, 172
Trophonieus 76, 180, 181
Trophonius 169, 170
Troy 94–7; Lower Sanctuary 79, 81, 84, 86, 88, 93–4, 103, 118, 119, 122, 128, 139; Upper Sanctuary 79, 80, 81–2, 84–90, 93–9, 100–4, 105; West Sanctuary 79, 80, 81–91, 93–9, 100–4, 105
Trygaeus 52
trygon 179
Tullia 250, 255
Typaneai 138
Tzetzes 179, 183, 184

Underworld 25, 33, 34, 40, 170, 172, 174, 177, 178, 179, 180, 181, 182, 196, 233
Upper Tholos, Kabeirion, Thebes 133, 134

Varro 35, 68, 72, 101
Vettius Agorius Praetextatus 253, 255

wizardry 53
Wright, J.C. 15, 16, 19, 20

Xantriai 236
Xerxes 92, 114
Xoanon 39

Zalmoxis 170, 171, 172, 177
Zethos 123
Zeus Herkeios 92
Zeus *meilichios* 221
Zeus Panameros 250–1
Zeus Polieus 92